I0517708

哲学兵法：中国兵道思想反恐

Philosophical Art of War:
Anti-Terrorism with Chinese Military Ideology

张子良　著

王　勇　译

Written By Ziliang Zhang

Translated By Yong Wang

ASIAN CULTURE
PRESS

本书由美国亚洲文化出版社(Asian Culture Press)在博尔德出版

1942 Bradway, Suite 314c,

Boulder, CO 80302,

United States

封面排版设计 : Asian Culture Press

翻译 : 王勇 (Yong Wang)

Published in the United States of America

First paperback edition September 2025

本书2025年9月在美国第一次出版

目录

CONTENTS

前言
Preface

21 世纪既是一个阶级社会，又是一个文明社会。任何人要想在这种社会中生存和生活，做人就要既有阴柔又有阳刚的一面。

The society in the 21st century is not only class-based but also civilized. Anyone who wants to survive and live in this society must possess gentle and virile traits.

自古以来，每个国家与地区的社会秩序和国家等级都是有所不同的。然而，人类活动空间有限，危险和机遇却是无限的，生存和生活充满了诸多的不确定性。于是，代表阴柔的哲学和代表阳刚的兵法，就大有用处地登上了人类活动的舞台。

Since ancient times, each country or region has distinctive social order and national hierarchy. Although the space for human activities is limited, there are infinite dangers and opportunities, making survival and life full of uncertainties. Therefore, philosophy, which represents gentleness, and the art of war, which represents virility, are greatly applied on the stage of human activities.

中国兵道思想是以"道"为最高原则，以"兵"为最低能力，进行相融合的哲学兵法。兵道思想是建立在有朝代背景基础上的哲学思想，将知识进行科普成为一种兵法，能够运用于现代社会，屹立于工业革命时代。比如说，每个国家的兴衰成败都有自己独特的潜在规律。国家不是太多太大太强就好就坏，也非太少太小太弱就好就坏，而是依道靠德在自行变化之中。

The Chinese military thought is a philosophical art of war, which combines "Tao" as the highest principle with "military strategy" as the basic ability. The Chinese military thought is a philosophical one based on the background of dynasties. Popularizing this knowledge as a form of military strategy enables it to be applied in modern society and stand firm in the era of the Industrial Revolution. For example, the rise and fall of each country follow its own unique underlying laws. The quality of a country cannot be judged solely by the size of its territory, the number of its population, or the strength of its national strength. Instead, it is self-evolving in line with Tao and morality.

从中国古代开始，一旦中国被异民族或者被傀儡政府统治，异域文化就会与汉文明起文化冲突。于是，在中国历朝历代，卖弄文章、吟诗作对、点评和创作小说戏曲以及著写史书等文化攻势就成为一种对敌的攻防利器。

In ancient times, once China was ruled by alien ethnic groups or puppet governments, there were cultural conflicts between alien cultures and the Han civilization. Therefore, in all dynasties of China, cultural attacks such as showing off literary skills, composing poems, commenting on and creating novels and operas, and writing historical records became a powerful weapon for defense and offense against enemies.

魏晋时期"文"作为"文章"的意义被全面凸现，这在《典论·论文》《文赋》《文章流别论》《翰林论》等有关文体的论述中，都显而易见。但魏晋人所谓"文章"，其范围依然广泛，除单篇应用文章外，还包括史书和子书。[1]

1　曾羽霞撰《魏晋南北朝散文文体批评研究》，来源《湖北师范大学》，2011 年 5 月

During the Wei and Jin Dynasties, the meaning of "wen" as "literary works" was fully highlighted. This is evident in theoretical works on literary styles such as *Discourses on Canonical Writings: On Literature*, *The Art of Literature*, *On the Genres of Literary Works*, and *On the Hanlin Academy*. However, the so-called "literary works" in the Wei and Jin Dynasties had a broader scope. In addition to single-piece practical writings, they included historical records and philosophical works.[1]

在中国文学史上，许多朝代都是以当时最具代表意义的某种文体作为这一时代文学的标志的，例如唐诗、宋词、元曲，而与此并称的，明清时代则是小说。明清两代，传统的诗、文、词等各种文学形式仍有大量的作品，但成就既不能与这些形式的前代相比，也不能与同一时代的小说相比。[2]

In the history of Chinese literature, the literature of many dynasties was marked by a certain literary style that was most representative of that era. For example, there were Tang Poetry, Song Ci, and Yuan Opera. In the same vein, novels were the symbol of the Ming and Qing Dynasties. During the Ming and Qing Dynasties, there were still a large number of works in traditional literary forms such as poetry, prose, and ci, but their achievements could not compare with those of previous generations, nor could they rival the novels of the same period.[2]

文学史说明，小说、戏曲等俗文学的发展与经济文化繁荣有密切关系。明代中期后，资本主义的生产因素最早在吴越地区萌芽，经济的繁荣，促使了文人心灵最先感受到时代的变革，多姿多彩的生活和开放发展的环境，进一步催生了俗文学的繁荣，小说、戏曲空前发展。单就小说来说，明清两代，文言小说和通俗小说的总数在 2000 余种，《中国通俗小说总目提要》提到通俗小说的作者为

2　孙文婧、丛何主编《明清小说研究》，长春：吉林大学出版社，2015 年 5 月

604 人，吴越文化区域的作者即高达 200 多人，占了总数的 1/3。[3]

The history of literature indicates that the development of popular literary works such as novels and operas is closely associated with economic and cultural prosperity. After the mid-Ming Dynasty, capitalist factors of production first emerged in the Wu and Yue regions. The economic prosperity enabled literati to perceive the changes of the era first. The colorful life and the open and developing environment further gave birth to the prosperity of popular literature, especially the unprecedented development of novels and operas. As far as novels alone are concerned, there were altogether more than 2,000 classical Chinese and popular novels during the Ming and Qing Dynasties. As mentioned in *An Introduction to the General Catalogue of Chinese Popular Novels*, there were 604 authors of popular novels, with more than 200 of them from the Wu and Yue cultural regions, accounting for one-third of the total.[3]

清朝是中国北方少数民族入主中原的朝代。清王朝一方面继承了明代的绝对君主制度，另一方面又加入了残酷的民族压迫政策，两者结合即构成了清代封建专制制度的基本特征。由此而派生的文化政策，是以扼杀汉民族反抗意识，巩固清王朝的绝对统治地位为目标的。清代盛行文字狱也是为此目标服务的。清代文字狱与明代有所不同，它多因镇压汉民族的反抗意识而发难。清代当权者认为，汉人反抗一日不消灭，清王朝的统治地位就不会巩固。而汉民族意识的宣扬和传播者主要是汉族文人，因此对他们要严加管制，这正是清代前期文字狱愈演愈烈的重要原因。[4]

The Qing Dynasty was established by the Manchu people, a

---

3 甘露撰《吴越文化与明清小说》，来源《河池学院学报》，2004 年第 5 期

4 黄少卿撰《明清文字狱及其对文化发展的影响》，来源《沧州师范专科学校学报》，2003 年 1 期

northern ethnic minority of China, when they occupied and dominated the Central Plains. On the one hand, the Qing Dynasty inherited the absolute monarchy of the Ming Dynasty. On the other hand, it adopted cruel ethnic oppression policies. The combination of the two constituted the basic characteristics of the feudal autocratic system of the Qing Dynasty. The resultant cultural policies aimed to suppress the Han people's resistance consciousness and consolidate the absolute ruling position of the Qing Dynasty. The prevailing literary inquisitions in the Qing Dynasty also served this purpose. Different from those in the Ming Dynasty, literary inquisitions in the Qing Dynasty were mostly launched to suppress the Han people's resistance consciousness. According to the rulers of the Qing Dynasty, their ruling position could not be consolidated unless the Han people's resistance consciousness was eliminated. Since the propagandists and spreaders of Han ethnic consciousness were mainly Han literati, they must be strictly controlled. It serves as an important reason for the growing intensity of the literary inquisition in the early Qing Dynasty.[4]

乾隆时期，作为外族统治者的清政府为了压制反清复明运动，将文字狱发展到了极致。康熙、雍正、乾隆三朝兴起了大小文字狱多次，数乾隆一朝最多，也最为严苛。例如若有人提到"乾三爻不象龙说"或"一把心肠论浊清"等语，便会引起乾隆皇帝的大怒，认为这种话是辱没大清朝，甚至有叛逆的嫌疑，说这话的人便极有可能遭来杀身之祸。在一些大的文字狱中，不但作者、出版者获罪，往往连受雇的刻工、印工或书商、买书人也极易受到牵连，被流放或杀戮。乾隆皇帝还借助修纂《四库全书》之名，广收天下书籍，进行大规模的检查和毁坏，书中凡是有不利于清朝统治政府的只言片语，或带有"胡""蛮"等字样者，统统被列为禁书。据统计，这一次浩劫中，被全毁或抽毁的书籍"多达数千种（一说2855

种，一说 8000 种，又书板 68000 片）以杜绝汉人的反满思想"，作为反映社会现实的戏曲和小说首当其冲，位于被禁之列，如雍正一朝，中央共下 16 次禁令，乾隆一朝，中央又下 17 次禁令，嘉庆时 18 次，道光年间 18 次，地方禁令更是不计其数。作为小说产量极高，坊刻事业发达的苏州自然处于被关注之列，雍、乾、嘉等朝都有直接针对苏州府的禁令，如雍正三年五月"禁江南苏松两府因蠲免浮粮聚众演戏"；地方法令中，直指苏州府的也不在少数，如兼署江南按察使司按察使苏松太道周为禀求谕禁事"禁苏州刊行淫书小说"。在这种严苛的条件下，文人墨客不敢再言小说，为求自保，转而开始研究无关现实政治的"考证学"，致使考证学独占学术势力。乾嘉学派倡导严谨的学风，追求言之有据，博大精深，雍容和顺的学者之风，这与通俗小说以虚构为生命，追求通俗化、市民化的趣味可谓水火不容，在这种环境下，就算是有新作产生，也多以炫耀学识才情为旨。这种学术风气逐渐蔓延到书坊，影响到了书坊主的经营策略，书坊主一则怕惹祸上身，二则受乾嘉学派的影响，不再以刊刻通俗小说为中心，转而开始刊刻既能保身又易获利的学术书籍，以满足当时文坛的需求，因此，小说传播的各个环节逐渐脱节，文人不再大规模地投身于小说创作当中，商人也不再大规模进行小说的买卖，读者群亦不再以阅读小说为乐，书坊在来源和销路上都受到巨大打击，书坊对小说的刊刻事业自然开始走下坡路。[5]

During Emperor Qianlong's Reign, in order to suppress the Movement to Overthrow the Qing and Restore the Ming, the Qing government, as an alien-ethnic ruler, pushed literary inquisitions to the extreme. During the reigns of Emperors Kangxi, Yongzheng, and Qianlong, a large number of literary inquisitions of different scales were

---

5　季孟瑶撰《苏州书坊与明清小说》，来源《东北师范大学》，2013 年 5 月

launched, with those in the Qianlong period being the most numerous and severe. For example, if anyone mentioned statements like "The three lines of Qian hexagram do not resemble a dragon" or "With all my heart, I discuss the murkiness and clarity of things", Emperor Qianlong would be greatly offended, deeming these words an insult to the Qing Empire and even suspecting them of being rebellious. The person who uttered these words was very likely to incur the misfortune of being killed. In some larger literary inquisition cases, not only the authors and publishers were convicted, but often the hired engravers, printers, booksellers, and buyers were also implicated, exiled or killed. Emperor Qianlong also, under the pretext of compiling *The Complete Library of the Four Treasuries*, gathered a large number of books from all over the country, but then carried out large-scale inspections and destruction. Any book with a single word unfavorable to the Qing government or with words like "Hu" (barbarian) or "Man" (a derogatory term for ethnic minorities in ancient times) would be banned. According to statistics, during the catastrophe, "as many as several thousand books (one source gives 2,855 and another 8,000. In addition, 68,000 printing blocks were destroyed.) were completely or partially destroyed to "eliminate the Han people's anti-Manchu thoughts". As a reflection of social reality, operas and novels were among the first to be banned. For example, during the Yongzheng period, the central government issued 16 bans; during the Qianlong period, 17 bans; during the Jiaqing period, 18 bans; during the Daoguang period, 18 bans. In addition, local bans were too numerous to count. As a place with a very high output of novels and a developed block-printing industry, Suzhou was naturally under close supervision. During the Yongzheng, Qianlong, and Jiaqing periods, direct bans targeting Suzhou were issued. For example, in the Fifth Month of the Third Year of Emperor Yongzheng's Reign, "assemblies for opera watching due to the exemption of excessive grain taxes in Suzhou and Songjiang Prefectures south of the Yangtze River were prohibited". Among local decrees, many were directly targeting Suzhou. For example, Zhou, concurrently acting as the Surveillance Commissioner of the Jiangnan Surveillance Commissioner's Office and the Intendant of the Suzhou-Songjiang-Taicang Circuit, submitted a petition for an order to "prohibit the publication and circulation of pornographic books and novels in Suzhou". Under these harsh circumstances, literati dared not write novels anymore. To protect themselves, they turned to "textual research", which was irrelevant to practical politics. As a result, textual research became a dominant academic force. The Qian-Jia School advocated a rigorous academic style, pursuing evidence-based arguments, profound knowledge, and an elegant and amiable academic demeanor. All these were completely incompatible with the characteristics of popular novels, which took fiction as their lifeblood and pursued a popular and a civilian-oriented taste. In this environment, even if new works were created, most of them aimed to show off learning and talent. This academic atmosphere gradually spread to bookstores, affecting the business strategies of bookstore owners. On the one hand, they feared getting into trouble. On the other hand, under the influence of the Qian-Jia School, they no longer focused on the publication of popular novels, but turned to academic books that could not only protect them but also generate profits easily, so as to meet the needs of the literary world at that time. Therefore, the diverse elements in the dissemination of novels gradually became disconnected. Literati no longer engaged in large-scale novel creation, merchants no longer engaged in large-scale novel trading, and the group of readers no longer took pleasure in reading novels. As a result, bookstores were severely hit in terms of sources and sales. Naturally, their business of publishing novels began to decline.[5]

隔行如隔山。倘若说中国魏晋时期的文化路线以文章为主，文化人写文章可以促进当时中国文房四宝等软件和硬件的销路和销量。那么，中国明清时期的文化路线以小说为主，文化人写小说进行流传和流通，则是对当时中国的商品经济有影响。

There is a gulf between different professions. If we say that the cultural route in the Wei and Jin Dynasties focused on essays, and that the writing of essays by cultural people could broaden the sales channels and improve the sales volumes of the Four Treasures of the Study or other stationery and related items in those periods, then, similarly, the cultural route in the Ming and Qing Dynasties mainly focused on novels, and the circulation of novels written by cultural people had an impact on the then commodity economy.

国家战争的胜负成败，可以象征为先进的社会生产力取代落后的社会生产力。优秀的文化氛围，可以促使一个国家提早迈入先进国家队伍之列。这种非军事的作战取胜条件，乃是兵道思想所重视的。

The victory of a national war symbolizes the replacement of backward social productive forces by advanced ones. An excellent cultural atmosphere can prompt a country to join the group of advanced countries earlier. This non-military condition for winning a war is what the Chinese military thought attaches importance to.

兵道思想是以哲学在上，兵法为下的哲学兵法。兵道思想中哲学部分多依靠中国诸子百家道家思想，兵法层面多吸收中国诸子百家兵家思想，动用自然规律推导兵法准则，化为中国哲学的尘埃。

The Chinese military thought is a philosophical art of war with philosophy on top and military strategy at the bottom. The philosophy in the Chinese military thought mainly relies on the Taoist thought among the Hundred Schools of Thought, and the art of war mainly draws on the military thought among the Hundred Schools of Thought. It deduces the principles of military strategy based on natural laws, and integrates them into the realm of Chinese philosophy.

从古到今，中国哲学都是符合客观，在认识基础上重新有所认识的系统体系，这是后人给哲学下定义"绕不过去"的方向。兵法是用兵的法则，其中"兵"有狭义和广义之分，狭义的"兵"是指军人、武器、军事和战争等与国家武装力量有关系的事物，广义的"兵"泛指一切有作战属性的事物。

Since ancient times, Chinese philosophy has been a system that conforms to objectivity and gains new understanding based on the previous understanding. This is an orientation that later generations "cannot bypass" when defining philosophy. The art of war refers to the rules of applying military forces. The term "military forces" has a narrow and a broad sense. In the narrow sense, "military forces" refers to things related to a country's armed forces, such as soldiers, weapons, military affairs, and wars. In the broad sense, "military forces" refers to all things with combat attributes.

兵道思想只是道家的一种类别，兵家的一个分支。兵家和道家思想都是中国古代史的文化领域，是诸子百家的一部分。诸子百家有超度社会的作用，是中国文化的根基，兵家和道家都是诸子百家的代表流派。

The Chinese military thought is only a category of Taoism and a branch of the art of war. Both the art of war and Taoism belong to the cultural realm of ancient Chinese history and are part of the Hundred Schools of Thought. As the foundation of Chinese culture, the Hundred Schools of Thought have the function of guiding society to break through certain limitations. Both the art of war and Taoism are representatives of the Hundred Schools of Thought.

西周末年，奴隶制度厉盛而衰，出现崩溃趋势。从公元前 770 年周平王继位，至公元前 221 年秦统一中国，史称春秋战国时期。[6]

At the end of the Western Zhou Dynasty, the slave system declined from prosperity and showed a tendency to collapse. Historically, this period from 770 BC, when King Ping of Zhou ascended the throne, to 221 BC, when the Qin Dynasty unified China, is known as the Spring and Autumn and Warring States periods.[6]

诸子百家是先秦至汉初各个学派的总称。诸子指各派的代表人物，百家指各学派。据《汉书·艺文志》上说，数得上名家的共有 189 家，4324 篇著作。但是，绝大多数都无法说出他们的代表人物、主要著作和观点，可据《诸子略》记载，诸子百家可罗列而论的是 10 家，即儒家、道家、阴阳家、法家、名家、墨家、纵横家、杂家、农家、小说家。[7]

The Hundred Schools of Thought is a general term for various schools of thought from the pre-Qin period to the early Han Dynasty. "Zhuzi" refers to the representative figures of each school, and "Baijia" refers to the various schools. According to *The Treatise on Literature, The History of the Han Dynasty*, there are 189 well-known schools with 4,324 works. However, for the vast majority of them, there is no way to name their representative figures, main works, and viewpoints. According to *Outline of the Masters*, 10 schools from the Hundred Schools of Thought can be listed and discussed, namely the Confucian School, the Taoist School, the Yin-Yang School, the Legalist School, the Logician School,

---

6　孙光圻撰《中国航海历史的形成时期——春秋战国（公元前 770 年—前 221 年）》，来源《世界海运》，2011 年 3 期

7　范世忠撰《诸子百家说》，来源《华夏文化》，1998 年 2 期

the Mohist School, the School of Diplomacy, the Syncretist School, the Agrarian School, and the School of Fiction.[7]

道家，是指以先秦老子、庄子关于"道"的学说为中心的一个学术派别。传统的看法：老子是道家创始人，庄子则继承和发展了老子的道家思想。汉代司马谈的《论六家之要指》称这一学术派别为"道德家"。《汉书·艺文志》则直呼为道家。[8]

The Taoist School refers to an academic school centered on the theory of "Tao" proposed by Laozi and Zhuangzi, two famous thinkers in the pre-Qin period. According to the traditional view, Laozi is its founder, and Zhuangzi inherited and developed Laozi's Taoist thought. In *On the Essentials of the Six Schools* written by Sima Tan in the Han Dynasty, this academic school is referred to as the "School of Morality". In *The Treatise on Literature, The History of the Han Dynasty, it is* directly referred to as the Taoist School.[8]

道家思想是中国古代哲学的瑰宝之一。春秋时期《老子》一书的问世，标志着道家思想的产生，此后的《庄子》《列子》《管子》《淮南子》等著作进一步继承和阐发了道家思想，强调"道常无为而无所不为""道法自然""天地万物生于有，有生于无"等观点，一直为后世所推崇。[9]

Taoist thought is one of the treasures of ancient Chinese philosophy. The emergence of the book *Laozi* in the Spring and Autumn Period marked the birth of Taoist thought. Subsequently, works such as *Zhuangzi, Liezi, Guanzi,* and *Huainanzi* inherited and further expounded Taoist thought, emphasizing viewpoints such as "Tao often accomplishes everything by doing nothing", "Tao follows nature", and "All things in

---

8　邓黔生撰《道家与道教》，来源《学习月刊》，1997 年 12 期

9　臧笑薇撰《道家思想对中医学理论发展的影响源流考》，来源《中医药学刊》，2004年 8 期

heaven and earth are born from being, and being is born from non-being", which have been consistently venerated by later generations.[9]

"道"字的形义及其演变显示，其本义似应为"路"，现代汉语中主要衍生出"道路""道德""道理""道义""道家""道学""道统""人道""道白""正道""道教"等词汇。从哲学上来看，"道"的本义引申为"途径""方法"，再引申为"思想体系""规律""原则""学说""道理"等；在中国哲学史上道家是与儒家相辅相成的主要思想流派，道家的"道"及其体系影响了中国哲学思想的发展，而且在世界上也影响深广，特别是对西方现代存在主义哲学家海德格尔的学说发展有着重要作用[10]。

The form, meaning and evolution of the Chinese character "Dao" suggest that its original meaning should be "road". In modern Chinese, it has mainly given rise to terms such as "daolu (road)", "daode (morality)", "daoli (reason)", "daoyi (morality and justice)", "daojia (Taoism)", "daoxue (Taoist learning)", "daotong (the succession of the Confucian orthodoxy)", "rendao (humanity)", "daobai (spoken parts in an opera)", "zhengdao (the right path)", and "daojiao (Taoist religion)". Philosophically, "Dao" was extended from its original meaning to "path" and "method", and further to "ideological system", "law", "principle", "theory", "reason", and so on. In the history of Chinese philosophy, Taoism is a major ideological school that complements Confucianism. The "Dao" and its system have influenced the development of Chinese philosophical thought. Moreover, they have a profound and extensive impact worldwide, especially playing an important role in the development of the theory of the Western modern existentialist philosopher Heidegger.[10]

10　黄卫星、张玉能撰《"道"的文化阐释》，来源《美育学刊》，2017 年第 2 期

　　春秋战国由于诸侯争霸的存在，从事军事研究、总结军事方面经验教训的人较多，研究制胜规律的一批有识之士被称为兵家。而兵家对战争谋略方面进行论述的书籍则被称为兵书。从《汉书·艺文志·兵书略》的记载来看，兵书主要分为四家，分别是权谋、形势、阴阳以及技巧。[11]

　　During the Spring and Autumn and Warring States periods, due to rivalries among the feudal lords, many people were engaged in military research, and summarized military experiences and lessons. The insightful people who studied the laws of victory were called the Military Strategists. And the books in which the Military Strategists expounded on military strategies were called military treatises. According to *Overview of Military Works, The Treatise on Literature, The History of the Han Dynasty*, military treatises can mainly be divided into four categories: Tactics of Power and Strategy, Strategic Positions and Advantages, Yin and Yang Theory, and Military Skills.[11]

　　长期以来，学术界对"百家争鸣"的"百家"有一种成见，少有人把兵家纳入"百家"范畴，因此也就把"兵家"排斥在"争鸣"之外，给人的印象好像是兵家没有参与"百家争鸣"，这是不符合当时的思想文化历史实际的。究其原因，既有兵家学派自身的，也有兵家学派之外的，也就是内因与外因。内因是兵家学派重实践、重功用，兵家不是清谈家、玄想家，而是谋略家、实践家，这与儒、道、墨、法、名、阴阳诸家有很大不同。儒家关注政治伦理，道家玄想宇宙和人生，墨家贱己爱人，法家刻薄寡恩，名家执着于逻辑，阴阳家将神秘的自然现象比附于人事。兵家的实践性大于理论性，而其他各家则是理论性大于实践性。外因也是由内因而起的，正因为兵家的实践性大于理论性，是王者政治斗争和军事斗

11　钟斌撰《先秦兵家管理哲学探析》，来源《沈阳师范大学》2011 年

争的工具，它的重要地位由此凸显出来，大大超过其他各家。[12]

For a long time, the academic circle has held a prejudice regarding the "hundred schools" in the "contention of a hundred schools of thought". Few people include the Military Strategists in the category of "hundred schools", thus excluding the "Military Strategists" from the "contention". It gives the impression that the Military Strategists did not participate in the "contention of a hundred schools of thought", but this does not conform to the historical facts of the then ideological and cultural situation. The reasons can be attributed to the Military Strategist school itself and elements outside the school, that is, internal and external factors. The internal factor is that the Military Strategist school emphasizes practice and utility. Quite different from the Confucian, Taoist, Mohist, Legalist, Logician, and Yin-Yang schools, the Military Strategists are not idle talkers or visionaries, but strategists and practitioners. The Confucian school focuses on political ethics, the Taoist school contemplates the universe and life, the Mohist school advocates self-sacrifice and love for others, the Legalist school is harsh and unfeeling, the Logician school is obsessed with logic, and the Yin-Yang school associates mysterious natural phenomena with human affairs. The practical nature of the Military Strategist school outweighs its theoretical nature, while it is quite the opposite for other schools. The external factors stem from internal ones. It is because the practical nature of the Military Strategist school outweighs its theoretical nature, and it serves as a tool for the political and military struggles of the rulers that its important position is highlighted, far exceeding that of other schools.[12]

道家与兵家本属不同学派，两派宗旨也大相径庭，但老子书中

12　李桂生撰《先秦兵家研究》，来源《浙江大学》，2005 年

概括了一系列军事战略战术，致使后世言兵者多受老子影响。这种影响主要体现在：第一，反战论；第二，不得已而战；第三，以奇用兵；第四，柔弱胜刚强。由此形成了道家与兵家的密切联系。[13]

Originally, the Taoist and Military Strategist schools were different academic schools, and their tenets were poles apart. However, a series of military strategies and tactics are summarized in *Laozi*, thus influencing many people who discussed military affairs in later generations. This influence is mainly reflected in the following aspects: First, the anti-war theory; second, fighting only when there is no alternative; third, using surprise tactics in warfare; fourth, the weak overcoming the strong. In this way, a close connection is formed between the Taoist and Military Strategist schools.[13]

《孙子兵法》是中国兵学的文化瑰宝，在世界军事史上有着不朽的地位，是一部划时代的巨著。它不仅成书早，而且还形成了自己独特的军事哲学思想理论体系，并被世人广泛流传，享有崇高的地位。《孙子兵法》共 13 篇，包括计篇、作战篇、谋攻篇、行篇、势篇、虚实篇、军争篇、九变篇、行军篇、地形篇、九地篇、火攻篇、用间篇。一部《孙子兵法》虽然只有 5000 余言，但其在总结军事实践和战争经验的同时，又阐述了丰富的哲学道理。这些道理与军事行动有密切的关系，故一般人称之为"军事哲学"。书中总结了商周以来特别是春秋时期的战争经验，论述了军事领域若干重大问题，揭示了战争和军事的规律，形成了系统的军事理论体系。它是中国古代流传下来的最早、最杰出的军事名著，在中国军事史上乃至世界军事史上都占有重要地位，其军事思想对中国历代政治家和军事理论家的影响非常深远，素有"兵家圣典""东方兵学的鼻祖"之称，又被人誉为"武学之圣典，兵家之绝唱"。同时，《孙

13　张运华撰《道家与兵家》，来源《五邑大学学报（社会科学版）》，1998 年 01 期

子兵法》也是世界上最早的兵书。[14]

As a cultural treasure of Chinese military science and an epoch-making masterpiece, *The Art of War* holds an immortal position in the world military history. It was written early, and more importantly, the theoretical system of military philosophy contained is quite unique, has been spread worldwide and enjoys a lofty status. *The Art of War* can be divided into 13 chapters, including "On Assessments", "On Waging Battle", "Planning the Attack", "Strategic Positions", "Strategic Advantage", "Weak Points and Strong Points", "Armed Contest", "Adapting to the Nine Contingencies", "Deploying the Army", "The Terrain", "The Nine Kinds of Terrain", "Incendiary Attack", and "Using Spies". With only more than 5,000 words, the book expounds on rich philosophical principles while summarizing military practices and war experiences. These principles are closely related to military actions, so they are generally called "military philosophy". It summarizes the war experiences starting from the Shang and Zhou Dynasties, especially during the Spring and Autumn period, discusses several major issues in the military field, reveals the laws of wars and military affairs, and forms a systematic military theoretical system. As the earliest and most outstanding military masterpiece handed down from ancient China, it occupies an important position in the Chinese and world military histories. Its military thought has had a profound impact on Chinese politicians and military theorists of all dynasties. It is known as the "holy book of the military strategists" and "originator of eastern military science", and is praised as the "sacred scripture of martial arts and peerless masterpiece of military strategists". At the same time, it is the

---

14 韩亚轩、郭玲霞撰《＜孙子兵法＞军事哲学思想研究》，来源《沧桑》，2013 年 6 期

earliest military treatise in the world.[14]

春秋时期，道家开创者老子著书《老子》（又名《道德经》），其书含有丰富的辩证法哲学思想，从而老子被尊为"中国哲学之父"。[15]

During the Spring and Autumn period, Laozi, the founder of the Taoist school, wrote the book *Laozi* (also known as *Tao Te Ching*), which contains rich dialectical philosophical thoughts. Therefore, Laozi is honored as the "Father of Chinese Philosophy".[15]

老子与他的著作《道德经》，在古今中外都备受推崇。诸葛亮说："非淡泊无以明志，非宁静无以致远。"其境界道出了《道德经》的精髓，以智慧的出世思想做积极的入世人生。[16]

Laozi and his work *Tao Te Ching* have been highly respected at all times and in all countries. Zhuge Liang said, "Without a simple and unadorned mind, one cannot achieve lofty goals; without a peaceful mind, one cannot reach far." This realm reveals the essence of *Tao Te Ching*, that is, to lead a proactive life in the mundane world with a sagacious transcendental mindset.[16]

在 21 世纪，人类处理战争与和平，主要依靠三大力量：上战场和下政策以及工业革命。工业革命是西方人的强项，下政策是东方人的优势，上战场则属于你情我愿的选择。在中国，哪怕现代中国人下政策再怎么千变万化，都包含着诸子百家的"影子"。

In the 21st century, humanity relies mainly on three forces to handle war and peace: going to the battlefield, formulating policies, and the Industrial Revolution. The Westerners excel in the Industrial Revolution, while the Easterners have an advantage in formulating policies. Going to

---

15 蔡雨恬撰《< 老子 > 教育思想的探究》，来源《汉字文化》，2022 年 8 期

16 姚荻琳撰《< 道德经 > 与企业管理哲学》，来源《人力资源管理》，2014 年 12 期

the battlefield is a choice out of personal volition. In China, regardless of the great diversity in the policies formulated by modern Chinese, they all bear the "shadow" of the Hundred Schools of Thought.

兵家有讲道，道家有言兵。兵家包含道家成分，道家包含兵家成分。这为它们之间进行"合体"铺平了实际化的理论。

The Military Strategists also talk about Taoism, and the Taoists also discuss military affairs. Therefore, the Military Strategist school contains elements from the Taoist school, and the Taoist school contains elements from the Military Strategist school. This has paved the way for the practical combination of the two in terms of theory.

兵道思想以反恐为载体，建立在历史哲学基础之上，通过分析政府治理国家的得失成败，将这套哲学兵法"有轨迹，无诡计"式地融入世界历史的一部分。

The Chinese military thought, with anti-terrorism as its carrier, is based on historical philosophy. By analyzing the gains and losses of the government in governing the country, we can integrate this set of philosophical military strategies into the world history in a way that is "traceable and without trickery".

历史哲学，顾名思义，是历史学与哲学的有机构成，是一门既古老又新颖的边缘学科。历史哲学萌芽的出现与史学理论的产生同样源远流长。史学研究主要通过对史料的甄别、澄清历史事实、评定历史人物的功过是非，来总结历史活动的经验和教训。当人们一旦将思维视野转向探讨历史过程内部种种复杂的因素，以及它们之间的相互关系，并试图探寻历史表象背后本质性的东西时，历史哲学思想便应运而生了。历史哲学试图解决哲学和历史学共同关注的问题，因而既带有历史学的一般特点，又带有哲学的一般特点。但它又与单独的历史学、哲学不一样，整体不是部分的机械相加，而是部分之间的有机结合。[17]

Historical philosophy, as the name implies, is an organic combination of history and philosophy. It is an ancient yet novel interdisciplinary subject. The emergence of the germ of historical philosophy dates back to ancient times, as does the birth of historical theory. In historical research, the experiences and lessons of historical events are summarized mainly through distinguishing historical data, clarifying historical facts, and evaluating the merits and demerits of historical figures. When people turned their mental perspectives to exploring various complex factors within the historical process, as well as their interrelationships, and attempted to explore the essential elements behind historical manifestations, the thought of historical philosophy came into being. Historical philosophy attempts to solve problems that are of common concern to philosophy and history. Therefore, it bears both the general characteristics of history and those of philosophy. However, it is different from history or philosophy alone. The whole is not a mechanical superposition of parts but an organic integration of them.[17]

在中国，中华民族是由汉族和少数民族组成的。从中国古代史开始，论综合实力，中国少数民族上战场胜过汉族，汉族在下政策方面胜过少数民族。

In China, the Chinese nation is composed of the Han nationality and ethnic minorities. Since ancient times, in terms of comprehensive strength, ethnic minorities outperformed the Han nationality in going to the battlefield, while the Han nationality outperformed ethnic minorities in formulating policies.

---

17 王杰撰《中国历史哲学：一个值得关注的重要课题》，来源《理论前沿》，2000 年第 05 期

回顾中国古代历史，曾经出现过三种少数民族政权：第一，建立了强大的政权却没有入主中原的少数民族政权，有匈奴、柔然、突厥、回鹘等；第二，受中央政权的雇佣介入中原的斗争最终建立了北朝政权，有十六国时期的北朝少数民族政权、北魏（鲜卑族建立）政权；第三，入主中原的少数民族政权，有辽、西夏、金、元、清。[18]

Looking back at ancient Chinese history, there were three types of regimes established by ethnic minorities: First, those establishing powerful regimes but failing to enter and rule the Central Plains, e.g. the Xiongnu, Rouran, Turkic, and Uyghur. Second, those getting involved in the struggles in the Central Plains through the employment by the central government and eventually establishing regimes in the North, e.g. the regimes established by ethnic minorities in the Sixteen Kingdoms period and the Northern Wei Dynasty (established by the Xianbei ethnic group). Third, those entering and ruling the Central Plains, e.g. the Liao, Western Xia, Jin, Yuan, and Qing dynasties.[18]

秦汉以后，在北方先后兴起的游牧民族包括汉代的匈奴、丁零，魏晋北朝的鲜卑、柔然，隋唐的突厥，北宋的契丹，南宋的女真，此后是蒙古和满洲。尽管中原汉人以征战、长城、联姻、册封、任用、内迁等一系列方式阻挡游牧民族的南下滋扰，但是北方游牧民族仍然呈周期性地向中原农耕文明区进犯，一次次逐鹿中原，屡屡在中原地区建立民族政权。从秦始皇结束东周王朝统一中国（前 221）到清帝皇冠落地（1911）的 2132 年间，北方少数民族统治中原或北方全境长达 840 年之久，这还不包括具有鲜卑血统的隋唐的 326 年统治。尤其是近古时期，从辽、金、元到清的北方

18　陈天宇撰《中国古代强悍北狄入主中原及其原因探究》，来源《通化师范学院学报》，2015 年 9 期

民族政权连绵不绝，造成了中国历史演变的复杂画卷。[19]

After the Qin and Han Dynasties, the nomadic ethnic groups that emerged successively in the north included the Xiongnu and Dingling in the Han Dynasty, the Xianbei and Rouran in the Wei, Jin, and Northern Dynasties, the Turks in the Sui and Tang Dynasties, the Khitan in the Northern Song Dynasty, and the Jurchen in the Southern Song Dynasty, followed by the Mongols and the Manchus. Although the Han people in the Central Plains tried a series of methods such as warfare, the Great Wall, intermarriage, conferring titles, appointment, and internal migration to prevent the southward harassment of the nomadic ethnic groups, they still periodically invaded the agricultural civilization areas in the Central Plains. They repeatedly vied for hegemony in the Central Plains, and frequently established ethnic regimes there. During the 2,132 years from 221 BC, when Emperor Qin Shi Huang destroyed the Eastern Zhou Dynasty and unified China, to 1911 AD, when the reign of the Qing emperors came to an end, the northern ethnic minorities ruled the Central Plains or the entire northern region for 840 years. This does not include the rule of the Sui and Tang Dynasties with Xianbei blood, which lasted for 326 years. Especially, in the late ancient period, the northern ethnic groups established a series of regimes, ranging from the Liao, Jin, Yuan to the Qing Dynasty, creating a complex picture of the evolution of Chinese history.[19]

中国历史上存在的民族压迫，较长时期是汉族统治者压迫少数民族人民，但在有些时候、有些地区却是某些少数民族统治者压迫汉族和其他各族人民。如元朝和清朝统一全国时是这样，匈奴、鲜卑、突厥、吐蕃、西夏等统治中国一部分地区时也是这样。尽管在

19　崔桦撰《农牧视野下的中国古代战争研究》，来源《西北农林科技大学》，2011 年
5 月

中国长期的古代史中，朝代不断更替，统治民族也有过更换，但民族压迫一直存在。这种民族压迫长期存在的根本原因，是由于剥削压迫的社会制度造成的。另外，大汉族主义与狭隘的民族主义也助长了民族压迫。[20]

For the vast majority of periods in Chinese history, ethnic oppression was mainly imposed by the Han rulers on ethnic minorities. However, in some periods and in some regions, certain ethnic minority rulers oppressed the Han people and other ethnic groups. This was the case when the Yuan and Qing Dynasties unified the whole country, as well as when the Xiongnu, Xianbei, Turks, Tubo, and Western Xia ruled parts of the country. Although dynasties and the ruling ethnic groups changed frequently during China's long ancient history, ethnic oppression continued to exist. Fundamentally speaking, the long-term existence of this ethnic oppression was caused by the exploitative and oppressive social system. In addition, Han chauvinism and narrow nationalism also contributed to ethnic oppression.[20]

在维护和推动国家统一的过程中，文化是构筑民族共同心理、维系和发展民族感情、巩固国家统一意志的纽带。中原文化是中华传统文化的核心和代表，在维护和推动国家统一的进程中起到了重要的纽带作用。在中国古代历史中，中原文化是中华民族凝聚力的源泉和统一的多民族国家形成的文化基础。[21]

In the process of maintaining and promoting national unity, culture is a bond for building mutual psychology among ethnic groups, maintaining and developing ethnic feelings, and consolidating the will

---

20　方立军撰《试论中国历代王朝民族政策的特点》，来源《西北第二民族学院学报（哲学社会科学版）》，2002 年 2 期

21　王保国撰《论中原文化在国家统一进程中的作用》，来源《贵州师范大学学报（社会科学版）》，2006 年 4 期

of national unity. As the core and representative of traditional Chinese culture, the Central Plains culture played an important bonding role in the process of maintaining and promoting national unity. In ancient Chinese history, the Central Plains culture was the source for the cohesion of the Chinese nation, as well as the cultural foundation for the formation of a unified multi-ethnic country.[21]

历史上最早建立的夏、商、周三个王朝均以中原地区为中心腹地，这直接推动了中国文明的最后形成；此后一直到北宋时代，中原地区始终是以汉族为主体的中华民族活动的中心地区。中原地区形成的儒、道、释思想是两千年来中华民族的主导思想与生活信念。[22]

As the earliest-established dynasties in history, the Xia, Shang, and Zhou all took the Central Plains as their central hinterland. This directly promoted the final formation of Chinese civilization. Subsequently, until the Northern Song Dynasty, the Central Plains remained central for the ctivities of the Chinese nation with the Han people as the main body. The Confucian, Taoist, and Buddhist thoughts formed in the Central Plains have been the dominant thoughts and life beliefs of the Chinese nation for two thousand years.[22]

在中国，汉族和少数民族各自所掌握的民族文化有显著不同。汉族上战场是为下政策服务，少数民族下政策是为上战场服务。汉人通过舞文弄墨来使自己成长，提高自己的综合品质。少数民族通过金戈铁马来强大自己，上升自己的社会地位。

In China, there were significant differences between the ethnic cultures of the Han people and those of ethnic minorities. The Han people

---

22　康国章撰《论中原文化内涵研究的体系性》，来源《河南师范大学学报（哲学社会科学版）》，2013 年 1 期

went to the battlefield to serve the purpose of formulating policies, while ethnic minorities formulated policies to serve the purpose of going to the battlefield. The Han people developed themselves and improved their comprehensive qualities through literary and cultural activities, while ethnic minorities strengthened themselves and raised their social status through military exploits.

国家灾难不断，政局动荡不安，人民流离失所，就使不合时宜的事物产生了动摇，进而人类要学习更多的新事物，来充实自己。就像中国清朝末年，清官员吴大澂对付沙俄和日本这两位侵略者，就是一位有成有败的争议人物。

Constant national disasters, political unrest, and the people's homelessness and vagrancy shook things that were out of date. Therefore, people needed to learn more new things to enrich themselves. For example, during the late Qing Dynasty, Wu Dacheng, an official marked by both triumphs and defeats in dealing with the two invaders, namely Tsarist Russia and Japan, was a controversial figure.

晚清东北边务的问题，是 19 世纪 70 年代末在中俄伊犁交涉过程中产生的。1880—1883 年间，吴大澂以三品京官身份奉命经略东北边务，先后推行了编练边防军、招抚边地金匪、筹措边地屯垦等有效措施，加强了东北边防；同时，他还针对中俄边境出现的新问题，提出了在海参崴设中国领事公所，保护朝鲜以钤制日本等主张，为加强东北边务献计献策。1886 年，吴大澂再度奉命出关，与俄国重勘东部边界，收回了部分被俄国侵占的领土，为捍卫国家领土主权做出了重要的贡献[23]。

It was during the negotiations concerning Ili between China and

---

23　陈可畏撰《吴大澂与晚清东北边务》，来源《清华大学学报（哲学社会科学版）》，
　　2018 年第 5 期

Russia in the late 1870s that the Northeast China border issues in the late Qing Dynasty emerged. From 1880 to 1883, Wu Dacheng, as a third-rank official in the capital, was ordered to manage the border affairs in Northeast China. He strengthened the border defense in Northeast China by successively implementing effective measures such as training border defense troops, pacifying the gold bandits in the border areas, and raising funds for borderland reclamation. At the same time, in response to new problems that emerged on the China-Russia border, he put forward suggestions such as setting up a Chinese consular office in Vladivostok and protecting Korea to curb Japan, and offered strategies for strengthening the border affairs in Northeast China. In 1886, Wu Dacheng was again ordered to go out of the pass. He re-surveyed the eastern border with Russia, and recovered some of the territory occupied by Russia, thus making an important contribution to safeguarding national territorial sovereignty.[23]

在参与甲午中日战争的诸多晚清大员中，吴大澂是个悲剧人物。他曾治黄河有功而被朝廷赏赐头品顶戴，又因甲午战争中主动请缨援辽惨败而落得个"言大而夸""一味吹牛"的讥评。先是被撤去帮办军务大臣之职，虽在同乡翁同龢的疏通下，得以革职留任，但还难免屡遭参劾。戊戌政变他被视为"翁党"革职回乡，诏书称"开缺巡抚吴大澂，居心狡诈，言大而夸，遇事粉饰，声名恶劣，着即革职，永不叙用"。官方评价如此，民间也同样恶评不断。与他同时代的诗人黄遵宪就写下《渡辽将军歌》讥讽他："两军相接战甫交，纷纷鸟散空营逃。弃官脱剑无人惜，只幸腰间印未失。"1902 年（光绪二十八年）他在贫病中去世，终年 68 岁。光绪三十年甲辰寒松老人张鸣珂在怀念吴大澂的《怀人感旧诗》中依然不无叹息地提到这次战败："许书列小篆，君以籀文补。又编古玉图，令人识璜琥。惜哉统孤军，一溃难再鼓。"《清史稿》则将上述印象汇集为对他的盖棺论定："大澂治河有名，而好言兵，才气自喜，卒以虚骄败。"[24]

Among the many high-ranking officials in the late Qing Dynasty who participated in the First Sino-Japanese War, Wu Dacheng was a tragic figure. He had been rewarded with the first-rank official headdress by the imperial court for making contributions to the governance of the Yellow River, but was later criticized as "boastful" and "always bragging" due to a crushing defeat in the First Sino-Japanese War when he volunteered for a mission to assist Liaoning. At first, he was removed from the position of assistant military affairs minister. Although through the mediation of his fellow-townsman Weng Tonghe, he was allowed to retain his post, he was repeatedly impeached. During the Wuxu Coup in 1898, he was regarded as a member of the "Weng clique". As a result, he was dismissed from office and returned to his hometown. The imperial edict stated, "Wu Dacheng, the ousted provincial governor, is full of cunning intentions, boastful, fond of glossing over problems when dealing with matters, and notorious. Hereby, he will be dismissed from office and never be re-employed." In addition to the negative official evaluation, common people also gave harsh opinions continuously. Huang Zunxian, a poet of the same era, wrote in *Song of the General Crossing the Liao River* to satire him: "When the two armies met and the battle just started, they scattered like birds, leaving the camp empty. No one showed regret when he abandoned his official post and laid aside his sword, only feeling relieved that the seal at the waist was not lost." In 1902 (the 28th year of Emperor Guangxu's Reign), he died of poverty

---

24 王耘撰《清末边疆能吏吴大澂学政述评——兼论晚清经世之学与治政实践》，来源《东北史地》，2011 年第 4 期

and illness at the age of 68. In the 30th year of Emperor Guangxu's Reign or the year of Jiachen in the sexagenary cycle, when Zhang Mingke, titled as Hansong Laoren, wrote *Poem of Yearning for Old Friends and Reminiscing about the Past* to commemorate Wu Dacheng, he mentioned this defeat with a sigh: "You supplemented and improved the content of small seal script in Xu Shen's *Shuowen Jiezi* with zhouwen (a kind of large seal script). You also compiled an atlas of ancient jades, enabling people to recognize the shapes of ancient jade artifacts such as huang (semicircular jade pendant) and hu (tiger-shaped jade). But it's a pity that you led an isolated and unsupported army. Once it was routed, it could hardly be rallied and recovered." *Draft of the Qing History* summarized the above impressions as a final comment on him: "Wu Dacheng was famous for governing the Yellow River, but fond of talking about military affairs. He was complacent about his talent, and finally defeated for his overweening arrogance."[24]

1868 年，吴大澂考中进士，从此开始步入仕途。他先后担任过翰林院编修、陕甘学政、河南河北道、吉林边防会办、北洋事务会办、广东巡抚、河道总督、湖南巡抚等职，侧身官场几近 30 年，仕途顺达亦颇有政绩。1894 年中日甲午战争爆发时，吴大澂正在湖南巡抚任内。面对日本侵略者的嚣张气焰，一贯坚持主战而又以"知兵"自誉的吴大澂激于爱国义愤，"自请赴敌"，连续电奏清廷，要求"统帅湘军赴朝督战"。日军侵入辽东后，吴大澂奉命督师出关，但结果却是在辽东前线一败再败，不仅丧师失地，给战争全局带来灾难，也使自己身败名裂，遗羞后世[25]。

In 1868, Wu Dacheng was admitted as a Jinshi through the imperial

---

25 曹立前撰《吴大澂评述》，来源《山东师范大学学报（人文社会科学版）》，2004 年第 2 期

examination, and started his official career. He served as Compiler of the Hanlin Academy, Educational Inspector of Shaanxi and Gansu, Intendant of Henan-Hebei Circuit, Assistant Director of Jilin Border Defense, Assistant Director of Beiyang Affairs, Governor of Guangdong, Governor of the Yellow River Conservancy, and Governor of Hunan successively. He was in the officialdom for nearly 30 years, with a smooth official career and many achievements. When the First Sino-Japanese War broke out in 1894, Wu Dacheng was serving as Governor of Hunan. Facing the swaggering arrogance of the Japanese invaders, Wu Dacheng, who had always advocated war and boasted of being "knowledgeable in military affairs", was inspired by patriotic indignation and "volunteered to go to the front line". He continuously telegraphed the Qing Court, requesting to "lead the Hunan Army to Korea and supervise the battle". After the Japanese army invaded Liaodong, he was ordered to lead the army out of the pass. However, he suffered from successive defeats on the Liaodong front. He not only lost the troops and territory, bringing disaster to the overall situation of the war, but also lost his reputation, leaving a legacy of shame for future generations.[25]

在中国近代，俄国和日本恐怖侵略中国，中国清末人物吴大澂下政策抗俄有成，上战场抗日有败，能够侧面说明实践出真知有不老之处。

In modern Chinese history, when Russia and Japan brutally invaded China, Wu Dacheng, a figure in the late Qing Dynasty, achieved success by formulating policies against Russia but failed when going to the battlefield against Japan. This indirectly shows that the principle of "gaining true knowledge through practice" remains valid.

在后来，后人将"上战场和下政策之间的关系"延伸为"研究两线作战，只能一线作战"的高度，也有自圆其说的论点。

Later, people elevated the "relationship between going to the battlefield and formulating policies" to the height of "studying two-front warfare, but only being able to engage in one-front warfare". There are also self-justifying arguments to support that.

中国作为一个文明古国，有着几千年灿烂夺目的国家文化。在中国古代，就有四面受敌的汉人朝廷。以两宋为例子，宋代对外联盟政策，是导致本朝覆灭的直接原因之一，这说明当代政府要把国家安全放在自己身上，不能过分依赖外国。

As a country with ancient civilization, China has a splendid national culture with a history of several thousand years. In ancient China, there were regimes of Han people that were surrounded by enemies on all sides. Taking the Song Dynasty as an example, its policy of external alliance was a direct reason for its collapse. This shows that contemporary governments should assume full responsibility for national security instead of overly relying on foreign countries.

10—13 世纪东亚政治格局存在着剧烈动荡与变化，格局的"主角"此消彼长，10—11 世纪的大国是辽、北宋，12 世纪初随着辽、北宋国力相继减弱，金成了主导东亚政治格局发展的主要力量，随着金的力量从顶峰迅速衰落，至 12 世纪下半期东亚格局中形成了南宋与金对峙的局面，1234 年金亡后，蒙古（元）又成了主宰这一区域的"主角"，东亚政治格局的变动决定着两宋的外交。[26]

There were drastic upheavals and changes in the political pattern of East Asia from the 10th to the 13th century, with ebbs and flows of "leading roles". The major powers in the 10 - 11th centuries were the Liao Dynasty and the Northern Song Dynasty. In the early 12th century, as the national strength of the Liao Dynasty and the Northern Song

---

26　张云筝撰《宋代外交思想研究》，来源《河南大学》，2010 年

Dynasty weakened successively, the Jin Dynasty became the main force dominating the development of the political pattern in East Asia. After the strength of the Jin Dynasty declined rapidly from its peak, a confrontation between the Southern Song Dynasty and the Jin Dynasty was formed in the political pattern of East Asia in the second half of the 12th century. After the Jin Dynasty perished in 1234, the Mongols (Yuan Dynasty) became the "leading role" dominating this region. The changes in the political pattern of East Asia determined the foreign policies of the two Song Dynasties.[26]

宋朝（960—1279）是中国历史上承五代十国、下启元朝的时代，分北宋和南宋。960 年，后周大将赵匡胤，黄袍加身，建立宋朝。宋真宗、宋仁宗时期步入了盛世，北宋初期加强了中央集权，解决了藩镇割据问题。1127 年靖康之耻，北宋灭亡。宋高宗赵构南迁，建立了南宋。后期抗蒙战争连年，到 1276 年，元朝军队攻占临安，1279 年，8 岁小皇帝赵昺，被大臣陆秀夫背着跳海而死，崖山海战后，宋朝彻底灭亡[27]。

The Song Dynasty (960 - 1279) was an era in Chinese history that followed the Five Dynasties and Ten Kingdoms period and preceded the Yuan Dynasty. It can be divided into the Northern Song Dynasty and the Southern Song Dynasty. In 960, Zhao Kuangyin, a general of the Later Zhou Dynasty, staged a coup by putting on a yellow robe and established the Song Dynasty. During the reigns of Emperor Zhenzong and Emperor Renzong, the dynasty ushered in a prosperous period. In the early years of the Northern Song Dynasty, the centralization of power was strengthened, and the problem of separatist warlords was solved. In 1127, due to the Jingkang Incident, the Northern Song Dynasty perished.

27　吴斌撰《宋朝：养鸽玩鸽的流金岁月》，来源《中华信鸽》，2013 年第 5 期

Zhao Gou, Emperor Gaozong, moved south and established the Southern Song Dynasty. Later, there were continuous wars against the Mongols. In 1276, the Yuan army captured Lin'an. In 1279, Minister Lu Xiufu carried the eight-year-old emperor Zhao Bing on his back, and then jumped into the sea, meeting their end. After the Battle of Yashan, the Song Dynasty completely perished.[27]

宋代吸取前代的教训，采取设置文官分权以及完善科举制度等措施防止武将专权，偏重提高文人的社会地位，形成"重文轻武"的国策而且在社会上形成风气。这就使得宋代的精神文化得到发展，拓宽了社会上升流动的渠道，另外过度分权不重武将却又使国防军备孱弱，在与其他民族政权的战争中屡屡失败，社会精神走向衰微。[28]

Drawing lessons from previous dynasties, the Song Dynasty adopted measures such as appointing civil officials to share power, and improving the imperial examination system to prevent military generals from seizing power. It paid attention to raising the social status of literati, and formulated the national policy of "emphasizing literature over military affairs". This also became a social trend. As a result, the spiritual culture of the Song Dynasty thrived and the channels for social upward mobility were broadened. However, excessive decentralization and neglecting of military generals weakened national defense and military preparations. As a result, the dynasty repeatedly failed in wars against other ethnic regimes, and the social spirit declined.[28]

宋代是经晚唐至五代中国分裂割据之后又重新出现统一局面的时代。因此，宋代统治者十分重视唐代藩镇割据的历史经验，在中央与地方的权力分配问题上厉行中央集权，采取了新的措施防

28　钮敏、李仁霞撰《试论宋代"重文轻武"的社会风气》，来源《兰台世界》，2015年

范、限制地方坐大离心。这虽然对维护统一、稳定起了作用，但这都是站在中央和皇帝的角度着想，因此走向剥夺地方，强干弱枝的极端。中央权力一旦压倒地方，使地方缺乏生息经营的自主权和活力，便会限制和破坏地方的经济文化建设。而州府以至县乡，是中央政权的基础，基础既虚，大厦倾覆也在旦夕。宋代是外患最多的时期之一，有来自契丹、辽、夏、金的侵略，而北宋统治者抵抗无力，至于南渡偏安，其中地方无实力，易于虚弱瓦解是其重要原因之一。[29]

The Song Dynasty emerged as a reunified era after the fragmentation of China during the late Tang Dynasty and the Five Dynasties period. Therefore, its rulers attached great importance to the historical lessons of the separatist warlords in the Tang Dynasty. When it came to the distribution of power between the central and local governments, they strictly implemented centralization of power, and adopted new measures to prevent and restrict local authorities from growing too powerful and becoming separatist. This contributed to the maintenance of unity and stability, but it was entirely from the perspective of the central government and the emperor. As a result, they took things to extremes by stripping power from local authorities and excessively strengthening the central government. Once the power of the central government overwhelmed that of the local, and the local authorities were deprived of the autonomy and vitality for development and management, the local economic and cultural construction would be restricted and destroyed. After all, prefectures, counties and towns were the foundation of the central regime. If the foundation was weak, the collapse of the regime

---

29 林英男撰《唐宋时代地方行政体制和强干弱枝传统的形成》，来源《深圳大学学报（人文社会科学版）》，1988 年 3 期

would be only a matter of time. The Song Dynasty was one of the periods with the most external threats, suffering from invasions from the Khitan, Liao, Xia, and Jin. The rulers of the Northern Song Dynasty were weak in resistance, and eventually, they had to retreat southward and seek temporary safety in a corner. One of the important reasons was that the local authorities lacked strength and were prone to being weakened and disintegrated.[29]

南宋与北宋类似，同样犯了联强攻弱的地缘政治战略方面的错误，具体是北宋时的联金攻辽和南宋时的联蒙攻金战略。就联强攻弱这一战略本身而言，不仅不符合地缘战略联弱事强的规律，而且还与宋朝当时的地缘政治形势不相符合。宋朝统治者两次实行联强攻弱的战略，其根源在于对当时的地缘政治形势不了解，以及南宋统治者软弱无能和苟且偷安，他们把国家的安危及收复失地的愿望寄托在别人身上，最终使自己陷入难以自拔的境地。[30]

Similar to the Northern Song Dynasty, the Southern Song Dynasty wrongly adopted a geopolitical strategy of allying with the strong against the weak. Specifically, the Northern Song Dynasty allied with the Jin to attack the Liao, and the Southern Song Dynasty allied with the Mongols to attack the Jin. In terms of the strategy itself, it not only did not conform to the law of the geopolitical strategy of allying with the weak and serving the strong but also did not match the geopolitical situation at that time. The root cause for the two implementations of the strategy of allying with the strong against the weak was that they knew little about the geopolitical situation, and that the rulers of the Southern Song Dynasty were weak and incompetent, and sought only temporary ease and comfort. They pinned the safety of the country and the hope of

---

30　于爱华撰《南宋地缘政治关系研究》，来源《云南大学》，2010 年 5 月

recovering lost territories on others, but eventually found themselves in an inescapable situation.[30]

在中国封建社会发展史上，宋朝占有十分重要的地位。在其统治的 320 年间，把物质文明和精神文明提高到一个新的高度。同时，由于复杂的时代与历史方面的原因，宋朝实行"守内虚外"的治边政策，有效地维持了内部统治的长期稳定，但也造成了对外军事能力的软弱和对外交往的封闭保守。[31]

The Song Dynasty occupied a very important position in the development history of Chinese feudal society. During its rule for 320 years, it elevated the material and spiritual civilizations to a new height. At the same time, due to complex reasons of the era and history, it implemented a border policy of "defending the interior and neglecting the exterior", which effectively maintained the long-term stability of internal rule, but led to weakness in external military capabilities, and the closure and conservatism in foreign affairs.[31]

辽代和金代分别是由契丹贵族和女真贵族建立的少数民族政权。从公元 10 世纪初至 13 世纪前期，辽与五代十国和北宋、金与南宋先后对峙长达 300 年之久，继南北朝之后在中国历史上形成了又一个南北分治的局面。辽金时期占据统治地位的是契丹和女真的上层贵族，但是在其统治下有大量的汉人以及汉化程度较高的其他民族，辽金两代的 300 多年，契丹人和女真人虽为统治阶级，但是仍然无法阻挡本民族融入中华民族的历史潮流。[32]

The Liao Dynasty and the Jin Dynasty were ethnic-minority regimes established by Khitan aristocrats and Jurchen aristocrats respectively.

---

31 方铁撰《论宋朝以大理国为外藩的原因及其"守内虚外"治策》，来源《中央民族大学学报》，2000 年 6 期

32 邵海波、吴敬撰《辽代契丹人与金代女真人汉化过程的对比研究——以陵墓材料为线索的考古学观察》，来源《草原文物》，2011 年 2 期

For more than 300 years from the beginning of the 10th century to the early 13th century, the Liao Dynasty confronted the Five Dynasties and Ten Kingdoms and the Northern Song Dynasty, and the Jin Dynasty confronted the Southern Song Dynasty, leading to another north-south division in Chinese history following the Northern and Southern Dynasties. During the Liao and Jin periods, the upper aristocrats of Khitan and Jurchen were in a dominant position, but there were a large number of Han people and other highly-Sinicized ethnic groups under their rules. For the more than 300 years of the Liao and Jin Dynasties, although the Khitan and Jurchen aristocrats were the ruling class, they could not stop the historical trend of their own ethnic groups integrating into the Chinese nation.[32]

元代是中国非常重要的一个朝代，它以漠北少数民族入主中原，并最终建立了一个大一统帝国。为了巩固大一统帝国，元朝统治者尤其是忽必烈主动认同以儒学为核心的中华文化，推行汉化政策，由此赢得了中原地区民众对其政权的认同。[33]

The Yuan Dynasty was a very important dynasty in China. It was a unified empire established by an ethnic group from the northern desert regions when they entered the Central Plains. In order to consolidate this unified empire, the rulers of the Yuan Dynasty, especially Kublai Khan, took an initiative to identify with Chinese culture centered around Confucianism and implemented Sinicization policies, thus winning the recognition of the people in the Central Plains for their regime.[33]

国家改头换面需要资金和时间的支持。宋朝敌国强于武力，弱于文化，他们愿意汉化，这已经代表契丹族、女真族、蒙古族等敌

33　姜海军撰《"元承金学"及程朱之学的北传》，来源《石家庄学院学报》，2013 年
　　1 期

人重视经济发展是迟早的事情。与此同时，国家的经济发展和经济政策又是密不可分。所以，"重文轻武"的大宋朝廷联外对付共同敌人，是在帮助潜在敌人省去了一部分下达经济政策的功夫和工夫。为此，在后来，赵宋朝廷"重文轻武"到底利弊如何评判还是未知之数。不过，北宋"联金抗辽"和南宋"联蒙抗金"的联外政策是肯定要被后人抨击的，这也是宋朝读书人的文化耻辱。

A country's transformation requires financial and temporal support. The enemies of the Song Dynasty were strong in military strength but weak in culture. Their willingness to be Sinicized indicated that enemies such as the Khitan, Jurchen, and Mongolian would attach importance to economic development sooner or later. At the same time, a country's economic development is closely related to its economic policies. Therefore, by allying with foreign powers to deal with common enemies, the Song Dynasty court, which emphasized literature over military affairs, was actually helping potential enemies save some of the effort and time in formulating economic policies. Therefore, there is still a dispute when it comes to evaluating the advantages and disadvantages of the policy of "emphasizing literature over military affairs" adopted by the Zhao Song Court. However, the policy of "allying with the Jin against the Liao" adopted by the Northern Song Dynasty and the policy of "allying with the Mongols against the Jin" adopted by the Southern Song Dynasty are definitely to be criticized by later generations, and they were a cultural disgrace for literati of the Song Dynasty.

变法与改革都需要文化作为后盾才能功成名就。虽然，两宋时期"重文轻武""强干弱枝""守内虚外"有不少的弊端，却也能让宋朝境内减少文盲。所以，这些国家政策不能算是宋朝的官方"败笔"。

Reforms will end in failure without cultural support. Although the policies of "emphasizing literature over martial arts", "strengthening the central government and weakening the local", and "defending the interior and neglecting the exterior" in the Song Dynasty had many drawbacks, they could help reduce illiteracy within the territory. Therefore, these national policies cannot be regarded as official "failures" of the Song Dynasty.

非我族类，其心必异。某国政权亲近外国和外国侵略都常常产生实质性的关联，终究酿成社会大患，国家悲剧层出不穷。就像以华制华和以洋制洋，都是因地制宜的一部分。只要是因地制地，就没有速战速决的可能，无论其历史结果是什么，都能证明做人要靠自己。

People of other races are likely to have alien intentions. There is often a substantive connection between a regime's close relations with foreign countries and foreign aggression. It will ultimately lead to major social disasters and endless national tragedies. Policies such as using the Chinese to control the Chinese and using foreigners to control foreigners are part of the strategy of adapting to local conditions. As long as this strategy is adopted, a quick victory will be impossible. No matter what the historical results are, it can prove that one should rely on oneself.

甲午战争中国战败后，日本成为中国最主要的敌人，清政府求助于欧洲列强以抗衡日本。李鸿章曾向卡西尼许诺，若俄能以力阻日，中国愿在军事上和交通上提供便利。俄国带头干涉还辽，加强了它在中国的政治影响，中俄《四厘借款合同》的签订又提高了俄国在清政府许多达官显贵心目中的地位。一时"联俄抗日"之气氛甚浓，不仅慈禧、李鸿章决心投入俄国怀抱，即使原来亲英、日的一些廷臣如刘坤一、张之洞等人，也一反旧辙，主张与俄国订立密约，共同对付日本。"这种有害的主张正好适应了沙俄对华扩张的需要，给他提供了一个在中国东北勒索'借地筑路'权的现成机会。"于是，俄国借口尼古拉二世在 1896 年 5 月 26 日举行加冕典礼，指名邀请亲俄派官僚李鸿章以"钦差头等出使大臣"身份前往祝贺。临行前，慈禧太后向李鸿章面授"联络西洋，牵制东洋"的外交宗旨。[34]

After China was defeated in the First Sino-Japanese War, Japan became the primary enemy of China. The Qing government turned to European powers to counter Japan. Li Hongzhang once promised Cassini that if Russia could use its military strength to prevent Japan from invading China, China would be willing to provide convenience in military affairs and transportation. Russia took the lead in forcing Japan to return the Liaodong Peninsula to China, and this action strengthened its political influence in China. In addition, The signing of *Four-Percent Loan Contract* between China and Russia enhanced Russia's status in the eyes of many high- ranking officials of the Qing government. For a time, the atmosphere of "allying with Russia against Japan" was very strong. Not only Empress Dowager Cixi and Li Hongzhang decided to side with Russia, but even some court officials who were originally pro-British and pro-Japanese, such as Liu Kunyi and Zhang Zhidong, changed their attitude and advocated signing a secret treaty with Russia to jointly deal with Japan. "This harmful claim coincidentally met the needs of Tsarist Russia's expansion in China, which provided it with a ready-made opportunity to extort the right to 'lease land for railway construction' in Northeast China." Therefore, on the pretext of the coronation ceremony of Nicholas II on May 26, 1896, Tsarist Russia specifically invited Li

---

34 马蔚云撰《俄国对华政策的演变与中东铁路的修筑》，来源《俄罗斯学刊》，2013 年 2 期

Hongzhang, a pro-Russian bureaucrat, to attend the ceremony as the "Imperial Special Envoy of the First Rank" and offer congratulations. Before his departure, Empress Dowager Cixi personally imparted the diplomatic tenet of "allying with Western powers to contain Japan."[34]

沙俄对于清政府当时流露出的"联俄"倾向十分高兴。因为"联俄"有助于俄国实施其所谓的"和平渗入"的侵略方针，即在经济和财政上扩大在华的势力范围，而不使用武力。其具体内容主要包括"要把持中国的税收、财政、货币，并在中国境内建造铁路、架设电线等，其中尤其以建造通往中国东北的西伯利亚大铁路最为重要"。[35]

Tsarist Russia was very pleased with the Qing government's inclination towards "allying with Russia". The reason was that "allying with Russia" was conducive to its implementation of the so-called "peaceful penetration" invasion policy, that is, expanding its sphere of influence in China economically and financially without using armed force. The detailed content mainly included "controlling China's taxation, finance, and currency, and building railways and laying telegraph lines within China's territory, among which the construction of the Trans-Siberian Railway leading to Northeast China was of particular importance."[35]

中日甲午战争后，晚清政府企图利用俄国来抵制日本的侵略扩张，这根本就是一种不切实际的主观幻想。俄国逼迫日本归还中国的辽东半岛，不是为了维护中国的主权与领土完整，而是为了独吞辽东半岛。它无论是以侵略者的面目，还是以救星的角色来涉足中国事务，其根本目的是永不改变的——对中国实施战略分割与

---

35 殷欣撰《从甲午战争到日俄战争：俄国远东政的嬗变（1895-1904）》，来源《南京大学》，2011 年 5 月

包围。[36]

After the First Sino-Japanese War, the late Qing government's attempt to leverage Russia to resist Japan's aggression and expansion was only an unrealistic subjective fantasy. Russia forced Japan to return the Liaodong Peninsula to China not to safeguard China's sovereignty and territorial integrity, but to seize the Liaodong Peninsula exclusively. Whether it involved itself in Chinese affairs as an invader or a savior, its fundamental goal remained unchanged - to implement strategic division and encirclement of China.[36]

李鸿章作为晚清重臣，在晚清外交中发挥了重要作用。[37]

As a high-ranking official in the late Qing Dynasty, Li Hongzhang played an important role in the diplomacy.[37]

"联俄制日"是李鸿章一贯倡导的"以夷制夷"外交策略的中心和关键环节。随着时势不同，"联俄"外交的基础和目的也不相同。1898 年前，李鸿章"联俄"策略主要是针对日本。1898 年后，"联俄"不仅是为了"制日"，还要防范其他列强。但是，以《中俄密约》的签订为标志的清末"联俄制日"政策的实施，并没给清廷带来预想的好处。沙皇政府非但没能帮助清廷免受其他帝国主义侵略者的欺凌，反而充当了祸害中国的头号罪魁。[38]

"Allying with Russia to curb Japan" was the core and key part of Li Hongzhang's consistent diplomatic strategy of "using barbarians to control barbarians". As the situation changed, the basis and purpose of the diplomatic policy of "allying with Russia" also changed. Before 1898,

---

36　雷大川撰《晚清政府"联俄政策"刍议》，来源《长白学刊》，2011 年 2 期

37　张玉芬撰《从联日到联俄　李鸿章与＜中俄密约＞的签订》，来源《南都学坛》，2016 年 3 期

38　张雨撰《＜中俄密约＞与清朝末年的"联俄制日"政策》，来源《黑龙江省社会科学院》，2008 年 11 月

Li Hongzhang's strategy of "allying with Russia" was mainly to deal with Japan. After 1898, this strategy was not only to "contain Japan" but also to guard against other imperialist powers. However, the implementation of the policy of "allying with Russia to curb Japan" in the late Qing Dynasty, marked by the signing of the Sino-Russian Secret Treaty, did not bring expected benefits to the Qing court. Instead of helping the Qing court to be free from the bullying of other imperialist invaders, the Tsarist government became the prime culprit in ravaging China.[38]

"请神容易送神难"。历史能够证明，政府把国家希望放在外国人身上，到底是象征能人所不能，还是自己灭自己的威风，以及是凡事留一线，日后好相见，后人最有发言权。

"It's easier to invite a deity than to send it away." History can prove that future generations are best positioned to judge whether a government's act of pinning the country's hopes on foreigners symbolizes an attempt to achieve what one cannot do alone, or undermines its own confidence, or serves as a diplomatic maneuver of "leaving some leeway in everything for future interactions."

在中国古代史上，一旦朝廷腐朽，不知所谓，当官就不会下政策，人民违法乱纪，军队上战场杀敌大打折扣，造就国家安全堕落，形成一种恶性循环。就像在中国明朝，大明多位皇帝都面临倭寇问题，是中国官民不会合作发展经济的范本。

In ancient Chinese history, once the imperial court became corrupt and incompetent, officials would not formulate proper policies, the people would break laws and violate disciplines, and the army would greatly lose its combat effectiveness on the battlefield. These situations would lead to the decline of national security and the formation of a vicious cycle. For instance, in the Ming Dynasty, several emperors faced the problem of Japanese pirates. It was a typical example of the lack of cooperation between Chinese officials and the people in economic development.

中国明朝倭患从开始到结束，都与中国的经济问题有紧密联系。世人用现代化眼光来看中国古代的倭寇，能将其行为定义为抱有恐怖主义的有组织犯罪。

From start to finish, the problem of Japanese pirates in the Ming Dynasty was closely related to China's economic issues. Viewing the Japanese pirates in ancient China from a modern perspective, we can define their actions as organized crimes with elements of terrorism.

20 世纪末出版的权威著作《中国历史大辞典》中有"倭寇"词条，将其明确定义为"明时骚扰中国沿海一带的日本海盗"。[39]

The term "Wokcu" in the authoritative work *Dictionary of Chinese History* published at the end of the 20th century is clearly defined as "Japanese pirates who harassed the coastal areas of China during the Ming Dynasty."[39]

元末明初的倭寇以日本人为主，但到了嘉靖年间，倭寇的主刀就是中国人了。[40]

At the end of the Yuan Dynasty and the beginning of the Ming Dynasty, the Japanese pirates were mainly Japanese. However, during Emperor Jiajing's Reign, the main force of the Japanese pirates was Chinese.[40]

对假倭的身份问题，明人郑晓是这样总结的："小民迫于贪酷，困于饥寒，相率入海从之。凶徒、逸囚、罢吏、黠僧，及衣冠失职、书生不得志、群不逞者，为之奸细，为之乡道。弱者图饱暖旦夕，强者忿臂欲泄其怒。"一句话：三教九流，无所不包。[41]

---

39 郭又惊撰《倭寇 一个王朝的谎言?》，来源《中国国家地理》，2012 年第 2 期

40 《海禁之祸：明朝倭寇大多数是中国人假扮》腾讯新闻（腾讯网），www.qq.com
    2011 年 2 月 21 日

41 同上

Regarding the identity of the so-called "false Japanese pirates", Zheng Xiao in the Ming Dynasty summarized it as follows: "Ordinary people, constrained by avarice and cruelty, and afflicted with hunger and cold, successively went to sea and followed them. Violent criminals, escaped prisoners, dismissed officials, crafty monks, as well as members of the upper class who lost their official positions, scholars who were frustrated in their ambitions, and a group of people who had evil intentions and always sought to disrupt served as spies and guides. The weak sought merely to satisfy their immediate needs for food and clothing, while the strong, driven by anger, were eager to vent their fury." In a word, they included people from all walks of life.[41]

明代的海防是因防御倭寇而形成的。倭寇对中国沿海的侵扰，出现于南宋，元末趋于严重，到明初则更为猖獗。1336 年，日本分裂为南朝和北朝，双方争战不已。明洪武二十五年（1392），南朝灭亡，战乱基本平息。在长期战乱中，许多溃兵、败将、武士以及失去生产手段的浪人和冒险商人相互勾结，在封建诸侯的组织和支持下，不断对中国和朝鲜沿海进行侵扰和掠夺。加上逃亡到沿海岛屿的张士诚、方国珍、陈友谅残余势力的勾结，倭寇对沿海的侵扰十分严重，宣德之后，才有所减弱。1467 年，日本发生了应仁文明之乱，进入了战国时期。众多诸侯纷争不已，延续了一百多年。战乱期间，诸侯争相同中国贸易，贸易不成，遂支持武士、浪人和商人进行劫掠。[42]

The coastal defense in the Ming Dynasty aimed to defend against Japanese pirates. The harassment of the Chinese coast by Japanese pirates emerged in the Southern Song Dynasty, became increasingly serious at the end of the Yuan Dynasty, and became more rampant at the beginning

---

42 范中义撰《明代海防述略》，来源《历史研究》，1990 年第 3 期

of the Ming Dynasty. In 1336, Japan split into the Southern and Northern Dynasties, with the two sides locked in an endless struggle. In the 25th year of Emperor Hongwu's Reign of the Ming Dynasty (1392), the Southern Dynasty perished, and the war basically ended. During the long-term chaos, many defeated soldiers, generals, samurais, as well as ronins who lost their means of production and adventurous merchants colluded with each other. Organized and supported by feudal lords, they kept on harassing and looting the coasts of China and Korea. Colluding with the remaining forces of Zhang Shicheng, Fang Guozhen, and Chen Youliang who fled to the coastal islands, these Japanese pirates harassed the coast more rampantly. This situation was not eased until Emperor Xuande's Reign. In 1467, the Onin-Bunmei War broke out, and Japan entered the Warring States period. The continuous strife between numerous feudal lords lasted for more than a hundred years. During the war-torn period, the feudal lords vied to trade with China. However, they failed to achieve their expected goals in the trades, so they supported samurais, ronins, and merchants to conduct plundering.[42]

明嘉靖年间，中国东南沿海以中国人为主的"倭寇"猖獗一时。考察其成因，明政府实行严厉的海禁政策虽是形成嘉靖"大倭寇"的主要原因。但除此之外，流民的影响、政治上的黑暗、军备的松弛，以及葡萄牙人东来和日本战国混乱等外部因素的刺激也是形成明"嘉靖大倭寇"的重要原因。[43]

During Emperor Jiajing's Reign of the Ming Dynasty, the "Japanese pirates", mainly composed of Chinese people, were extremely rampant along the southeast coast of China. Although the strict sea-ban policy implemented by the Ming government was the main reason for the

---

43 刘国华撰《明"嘉靖大倭寇"成因探析》，来源《乐山师范学院学报》，2004 年 7 期

"major Japanese Pirates", the influence of displaced people, the darkness of politics, and the relaxation of military preparations, as well as the stimulation of external factors such as the arrival of the Portuguese and the chaos of the Warring States period in Japan were also important factors contributing to the "major Japanese Pirates during Emperor Jiajing's Reign" in the Ming Dynasty.[43]

戚继光（1528—1588），字元敬，号南塘，晚号孟诸，山东蓬莱人，是中国历史上杰出的军事家，伟大的民族英雄。他南歼倭寇，屡战屡捷，扫平了长期为害的倭寇，保障了东南海疆的安宁；北御鞑靼，固我长城，保卫了北部疆域的安全，促进了汉蒙民族的和平发展。戚继光为保卫国家安全和人民的生命财产安全奋斗了一生，建立了不朽的功勋；所著的《纪效新书》《练兵实纪》等著名的军事著作，丰富了祖国的兵学宝库，为后人留下了宝贵的精神财富；重修的东起山海关西至居庸关长城，成为中华民族的瑰宝。[44]

Qi Jiguang (1528 - 1588), a native of Penglai, Shandong, also known as Yuanjing by courtesy name, Nantang by literary name, and Mengzhu by late-stage literary name, was an outstanding military strategist and a great national hero in Chinese history. In the south, he annihilated Japanese pirates, achieved successive victories, eradicated the long-standing threat of Japanese pirates, and ensured the peace of the southeast coastal areas. In the north, he resisted the Tatars, strengthened the Great Wall, safeguarded the security of the northern border, and promoted the peaceful development of the Han and Mongolian ethnic groups. He dedicated his entire life to safeguarding national security and the safety of people's lives and property, and established immortal feats. His famous military works such as *New Book Recording Effective Military Methods*

44　卢如平撰《浙东抗倭述略》，来源《台州学院学报》，2011 年 2 期

and *Practical Record of Military Training* enriched the treasure house of Chinese military science, serving as precious spiritual wealth for future generations. The Great Wall rebuilt by him, stretching from Shanhai Pass in the east to Juyong Pass in the west, has become a treasure of the Chinese nation.[44]

　　然而值得注意的是，戚继光于 1566 年才基本扫除倭寇，部分放开海禁的隆庆帝是 1567 年即位的。这说明戚继光通过军事打击并不能完全消灭海商集团，平定倭患的根本措施是开放海禁[45]。

Notably, it was not until 1566 that Qi Jiguang basically eradicated the Japanese pirates, but Emperor Longqing, who partially lifted the sea ban, ascended the throne in 1567. This indicates that Qi Jiguang could not completely eliminate the maritime merchant groups merely through military strikes, and that the fundamental measure for quelling the Japanese pirate menace was the lifting of the sea ban.[45]

　　所谓"海禁"，又称"禁海"，最早开始于元代，当时主要是禁止海上的一切活动，但只是临时性政策，遂禁遂开，禁海政策不具有连续性。到明朝禁海政策被继承和强化，其主要目的是禁止民间海外贸易，而官方贸易也受到严格限制，形成了比较完整的禁海政策体系，阻碍了中国对外贸易的发展。[46]

The so-called "sea-ban", also known as "maritime prohibition", was first launched in the Yuan Dynasty. At that time, all maritime activities were prohibited, but it was only a temporary policy, and the ban was lifted and imposed intermittently. That is to say, the sea-ban policy lacked continuity. In the Ming Dynasty, the policy was inherited and strengthened, mainly aiming to prohibit private overseas trade. The

---

45　赵玉敏撰《从戚继光抗倭看明朝的海禁政策》，来源《考试周刊》，2015 年第 44 期
46　韩庆撰《明朝实行海禁政策的原因探究》，来源《大连海事大学学报（社会科学版）》，2011 年 5 期

official trade was also strictly restricted. Therefore, a relatively complete sea-ban policy system was formed, which hindered the development of China's foreign trade.[46]

隆庆初年朝廷采纳福建巡抚都御史涂泽民"请开海禁，准贩东西二洋"（《饷税考》）的建议，允民海外贸易，开放海禁，使私人贸易合法化，自此，倭患才逐渐平息下去[47]。

In the early years of Emperor Longqing's Reign, the imperial court adopted the suggestion of Tu Zemin, then serving as Governor of Fujian and Superintendent of the Censorate. He proposed "lifting the sea-ban and permitting merchants to engage in trading activities in the East and West Oceans" (*Examination of Tax Revenue*). As a result, the people were allowed to engage in overseas trade, the sea ban was lifted, and private trade was legalized. After that, the Japanese pirate menace gradually subsided.[47]

士农工商能够发展为三百六十行，跟经济发达密切相关。经济矛盾掀起"大风大浪"，经济问题就浮出水面，三山五岳纷纷铤而走险，酿成社会问题。中国用海禁和反海禁造成倭寇兴衰成败，都能正反两面证明"收益越高，风险越大"。从古至今，无论是丰衣足食，还是大富大贵，做生意考虑成本和利润是不可缺少的要素。为此，追求荣华富贵去铤而走险的士农工商大有人在。

The evolution of the traditional four occupations (scholars, farmers, artisans, and merchants) into the so-called "360 trades" is closely related to the prosperity of the economy. When economic contradictions stir up "great waves", economic problems will emerge, and people from all walks of life may take risks and cause social problems. In China, the rise

---

47　王红、凌文超撰《论隆庆时期"南倭北虏"问题的缓和》，来源《忻州师范学院学报》，2006 年第 6 期

and fall of Japanese pirates caused by the sea-ban and the anti-sea-ban policies can prove from the positive and negative aspects that "the higher the return, the greater the risk". Since ancient times, whether for having ample food and clothing or for attaining great wealth, considering costs and profits is an essential element in doing business. Therefore, many people among scholars, farmers, artisans, and merchants took risks in pursuit of glory, wealth, and status.

中国历代王朝从起始到覆灭，都经历了各种各样的恐怖主义。在中国宋金元的战争史之中，中国全真教领导者丘处机劝诫成吉思汗，不要肆意多造无辜的杀戮，从而功德无量，侧面和局部减少了蒙古大军的暴行。

From the establishment to the downfall, all dynasties in Chinese history witnessed various forms of terrorism. In the history of wars during the Song, Jin, and Yuan Dynasties, Qiu Chuji, the leader of the Quanzhen School, admonished Genghis Khan not to indiscriminately kill the innocent, thus performing a great deed of merit and reducing the atrocities of the Mongolian army to some extent.

丘处机（1148—1227 年）是中国金元时期的道教重要支派全真道的创始人之一。他不仅是道教史上一位著名的宗教领袖，而且是一位对当时政局有着重大影响的风云人物。通观丘处机一生的重大活动，可以清楚地看到他对道教改革以及维护社会安定、抚恤民众所做出的特殊历史贡献。[48]

Qiu Chuji (1148 - 1227) was one of the founders of the Quanzhen School, an important branch of Taoism during the Jin and Yuan Dynasties. He was not only a famous religious leader in the history of Taoism but

---

48 翟如潜撰《丘处机的历史贡献》，来源《烟台师范学院学报（哲学社会科学版）》，1998 年 2 期

also a prominent figure who had a significant impact on the then political situation. By examining the major activities throughout his life, we can clearly see his special historical contributions to the reform of Taoism, the maintenance of social stability, and the consolation to the people.[48]

丘处机是金元时期伟大的道教思想家和实践家。他心系苍生，捍卫和平，以高龄之躯远赴大漠，劝诫成吉思汗止杀寡欲，保全黎民苍生；他以慈悲为本，在百姓罹难之际，超度亡灵，斋醮禳禁，给予苦难黎民精神慰藉，表达对和平的渴望；他苦己利人，感化民众，教导门徒，庇护百姓，广利有情；他立观度人，大开善门，分粮济馁，修观建场，安抚八方流民。此种济世为怀的气魄和风骨堪称侠之大者。此外，他还继承重阳真人遗志，光大门楣，为全真教的隆盛，乃至中国道教史的发展，做出了不可磨灭的贡献。[49]

Qiu Chuji was a great Taoist thinker and practitioner during the Jin and Yuan Dynasties. Caring about common people and being determined to defend peace, he went to the desert in his senior age to admonish Genghis Khan to stop killing and reduce desires, so as to protect the common people. Holding compassion in his heart, he performed rituals to release the souls of the deceased, and held Taoist ceremonies to pray for blessings and dispel disasters when the people were in distress. These actions provided the distressed people with spiritual comfort, and expressed his yearning for peace. He endured hardships to benefit others, influenced the people, taught his disciples, protected the common people, and showed kindness to all beings. He established Taoist temples to guide people, engaged extensively in charitable acts, distributed food to relieve the starving, built Taoist temples and venues, and appeased displaced people from across the country. With the spirit and mettle of relieving

---

49　郭蕴荞撰《论丘处机的宗教实践观》，来源《青春岁月》，2018 年第 20 期

the world's distress, he can be regarded as a great hero. In addition, he inherited the will of Wang Chongyang, expanded the influence of the sect, and made indelible contributions to the prosperity of the Quanzhen School and even the development of China's history of Taoism.[49]

某种意义上，成吉思汗个人的价值倾向导致了全真教的迅速崛起，丘处机的西行论道则满足了成吉思汗巩固政权、养生长生、重新审视汉法和加速统一天下的需求。西行之后，全真教成为道教正宗，全真道徒在社会上形成了一个特殊的阶层，"管理天下应有底出家善人"，在成员数量、地位和声望上巨增。丘处机等人更是利用这一机会以积极行善等方式来进一步扩大全真教在社会上的影响。就宗教与皇权的关系而言：皇权是宗教发展的巨大推动力量，没有帝王的扶植，宗教无法获得显赫的地位，其在民间社会中的传播也可能受到限制；宗教安抚民心和护持秩序的功能则有助于帝王更好地获取民心。对于一个国家来说，某一教团影响面的大小并无多大妨碍，而如果国家政权不能得到民众的支持，则将岌岌可危。概言之，成吉思汗与丘处机双方谋求互相适应的积极态度，是他们各自对皇权与宗教合作利弊深思熟虑的结果。然而，在中国传统社会中，社会实体是服从于皇权的，不管某派宗教的起源是出于生存的现实还是生活的理想，它总是依附性的。全真教即使达到了发展的顶峰，也不会对世俗权力结构产生深远和深刻的影响。[50]

In some sense, Genghis Khan's personal value inclination led to the rapid rise of the Quanzhen School, while Qiu Chuji's journey to the west to preach Taoism met Genghis Khan's needs for consolidating the regime, promoting longevity, re-examining the Han laws, and accelerating the unification of China. After his journey to the west, the Quanzhen School became the orthodox of Taoism, and Quanzhen Taoists became a special

---

50　同上

class in society, who "managed all the kindhearted people who have withdrawn from the secular life to pursue religious cultivation across China", and experienced a huge increase in terms of membership size, status and prestige. Qiu Chuji and others took this opportunity to further expand the influence of the Quanzhen School in society by actively doing good deeds. The relationship between religion and imperial power can be described as follows: Imperial power was a huge driving force for the development of religion. Without the support of the emperor, a religion could not become prominent, and its spread in folk society would be restricted. The function of religion to pacify people's minds and maintain order helped the emperor to win the people's support more effectively. For a country, the size of the influence of a certain religious group does not matter. However, if a regime cannot win the support of the people, it will be in jeopardy. In general, the positive attitude of Genghis Khan and Qiu Chuji seeking mutual accommodation was the result of their careful consideration of the advantages and disadvantages of the cooperation between imperial power and religion. However, in traditional Chinese society, the social entity was subordinate to imperial power. No matter whether a certain religious sect originated from the reality of survival or the ideal of life, it was in a subordinate position. Even when the Quanzhen School developed to its peak, it would not have a profound and far-reaching impact on the secular power structure.[50]

在这个世界上，总是有人欢喜，有人忧愁。中国哲学讲究对立统一，形成有阴必有阳，有阳必有阴的哲学理念。即便是多阴少阳，多阳少阴，也是阴阳共存共补的局面，"两面都没有阴阳"就不是中国哲学思想。

In this world, one man's joy is often another man's sorrow. Chinese philosophy emphasizes the unity of opposites, forming the concept that where there is *yin*, there must be *yang*, and where there is *yang*, there must be *yin*. Even the situation of more *yin* and less *yang* or more yang and less yin is one of *yin* and *yang* co-existing and complementing each other. The idea that "there is no *yin* and *yang* on either side" does not conform to Chinese philosophy.

一个人学好哲学，学习兵法可以提高自己的办事效率，使自己更上一层楼，不再原地踏步，提高或增加自己的技能，亦可以为他人之师。万事万物相通相连，就像两人对弈的策略型棋类游戏，就包含哲学和兵法。棋子各有七种十六颗的中国象棋，比棋子非黑即白的围棋，更加民间化，符合多姿多彩的社会形态。

Mastering philosophy and the art of war, one can improve his work efficiency, make further progress rather than staying stagnant, improve his skills, or become a teacher to others. All things in the world are interconnected. For example, a strategic board game played between two people involves both philosophy and art of war. Chinese chess, with sixteen pieces in seven types on each side, is more popular among common people and conforms better to diverse forms of society than Go, whose pieces are either black or white.

中国象棋的双方棋子都可以既能够横着竖着给对手致命一击，也能够又横又竖进行解杀还杀，暗符合纵连横的攻伐策略。也就是说，中国象棋棋手都懂得一些纵横家原理。只是，随着中国象棋棋手的功力深浅不同，所对应的纵横能力也是强弱有别。所以，越精通中国象棋的棋手，越能够有纵横家的能力。在讲究团体合作的现代社会，纵横学说多游说之道，一个人掌握纵横家的能力，才能够更好地联合和孤立他人，壮大自己。

In Chinese chess, either side can deliver a fatal blow to the opponent horizontally or vertically, and respond to an attack or counter-attack horizontally or vertically. This implicitly conforms to the offensive strategies of vertical and horizontal maneuvering. That is to say, Chinese chess players all understand some principles of the School of Vertical and Horizontal Alliance. However, depending on the players' levels of proficiency, their abilities of vertical and horizontal maneuvering vary. Therefore, the more proficient a Chinese chess player is, the more capable he is at vertical and horizontal maneuvering. In modern society, which emphasizes teamwork, the theory of vertical and horizontal maneuvering focuses on the art of persuasion. Only by mastering the skills of vertical and horizontal maneuvering can a person better unite with or isolate others, and strengthen himself.

所谓"纵横"，是"合纵连横"的简称。合纵，有连接直行之意，也泛指联合连横，又作"连衡"，有结盟、联合之意，也有比配、比肩的意思。战国时期"合纵连横"成为特指那些游说之士策略的一种专有名词。[51]

The so-called "vertical and horizontal" is the abbreviation of "vertical integration and horizontal alliance". "Vertical integration" means connecting in a straight line and generally refers to uniting. "Horizontal alliance", also written as "horizontal alliance for checks-and-balances", means forming an alliance or uniting, and also conveys the meaning of being comparable or on a par. During the Warring States period, "vertical integration and horizontal alliance" became a specific term for the strategies of those itinerant persuaders.[51]

纵横家在战国、秦汉之际并不是一个固定的称呼，在先秦时期被称为"游士""说士""辩士""智士""权变之士"，只是因为这些人以积极的态度参加战国时期的合纵连横斗争，才被后人称为纵横家。传统认为，合纵连横是诸国之间国际战略制定与实施的外交

51　程翔章撰《什么是纵横家》，来源《语文教学与研究》，1998 年 4 期

活动，纵横家是主要从事外交活动的外交家。然而认真考察战国史实，合纵连横以及纵横家的活动绝不仅仅局限于此。合纵连横是战国时期兼并与反兼并斗争主要的形式之一，其中有外交斗争，但不仅仅是外交斗争，更多的却是政治斗争、军事斗争乃至富国强兵的改革变法。所有这些斗争都有自己的独特内容，但又相互依存与支撑，具有千丝万缕的勾连，综合起来构成了战国兼并与反兼并斗争的广阔画面。这种情况，决定了合纵连横斗争内容的丰富性、范围的广阔性和参与者的多样性。[52]

During the Warring States period and in the interim between the Qin and Han Dynasties, the School of Vertical and Horizontal Alliance was not a fixed term. In the pre-Qin period, they were called "wandering scholars", "persuading scholars", "debating scholars", "wise scholars", or "resourceful scholars". It was only because they actively participated in the vertical and horizontal struggles during the Warring States period that they were called by later generations as the School of Vertical and Horizontal Alliance. Traditionally, vertical and horizontal maneuvering was regarded as the diplomatic activities of formulating and implementing international strategies among various states, and the School of Vertical and Horizontal Alliance was mainly composed of diplomats engaged in diplomatic activities. However, a careful examination of the historical facts of the Warring States period shows that the activities of vertical and horizontal maneuvering and the School of Vertical and Horizontal Alliance were not merely confined to this. Vertical and horizontal maneuvering was a major form of the annexation and anti-annexation struggles during the Warring States period. It involved diplomatic struggles, but not merely diplomatic struggles. More often, it involved

---

52 张彦修撰《纵横家新论》，来源《史学集刊》，1999 年 2 期

political struggles, military struggles, and even reforms and changes aiming at enriching the country and strengthening the military. All these struggles had their own unique contents, but they were interdependent and mutually supportive, with countless connections. Collectively, they constituted a broad picture of annexation and anti-annexation struggles in the Warring States period. This situation determined that the vertical and horizontal maneuvering involved rich contents, an extensive scope, and diversified participants.[52]

在大千世界，一个人要靠他人才能生活，更要靠自己才能生存。任何人去结交狐朋狗友都是在害人害己。所以，良性人少认识酒肉朋友，多塑造自己的内心品德，也是在教育他人，造福社会。

In this vast world, a person needs to rely on others to live, but more importantly, he must rely on himself to survive. Anyone who makes friends with people of little worth is harming both himself and others. Therefore, people of good nature should make the acquaintance of fewer fair-weather friends and devote more efforts to the cultivation of their inner virtues. It is also a way of educating others and benefiting society.

在中国现代教育时代，大致上可以将中国文化人划分为文科生和理科生两大类别。文科生和理科生都可以自学哲学和兵法，去进行反恐。

In the contemporary era of Chinese education, the cultural people can generally be divided into two categories: liberal arts students and science students. Both can study philosophy and the art of war by themselves to combat terrorism.

在中国历史学，国家社会的损耗和积累都是历史积累的一部分。文科生是研究人文社科的学人，理科生是研究理论科学的学人。文科生以学习历史、地理、政治为基本课程，理科生以学习数学、物理、化学为基本课程。

In the study of Chinese history, both the losses and accumulations of the country and society are considered as part of historical heritage. Liberal arts students study humanities and social sciences, while science students study theoretical sciences. Liberal arts students take history, geography, and politics as their basic courses, while science students take mathematics, physics, and chemistry as their basic courses.

于是，在中国现代社会，文科生是用"课外书喂出来的"，文科生的特长是独立研究知识，前提条件是文科生阅读了大量的课外书，家里需要配置书房，摆放文学和学术书籍。理科生是对工具有熟能生巧的应用，多借助实验室、团队合作去研究工业革命。文科生和理科生既各有所长，也各有所短，算是各有千秋。一旦文科生和理科生发生文化冲突，可以让他们在国家战争的前线和后方一较高下。

Therefore, in modern Chinese society, liberal arts students are "fed by extracurricular books". Liberal arts students are good at studying knowledge independently on the precondition that they have read a large number of extracurricular books, so their homes need to be equipped with a study for literary and academic books. Science students should be proficient in employing tools, and rely more on laboratories and teamwork to study the Industrial Revolution. Liberal arts students and science students have their own strengths and weaknesses, and each has their unique charm. Once a cultural conflict occurs between them, they can have a showdown at the front and rear of a national war.

在 21 世纪，恐怖主义是一个东西方世界都没有解决的国际问题。国家反恐是在捍卫国家安全，付诸实际行动才能说明一切，所以，不管国家反恐运用上战场和下政策是成是败，都是在彰显本国在全球舞台的地位。

In the 21st century, terrorism is an international problem that either

Eastern or Western countries fail to solve. National counter-terrorism aims at defending national security. Only by taking real action can this target be achieved. Therefore, regardless of whether the strategy of going to the battlefield or formulating policies in national counter-terrorism leads to success or failure, it demonstrates the country's status on the global stage.

第一章　中国兵道思想对恐怖主义的剖判

Chapter 1: Analysis of Terrorism Based on Chinese Military Thought

在 21 世纪，学术界阐述什么是"恐怖主义"，是从哲学与法学这两个维度出发。

In the 21st century, the academic community elaborates on "terrorism" from two dimensions: philosophy and law.

由英国学者依高·普里莫拉兹所编，中国学者周展、曹瑞涛、王俊翻译的《恐怖主义研究——哲学上的争议》一书中，从哲学的角度给予"恐怖主义"的定义是："结果，讨论恐怖主义及其相关的道德、政治和法律问题时，困难重重。仅有两件事情是清楚的：恐怖主义是一种暴力；恐怖主义是件坏事，并非什么可以值得自豪和值得支持的事情。没有人把'恐怖主义'一词用在自己身上，没有人会把自己的行为称为恐怖主义，也没有人会把该词用在自己所同情的那些人身上，或把自己所支持的行为称为恐怖主义。正如老生常谈的那样，一个人眼里的恐怖分子是另一个人眼里的自由斗士。这说明，关于恐怖主义的讨论，正如许多公共性的讨论，有双重标准：一种'我们对他们'的形式。"

In *Terrorism: The Philosophical Issues*, a book compiled by British scholar Lgor Primorootz and translated by Chinese scholars Zhou Zhan, Cao Ruitao, and Wang Jun, "terrorism" is defined from a philosophical perspective: "As a result, when discussing terrorism and relevant moral, political, and legal issues, we will encounter numerous difficulties. Only two things are clear: terrorism is violence; terrorism is a bad thing, not something to be proud of or deserving of support. No one applies the term 'terrorism' to himself, no one calls his own action terrorism, no one applies the term to any person he sympathizes with or any action he supports. As a common saying goes, a terrorist in the eyes of one person is a freedom fighter in the eyes of another. This shows that there is a double standard, a form of 'us versus them' for the discussion of terrorism, just as in many public discussions."

中国学者朱威烈在著作《中东反恐怖主义研究》一书中从法学角度给"恐怖主义"下的定义是："恐怖主义是在某种极端信念或意识形态理论驱使下的社会组织或群体，用暴力和威胁等非法手段袭击非战斗人员特别是平民及民用目标，以期产生恐惧的社会心理，借此达到特定政治目的的犯罪行为。"

In *Research on Counter-Terrorism in the Middle East*, a book written by Chinese scholar Zhu Weilie, "terrorism" is defined from a legal perspective: "Terrorism is a criminal act carried out by social organizations or groups, who, driven by certain extreme beliefs or ideological theories, use illegal means such as violence and threat to attack non-combatants, especially civilians and civilian targets, aiming to create a fearful social psychology and thereby achieve specific political goals."

无论是从哲学还是从法学角度，学术界至今都无法给"恐怖主义"这一词语下准确的定义。这造成了世人对恐怖主义有不同的理解和表达。例如，谁是恐怖分子？什么样子才是恐怖袭击？恐怖主义到底是什么？

Whether from a philosophical or legal perspective, the academic community has failed to define the term "terrorism" accurately so far. This leads to different understandings and expressions of terrorism among people. For example, who is a terrorist? What kind of behavior counts as a terrorist attack? What on earth is terrorism?

在人类的发展历史中，无论是古代还是现代，无论是国内还是国外，恐怖活动犯罪都贯穿其中。在中国，最早也是最著名的恐怖活动犯罪莫过于荆轲刺秦王，尽管一代代的文人墨客以及史学家对此进行了种种美化，然而都无法掩盖其恐怖活动犯罪的本质[53]。

Throughout the history of human development, whether in ancient or modern times, in China or foreign countries, terrorist activities and crimes have persisted. In China, the earliest and most famous terrorist activity crime is undoubtedly Jing Ke's attempt to assassinate the King of Qin. Although this event has been glorified by generations of literati and historians in various ways, its nature as a terrorist crime cannot be concealed.[53]

公元前 689 年亚述帝国皇帝辛那赫里布攻克巴比伦后怒焚全城并大水漫灌，还煞有介事立碑传播以便威加四方。41 年后，其孙巴尼帕尔再克巴比伦，将大批反叛者拔舌碎尸抛喂飞禽走兽，并广而告之以儆效尤。12 世纪，西亚"阿萨辛"极端宗派专门暗杀各路政敌首脑，作乱百年，风声鹤唳，以致"阿萨辛"成为英语"暗杀"一词的词源。此后蒙古三次大西征，沿途杀人无数，帖木儿等在中亚动辄堆尸成山，枭首聚塔，恐怖气氛不胫而走，欧亚诸多城市军民闻风丧胆[54]。

In 689 BC, after Sennacherib, the king of the Assyrian Empire, conquered Babylon, he angrily burned the whole city and flooded it. He also erected a stele on purpose to spread the news to intimidate others. Forty-one years later, when his grandson Banipal conquered Babylon once more, he cut the tongues of a large number of rebels, dismembered their bodies, and threw them to be eaten by birds and beasts, and spread the news far and wide as a warning. In the 12th century, an extreme

---

53　王鉴撰《恐怖活动犯罪研究》，来源《江西财经大学》，2015 年

54　《恐怖主义：当从历史长河明辨其踪》，新华网 www.xinhuanet.com，2016 年 3 月 26 日

sect called "Assassins" in West Asia focused on assassinating political enemies and leaders. The disturbance lasted for a hundred years, thrusting people into a state of extreme nervousness. As a result, "Assassins" became the etymology of the English word "assassination." After that, during the three large-scale Western Expeditions conducted by the Mongols, countless people were killed along the way. As Timur and his party piled up corpses into mountains and amassed severed heads into towers in Central Asia, the terrorist atmosphere spread far and wide. The soldiers and civilians in many cities in Europe and Asia were terrified at the news.[54]

古罗马的恺撒被刺、1881 年沙皇亚历山大二世被刺、1914 年奥匈帝国斐迪南大公被刺、1995 年以色列总理拉宾被刺等事件都是历史上比较著名的例子[55]。

Events such as the assassination of Caesar in ancient Rome, the assassination of Tsar Alexander II in 1881, the assassination of Archduke Franz Ferdinand of Austria-Hungary in 1914, and the assassination of Israeli Prime Minister Yitzhak Rabin in 1995 are all famous examples in history.[55]

翻阅记录在案的人类历史，人们发现疾病早就被作为战胜敌人或竞争对手的武器：欧洲白人有目的地将天花或麻疹病人用过的毛毯卖给印第安人；日本承认在第二次世界大战中对中国人民使用了细菌战；人为营造疾病暴发的条件以战胜对方的"间接生物战"也是人类战争中常用的战术。生物技术的飞速发展给人类带来控制和消灭某些危害性极大传染病的希望，但同时也给生物武器的研制创造了条件，恐怖主义者可以利用已消灭的传染性强的微生物或"制

55　吕恒远、韩旭东撰《"制恐"与"反恐"在走向军事化》，来源《环球军事》，2003 年第 14 期

造重组"的新型微生物。因此用于研制生物武器的生物学被称为
"黑色生物学"（Black Biology）。在人们谴责生物武器的同时，必
须"知己知彼"，有备无患[55]。

Looking through the records of human history, we find that diseases
have long been used as weapons to defeat enemies or competitors:
European whites deliberately sold blankets used by smallpox or measles
patients to Native Americans; Japan admitted have used germ warfare
against the Chinese people during the Second World War; "indirect
biological warfare," which involves artificially creating conditions for
the outbreak of diseases to defeat the opponent, is also a common tactic
in human wars. The rapid development of biotechnology has brought
hope for humans to control and eliminate some extremely harmful
infectious diseases, but at the same time, it has created conditions for the
development of biological weapons. Terrorists can make use of eradicated
highly contagious microorganisms or "reorganized" new microorganisms.
Therefore, the biology used for the development of biological weapons is
called "black biology." While condemning the development of biological
weapons, we must "know ourselves and know our enemy". Only in this
way can we be well-prepared to ward off any untoward incidents.[56]

尽管，有人对恐怖主义有分歧，但是，这不妨碍找到恐怖主义
的必要性。就如同"恐怖主义是毒药，恐怖主义需要解药"。即使
恐怖主义的定义比较抽象，但恐怖主义产生的罪恶却是实在的。一
般人了解恐怖主义的史例，比了解恐怖主义的含义更加重要，这能
够更深层次地让人明白恐怖主义对世界造成的破坏有多大。

Although there are different opinions regarding terrorism, this does

---

56 瞿涤撰《警惕21世纪"人造"疾病的威胁》，来源《国外医学（微生物学分册）》，
    1999年第6期

not impede the necessity of finding a way against it. As the saying goes, "terrorism is poison, and it needs an antidote." Even though the definition of terrorism is abstract, the evils it generates are real. For the general public, understanding historical examples of terrorism is more important than grasping its meaning. This helps people to understand, at a deeper level, the extent of the damage that terrorism has inflicted on the world.

社会光怪陆离，不是所有的恐怖主义都能够轻而易举得到判定。出于对政治考量、经济政策、军事理念、外交政策、爱国情怀等方面的理解，使得给"恐怖主义"下永恒不变的明确定义是件难事。不过，世人怎样解释"恐怖主义"依旧有迹可循。

In this complex and diverse society, not all forms of terrorism can be easily identified. Due to different understandings in political considerations, economic policies, military concepts, foreign policies, and patriotic sentiment, it is difficult to provide a definite and eternal definition of "terrorism." However, regarding how people interpret "terrorism", there are still traces to follow.

荷兰学者亚历克斯·施密德（Alex Schmidt）做了一件很有意义的工作。他在 1988 年出版的《政治恐怖主义》一书中对 1936—1981 年（主要是 60—70 年代）专业领域内的学者专家给出的 109 个恐怖主义定义进行归纳分析，将界定中出现的各要素剥离出来，并按它们在定义中出现频率的统计数值依次做了如下排列：暴力、武力（在定义中的出现率占 83.5%）；政治性（65%）；恐惧、恐怖（51%）；威胁（47%）；心理影响和预期出现的反应（41.5%）；打击目标和直接受害者之间的差异（37.5%）；有目的、有计划、系统化、有组织的行为（32%）；战斗方法、战略与战术（30.5%）等[57]。

57　余建华等著《恐怖主义的历史演变》，上海：上海人民出版社，2015 年 1 月第 1 版

Dutch scholar Alex Schmidt did a meaningful job. In his book *Political Terrorism* published in 1988, he conducted an inductive analysis of the 109 definitions of terrorism given by scholars and experts in professional areas from 1936 to 1981 (mainly in the 1960s and 1970s). He separated various elements from the definitions and arranged them in the following order according to their frequency of occurrence in the definitions: violence, force (the frequency of occurrence in the definitions being 83.5%); political nature (65%); fear, terror (51%); threat (47%); psychological impact and expected response (41.5%); difference between the target of attack and the direct victim (37.5%); purposeful, planned, systematic, and organized behaviors (32%); methods of combat, strategies, and tactics (30.5%), etc.[57]

美国学者杰西卡·斯特恩（Jessica Stern）曾指出："文献中提出了数百个恐怖主义的定义。"另外，1983 年，美国学者 Schmid 仅从 1936—1983 的文献中就引用了一百个以上的恐怖主义的定义[58]。

American scholar Jessica Stern once pointed out, "Hundreds of definitions of terrorism can be found in the literature." In addition, in 1983, American scholar Schmid cited more than a hundred definitions of terrorism just from the literature published between 1936 and 1983.[58]

恐怖主义有主观味道。倘若用"取其精华，去其糟粕"来给恐怖主义下定义，世人可以得出"恐怖主义"至少有"袭击平民（或非作战人员），无道无德的违法行为"的含义。

The definition of terrorism is subjective. If defined in a way of "selecting the essence and discarding the dross," "terrorism" at least implies "immoral and illegal acts against civilians (or non-combatants)."

不明确恐怖主义的定义，就不明确恐怖主义的方圆。恐怖主义

58　何秉松著《恐怖主义·邪教·黑社会》，北京：群众出版社，2001 年 12 月第 1 版

是政治、经济、军事、外交、宗教、科学等恶性结合体，无差别攻击还是很多人对恐怖主义的认知。如同在 2018 年，日本"奥姆真理教"的教主麻原彰晃因实施过恐怖主义而伏法，就是一件天公地道的事情。

Without a clear definition, the boundaries of terrorism will be unclear. Terrorism is a malignant combination involving politics, economy, military, diplomacy, religion, science, and so on. People generally believe that terrorism means indiscriminate attacks. For example, it was just and fair that Shoko Asahara, the leader of the Japanese "Aum Shinrikyo" cult, was executed for conducting terrorist acts in 2018.

2018 年，日本 NHK 电视台 7 月 6 日报道，据相关人士透露，日本"奥姆真理教"原教主麻原彰晃已于当日被执行死刑。[59]

On July 6, 2018, NHK, the Japanese television station, reported that according to relevant sources, Shoko Asahara, the former leader of the Japanese "Aum Shinrikyo" cult, was executed that day.[59]

麻原彰晃，本名为松本智津夫，是日本邪教组织"奥姆真理教"原教主。他被认为是 1989 年坂本堤律师灭门惨案、1994 年松本沙林毒气事件以及 1995 年东京地铁沙林毒气袭击等一系列案件的主谋，于 1995 年被捕。[60]

Shoko Asahara, originally called Matsumoto Chizuo, was the former leader of the Japanese cult "Aum Shinrikyo." He was considered the mastermind behind a series of cases, including the murder of Lawyer Tsutsumi Sakamoto and his family members in 1989, the Matsumoto sarin gas incident in 1994, and the Tokyo subway sarin gas attack in

---

59　《日本邪教组织教主麻原彰晃被执行死刑 为沙林毒气事件主谋》新浪军事（新浪网）www.sina.com.cn，2018 年 07 月 06 日

60　同上

1995. He was arrested in 1995.[60]

2013 年，据日本《产经新闻》7 月 10 日报道，日本公安厅调查显示，曾策划过东京地铁沙林毒气事件等恐怖事件的"奥姆真理教"的后续团体"阿莱夫"和"光之轮"去年新入教 255 人。近畿地区人数最多达 98 人，其中大阪和京都的入教人数占八成以上，大多数是"阿莱夫"的教徒。日本公安当局认为，"阿莱夫"把对过去一系列事件不知情的年轻人当作主要发展对象，在拥有很多大学的大阪和京都积极传教[61]。

On July 10, 2013, according to the report of *Sankei Shimbun*, an investigation by the Japanese Public Security Agency showed that "Aleph" and "Hikari no Wa," the successor groups of the "Aum Shinrikyo" that had planned the Tokyo subway sarin gas incident and other terrorist incidents, recruited 255 new members in the previous year. The vast majority of them were from the Kinki region, numbering 98. Among them, more than 80% were from Osaka and Kyoto, and most of them were members of "Aleph." According to Japanese public security authorities, "Aleph" mainly targeted young people who were unaware of the previous series of events for recruitment, and actively preached in Osaka and Kyoto, where there are many universities.[61]

2019 年 4 月 10 日，日本东京地方法院判决，"奥姆真理教"后继组织"阿莱夫"（Aleph）需要向"奥姆真理事件"的受害者及家属支付 10.2 亿日元（约人民币 6100 万元）的赔款[62]。

On April 10, 2019, the Tokyo District Court ruled that "Aleph," the successor organization of the "Aum Shinrikyo," had to pay a

---

61 《日本邪教奥姆真理教后续教派瞄准大学生发展信徒》，新浪新闻（新浪网）www. sina.com.cn，2013 年 7 月 11 日

62 《25 年了，奥姆真理教受害者及家属终获赔 10 亿日元》，新浪军事（新浪网）www. sina.com.cn，2019 年 4 月 11 日

compensation of 1.02 billion *yen* (about RMB 61 million yuan) to the victims of the "Aum Shinrikyo Incident" and their families.[62]

如果有人冥顽不灵，不知悔改，就会遭人唾弃，反之，悬崖勒马，为时不晚，就会时望所归。世道混沌，每个人都有不光彩的过去，却照样分化出截然不同的人生结局。由此可见，一个人自甘堕落就只剩下失败，没有成功的可能。

Anyone who is stubborn and unrepentant will be spurned by others. On the contrary, if one halts on the brink of the abyss, it will never be too late to win public approval. The world is chaotic. Everyone has a disgraceful past, yet different people can have entirely different life outcomes. Hence, it can be seen that if a person gives in to depravity, he will be doomed to failure and have no chance of success.

"道远知骥，世伪知贤"。事物是由内在属性和外在属性组成的，由此产生内在美和外在美。在整个自然界，无道无德的兵锋所指，必有不服，一来二往，容易形成恐怖主义。在中国古代，有一个历史故事叫做"周处除三害"。这个故事告诉世人，恐怖分子不是英雄，英雄也可能与恐怖分子只有一步之遥。"知耻而后勇"，常人不去学习读书，不努力改变自己的短处，不增加自己的长处，只能沦为社会垃圾。

"Only through a long and arduous journey can we identify a fine horse, and only in a world full of falsehood can we recognize a true talent." Everything is composed of internal and external attributes, which give rise to internal and external beauty. In the entire natural world, a resort to force without morality and righteousness will not be convincing. If such things take place frequently, terrorism is likely to occur. In ancient China, there was a historical story called "Zhou Chu Eliminating the Three Evils." It tells us that a terrorist is not a hero, and a hero may be only one step away from being a terrorist. "Realizing shame, one gains courage." If an ordinary person fails to study, refuses to correct his shortcomings and increase his strengths, he will degenerate into social trash.

周处（236—297），字子隐。义兴阳羡（今江苏宜兴）人，鄱阳太守周鲂之子。西晋周处年少时纵情肆欲，横行乡里，人们将他与山中猛虎、水中蛟龙合称为"三害"，深恶痛绝。周处得知后，未泯的羞耻心使其幡然醒悟，随即入水搏杀蛟龙，入山手刃猛虎，并痛改前非，跟随当时著名的学者陆云学习，勤奋读书，励志图强，终于成为一代能臣名将[63]。

Zhou Chu (236 - 297), also known as Ziyin by courtesy name, was a native of Yangxian, Yixing (now Yixing, Jiangsu), and was a son of Governor Zhou Fang of Poyang. In his youth, he indulged in desires and rampaged through the village. He, referred to as one of the "three evils", the other two of which being a fierce tiger in the mountains and a dragon in the sea, was abhorrent to others. After learning that, he came to his senses due to an unextinguished sense of shame. So he fought against the dragon in the sea, and killed the tiger in the mountains. He also thoroughly reformed his ways. Following Lu Yun, a famous scholar at that time, to study diligently, and making a determined effort to improve himself, he eventually became an outstanding statesman and general.[63]

人心善恶难辨，就算人的本性是犯罪，但决定比本性更重要。一个人犯下恐怖主义是行为决定的，付诸了实践行动。而且，一个人实施了恐怖主义，就无法跟歹徒划清界限，这辈子此人就是一个犯罪者。所以，无论是从道德还是法律两个层面来说，恐怖主义是错误的，没有任何情面可讲。

It is difficult to tell whether a heart is good or evil. Even if human

---

63 《"改邪归正"的周处曾在南京苦读》，新浪财经（新浪网）www.sina.com.cn，2019年4月19日

nature is inclined to sin, decision-making is more important than nature. Whether a person has committed a terrorist crime is determined by whether his actions have been put into practice. Moreover, if a person has committed a terrorist crime, he cannot make a clean break with gangsters, and will remain a sinner for the rest of his life. Therefore, whether from the moral or the legal perspective, terrorism is wrong and there is no room for leniency.

恐怖分子不是英雄，不是自由斗士，不是民族解放者，而是行凶的歹徒。上自政府，下至平民，都会有人沦为恐怖分子。哪怕是一念之差酿成恐怖袭击，仅仅一次，也无法改变这种犯罪事实。像1918年日本发生的"米骚动"就是日本国内各个阶层都有人当恐怖分子的史例。

A terrorist is neither a hero, nor a freedom fighter, nor a national liberator. Instead, he is a violent criminal. Whether in governments or among ordinary civilians, there will be some people who become terrorists. Even if a terrorist attack is caused by a momentary lapse and is launched only once, the criminal fact cannot be changed. The "Rice Riot" that occurred in Japan in 1918 serves as a historical example that terrorists can emerge from any social class in Japan.

所谓的"米骚动"经常见之于中国和日本等东方国家，主要表现为大米短缺或价格腾贵之后的民众暴动。这里所说的"米骚动"则是特指1918年下半年发生于日本的抢米风潮事件。根据井上清和渡部徹的《米骚动研究》，早在1918年7月上旬，"米骚动"就已发端。但是，真正有组织地展开还是从7月下旬开始的，而其最先的发源地是位于北陆地区的富山县 [64]。

64　张轶撰《"米骚动"和日本媒体在其中所扮演的角色》，来源《文史天地》，2016年
　　第1期

The so-called "rice riots" often occurred in Eastern countries such as China and Japan, mainly manifested as mass riots after a shortage of rice or a sharp increase in its price. The "Rice Riot" mentioned here specifically refers to the rice-looting tide in Japan in the second half of 1918. According to *Study on the Rice Riot* written by Ikegami Kiyoshi and Watanabe Tetsu, the "Rice Riot" sprouted as early as the beginning of July 1918. However, it was carried out in an organized manner in late July, and it first originated from Toyama Prefecture in Hokuriku Region.[64]

从 1918 年 7 月 23 日富山县新川郡鱼津町的渔村妇女要求停止运米出境和贱价出售开始, 直到 9 月 19 日煤矿工人的暴动被镇压为止的 57 天中, 日本全国一道三府三十三县都发生了暴动, 其余各县也无不发生群众斗争。参加暴动的既有农民, 也有工人和城市贫民, 既有社会最底层的部落民, 也有监狱的看守、城市里的警察以及海军士兵等, 总人数累计达 1500 万, 约占当时全国人口的四分之一。这次暴动, 因为最初从米粮问题引起, 而且各地暴动一般已是以 "要求米谷商或谷物仓库廉价出售谷物的和平示威运动为开端的", 故日本历史上习惯称为 "米骚动"[65]。

During the 57 days from July 23, 1918, when women of fishing villages in Uozu Town, Shinokawa County, Toyama Prefecture demanded the halt of rice transportation out of the country and its sales at low prices, until September 19, when the coal miners' uprising was suppressed, riots broke out in one circuit, three prefectures, and thirty-three counties across Japan, and mass struggles occurred in the remaining counties. The riot participants included farmers, workers, and urban poor, as well as Burakumin at the bottom of society, prison guards, urban

---

65 叶昌纲撰《谈日本"米骚动"的社会背景》, 来源《山西大学学报 (哲学社会科学版)》, 1984 年第 3 期

policemen, and navy soldiers. The total number of participants reached 15 million, accounting for approximately one-quarter of Japan's population at that time. Since it was first aroused by rice issues, and the uprisings in each area generally began with "peaceful demonstration movements demanding rice merchants or grain warehouse owners to sell grains at low prices," it is habitually referred to as the "Rice Riot" in Japanese history.[65]

其实，这场看似突然爆发的米价危机，在很早之前就被埋下伏笔。自明治维新以来，日本就长期对进口大米课以高额关税，以便让进口货无法在市场上同本地大米竞争。作为调剂手段，就是从自己控制下的朝鲜和台湾补货，确保市场永远处于一种非常紧的平衡状态。但只要稍有风吹草动，这层脆弱的体系就会出现漏洞，将几十年的旧账都瞬间暴露出来。[66]

In fact, the seemingly sudden rice price crisis had been foreshadowed long before. Since the Meiji Restoration, the Japanese government had long imposed high tariffs on imported rice to prevent it from competing with local rice in the market. As a means of adjustment, it replenished the supply from the Korea and Taiwan regions under its control, ensuring that the market was always in a very tight balance. However, even with the slightest disturbance, this fragile system would have loopholes and reveal decades-old problems all at once.[66]

最后，1918 年的米骚动还有一个更为直接的诱因。当时的日本为继续巩固强国地位，决定参与列强的武装干涉俄国行动。[67]

Finally, there was a more immediate trigger for the 1918 Rice Riot. At that time, in order to continue to consolidate its status as a powerful

---

66 《1918 米骚动：日本军国主义制造的粮食危机》凤凰网历史（凤凰网）www.ifeng.com，2020 年 7 月 31 日

67 同上

country, Japan decided to participate in the powers' armed intervention in Russia.[67]

1917 年 11 月 7 日（俄历 10 月 25 日），俄国爆发了十月革命，建立了世界上第一个社会主义国家——苏维埃俄国。日本以解救捷克斯洛伐克军团为由，于 1918 年 7 月接到美国的邀请之后，决定出兵西伯利亚。[68]

On November 7, 1917 (October 25 in the Russian calendar), the October Revolution broke out in Russia, and the Soviet Russia, the first socialist country in the world, was established. On the pretext of rescuing the Czechoslovak Legion, Japan decided to dispatch troops to Siberia after receiving an invitation from the United States in July 1918.[68]

十月革命胜利后，帝国主义列强对苏俄进行了武装干涉，其中，日本出兵西伯利亚，在武装干涉中时间最长，兵力最多，从东部严重地威胁着苏俄。苏俄人民经过 4 年多的英勇抗战，最后把日本侵略者赶出西伯利亚，保卫了苏维埃政权[69]。

After the victory of the October Revolution, the imperialist powers launched armed intervention against Soviet Russia. Among them, Japan's military intervention in Siberia lasted the longest and involved the largest number of troops, thus seriously threatening Soviet Russia from the east. After more than four years of heroic resistance, the Russian people eventually drove the Japanese invaders out of Siberia and defended the Soviet regime.[69]

这个世界空间是有限的，对立和统一缺一不可，有用的东西都未必能被社会所容纳，无用的东西是肯定要被社会淘汰的。在道德和法律的双重约束之下，一个人要牢牢严格要求自己，就算自己不

68　谭敏撰《日本从远东共和国撤兵问题研究》，来源《首都师范大学》，2011 年 5 月 10 日

69　张义德撰《日本在西伯利亚武装干涉的破产》，来源《历史教学》，1983 年第 7 期

是英雄，也绝对不能去当恐怖分子。

The space in this world is limited, and neither opposition nor unity can be dispensed with. Useful things may not necessarily be accepted by society, but useless things are bound to be eliminated by society. Under the dual constraints of morality and law, a person should be strict with himself. Even if he cannot be a hero, he must never be a terrorist.

这个世界不是"非黑即白"的，人一生下来立足于"灰色"的天地之间。无论人性到底是"性善论"或者"性恶论"，都敌不过人做好事困难，做坏事容易，人做好事和做坏事都是愿买愿卖，怨不得其他人。

The world is not just "black or white." People are born and exist in a "gray" belt. Whether human nature is good or evil, it can't change the fact that it's difficult to do good deeds but easy to do bad ones. Whether people do good or bad deeds is a matter of their own choice, and no one else should be blamed.

论起源，恐怖主义一开始就不是纯粹的负面词语，从"灰色"沦落为"黑色"也有一个长的过程。就像法国大革命期间，罗伯斯庇尔等人所主宰的雅各宾派开始"恐怖统治"法国，后来拿破仑结束"恐怖统治"法国。

Regarding its origin, terrorism was not initially a purely negative term, and it underwent a long process of declining from "gray" to "black." For instance, during the French Revolution, the Jacobins led by Robespierre and his party initiated the "Reign of Terror" in France, and later Napoleon ended this "Reign of Terror".

18 世纪末期，古老的法兰西大地上发生了一场震惊欧洲和整个世界的大革命。这场革命历时 5 年有余，以首都巴黎为中心，波及整个法兰西乃至大部分欧洲地区，它彻底改变了法国的政治格局，影响了国家的发展进步[70]。

In the late 18th century, a great revolution that shocked Europe and the whole world took place on the ancient land of France. It lasted for more than five years, centering around the capital Paris, and spreading throughout France and most of Europe. It has thoroughly changed the political pattern of France and influenced its development and progress.[70]

两百多年来，无数专家对法国大革命的功过进行了分析、探讨，否定者不计其数，肯定者也大有人在[71]。

Over the past two hundred years, numerous experts have analyzed and discussed the merits and demerits of the French Revolution. Many people speak highly of the revolution, yet there are still many people who hold opposing views.[71]

罗伯斯庇尔（1758—1794），法国革命家，法国大革命时期雅各宾派政府的实际首脑之一。他在执政后期，改组革命法庭，简化审判程序，实行雅各宾专政和"恐怖统治"。最终，他身亡于法国大革命时自己织造的"恐怖统治"中[72]。

Robespierre (1758-1794) was a French revolutionary, and one of the actual leaders of the Jacobin government during the French Revolution. In the later period of his tenure, he reorganized the revolutionary tribunal, simplified the trial process, and implemented Jacobin dictatorship and the "Reign of Terror". Eventually, he died from the "Reign of Terror" organized by himself during the French Revolution.[72]

罗伯斯庇尔的敌人以及"金色青年"咒骂他是"伪善成性"的人；阿道夫·梯也尔称他为"嗜血的教主"；近代资产阶级史学

70　楚梦撰《罗伯斯庇尔与法国大革命》，来源《同舟共进》，2016 年第 5 期
71　同上
72　杨宇冠撰《法国革命领袖罗伯斯庇尔：实施暴政自食其果》，来源《法律与生活》，2014 年第 22 期

家，也对他（主要是对其恐怖政策）大加责骂，其中以法国的米涅最为激烈。在米涅的笔下，罗伯斯庇尔"极为狂妄"，使"恐怖笼罩全国，且加倍残酷"。罗伯斯庇尔简直成了以杀人为乐的"暴君，恶虎"[73]。

Robespierre's enemies and the "Golden Youth" cursed him as a "hypocrite"; Adolphe Thiers called him a "bloodthirsty cult leader"; modern bourgeois historians also severely criticized him (mainly for his terror policies), with Mignet of France rebuking him most fiercely. In Mignet's description, Robespierre was "extremely arrogant", making "terror pervade the whole country with double cruelty". He almost became synonymous with "tyrant or fierce tiger" who took pleasure in killing.[73]

与之相反，罗伯斯庇尔的战友和拥护者却大力颂扬他的"不可腐蚀"的美德和作为资产阶级利益的坚决捍卫者、"平民代言人"的伟大功绩[74]。

On the contrary, Robespierre's comrades-in-arms and supporters spoke highly of his "incorruptible" virtues and his great achievements, regarding him as a resolute defender of the interests of the bourgeoisie and a "spokesperson for the common people".[74]

法国大革命时期恐怖主义的概念正式产生。当时的法国执政党雅各宾派推行恐怖政策，被认为是人类历史有记载的第一次由政府系统解释并运用恐怖主义战略的实践活动，故堪称近代恐怖主义概念之先驱，领导人罗伯斯庇尔被称为"恐怖主义之父"。据估计，在雅各宾派统治的 1 年多时间里（1793—1794），约有 1.7 万到 4 万人被处死，30 万到 50 万人被捕，其中 20 万人死于监狱的酷刑与

73　李滨撰《"恐怖政策"与罗伯斯庇尔》，来源《西南民族大学学报（人文社科版）》，1984 年第 3 期
74　同上

饥饿。英国政治家 Edmund Burke 创造性地使用了"Terrorism"一词来描述这一时期的恐怖统治（Reign of Terror）[75]。

The concept of terrorism formally emerged during the French Revolution. The implementation of terror policies by the then ruling Jacobin Party in France was considered the first practice in human history where a government systematically explained and applied the terrorist strategy. Therefore, it can be regarded as the embryo of the modern concept of terrorism, and its leader, Robespierre, was called the "father of terrorism". It is estimated that during the more than one-year rule of the Jacobin Party (1793-1794), about 17,000 to 40,000 people were executed, 300,000 to 500,000 people were arrested, and 200,000 of them died from torture and starvation in prison. The British politician Edmund Burke creatively used the word "terrorism" to describe the Reign of Terror during that period.[75]

发生于 18 世纪末 19 世纪初的法国大革命是人类历史上第一场最为彻底的西方资产阶级革命，它不仅彻底推翻了法国的封建阶级统治，而且还建立起了一套相对比较完整的现代国家理论框架与实践模式。拿破仑帝国不仅坚定地维护了资产阶级的统治，而且随着持续不断的拿破仑战争，对西方国际关系与人类民主进程产生了深远的影响[76]。

The French Revolution that took place at the end of the 18th century and the beginning of the 19th century was the most thorough Western bourgeois revolution in human history. It not only completely overthrew the feudal rule in France but also established a relatively

---

75　兰迪撰《国际恐怖主义犯罪的历史溯源与现状描摹》，来源《广西警官高等专科学交学报》，2016 年第 1 期

76　欧阳国杏撰《法国大革命与拿破仑战争时期的国际关系》，来源《魅力中国》，2010 年第 29 期

complete theoretical framework and practical model of modern countries. The Napoleonic Empire not only firmly safeguarded the rule of the bourgeoisie but also, as the Napoleonic Wars continued, had a profound impact on Western international relations and the process of human democracy.[76]

　　罗伯斯庇尔等雅各宾派统治法国的确是有功劳的。但对法国的恐怖统治则是以"以丑为美""反派当正派演""颠倒黑白"在历史长河中留下印记。因为，政府只要向人民征了税，政府就有义务保护人民，"疑罪从无"注定取代"宁枉勿纵"。以"宁可错杀，不可放过"的政府领导国家命运，社会和天下都注定大乱。这种政府的领导者是对国家和人民的不负责。

　　Robespierre and other members of the Jacobins did have contributions to the governance of France. However, in the long course of history, the Reign of Terror in France impresses people as "taking the ugly as the beautiful", "playing the villain as the hero", and "reversing black and white". As long as a government levies taxes from the people, it has the obligation to protect them, and "presumption of innocence" is destined to replace "preferring to wrong the innocent than let the guilty go unpunished". If a government following the principle of "it is better to kill by mistake than to let go" leads the country's destiny, there will undoubtedly be chaos in society and the world. The leaders of such a government are irresponsible to the country and the people.

　　国家有一年后遗症，需要用五年时间来解决。在这种情况下，用"快刀斩乱麻"来解决问题只能使"糊涂账"有增无减。有人认为恐怖主义是正确行为，是在"钻牛角尖"，将会证明此人不愿意吃亏，脑子里面只想着如何只赚不赔。恐怖主义只有"错"的成分，没有"对"的成分。一个人就算有再大的理由，来实行恐怖主义都是站不住脚的。

It will take five years to solve the aftereffects of a country left over from the previous one-year period. In this case, if problems are solved "with a bold and quick stroke", such an approach will only create more "messy accounts". If a person considers terrorism a correct behavior, he is "stubbornly fixated on an irrational idea". It will only prove that he is only concerned about making profits without suffering losses. Terrorism only contains elements of "wrong" without the slightest element of "right". No matter how reasonable it seems, implementation of terrorist acts is unjustifiable.

这个世界的社会观经常都在变化之中，无道无德的观点却不会改变。在恐怖主义的案例中，有人被贴上"恐怖分子可能是英雄，英雄可能是恐怖分子"标签很常见。但是，在道和德冲刷下，恐怖主义早晚原形毕露，恐怖主义事件的当事人"到底是英雄，还是恐怖分子"，终究还是纸包不住火。

The social values of this world are constantly changing, but immoral views remain unchanged. In cases of terrorism, it is common for people to be labeled as "terrorists may be heroes, and heroes may be terrorists". However, under the scrutiny of morality, terrorism will eventually be exposed. Whether the parties involved in terrorist incidents are "heroes or terrorists", the facts will eventually surface.

爱德华·约瑟夫·斯诺登（Edward Joseph Snowden），美国人，1983 年 6 月 21 日出生。虽高中未毕业，但在 2003 年开始了自己在美国国家安全局（NSA）的第一份工作——为马里兰大学某 NSA 秘密机构当保安[77]。

Edward Joseph Snowden was an American, born on June 21, 1983

---

77 《斯诺登："英雄"还是"叛徒"?》，《青年参考》第 9 版：特别报道，2013 年 6 月 19 日

Although he did not graduate from high school, he started his first job at the National Security Agency (NSA) of the United States in 2003, serving as a security guard for a secret NSA agency at the University of Maryland.[77]

有资料显示，斯诺登曾是美国情报局前雇员，在他手中，几乎掌握了美国多达 10 万份机密文件，有一天，斯诺登突然将这些情报公开，曝光了美国网络监听各国政要的巨大丑闻，一时间让美国与盟友间关系变得岌岌可危，随后，该举动被称为"棱镜门事件"。[78]

Data show that Snowden was a former employee of the US Intelligence Agency. He possessed up to 100,000 confidential documents of the United States. One day, he suddenly made these documents public, exposing the huge scandal of the US network eavesdropping on political leaders of different countries. For a time, the relationship between the US and its allies became precarious. Subsequently, this act was called the "Prism Incident".[78]

"棱镜门"事件折射出美国国家安全观念正在发生一些微妙变化。一是"棱镜"计划监控对象的泛化。根据斯诺登先前透露，"棱镜"计划不仅针对美国人所认为的恐怖分子、对手国家或潜在对手国家，而且对德国等北约军事盟友以及拉美国家进行监控。斯诺登在一次爆料中谈到，美国国家安全局的"Xkeyscore"监控计划"几乎可以涵盖所有网上信息"，可以"最大范围收集互联网数据"，内容包括电子邮件、网站信息、搜索和聊天记录等等。二是"棱镜"计划监控内容的泛化。据斯诺登爆料，美国"棱镜"项目不仅监控恐怖分子的信息，而且监控别国军事、政治、经济、能源乃至大学教育等多方面信息，说明美国追求的国家安全不仅是消除恐怖主义

78 《曝光美国棱镜门事件，"叛徒"斯诺登获俄国籍，会被征召上前线吗》，腾讯新闻（腾讯网），www.qq.com，2022 年 09 月 28 日

隐患、军事冲突等传统意义上的安全，而是追求在绝对信息优势基础上维护其世界领导者的超级大国霸权地位。以信息通信技术优势追求绝对安全，却因维护霸权和盲目推进本国利益的冲动滥用信息通信技术，从而招致国际国内信任的丧失和猜疑的上升，诱发新的不安全因素，这便是美、英等信息通信技术强国不得不面对的安全两难。[79]

The "Prism Incident" reflects some subtle changes in the US national security concept. The first is the generalization of the monitoring targets of the "Prism" program. According to Snowden's previous revelations, the "Prism" program not only targeted terrorists, rival countries or potential rival countries in the eyes of Americans, but also was used to monitor NATO military allies like Germany as well as Latin American countries. In one disclosure, Snowden mentioned that the NSA's "Xkeyscore" monitoring program "could cover almost all online information" and could "collect internet data on the largest scale", including emails, website information, and searching and chatting records. The second is the generalization of the monitoring contents of the "Prism" program. According to Snowden's revelations, the US "Prism" program was used not only to monitor the information of terrorists, but also to monitor information concerning the military, politics, economy, energy, and even university education of other countries. This shows that the national security the US pursues is not only security in a traditional sense, involving the elimination of terrorist threats and the settlement of military conflicts, but also the maintenance of its hegemony as a superpower and world leader based on absolute information superiority.

79　《"棱镜门"事件的棱镜效应》人民网科技（人民网）www.people.com.cn，2013年09月10日

The US pursues absolute security with its advantage in information and communication technology, but at the same time, it abuses this technology due to an impulse to maintain its hegemony and blindly safeguard its national interests, leading to a loss of trust and an increase of suspicion both internationally and domestically, and thus triggering new factors of insecurity. This is a security dilemma that countries with an enormous strength in information and communication technology such as the US and the UK have to face.[79]

2018 年，美国民意调查机构拉斯穆森报告（Rasmussen Reports）进行的一项民调结果显示，美国特工部门机密文件被泄事件 5 年过后，有 48% 的美国人既不认为美国国家安全局前雇员爱德华·斯诺登是叛徒，也不认为他是英雄[80]。

According to a public opinion poll conducted by the US polling agency Rasmussen Reports in 2018, five years after the leakage of the confidential documents of the US special agent department, 48% of Americans neither regarded Edward Snowden, a former employee of the NSA, as a traitor nor as a hero.[80]

从个人力量角度出发，远离恐怖主义比消灭恐怖主义更加贴合自己的实际情况。每个人都有被自己情感冲昏头脑的时候，自己在不断的强大之中才能不怕灾难，而不是去多管闲事。

From the perspective of individual strength, staying away from terrorism accords more with his actual situation than eliminating terrorism. Anyone is likely to be carried away by his emotions. Only through constantly growing stronger rather than meddling in others' affairs can one fear no disasters.

80　《民调：近半数美国人不认为斯诺登是叛徒也不是英雄》，新浪军事（新浪网）www.sina.com.cn，2018 年 8 月 16 日

恐怖主义是一种可以抹杀的邪恶文化。在 21 世纪，恐怖主义对全世界的危害越来越大。恐怖主义已经变成了卑鄙、残暴、丑恶和血腥的词语，沦为公害，一步又一步清晰明朗化。如同二战时期，德国和苏联都对波兰犯下恐怖主义，这是历史事实。这个史实不会随着后人对他国的情感变化而发生变化。

Terrorism is an evil culture that can be eradicated. In the 21st century, terrorism is causing more and more harm to the world. It is increasingly evident that terrorism has become a synonym for baseness, brutality, ugliness or sanguinariness, and degenerated into a public harm. For example, it is a historical fact that both Germany and the Soviet Union committed acts of terrorism against Poland during the Second World War. This fact will not change with the emotional changes of later generations towards other countries.

1939 年 9 月 1 日，德国由西向东进攻波兰，17 日，苏联由东向西出兵波兰。苏军俘虏了波兰东部的军人、警察及其他人员共约 25 万之众。他们有的被编入苏军、有的被释放、有的被送到劳动营，还有约 1.5 万军官、军士等被关押进苏联西部战俘营里，以后下落不明。[81]

On September 1, 1939, Germany attacked Poland from the west side. On September 17, the Soviet Union dispatched troops into Poland from the east side. The Soviet army captured about 250,000 people in eastern Poland, including soldiers, policemen and others. Some of them were incorporated into the Soviet army, some were released, and some were sent to labor camps. About 15,000 officers and non-commissioned officers were imprisoned in prisoner-of-war camps in the western Soviet Union, but their subsequent whereabouts were unknown.[81]

81　刘彦顺撰《"卡廷事件"的真相》，来源《历史教学》，2004 年 5 期

1939 年 11 月，德国人计划将波兰人"完全铲除"，到 1942 年，已经有 300 万—400 万人离开波兰，成了德国定居者的苦工。他们被禁止娶嫁，不能得到医疗救治，直到最后一名波兰人消失为止。二战时期，有约 250 万非犹太波兰人在战争中遇难，五分之四是波兰人。[82]

In November 1939, the Germans plotted to "completely eradicate" the Poles. By 1942, three to four million Poles had left their country and become forced laborers for German settlers. They were prohibited from getting married or receiving medical treatment until the last one of them disappeared. During the Second World War, about 2.5 million non-Jewish Poles died in the war, and four-fifths of them were ethnic Poles.[82]

第二次世界大战初期，大批波兰军官在苏联斯摩棱斯克以西的卡廷森林遭到集体屠杀，已被发现的尸体就有 4000 多具。法西斯德国官方曾宣扬，这是在 1940 年春天被苏联内务部杀害的。而苏联官方则声称，这是希特勒军队占领这个地区后于 1941 年 9 月枪杀的。长期以来围绕着这个事件，政治风波迭起，层层疑云密布。[83]

In the early days of the Second World War, a large number of Polish officers were massacred in the Katyn Forest west of Smolensk, the Soviet Union. More than 4,000 bodies were discovered. Nazi Germany officially claimed that they were killed by the People's Commissariat for Internal Affairs of the Soviet Union in the spring of 1940. The Soviet Union, on the other hand, officially claimed that they were shot by Hitler's army in September 1941 after they occupied this area. For a long time, political turmoils arose one after another due to this incident, with suspicion hanging over.[83]

---

82 《二战时德军在东欧有多暴虐？屠杀的斯拉夫人竟达数千万》腾讯新闻（腾讯网）www.qq.com，2022 年 3 月 8 日

83 鲁骥《卡廷事件真相》，来源《当代世界社会主义问题》，1990 年 2 期

随着波兰和苏联各自国内政治局势的变化，有关卡廷事件的记忆和追问再一次被唤起。1987 年之后，由两国历史学家组成的调查委员会开始对波、苏历史上诸多悬而未决的历史问题进行研究，并得出了不利于苏联的结论。1990 年，苏方在波兰总统雅鲁泽尔斯基将军访问之际，公开承认对卡廷大屠杀负有全部责任，并向波方转交了一些相关档案资料。1992 年，叶利钦派其特使飞往华沙，再次向波方转交了有关卡廷事件的部分档案 [84]。

As the political situations of Poland and the Soviet Union changed, memories and inquiries about the Katyn incident were once again awakened. After 1987, an investigation committee composed of historians from both countries began to study many pending historical issues in the history of Poland and the Soviet Union, and drew a conclusion unfavorable to the Soviet Union. In 1990, when General Wojciech Jaruzelski, the President of Poland, visited the Soviet Union, the Soviet government publicly admitted full responsibility for the Katyn Massacre, and handed over some relevant archival records to Poland. In 1992, Yeltsin dispatched to Warsaw his special envoy, who handed over more archives related to the Katyn incident to Poland.[84]

对于一个政权而言，己方歼灭敌人有生力量和夺取他国领土，都是证明自己有精兵强将的一种方法，其中"假以时日"是一个必不可少的客观条件。因为溃不成军可用以退为进；丧权辱国可用忍辱负重；人心涣散可用因势利导；百废待兴可用无中生有；国破家亡可用光复卷土重来。然而，后悔莫及则无药可救，恐怖主义只能酿成更多的人间惨剧。

For a regime, both the annihilation of the enemy's effective strength and the capture of other countries' territory can prove that it possesses

---

84 翟宇、彭勃撰《卡廷森林大屠杀》，来源《百科知识》，2007 年第 19 期

excellent troops and capable commanders. Among them, "given sufficient time" is an indispensable objective condition. Because a army that has been routed can adopt the strategy of retreating in order to advance; a regime that has surrendered national sovereignty and humiliated the nation can endure humiliation and bear the burden; a mind that has been shattered and dispirited can be guided according to the situation; industries that have been devastated can be restored from ruins; a country that has been broken can stage a comeback and restore its former glory. However, there is no remedy for regret, and terrorism can only lead to more human tragedies.

没有物质基础，人类显得微不足道，恐怖主义杀人毁物不值得原谅。就如以清代明治理中国，在有的汉人努力之下，大清朝不得不逐渐落实满汉一家的民族政策道路。这导致后人过分评价明朝和清朝以及中华民国，这互为过渡的三个朝代皆不可取。

Without a material foundation, human beings will be insignificant, so it is unforgivable to use terrorism to kill people and destroy things. When the Qing Dynasty replaced the Ming Dynasty to govern China, through the efforts of some Han people, it had to gradually implement the ethnic policy of "treating Manchus and Han people as a unified family". For anyone in later generations, it is rather one-sided to rate the ethnic policies of the Ming Dynasty, the Qing Dynasty, and the Republic of China as too good or too bad.

朱明王朝对待民族问题很讲策略，于初期他的"多封众建""分而治之""羁縻笼络"等都是行之有效的，所以形成了对周边有吸引力的中央王朝，并且达二百余年。但是随着时间的推移，各方情况都在发生变化，不变的政策必然不好使了。加之朱明王朝一向以续汉唐之正统而有别于夷狄的优势，带来了事实上的文化歧视，导致了其与东北女真人之间的对立、对抗状态，并且最终被

"东夷"所替代的结局。[85]

The Ming Dynasty under the rule of the Zhu family was very strategic in handling ethnic issues. In the early years, due to its effective policies such as "extensive enfeoffment and establishment of small-scale powers", "divide and rule", and "control through appeasement", it became a central dynasty, which exerted a strong appeal on its neighboring regions and lasted for more than two hundred years. However, as time passed, the situations changed, inevitably leading to the failure of unchanging policies. Moreover, taking advantage of inheriting the orthodoxy of the Han and Tang Dynasties and differing from peripheral ethnic minorities, the Ming Dynasty brought about de facto cultural discrimination, fell into a state of opposition and confrontation with the Jurchen people in Northeast China, and was eventually replaced by the so-called "Eastern Barbarians".[85]

清朝是以满族为首、满汉联合统治的国家。清朝对满汉民族的政策，是这个具有民族统治特色的政权奉行的一项基本国策，关系到有清一代的治乱兴衰。[86]

The Qing Dynasty was ruled jointly by the Manchus and the Han people with the Manchus playing a dominating role. Its ethnic policy regarding Manchus and Han people was a basic national policy of this regime with ethnic ruling characteristics, concerning the rise and fall, as well as the order and chaos of the whole dynasty.[86]

清朝满汉文化的矛盾与融合过程，其最典型时期约有 150 年，即从天命到乾隆中期。八旗汉军不仅是这种矛盾斗争的产物，也是

---

85 王冬芳撰《明朝对女真人的羁縻政策、文化歧视及对后世的深远影响》，来源《明史研究》，2005 年第 1 期

86 孙文良撰《论清初满汉民族政策的形成》，来源《辽宁大学学报：哲学社会科学版》，1991 年第 1 期

汉人满族化的例证，但仍是"在旗的汉人"。这种特殊身份，反映了汉军社会地位的双重性。汉军本身的改造和复杂的变化，使其成为瓦解八旗制度的最有力的因素之一。汉军人已经成为满族走向汉化的媒介与桥梁，而淹没在广大汉人之中的驻防汉军八旗的重新汉化，不仅是乾隆帝实行汉军出旗政策的重要依据，也是对旗人汉化的无可奈何的一种承认。清朝对汉军人的区别对待，并不具有民族差异的认识，完全是一种政治控制手段。乾隆以后允许部分汉军仍留在旗内，其实只是对汉人仍然采取分化政策的表现[87]。

As to the contradiction and integration between Manchu and Han cultures in the Qing Dynasty, the most typical period lasted about 150 years, that is, from Emperor Tianming's Reign to the middle of Emperor Qianlong's Reign. The Han Army of the Eight Banners was not only the product of this conflict and confrontation but also an example of the Manchuization of the Han people. However, the soldiers were still "Han people within the Eight Banners system". This special identity reflected the dual nature of the Han Army's social status. The transformation and complex changes of the Han Army made it one of the most powerful factors in disintegrating the Eight Banners system. The Han Army had become a medium and bridge for the Sinicization of the Manchus. The re-Sinicization of the garrisoned Han Army of the Eight Banners that was submerged among the vast number of Han people not only served as an important basis for Emperor Qianlong's policy of allowing the Han Army to leave the banners but also reflected his helplessness in acknowledging the Sinicization of the Banner people. The differential treatment of the Han Army in the Qing Dynasty was irrelevant to the understanding of

---

87 谢景芳撰《清代八旗汉军的瓦解及其社会影响——兼论清代满汉融合过程的复杂性》，来源《中央民族大学学报：哲学社会科学版》，2008 年第 3 期

ethnic differences. Instead, it was completely a means of political control. The fact that some Han Army troops were allowed to remain within the Eight Banners system after Emperor Qianlong's Reign was actually only a manifestation of the continuing policy of dividing the Han people.[87]

晚清重臣文庆执掌权柄之际，适值太平天国革命迅猛发展时期。一方面，文庆提出重用汉人之策，护佑胡林翼、曾国藩等人，影响了江南战局的变化；另一方面，文庆虽然屡次向咸丰帝密陈破除满汉畛域，但是清政府内部的满汉关系并没有发生实质性的变化。然而，正是由于文庆重用汉人的观念，成为清政府制定和推行以汉制汉政策的思想基础，才最终延缓了清王朝的统治的灭亡[88]。

The period when Feimo Wenqing, a high-ranking official in the late Qing Dynasty, was in power coincided with the rapid development of the Taiping Heavenly Kingdom Revolution. On the one hand, the strategy of attaching importance to Han people and protecting Hu Linyi and Zeng Guofan proposed by him influenced the war situation south of the Yangtze River. On the other hand, although he repeatedly secretly advised Emperor Xianfeng to remove the barriers between Manchus and Han people, there was no substantial change in the Manchu-Han relationship within the Qing government. However, his concept of relying on Han people became the ideological basis for the Qing government's formulation and implementation of the policy of using Han people to control Han people, and ultimately postponed the downfall of the Qing Dynasty.[88]

随着袁世凯集团势力的扩展，袁世凯与满族亲贵的矛盾也日益激化。恰在此时，李鸿章、刘坤一、张之洞等人相继过世，清朝统治阶层中失去了一批可以对各种社会势力进行平衡并可以在满汉

88　高中华撰《文庆与重用汉人之策》，来源《中国国家博物馆馆刊》，2013 年第 10 期

矛盾中起缓冲作用的人物。最终，满族亲贵与袁世凯的矛盾愈演愈烈，清廷采取措施削弱袁世凯的权势，导致袁世凯与清廷的决裂和清朝的覆亡[89]。

As the power of Yuan Shikai's clique expanded, the conflict between Yuan and the Manchu nobles intensified with each passing day. At that time, Li Hongzhang, Liu Kunyi, and Zhang Zhidong passed away successively, so the ruling class of the Qing Dynasty lost a significant number of people who could balance different social forces and play a buffering role in the Manchu-Han conflict. Eventually, as the conflict between the Manchu nobles and Yuan Shikai became increasingly intense, the Qing court adopted measures to weaken Yuan's power, which led to the break between Yuan and the Qing court and the downfall of the Qing Dynasty.[89]

辛亥革命后各阶层重新寻找自身位置，经过短暂波动后社会很快趋于平静，各方政治势力最终被暂时性地归于中华民国。[90]。

After the Xinhai Revolution, the social classes began to re-seek their own positions. After a brief spell of upheaval, society reverted to peace, and ultimately, all political forces were temporarily incorporated into the Republic of China.[90]

1912 年 1 月 1 日，南京临时政府成立，孙中山就任临时大总统。这时他已逐渐淡化反满排满情绪，接受"五族共和"观念，确立民族平等思想，作为处理国内民族问题的施政纲领。"五族共和"即中国境内汉、满、蒙、回、藏五大民族平等联合起来，推翻大清封建王朝，把中国改造成为一个多民族统一的资产阶级民主共和国。以"五族共和"为标志，孙中山民族思想逐步转型为近代民族

---

89 梁其承撰《"东南互保"研究》，来源《吉林大学》，2004 年

90 郭辉撰《民国国家仪式研究》，来源《华中师范大学》，2012 年

主义,体现资产阶级民族平等,使民主共和观念深入人心。[91]

On January 1, 1912, the Nanjing Provisional Government was established, and Sun Yat-sen assumed the position of Provisional President. At that time, he gradually diluted his anti-Manchu sentiment, accepted the concept of "founding a republic based on the unity of five ethnic groups", and established the idea of ethnic equality as a guiding principle for handling domestic ethnic issues. "Founding a republic based on the unity of five ethnic groups" meant that the five major ethnic groups in China, namely the Han, Manchu, Mongolian, Hui, and Tibetan ethnic groups, should unite on an equal footing to overthrow the feudal Qing Dynasty and transform China into a unified multi-ethnic bourgeois democratic republic. Marked by this concept, Sun Yat-sen's ethnic thought gradually turned to modern nationalism, embodying the ethnic equality advocated by the bourgeoisie and making the concept of democratic republic deeply rooted in the hearts of the people.[91]

中国满汉地位是中华民族史的一部分,折射了中国男性和女性的美丽与丑陋,成为国家对内对外的历史形象。在中国,汉文明希望永远都是在敢于反抗的中国人身上,懦弱的中国人永远是国家的耻辱。如果中国人形象尚佳,政府才有解决恐怖主义的社会底气,中国政府支持恐怖主义有低潮。反之,如果中国人形象难堪,政府就没有解决恐怖主义的社会底气,中国政府支持恐怖主义有高潮。并且,国家恐怖主义常常和钱扯上关系,由于中国社会形象是由其官方和民间合力组成的,故此,从中国恐怖主义"高潮和低潮"程度就能看出中国经济恶化程度。

As one part of the history of the Chinese nation, the positions of

---

91 杨顺清撰《从"因俗而治"到"五族共和"——中国民族治理模式的近代嬗变》,来源《贵州民族学院学报(哲学社会科学版)》,2011 年 6 期

the Han and Manchu ethnic groups reflected the beauty and ugliness of Chinese men and women, and became China's historical image internally and externally. In China, the hope of Han civilization always lied with those who dared to resist, while those who were cowardly were always a shame to the country. When the image of the Chinese was good, the government would have the social confidence to deal with terrorism, and the support for terrorism by the Chinese government would be at a nadir. On the contrary, if the image of the Chinese was bad, the government would lack the social confidence to deal with terrorism, and the support for terrorism by the Chinese government would be at a climax. Moreover, national terrorism was often associated with money. Since the social image of China was jointly shaped by official and civilian sectors, the degree of economic deterioration could be seen from the "climax or nadir" of terrorism.

工业革命以后，社会更加息息相通，不管一个人有钱没钱，都做不到独善其身，飘然于世，自顾自地逍遥快活过日子。在21世纪，恐怖主义不除，则"鸡犬相闻"变成"鸡犬不宁"。

After the Industrial Revolution, society became more closely interconnected. Whether one is rich or poor, he cannot look after his own interests only, stay aloof from the world, and live a carefree life. In the 21st century, if terrorism is not eliminated, the idyllic scene in which "cocks crow and dogs bark are audible in the vicinity" will turn into a state of chaos.

在20—21世纪，全世界都充斥着各种各样的国家后遗症。随着时间的推移，这些后遗症能够逐渐变成恐怖主义的一部分。比如，1994年非洲中东部国家卢旺达发生的"卢旺达大屠杀"，就是一次掺杂了民族矛盾诱发的国家恐怖主义。

In the 20th and 21st centuries, the whole world has been filled with different forms of national aftereffects. As time goes by, the aftereffects are likely to gradually evolve into a part of terrorism. For example, the "Rwandan Genocide" that occurred in Rwanda, a country in the east-central part of Africa in 1994, was a case of national terrorism triggered by ethnic contradictions.

卢旺达自古以来都是一个部族矛盾严重的国家，境内主要分布三种族裔：胡图族、图西族和特瓦族。15 世纪，成群游牧的图西人来到这一地区，建立了图西人占据统治地位的卢旺达王国，并在随后的几个世纪里，逐步扩大了王国的统治范围。19 世纪 90 年代，德国人占领中非地区，卢旺达遂成为殖民地。第一次世界大战后，德国人撤离其殖民地，比利时按国联指示接管卢旺达。20 世纪 50 年代末，比利时开启非殖民地化进程。1959 年，史称"胡图人农民革命"爆发，卢旺达国王被推翻。1962 年，比利时托管结束，卢旺达筹备独立后的第一次选举。1963 年，选举前夕发生了大规模的暴力事件，数十万图西人逃离卢旺达。1973 年，哈比亚利马纳发动政变成为卢旺达总统，对外拒绝图西人返回的要求，对内实行种族歧视政策。1979 年，流亡的图西难民建立"卢旺达全国统一联盟"，后应乌干达抵抗军领袖穆塞韦尼邀请参军，卷入乌干达内战，这一组织于 1987 年更名为"卢旺达爱国阵线"。1990 年，卢爱阵部队与卢旺达政府军交火，战争爆发。1993 年 8 月，通过联合国和邻国的斡旋，双方在阿鲁沙签订停战协议。[92]

Since ancient times, Rwanda has been a country with serious tribal conflicts, with the Hutu, Tutsi, and Twa being its three major ethnic groups within its territory. In the 15th century, nomadic Tutsi people migrated in groups to this area, and established the Kingdom of Rwanda where the Tutsi people held the dominant position. In the following

---

92 郑正撰《联合国卢旺达维和行动研究》，来源《苏州大学》，2011 年 4 月

centuries, the kingdom gradually expanded its ruling scope. In the 1890s, the Germans occupied the central African region, and Rwanda became its colony. After the First World War, the Germans withdrew from the colony, and Belgium took over Rwanda according to the instructions of the League of Nations. In the late 1950s, Belgium launched the process of decolonization. In 1959, an event historically known as "Hutu Peasant Revolution" broke out, and the rule of Rwanda's King was overthrown. In 1962, the trusteeship by Belgium ended, and Rwanda prepared for its first election after independence. In 1963, on the eve of the election, a large-scale violent incident took place, and hundreds of thousands of Tutsi people fled Rwanda. In 1973, Habyarimana launched a coup, and became the President of Rwanda. He refused the request of the Tutsi people to return to Rwanda, and implemented a policy of ethnic discrimination at home. In 1979, the exiled Tutsi refugees established the "National Unity Alliance of Rwanda", which later got involved in the Ugandan civil war at the invitation of Yoweri Museveni, the leader of the Ugandan Resistance Army. In 1987, this organization was renamed the "Rwandan Patriotic Front". In 1990, the Rwandan Patriotic Front forces clashed with the Rwandan government army, and the war broke out. In August 1993, through the mediation of the United Nations and neighboring countries, the two parties signed a ceasefire agreement in Arusha.[92]

1994 年 4 月 6 日，由于胡图族总统哈比亚利马纳乘飞机遇难，再次引发了胡图族极端分子对图西族人的仇杀。从 4 月 7 日起至 7 月，约有 80 万人被屠杀，约占总人口的九分之一，400 万人无家可归，酿成了举世震惊的人道主义灾难[93]。

93　颜旭撰《卢旺达大屠杀中美国政府的"不作为"政策及其原因》，来源《大庆师范学院学报》，2007 年第 4 期

On April 6, 1994, the death of Hutu President Habyarimana in a plane crash again triggered the killing of Tutsi people by Hutu extremists From April 7 to July, about 800,000 people were killed, accounting for about one-ninth of the total population, and 4 million people became homeless. It was a humanitarian disaster that shocked the world.[93]

1994 年 10 月 3 日，联合国确认卢旺达发生大屠杀。这一天，联合国安理会公布了一个调查报告，确认卢旺达的胡图部落对处于少数地位的图西部落进行了大屠杀，至少有 50 万人遇害[94]。

On October 3, 1994, the United Nations confirmed that a massacre had occurred in Rwanda. That day, the United Nations Security Council released an investigation report, confirming that the Hutu tribe in Rwanda had carried out a massacre against the Tutsi tribe, which was a minority, and at least 500,000 people were killed.[94]

敌对双方势不两立，敌我之间比的不是谁对更多，而是比谁错更少。在以后，恐怖主义积极对待世人和世人消极对待恐怖主义，哪一样更令人作呕，时间总有一天能够证明。

The opposing sides are implacable enemies. Between us and the enemy, the competition should be about which side has committed fewer mistakes rather than about which side has done more correct things. In the future, it will be proved one day whether terrorism's positive attitude towards common people is more disgusting than common people's negative attitude towards terrorism, or the contrary is the case.

世人用联系的观点看问题，能发现迷宫出口和迷宫入口有关系。所以，每次能够正确成功分析出问题也是解决问题的方法。就好比许多组织一旦"变质"使用，经过辩证论道，都有可能变成恐

94　长平撰《卢旺达屠杀，所有人的耻辱》，来源《时代教育（先锋国家历史）》，2007年第 19 期

怖主义的产品。

Viewing problems from a perspective of connection, we will find that the exit of a maze is related to its entrance. Therefore, analyzing a problem correctly and successfully each time is also a way to solve it. For instance, many organizations, once "used in a corrupt way", are likely to become products of terrorism through dialectical analysis.

据英国媒体报道，ISIS 的全名叫"伊拉克和黎凡特伊斯兰国"，是伊拉克宗教极端武装。2011 年前，它还是一支常被打得丢盔弃甲的武装力量。2011 年，叙利亚内战爆发，这群武装分子通过伊叙边境进入叙利亚，随后在叙利亚组建了一支名为"胜利阵线"的激进组织，并在内战期间迅速扩张，吞并部分叙利亚反对派组织[95]。

According to a report of the British media, ISIS, fully called the Islamic State of Iraq and al-Sham, is a religious extremist armed group in Iraq. Before 2011, it was an armed force that was often defeated and fled in disorder. When the Syrian civil war broke out in 2011, this group of militants entered Syria through the Iraqi-Syrian border. Subsequently, they established a radical organization called "Victory Front" in Syria, expanded rapidly during the civil war, and absorbed some Syrian opposition organizations.[95]

自动驾驶汽车可谓时下汽车领域最热门的话题之一，而随着自动驾驶技术的发展，自动驾驶汽车未来甚至有可能颠覆整个交通运输系统，不仅解放了司机，而且对于不会开车的人来说也更加方便。不过遗憾的是，自动驾驶技术带来的也不一定是好事，根据国外媒体的报道，恐怖组织也有可能正在利用无人驾驶汽车制作汽车

---

95 《揭秘 ISIS：成员统一套着黑色头罩 众多萨达姆亲信加入》，凤凰资讯（凤凰网）www.ifeng.com，2014 年 8 月 9 日

炸弹[96]。

The autonomous driving car is one of the hottest topics in the automotive field nowadays. With the development of autonomous driving technology, autonomous driving cars may even subvert the entire transportation system in the future. They can not only liberate drivers but also bring more convenience to those who are unable to drive. However, what the autonomous driving technology brings is not always good. According to the reports of some foreign media, terrorist organizations may use self-driving cars to make car bombs.[96]

由于自动驾驶汽车可以自动行驶至目的地，或者通过遥控的方式进行操作，因此对于恐怖组织来说，相当于不再需要自愿者。而 Mikko Hypponen 表示，ISIS 可能是 2016 年唯一有能力研发自动驾驶汽车炸弹的恐怖组织，而且除了炸弹的用途之外，自动驾驶汽车甚至还能用于其他破坏性目的，这不免让人更加担心[97]。

Since an autonomous driving car can go to the destination automatically or be operated in a remote manner, it means that terrorist organizations no longer need volunteers. According to Mikko Hypponen, ISIS may be the only terrorist organization capable of developing autonomous car bombs in 2016. Apart from being used as bombs, autonomous driving cars can be used for other destructive purposes. This inevitably makes people more worried.[97]

根据之前的相关调查，由于自动驾驶汽车内部有更加复杂的软件系统，因此被遥控操作劫持的可能性也会大大增加。在 FBI 2014 年出具的一份报告中，FBI 表示，虽然自动驾驶汽车可能会为警察

96　《传恐怖组织 ISIS 正在研制无人驾驶汽车炸弹》，腾讯数码（腾讯网）www.qq.com，2016 年 3 月 18 日

97　同上

执行任务时带来诸多便利，但同样有成为致命武器的潜在风险[98]。

According to previous relevant investigations, autonomous driving cars contain more complex software systems, thus increasing the likelihood of being remotely hijacked. The FBI stated in a report issued in 2014 that although autonomous driving cars may bring many conveniences to policemen performing tasks, they have the potential risk of becoming lethal weapons.[98]

不偏不倚地分析问题能将是非曲直升级为道和德。就如同做生意讲究售后服务，甚至售后比售前和售时更加重要。某人赚取战争财并不能纯粹地说明此人道德值是高是低，展现出的乃是这种社会生存环境是否残酷。不过，连累其他无关人士就是大错特错了。

Analyzing problems impartially can elevate the issues of right and wrong to a moral height. Just like in business, after-sales service should be emphasized, and sometimes after-sales service is even more important than pre-sales and in-sales services. The fact that someone makes a fortune from war does not necessarily mean that his moral standard is high or low; instead, it reveals whether the social living environment is tough. However, it is a huge mistake to involve other innocent people.

"打左灯，向右转"。越确定的事情可造成的结果，却能宛如眼花缭乱的蜘蛛网一般，可以越不肯定的。因为，某个事件对政治、经济、军事、外交等有不同层面的影响是常事。就像在 21 世纪，武侠文化对中国人的吸引力在逐渐降低。关于这个现象，有人总结原因之一是武侠文化跟当代法律格格不入，起了尖锐的冲突。

"Turn on the left indicator lamp, but turn right." The result of a seemingly definite thing may be as complex and uncertain as a dazzling spider web. The reason is that a certain event can often have impacts

---

98 同上

of different levels on politics, economy, military and diplomacy. For example, in the 21st century, martial arts culture is becoming less attractive to the Chinese. Regarding this phenomenon, some people summarize one of the reasons as the incompatibility and acute conflict between martial arts culture and contemporary laws.

韩非子在《五蠹》中说"儒以文乱法，侠以武犯禁"，"法家认为游侠的存在是扰乱社会治安、妨害社会管理的不安定因素"，侠客超脱社会管理体系除暴安良，实际上是对法律制度的伤害[99]。

In *Five Worms,* Han Feizi said, "Confucians use literature to disrupt the law, while vigilantes resort to force to violate prohibitions." "Legalists believe that the existence of vigilantes is an unstable factor for disrupting social order and hindering social management." Eliminating evil and upholding justice outside the social management system, the vigilantes actually cause harm to the legal system.[99]

在法律秩序的社会里，侠客除暴安良往往需要使用武力犯法伤人、杀人才能成功，于是，有的人认为以武为侠的人士涉嫌非法和违法也是恐怖分子。

In a society with legal order, to realize the so-called goal of eliminating evil and upholding justice, vigilantes usually have to violate laws by using force to harm or kill people. Therefore, some people think that those vigilantes resorting to force are suspected of breaking the law, so they are also terrorists.

然而，有这个想法的人是只知其一，不知其二。在 21 世纪，中国男女或不去早恋，或从一而终，或真心付出的人少之又少。比起法律层面的原因，中国女人愿意做残花败柳，缺少冰清玉洁，没

99　《武侠与法律：刀光剑影中的正义追求》，《人民法院报》第 5 版：法律文化周刊，2015 年 3 月 27 日

有女性品德。中国读者不想浪费自己的时间，无意关注武侠世界里面的侠骨柔情，进而无心关注武侠作品，这是致使武侠文化没落的一个原因。

However, those who hold this view only know one aspect of the matter. In the 21st century, few Chinese people, men and women, are willing to have puppy love, be faithful to their partners to the end, or devote love wholeheartedly. The reason is not just related to the legal level. Chinese women are willing to descend into a state of withered beauty, lack noble purity, and do not have female virtues. Chinese readers are unwilling to waste their time, having no intention of paying attention to the chivalrous spirit and tender affection in the world of martial arts, and thus have no interest in martial arts novels. This is one of the reasons for the decline of martial arts culture.

2015 年，据美国《华尔街日报》网站 12 月 8 日报道称，世界卫生组织（WHO）认为，中国年轻人面临意外怀孕、流产和性传播疾病等问题。WHO 在最近的声明中说，在中国，每五个性活跃年轻女性中，就有一个曾经意外怀孕，那些怀孕中，大部分最后都以流产告终。[100]

According to a report issued on the website of *Wall Street Journal* on December 8, 2015, the World Health Organization (WHO) thinks that Chinese young people are facing problems such as unplanned pregnancies, abortions, and sexually transmitted diseases. In a recent statement, WHO said that in China, one in every five sexually active young women has an unplanned pregnancy, and most of them end in abortion.[100]

---

100 《美媒：中国少女意外怀孕比率高 大部分选择堕胎》，腾讯新闻（腾讯网）www.qq.com，2015 年 12 月 13 日

在中国，自古现实社会和虚构世界都有"英雄美人形影不离"的传统。艺术来源于生活，却又高于生活。任何超高艺术的童话都难以脱离合理的现实生活为基础。

Since ancient times, both the real and fictional worlds in China have held the tradition that "heroes and beauties are inseparable." Art originates from life, but is superior to life. Any highly artistic fairy tale can hardly be separated from reasonable real life.

武侠是一种极为中国化的传统文化，"侠骨柔情"对读者的影响深远，结合英雄美女的搭配，通常能收到意想不到的传播效果[101]。

Martial arts is a traditional culture with strong Chinese characteristics, and the influence of "chivalrous spirit and tender affection" on readers is profound. Combined with the pairing of heroes and beauties, it can usually achieve an unexpected effect in spreading.[101]

素有浪漫主义精神的武侠，含有打打杀杀的情节，却能够快意恩仇，酣畅淋漓。

Martial arts with a romantic spirit contains scenes of fighting, but it can bring a sense of satisfaction from avenging wrongs and achieving justice.

然而，在21世纪，武侠文化走上了一条"墙内开花墙外香"的道路，并非彻底"凋零枯萎"。

However, in the 21st century, martial arts culture has gained more popularity abroad than at home, just as "a flower blooming inside the wall spreads its fragrance outside", but it has not completely "withered".

在文学世界里，少不得要哗众取宠，热度渐冷的武侠文化也由此因祸得福，并没有在恐怖主义的类型中"发扬光大"，还合法传

---

101 门薇薇撰《武侠小说及武侠文化在体育新闻中的展现》，来源《第五届中国体育博士高层论坛论文集》，2014年

播到外国。

In the literary world, there is always a need to please the public with claptrap. Therefore, the martial arts culture, which is gradually losing its popularity, has gained advantages from misfortunes. Instead of "flourishing" in the category of terrorism, it has been legally spread abroad.

20 世纪 50 年代初期，武侠小说在香港以新的面貌再度萌生、复兴之后，旋即像厉风狂涛般地席卷了台湾、东南亚及海外华人区。80 年代初期以来，又很快地风靡了中国大陆。可以毫不夸张地说，武侠小说流布地区之广、拥有读者之多，在中国文化史上也是较为罕见的 [102]。

After martial arts novels emerged and revived in a new look in Hong Kong in the early 1950s, they swept through Taiwan, Southeast Asia, and overseas Chinese communities like fierce winds and raging waves. After the early 1980s, they quickly became popular in China's mainland. It is no exaggeration to say that the extensive distribution areas and vast number of readers of martial arts novels were quite rare in Chinese cultural history.[102]

2017 年，港媒称，一名前美国外交官开办了一家武侠小说网站，向西方读者介绍中国的武侠小说，引起巨大反响 [103]。

In 2017, Hong Kong media reported that a former US diplomat established a martial arts novel website to introduce Chinese martial arts novels to Western readers, causing a huge stir.[103]

他是美国前外交官赖静平，是 "武侠世界" 网站的创办者，他

102　孙玉明撰《武侠小说与人类的超人崇拜心理》，来源《文史知识》，1993 年第 3 期

103　《美国前外交官痴迷武侠 办网站向西方推广武侠小说》，中国青年网 www.youth. cn，2017 年 5 月 7 日

向如饥似渴的读者们提供翻译的网络武侠小说[104]。

The founder of the website "the World of Martial Arts" is Lai Jingping, a former US diplomat, who provides translated online martial arts novels to eager readers.[104]

报道称，在北美、西欧和东南亚，越来越多的读者开始了解中国的这类武侠小说。与更现实性、现代的功夫电影不同，武侠小说凭借古代中国历史背景下的武人奇遇吸引粉丝[105]。

According to a report, more and more readers in North America, Western Europe, and Southeast Asia have begun to understand Chinese martial arts novels. Different from realistic and modern kung fu movies, martial arts novels attract fans with the adventures of warriors in the historical context of ancient China.[105]

在 21 世纪，中国武侠文化在低谷徘徊不进，只是，这不能说明"武侠已死，只剩绝唱"的观点就能成立。将来中国武侠文化可能由于遭受巨大的挫折，反倒是有机会产生一种哲学武侠 VS 套路武侠的新文化。

In the 21st century, Chinese martial arts culture is lingering at a low ebb, but this does not necessarily mean that "the age of martial arts novels has passed, leaving only timeless masterpieces." Despite potential great setbacks in the future, Chinese martial arts culture may have the opportunity to generate a new culture in which philosophical martial arts compete with formulaic martial arts.

比起团结就是力量的军事作战，武侠文化更加适合个人成长，后者更加能够做到自己独自一人对付仇人，不波及更多人士。至于武侠文化到底利弊各与多少，就留给中国海内外人士来评说。

104　同上

105　同上

Compared with military operations highlighting the strength of unity, martial arts culture is more suitable for personal growth. In martial arts culture, one can deal with enemies alone without involving more people. As to the proportion of the advantages or disadvantages of martial arts culture, it can be evaluated by people at home and abroad.

在某些时候，借刀杀人和见死不救并不能得到法律的惩罚，只能得到世人道德的谴责。故此，只要国家的政府法律有太多的灰色和黑色，中国武侠文化就有立足之地，难以扼杀。

At certain times, the act of using a third party to get rid of an opponent or turning a blind eye to someone in desperate need will not be punished by the law, but only be morally condemned by the people. Therefore, as long as there are so many gray and black areas in the laws of a country's government, Chinese martial arts culture will have a foothold and can hardly be stifled.

不管一个人是文科生还是理科生，自己都要用丰富的知识武装自己，以防对很多事物一问三不知。

Either liberal arts students or science students should arm themselves with rich knowledge lest they become ignorant about many things.

知识之上的命运和命运之下的知识，有着两种截然不同的结果。社会竞争残酷激烈，将敌人不利的砝码，变成自己有利的筹码，使自己赢在胜利的起跑线，对手一败涂地。就像在12世纪，宋金对峙期间发生采石矶之战。该战役金强宋弱，结果却是以弱胜强，属于骄兵必败，哀兵必胜的典型战例。

Fate above knowledge and knowledge beneath fate will lead to entirely different results. In fierce and brutal social competition, if one can turn factors unfavorable to the enemy into ones favorable to himself, he is likely to win at the starting point for victory and thoroughly defeat his opponent. For example, in the Battle of Caishi that took place during the confrontation between the Song and Jin Dynasties in the 12th century, the Jin Dynasty was more powerful than the Song Dynasty, but the result was that the weak defeated the strong. It is a typical example of illustrating the principle that an army full of arrogance is bound to be defeated while an army with desperate courage is bound to win.

公元 1149 年 12 月，金王朝发生内讧，海陵王完颜亮谋权篡位，自立为帝。经过多年改革，公元 1161 年 9 月，完颜亮认为跟宋朝干上一架的时机到了，就发动 40 万大军，攻击南宋。出发前，完颜亮夸下海口："从前我们进攻宋朝，费了多少时间都没能胜利。这次我出征，多则一百天，少则一个月，我一定把南宋拿下！"[106]

In December 1149, an internal conflict occurred in the Jin Dynasty. Wanyan Liang, Prince of Hailing, schemed to usurp the throne and proclaimed himself emperor. After years of reforms, in September 1161, he believed that it was time to fight against the Southern Song Dynasty, so he launched an army of 400,000. Prior to the departure, he boasted, "When we attacked the Song Dynasty in the past, we spent a long time but failed to win. This time, going on an expedition by myself, I will definitely conquer the Southern Song Dynasty within one month, at most a hundred days!"[106]

尽管如此，形势并非不可改变。其一，完颜亮发动的这场非正义的掠夺性战争，内部隐藏严重的危机。就在十月初八，金东京留守乌禄宣布在辽阳称帝，迫使完颜亮既失后方支援，且有后顾之忧，消息传开，军心越发不稳；其二，南宋广大军民决心抗战，各地捷报频传，更使军民斗志昂扬；其三，滔滔长江天堑是天然屏障。不过，能否变被动为主动，扬长避短，关键还在于战争领导者

106　谢林海撰《虞允文：慷慨磊落有大志　智勇双全无私心》，来源《课堂内外创新作文（初中版）》，2012 年 11 期

的决心和指挥。[107]

However, the situation was not unchangeable. First, the unjust and predatory war launched by Wanyan Liang was fraught with serious crises. On the eighth day of the tenth lunar month, Wulu, Military Governor of Dongjing in the Jin Dynasty, proclaimed himself emperor in Liaoyang, making Wanyan Liang lose his rear support and worry about the matters left unattended. When the news spread, the military morale became more unstable. Second, the vast number of military and civilian people in the Southern Song Dynasty were determined to resist, and reports of victories came from all directions, which further boosted their fighting spirit. Third, the surging Yangtze River served as a natural barrier. However, whether it was possible to turn passivity into initiative and make the best use of his own advantages and avoid the disadvantages of his opponents depended on the determination and command of the war leader, which played a crucial role.[107]

完颜亮（1122—1161），字元功，本名迪古乃，太祖阿骨打之孙，1149 年弑熙宗篡立，1161 年被部将杀于南侵途中。[108]

Wanyan Liang (1122—1161), known as Yuangong by courtesy name and Digunai by original name, was the grandson of Aguda, the founding emperor of the Jin Dynasty. In 1149, he murdered Emperor Xizong and usurped the throne. In 1161, he was killed by his subordinate general during the southward invasion.[108]

完颜亮为了伐宋之需，进行了大规模的扩军备战，由此所引起的横征暴敛激发了大范围的人民起义，其中以东海县起义、大名府起义以及契丹大起义的规模、影响最大，严重地动摇了完颜亮的统

107　林建曾撰《采石之战及其指挥者虞允文》，来源《南充师院学报（哲学社会科学版）》，1982 年 2 期

108　王红娟撰《近二十年完颜亮研究综述》，来源《文史知识》，2007 年 2 期

治基础。[109]

In order to attack the Southern Song Dynasty, Wanyan Liang conducted a large-scale military expansion, made preparations for the war, and extorted excessive taxes and levies, thus triggering widespread people's uprisings. Among them, the Donghai County Uprising, the Daming Prefecture Uprising and the Great Khitan Uprising were the largest in scale and influence, seriously shaking his ruling foundation.[109]

虞允文（1110—1174 年），字彬父，一作彬甫，南宋名臣，隆州仁寿县（今四川省眉山市仁寿县）人。绍兴二十四年（1154 年）进士，历任彭州通判、中书舍人、督视江淮军马府参谋军事、兵部尚书、右仆射同中书门下平章事兼枢密使、左丞相、川陕宣谕使等职。绍兴三十一年（1161 年），虞允文奉命前往采石前线劳军，在军情紧急主将缺位的情况下，自任统帅，指挥三军以少胜多，大破金主完颜亮，创造了采石大捷奇迹，堪称千古军事神话。[110]

Yu Yunwen (1110-1174), known as Binfu by courtesy name, was a famous minister of the Southern Song Dynasty, and a native of Renshou County, Longzhou (now Renshou County, Meishan City, Sichuan Province). He was admitted as a Jinshi through the imperial examination in the 24th Year of Emperor Shaoxing's Reign (1154), and served as Assistant Magistrate of Pengzhou, Secretary in the Central Secretariat, Staff Officer of the Military Command for Supervising Armies in Jianghuai Region, Minister of War, Right Minister of the Imperial Secretariat and Concurrent Minister of the Central Secretariat and the Chancellery and Minister of the Privy Council, Left Prime Minister, and

---

109　周峰撰《论金海陵王完颜亮时期的人民起义》，来源《哈尔滨学院学报（社会科学）》，2002 年 9 月

110　刘立祥撰《虞允文：自任统帅创千古奇迹的一介书生》，来源《文史天地》，2013 年 6 期

Imperial Envoy for Public Announcement in Sichuan-Shaanxi Region successively. In the 31st Year of Emperor Shaoxing's Reign (1161), he was ordered to go to the front line at Caishi to console the troops. When the military situation was urgent and the main general was absent, he took on the role of the commander by himself, and won a victory against the numerically superior enemy commanded by Wanyan Liang, the Emperor of the Jin Dynasty. It was called the Great Victory at Caishi, a miracle and unparalleled military myth in history.[110]

在南宋当时的形势下，一旦采石失守，金军将长驱直入江南，南宋将面临灭亡。因此，采石之战的胜利成功遏制了金的南侵，最终拯救了整个长江防线免于崩溃，给南宋以喘息之机，对南宋存亡有至关重要的作用。此外。采石之战在心理上造成的影响是不可忽略的，宋朝因此而获得了信心，大大提振了宋军士气。另一方面，加速了完颜亮统治集团的分裂和崩溃，间接导致了金朝的政权更迭。[111]

Given the situation of the Southern Song Dynasty at that time, if Caishi had been lost, the Jin army would have marched straight into the regions south of the Yangtze River, and the Southern Song Dynasty would have been on the brink of extinction. Therefore, the victory of the Battle of Caishi successfully curbed the southward invasion of the Jin army, and ultimately prevented the collapse of the entire defense line along the Yangtze River. It gave the Southern Song Dynasty a chance to catch its breath, and played a crucial role in the continuation of the regime. In addition, the Battle of Caishi had a significant psychological impact, because it afforded the Song Dynasty confidence, and remarkably boosted the morale of the Song army. On the other hand, it accelerated

---

111　张香宁撰《虞允文研究》，来源《浙江大学》，2011 年

the division and collapse of Wanyan Liang's ruling clique, indirectly leading to the shift of political power in the Jin Dynasty.[111]

完颜亮遇弑，标志着战场局势发生了有利于南宋的重大变化。此时，扬州一带的金军主动向南宋提和，上下亟于北返，已经无心恋战。不过，正所谓"归师莫遏"，对南宋的主动态势也不能估计太高，毕竟金军未乱，主力犹在，近三十万金军绝非易与之辈，南宋绝无轻易战而胜之的把握。[112]

The assassination of Wanyan Liang marked an important change in the military situation that was favorable to the Southern Song Dynasty. At that time, the Jin army in the Yangzhou area took an initiative to sue for peace with the Southern Song Dynasty. The soldiers were eager to return north and had no intention of continuing the war. However, as the saying goes, "Do not attempt to halt an army that is returning to its native land", so the initiative of the Southern Song Dynasty should not be overestimated. After all, the Jin army was not in chaos, and its main forces were still intact. The nearly 300,000 soldiers of the Jin army were absolutely a tough enemy, and the Southern Song Dynasty had no confidence at all in achieving an easy victory.[112]

"阴阳对立统一，阴近则阳退，阳退则阴近"。宋金两国的采石矶之战，表面上是敌我双方在前方和后方的军事较量。更深层次分析，乃是国家恐怖主义产生"得道多助，失道寡助"的战争局面。这充分说明，恐怖主义不仅使受害者增加了反压迫的勇气和力量，也削弱了加害者的底气和实力。

"Yin and Yang are a pair of opposites in unity. When Yin approaches, Yang retreats; when Yang retreats, Yin approaches." The

---

112　范学辉撰《宋金绍兴辛巳战事新探——以南宋三衙诸军为中心》，来源《济南大学学报（社会科学版）》，2016 年 4 期

Battle of Caishi between the Song and Jin Dynasties was apparently a military confrontation between the two sides in the front and rear areas. However, a further analysis reveals that it was a war situation in which "one can win popular support by upholding justice or lose popular support by doing the opposite", which was caused by national terrorism. This fully shows that terrorism can not only increase the victims' courage and strength to resist oppression but also can weaken the confidence and strength of the aggressors.

侵略战争发生恐怖主义，恐怖主义引发的反抗已经成为历史常态。并且，即使是在多年以后，这些反抗还会产生连锁反应的后遗症。以至于，一场战争过后，更多人只记住战争留下人间悲剧，战争创伤有多无少，重建家园有苦难。

Historically, it was often the case that terrorism associated with invasion wars would cause resistance. In addition, even many years later, the resistance would cause aftereffects through a chain reaction. Therefore, after a war, most people only remembered the human tragedies, the numerous war traumas, and the difficulty in rebuilding their homes.

恐怖主义夹杂政治，官字两张口，恐怖主义可能渐渐政治化，官场反恐亦阴亦阳。比如，恐怖分子头目本·拉登被美军击毙，巴基斯坦官方对本·拉登的说法有真有假就是例子。

Terrorism is intertwined with politics. Officials often interpret things in two different ways. Therefore, terrorism may gradually be politicized, and counter-terrorism efforts in the official arena have a dual nature. For example, when Osama bin Laden, the leader of a terrorist organization, was killed by the US military, the official statements of the Pakistani government about Osama bin Laden were a blend of truth and misinformation.

2011 年 5 月，当地时间 1 日晚 11 时 30 分左右，美国总统奥巴马在白宫发表全国电视演讲，宣布"基地"组织领导人、"9·11"恐怖袭击的元凶本·拉登已在美方特别行动中被击毙，其尸体已在美方控制中 [113]。

At around 23:30 local time on May 1, 2011, the US President Barack Obama delivered a national television speech at the White House, announcing that Osama bin Laden, the leader of the al-Qaeda organization and the mastermind of the September 11 terrorist attacks, had been killed in a special operation by the US military, and his body was controlled by the US side.[113]

2011 年 5 月，巴基斯坦总理优素福·拉扎·吉拉尼 9 日在伊斯兰堡发表公开讲话，首次回应美军在巴境内突袭击毙"基地"组织头目乌萨马·本·拉登事件及相应说法。吉拉尼极力驳斥外界有关巴基斯坦藏匿本·拉登的怀疑论，但承诺彻查军情部门对本·拉登下落毫不知情的原委 [114]。

On May 9, 2011, Pakistani Prime Minister Yousaf Raza Gilani made a public speech in Islamabad, responding for the first time to the US military's raid that killed Osama bin Laden, the leader of the al-Qaeda organization, within Pakistan and the corresponding statements. He strongly refuted the suspicion that Pakistan was harboring bin Laden but promised to thoroughly investigate the reasons why the Pakistani military intelligence department knew nothing about bin Laden's whereabouts.[114]

2015 年 10 月 14 日，据《印度斯坦时报》报道，巴基斯坦前国防部部长乔杜里·艾哈迈德·穆赫塔尔表示，早在美军击毙本·拉登之前，包括总统在内的巴基斯坦领导层就已经知道了本·拉登的

113　《奥巴马宣布本·拉登被击毙》，《光明日报 07 版：国际新闻》，2011 年 05 月 03 日

114　《巴基斯坦总理驳斥庇护说 称本·拉登非请自来》，腾讯新闻（腾讯网）www.qq.com，2011 年 5 月 11 日

藏身之处 [115]。

On October 14, 2015, according to *Hindustan Times*, Chaudhry Ahmad Mukhtar, the former Pakistani Minister of Defense, said that the Pakistani leadership, including the president, had already known the hiding place of Osama bin Laden before the US military killed him. [115]

穆赫塔尔称，不少高层人士都参与了涉及本·拉登的行动，包括：总统扎尔达里、军队最高指挥官卡雅尼以及联合参谋长。官员们及其团队早已做好准备，只待一声令下，就采取行动，并为其他盟友提供相关情报。穆赫塔尔还表示，除了巴基斯坦军方，也有其他势力知晓本·拉登的所在。他们一直在寻找体形和本·拉登相仿的人 [116]。

Mukhtar claimed that many high-ranking officials, including President Zardari, the Superior Military Commander Kayani, and the Joint Chief of Staff, were involved in the operations related to Osama bin Laden. The officials and their teams had been well-prepared. They were just waiting for the order to take action and provide relevant intelligence to other allies. Mukhtar also said that apart from the Pakistani military, there were other forces that knew the whereabouts of Osama bin Laden. They had been seeking people with a similar body shape to that of bin Laden. [116]

2019 年，巴基斯坦总理伊姆兰·汗在接受福克斯新闻采访时表示，美国当年是在巴情报部门的帮助下才击毙"基地"组织头目本·拉登的 [117]。

---

115 《巴基斯坦首次承认早知晓本·拉登藏身之处》，新浪新闻（新浪网）www.sina. com.cn，2015 年 10 月 14 日

116 同上

117 《巴总理再改立场：当年是我们帮助 CIA 击毙本·拉登》，观察者 www.guancha. cn，2019 年 7 月 23 日

When Pakistani Prime Minister Imran Khan was interviewed by Fox News in 2019, he claimed that it was with the help of the Pakistani intelligence agency that the US military killed Osama bin Laden, the leader of the al-Qaeda organization.[117]

这一表态再次改写了巴基斯坦官方在该事件上的立场[118]。

The statement once again changed the stance of the Pakistani government on this incident.[118]

近朱者赤，近墨者黑，具体依靠实体胜过虚体进行表现。在官场上，高官大员为了捞取政治资本尔虞我诈。由于不管官员的左膀右臂是不是心腹，都能成为心腹大患，于是常人在政治领域进行反恐，常常不仅要政治化，还要沦为政客，才能与政治家沆瀣一气。

A man is known by the company he keeps. This is revealed by the fact that tangible entities prevail over intangible ones. In the officialdom, high-ranking officials often cheat and scheme against each other to seize political capital. Whether people around an official are trustworthy or not, they may become a serious threat. Therefore, if ordinary people intend to carry out counter-terrorism operations, it is often the case that they not only have to politicize terrorism but also have to degrade themselves. Only in this way can they act in collusion with the politicians.

"有道有德可以用兵，无道无德不可用兵"。在世界古代史，人类入世和出世都要克制住自己享福的心态，多培养自己民用和军用技能，以备解决突发情况。就像秦末汉初的人才张良，也曾经搞过暗杀类型的恐怖主义。张良此人先去刺杀秦始皇，再去辅佐刘邦，而非先去辅佐刘邦，再去刺杀秦始皇。后世人解剖张良人生行动轨迹进行研究，则能发现少去碰运气，多来充实自己，这才是不世之才所走的康庄大道。

118　同上

"Those who adhere to moral principles are fit to wield military power, while those who abandon moral principles are unfit to wield military power." In the ancient history of the world, whether people were involved in worldly affairs or detached from them, they should restrain their desire for enjoyment and develop more civilian and military skills to deal with unexpected situations. Zhang Liang, a talented person at the end of the Qin Dynasty and the beginning of the Han Dynasty, also carried out an assassination as a terrorist act. He attempted to assassinate Emperor Qin Shi Huang before assisting Liu Bang, not in the opposite sequence. By analyzing his life trajectory, later generations find that only through enriching themselves instead of relying on luck can outstanding talents have a bright future.

张良为韩国贵公子，其祖与父相继为韩昭侯、宣惠王、悼惠王等五世相。秦灭韩后，张良图谋恢复韩国，散尽家财，重金收买刺客，在博浪沙狙击秦始皇未中，逃亡至下邳，遇齐国隐者黄石公传授兵书，刻苦攻读，十年积聚，胸藏兵法战策，后加入反秦农民起义中，追随刘邦，灭秦兴汉，屡出奇策，成为刘邦的主要谋士。汉立，被刘邦封为留侯。[119]

Zhang Liang was a nobleman of the State of Han, whose lineal ancestors, including Marquis Zhaohou, King Xuanhui, and King Daohui, served as prime ministers for five generations. After the Qin Dynasty destroyed the State of Han, he attempted to restore the State of Han, so he exhausted his family wealth to hire assassins. After he failed in an attempt to assassinate Emperor Qin Shi Huang in Bolangsha, he fled to Xiapi, and met Huang Shigong, a hermit from the State of Qi, who taught him military strategies. After studying assiduously for ten years, he gained a

---

[119] 刘玉娥撰《张良的成功人生》，来源《当代人：下半月》，2011 年第 6 期

profound knowledge of military strategies. Later, he joined the peasant uprising against the Qin Dynasty, following Liu Bang to overthrow the Qin Dynasty and establish the Han Dynasty. He repeatedly came up with ingenious strategies and became one of Liu Bang's main advisors. After the Han Dynasty was established, he was conferred the title of Marquis of Liu by Liu Bang.[119]

张良作为秦汉时期杰出的谋士，是为汉高祖刘邦筹谋天下的助手。史书中很少记载张良担任过的具体职务。据记载，张良体弱多病，归附刘邦后一直担任幕后策划的角色。从《史记·留侯世家》中可知，公元前 208 至公元前 196 年，张良先后被封为司徒、留侯以及少傅。作为参谋型秘书，张良的秘书事迹主要体现在他的能谋善谏、通达知变中。无论是斗智鸿门、火烧栈道，还是劝都关中、扶持太子，在他屡建奇功的背后，体现出了秘书理论与实践的具体结合。[120]

As an outstanding advisor in the Qin and Han Dynasties, Zhang Liang devised strategies for Liu Bang, the founding emperor of the Han Dynasty, to govern the country. Historical books reveal little about the specific positions he once held. It is recorded that he was physically weak and often ill. After attaching himself to Liu Bang, he played the role of an aide and advisor all the time. According to *Biographies of the Marquis of Liu, Records of the Grand Historian*, from 208 BC to 196 BC, he was successively conferred the titles of Grand Minister of Works, Marquis of Liu, and Junior Tutor. The deeds of Zhang Liang as an advisory secretary were mainly manifested in his ability to devise strategies and offer good advice, as well as his flexibility and adaptability. Behind his numerous remarkable achievements such as outwitting the enemy at Hongmen,

---

120 庄亦男撰《汉代谋士张良的秘书观解读》，来源《文教资料》，2018 年 36 期

setting fire to the plank roads, persuading Liu Bang to set up the capital in Guanzhong, and assisting the crown prince, there was a specific combination of secretary theory and practice.[120]

社会竞争激烈，一个人在没有步入社会以前，就要学着怎么步入社会。一个人有多少实际能力，不是与生俱来，是依靠后天勤学苦练得来的。一个人将历史事物重新排列，得出最新结论，也是需要经过其深思熟虑的决定，才能得出结果。

The social competition is very fierce, so one has to learn how to step into society before actually entering it. The practical ability of a person is not inborn but is acquired through hard work and practice later. For a person to rearrange historical events and draw the latest conclusions, it should be based on a decision made after careful consideration.

多充实自己胜过多释放自己，少释放自己胜过少充实自己，不充实自己就去释放自己是在自取其辱，这就是一种社会荣辱观。在中国历史，每当国家政权交替之际，有人选择淡泊名利，有人选择唯利是图，有人选择不忘初心，有人选择随遇而安，有人选择隐居遁世，这些选择都能够让人名声大噪，也影响国家未来的发展走向。不过，尽管如此，这最终也只能证明乃是此人需要国家，而非国家需要此人，大家都是心甘情愿做出自己的选择。就像在中国近代史，一个"招安"政策之下，名垂青史和遗臭万年的大小人物都会纷纷浮出水面。"招安"既能用于分裂，也能用于团结。招安能分裂敌方，就是在团结己方。反之，招安团结敌方，就是在分裂己方。

Enriching oneself more is better than releasing oneself more, releasing oneself less is better than enriching oneself less, and releasing oneself without enriching oneself first is tantamount to inviting humiliation. This is a social concept of honor and disgrace. In Chinese history, whenever there is a change of regime, some people are indifferent to fame and wealth, some people are greedy for profit, some people stay true to their original aspirations, some people accommodate themselves to the circumstances, and some people live in seclusion. All these choices can make people famous, and affect the country's development orientation in the future. Even so, it can only prove that people need the country, not the other way around. Everyone makes a choice of his own free will. For instance, in modern Chinese history, under the policy of "pacification by offering concessions", both illustrious and notorious figures emerged one after another. The policy of "pacification by offering concessions" can be used for division and unity. If this policy has the effect of dividing the enemy, it plays the role of uniting our own strength. Conversely, if this policy has the effect of uniting the enemy, it plays the role of dividing our own strength.

明清易代之际，明朝官绅面临着政治立场的多重选择。清军入关前，他们有的人加入起义军队伍，有的人为崇祯帝殉葬，有的人彷徨四顾。清军入关后，原明朝官员，有的转投南明政权，有的随农民军转战各地，更多的人则投靠新主清王朝。南明政权把明朝官员投降农民政权的行为称作"从贼"，清乾隆时期把降清的明朝官员称为"贰臣"。[121]

During the transition from the Ming Dynasty to the Qing Dynasty, the officials of the Ming Dynasty faced multiple choices in terms of political stance. Before the Qing army entered the Shanhaiguan Pass, some of them joined the rebel army, some sacrificed their lives for Emperor Chongzhen of the Ming Dynasty, and some were in a state of indecision. After the Qing army entered the pass, some of them turned to the Southern Ming regime, some followed the peasant army and

---

121 彭勇撰《"从贼的贰臣"与南明政局走向：以柳同春为个案的研究》，来源《明史研究》，2017 年第 1 期

fought from place to place, but more defected to the new regime. The regime of the Southern Ming Dynasty regarded the act of Ming officials surrendering to the peasant regime as "colluding with the rebels", while the regime of Emperor Qianlong of the Qing Dynasty called those who surrendered to the Qing Dynasty "turncoat officials".[121]

以武昌起义为标志性事件的辛亥革命，结束了中国两千年的封建统治，建立了亚洲第一个民主共和国，是中国乃至亚洲走向民主共和的开端，在中国历史中具有里程碑意义。[122]

After the Xinhai Revolution broke out with the Wuchang Uprising as its landmark event, the two-thousand-year-long feudal rule in China came to an end, and the first democratic republic in Asia was established. The Xinhai Revolution marked the beginning of the democratic republican system of China and Asia, and so holds a milestone significance in Chinese history.[122]

1911 年 10 月 10 日，打响武昌起义第一枪的便是湖北新军工程第八营的革命士兵。武昌起义之后，各省纷纷响应。其中，湖南、江西、陕西、山西和云南的起义均由新军发动，而在贵州、浙江、广西、安徽、福建、广东、四川和江苏等省的革命中，也得到了新军的有力支持。可以说，新军在革命各省推翻清王朝的武装起义中发挥了中流砥柱的作用。[123]

On October 10, 1911, the revolutionary soldiers of the Eighth Engineering Battalion of the Hubei New Army fired the first shot of the Wuchang Uprising. Other provinces responded successively. Among them, the uprisings in Hunan, Jiangxi, Shaanxi, Shanxi and Yunnan were launched by the New Army, and the revolutions of Guizhou,

---

122　汤水清装《对辛亥革命历史意义的新思考》，来源《江西社会科学》，2011 年 10 期

123　郑大华撰《论革命派在辛亥革命中的历史作用》，来源《高校理论战线》，2011 年第 10 期

Zhejiang, Guangxi, Anhui, Fujian, Guangdong, Sichuan and Jiangsu were vigorously supported by the New Army. It can be said that the New Army played a crucial role in the armed uprisings of the revolutionary provinces to overthrow the Qing Dynasty.[123]

辛亥革命发生、发展及结果，均与经济因素密切关联。清朝末年的新政虽取得了显著成绩，但在经济废墟上的改革是脆弱的。1907 年美国金融危机触发了中国的经济危机。武昌起义后列强停止对中国各方借款，南北双方均陷于经济困境。清政府因经济竭蹶不能及时平息事端，南方因财政窘迫无力北伐。在内外交困的情势下，各派妥协让步，南北议和，清帝退位。[124]

The occurrence, development, and outcome of the Xinhai Revolution were closely related to economic factors. The New Policies at the end of the Qing Dynasty had achieved remarkable results, but the reforms amid the economic ruins were fragile. In 1907, the US financial crisis triggered an economic crisis in China. After the Wuchang Uprising, the Western powers ceased providing loans to all parties in China, leading to economic predicaments of both the North and the South. The Qing government failed to quell the unrest in a timely manner due to its economic breakdown, while the South was unable to launch a northern expedition due to financial constraints. Amid these internal and external difficulties, all parties made compromises and concessions, sought to reach a peace treaty to end the conflict between the North and the South, and the Qing emperor abdicated.[124]

明末清初，很多明人争先恐后投降清政府，这虽然是明朝的不幸，加速了大清统一中国的步伐，却也为中国留下了大量的物质基础。这使后来的中华民国推翻清朝以后，有了建设国家的起码根基。

124　王爱云撰《经济困境与辛亥革命》，来源《史学月刊》，2012 年 10 期

At the end of the Ming Dynasty and the beginning of the Qing Dynasty, many people of the Ming Dynasty scrambled to surrender to the Qing government. Although it was a misfortune for the Ming Dynasty and an accelerator for the Qing Dynasty's unification of China, it left a great material foundation for China, serving as an essential basis for the national construction of the Republic of China after the collapse of the Qing Dynasty.

由于享受荣华富贵就要铤而走险，乃至卖国求荣的历史事迹在各个朝代都有上演。这段明末到中华民国更迭的中国王朝古近代历史，足以证明将中华民国打到台湾的中华人民共和国如何对待国内反对力量，以防现代中国的恐怖主义老调重弹能够获得成功。

In all dynasties, there were always some people who took risks, even betrayed their country for wealth and glory. The ancient and modern history from the end of the Ming Dynasty to the establishment of the Republic of China is sufficient to prove why the People's Republic of China, which drove the regime of the Republic of China to Taiwan, was able to achieve success in dealing with domestic opposition forces, so as to prevent the recurrence of modern Chinese terrorism.

在21世纪，恐怖主义再怎么变化莫测，不可捉摸，难以言明，而以全世界人数总量来算，恐怖分子也只是少数人。反恐以子弹对子弹、以爆炸对爆炸、以宣传对宣传、以一命换一命，恐怖分子则沦为"龟孙子"。

In the 21st century, no matter how unpredictable, elusive, and indescribable terrorism appears, in terms of the total global population, terrorists are only a minority of people. If the method of bullets against bullets, explosions against explosions, propaganda against propaganda, and life against life is applied in anti-terrorism, terrorists will be reduced to "spineless wretches".

然而，在现代社会，终究还是或有人成为恐怖分子，或有人屈服于恐怖分子的统治，或有人助纣为虐对恐怖分子提供支持，或有人对恐怖袭击漠不关心……这足以说明恐怖主义是一个社会问题。

However, in modern society, it is undeniable that some people become terrorists, some submit to the rule of terrorists, some become accomplices to terrorists by providing them with support, and some are indifferent to terrorist attacks... This is enough to show that terrorism is a social problem.

混乱时期的社会总是不明不白，当好人看见希望，坏人看见绝望，反恐也能成功，这是解决恐怖主义的一种常规方法。例如，在中华民国时期，1915 年开始的护国运动，云南军事人物蔡锷毅然决然起兵，推翻倒行逆施有独裁称帝行为的袁世凯，就是一场"领头羊"率领的反恐战争。

Society in a chaotic period is confusing. When kind-hearted people see hope and malicious people see despair, anti-terrorism efforts can be successful. This is a common approach to solving the problem of terrorism. For example, during the era of the Republic of China, the National Protection Movement that began in 1915, in which Cai E, a military figure from Yunnan, resolutely raised an army to overthrow the rule of Yuan Shikai, who was acting contrary to the will of the people and attempting to restore the monarchy and proclaim himself emperor, was a "counter-terrorism war" led by a "leader".

民国初年的"民心"就是一个谜：它曾经激扬澎湃于推倒帝制、保卫共和的历次战争中，也曾经销影遁形于一片政治失败、经济凋弊的乱局之中[125]。

The "popular sentiment" in the early years of the Republic of China

---

125 马少华撰《从"民心"到"人民程度"》，来源《读书》，1998 年第 10 期

was a mystery: It once surged in the wars to overthrow the monarchy and defend the republic, but at other times, it vanished in the chaotic situation of political failures and economic depressions.[125]

袁世凯在清末民初的中国政坛举足轻重。在帝制与共和交替过程中，他利用自己培植的政治、经济、军事势力拔掉了清政府这棵参天大树，同时实现南北和谈，避免了制度变革带来的大规模流血牺牲。"他本可以成为中国历史上为数不多的杰出政治家，本可以成为他期望的中国的华盛顿"。但当时中国的道路选择还处于探索初期，立宪君主制与新生共和制仍在较量。袁世凯本来就是一个亦旧亦新的人物，1916 年贸然选择复辟帝制，成为执舆论牛耳的国民党批判、讨伐的对象，"洪宪帝制"随着袁世凯的病逝而黯然收场[126]。

In the Chinese political arena during the late Qing Dynasty and the early Republic of China, Yuan Shikai played a crucial role. During the transition from monarchy to republic, he used the political, economic, and military forces he had cultivated to overthrow the Qing government, and achieved peace between the North and the South through negotiations, thus avoiding large-scale bloodshed caused by institutional changes. "He could have become one of the few outstanding statesmen in Chinese history, a figure like George Washington he aspired to be." But at that time, China was still in an initial stage in path exploration, and the constitutional monarchy was competing with the nascent republican system. As a person embodying both traditional and innovative traits, Yuan Shikai rashly chose to restore the monarchy in 1916. As a result, he was criticized by the Kuomintang, which dominated public opinion, and the "Hongxian Monarchy" came to an end with Yuan Shikai's death from illness.[126]

1915 年 12 月 25 日爆发的护国战争，是中国近代史上继辛亥

---

126 刘耀撰《袁世凯称帝的心理悲剧》，来源《南方论刊》，2015 年第 9 期

革命之后，为反对袁世凯复辟帝制、维护民主共和制度而进行的一场具有进步、爱国意义的战争。蔡锷为护国战争的策划、联络和发动发挥了极为独特而重要的作用[127]。

The National Protection War, which broke out on December 25, 1915, was a patriotic war with progressive implications in modern Chinese history. It was fought after the Xinhai Revolution to oppose Yuan Shikai's restoration of the monarchy and safeguard the democratic republican system. Cai E played a unique and important role in the planning, liaison, and initiation of the war.[127]

蔡锷（1882—1916），原名艮寅，字松坡，湖南邵阳人，中国近代史上杰出的民主革命家、军事家和爱国主义者。他在海内外都享有崇高的威望。在他1904—1916年的政治、军事生涯中，做出了辉煌大事，一是在辛亥革命时期，领导了云南的反清武装起义；二是在1915年发动和指挥了反对袁世凯复辟帝制的护国战争，其光辉业绩彪炳史册[128]。

Cai E (1882-1916), known as Genyin by original name, and Songpo by courtesy name, a native of Shaoyang, Hunan, was an outstanding democratic revolutionary, military strategist, and patriot in modern Chinese history. He enjoyed a high reputation at home and abroad. During his political and military career from 1904 to 1916, he accomplished two remarkable things. First, he led the anti-Qing armed uprising in Yunnan during the Xinhai Revolution. Second, he launched and commanded the National Protection War against Yuan Shikai's restoration of the monarchy in 1915. His glorious achievements are indelible in the

---

127　邓江祁撰《蔡锷与护国战争的发动——纪念护国战争100周年》，来源《邵阳学院学报：社会科学版》，2015年第6期

128　肖平撰《蔡锷将军——邵阳出来的文武全才》，来源《邵阳师专学报》，1996年第4期

historical records.[128]

1915 年，袁世凯复辟称帝，激起全国民众的反对。12 月 25 日，唐继尧、蔡锷、李烈钧在昆明联名通电全国，反对袁世凯称帝，宣布云南独立，建立云南都督府，组织讨袁护国军进兵四川、贵州等地。南方各省纷纷宣布独立，1916 年 3 月，袁世凯在内外压迫后宣布取消帝制。护国运动是中国近代史上一次伟大的革命，具有"辛亥革命，民革建立；护国讨袁，共和再现"的历史地位。护国运动延缓了中国半殖民地化加深的过程，避免了历史的大倒退，昭示了历史的潮流不可阻挡。护国运动促进了云南的社会发展，唤醒了广大民众的思想觉悟，推动了全国范围逐步兴起的革命高潮，是中国革命发展的又一重要标志[129]。

In 1915, Yuan Shikai restored the monarchy and proclaimed himself emperor, which aroused the opposition of the entire nation. On December 25, Tang Jiyao, Cai E, and Li Liejun issued a circular telegram to the whole country in Kunming, opposing Yuan Shikai's proclamation as emperor, declaring the independence of Yunnan, establishing the Yunnan Military Government, and organizing and dispatching the National Protection Army into Sichuan and Guizhou. The southern provinces successively declared their independence. In March 1916, Yuan Shikai was force to abolish the monarchy under internal and external pressure. The National Protection Movement was a great revolution in modern Chinese history, whose historical status can be summarized as "the establishment of the Republic of China after the Xinhai Revolution, and the restoration of the republican system after the launch of the National Protection Movement against Yuan Shikai". It delayed China's semi-

---

129 赵惠昆撰《护国运动百年的启示》，来源《云南社会主义学院学报》，2015 年第 4 期

colonization, avoided a major historical setback, and demonstrated an irresistible historical trend. It promoted the social development of Yunnan, awakened the ideological awareness of the vast majority of the people, and promoted the gradually-emerging nationwide revolution to the highest level. It was another important symbol of the development of the Chinese revolution.[129]

1915 年 12 月 12 日，袁世凯接受了所谓的民众劝进书，宣布登基，史称洪宪皇帝。1916 年 3 月 22 日，袁被迫下台，当了 83 天皇帝，6 月 6 日又因尿毒症弃世而去[130]。

On December 12, 1915, Yuan Shikai accepted the so-called petition from the people and proclaimed his accession to the throne, known as Emperor Hongxian in history. On March 22, 1916, he was forced to step down after being emperor for 83 days. On June 6, he died of uremia.[130]

中华民国的护国运动是一场武力保家卫国的战争，跟和平理性抗争有很大的区别。由于，袁世凯进行复辟称帝是为了"家天下"，而非为人民服务的宗旨，最终也致使袁世凯称帝美梦破损。所以，尽管护国运动是一场开展暴力行为的运动，与现代文明和平理性，用法律手段争取自身权益有很大的背离，却在现代中国依旧是一场有影响力的历史运动。

The National Protection Movement of the Republic of China was a war of safeguarding the country by force, which was quite different from peaceful and rational resistance. Since Yuan Shikai's restoration of the monarchy and proclamation as emperor was aimed at establishing a "family empire" rather than serving the people, his dream of becoming emperor ultimately shattered. Therefore, although it was a movement involving violent actions, which deviated greatly from the principles of

---

130　苏全有撰《袁世凯称帝的幕后推手》，来源《晚报文萃》，2010 年第 19 期

modern civilization that advocate peace, rationality, and the use of legal means to strive for people's rights and interests, it was still an influential historical movement in modern China.

在客观上，恐怖主义能勉强把全世界力量貌合神离地聚集在一起进行反恐，但无道无德的反恐照样会让国家分崩离析，社会大乱，各方力量无法聚沙成塔。就像在中国古代历史上，明朝嘉靖时期，明政府斩首中国海商兼倭寇领袖人物王直（汪直），导致中国海域安全愈发失控就是一个例子。

Objectively speaking, terrorist tactics can be used to barely unite the forces of the whole world in a seemingly harmonious but actually estranged manner for counter-terrorism purpose. However, immoral counter-terrorism measures will lead to the disintegration of a country, the disorder of society, and the failure in uniting various forces. For example, in ancient Chinese history, during Emperor Jiajing's Reign of the Ming Dynasty, the decapitation of Wang Zhi, the leader of maritime merchants and Japanese pirates, by the Ming government led to an even more out-of-control situation regarding maritime security.

汪直还是王直"必也正名乎"，王直姓汪还是姓王，一直有争论。《明史》作汪直，《辞海》作王直。据考，明代徽州府歙县柘林村，既有汪姓，也有王姓。王直的母亲被称为汪妪，王直的侄儿，姓汪名汝贤。这些材料都证实王直姓汪，非姓王。但王直对自己名字有明确说法。嘉靖三十六年（1557年），王直被诱捕后向嘉靖皇帝呈上《自明疏》中写道："带罪犯人王直，即汪五峰，直隶徽州府歙县民"。据说，王直原本叫汪直，后来入海为盗，因怕连累家族，改称王直。[131]

---

131 《王直，海商的使命与海盗的归宿》搜狐滚动（搜狐网），www.sohu.com，2015年11月26日

"It is necessary to ensure that everything is called by its proper and rightful name." There has been a debate about whether Wang Zhi was surnamed 汪 (Wāng) or 王 (Wáng). In *History of the Ming Dynasty*, his name is written as 汪直 (Wāng Zhí), but in *Cihai*, it is written as 王直 (Wáng Zhí). A research shows that there were both people surnamed 汪 (Wāng) and people surnamed 王 (Wáng) in Zhelin Village, She County, Huizhou Prefecture in the Ming Dynasty. His mother was called Madam 汪 (Wāng), and his nephew was called 汪汝贤 (Wāng Rǔxián) These materials all confirm that Wang Zhi was surnamed 汪 (Wāng), not 王 (Wáng). However, Wang Zhi had a clear statement about his own name. In *Memorial on Self-Justification* he submitted to Emperor Jiajing after he was lured into a trap in the 36th Year of Emperor Jiajing's Reign (1557), he wrote: "The criminal in custody, 王直 (Wáng Zhí), also known as 汪五峰 (Wāng Wǔfēng), is a native of She County, Huizhou Prefecture under the jurisdiction of the Central Secretariat." It is said that 王直 (Wáng Zhí) was originally called 汪直 (Wāng Zhí). Later, he became a pirate, and changed his surname to 王 (Wáng) for fear of involving his family members in trouble.[131]

王直武装走私集团的行为引起了明中央政府的高度关注，政府相继派朱纨等人清剿浙江沿海流民武装。他们派兵两路夹击汪直，王直只好将活动基地迁至日本。日本各诸侯的对外贸易政策为王直提供了客居的良好条件。王直善于拉拢、结交朋友，取得了许多日本人的信任，他定居日本平户（今属日本长崎县），挂起了"徽王"的旗号，以平户为基地吸收反明势力，不仅招集国内亡命之徒，而且还用巨资收买日本真倭的门多郎次郎、四助四郎等部为羽翼，并利用日本浪人向中国沿海地区发动多次跨海攻击。[132]

132　杨沐喜撰《略论游走于商寇之间的汪直》，来源《海洋文化与福建发展》，2011 年

The activities of Wang Zhi's armed smuggling group attracted the high attention of the central government of the Ming Dynasty. The government dispatched Zhu Wan and others to suppress the armed forces of the displaced people along the coast of Zhejiang. They sent troops to attack Wang Zhi from two directions, forcing him to relocate his base of operations to Japan. The foreign trade policies of the Japanese feudal lords provided favorable conditions for him to live in Japan. Good at courting friends and building connections, he won the trust of many Japanese people. He settled in Hirado (now in Nagasaki Prefecture, Japan), proclaimed himself "King of Huizhou," and used Hirado as a base to gather anti-Ming forces. He not only recruited fugitives from China but also used large amounts of money to win the support of real Japanese pirates such as Mon tarou jirou and Shi suke shirou, and employed Japanese ronin to launch several cross-sea attacks on China's coastal areas.[132]

嘉靖三十三年（1554 年），胡宗宪就任浙直总督。东南沿海的抗倭任务落在他的身上。和几个前任以剿为主、"四处救火"不同，胡宗宪上任后决计剿、抚并施，并把最大的目标毫不迟疑地对准了王直，面对茫茫大海，他说道："海上贼惟（王）直机警难制，其余皆鼠辈，毋足虑。"[133]

In the 33rd Year of Emperor's Jiajing Reign (1554), Hu Zongxian took office as the Governor of Zhejiang and Zhili, and assumed the responsibility of fighting against Japanese pirates along the southeast coast. Different from his predecessors who mainly focused on suppression and "putting out fires everywhere", Hu Zongxian decided to adopt a strategy that combined suppression with appeasement. He targeted Wang

---

133 彭治国撰《越境者王直 从商人到"倭寇"》，来源《优品》，2016 年第 3 期

Zhi as his main objective without hesitation. Facing the vast sea, he said, "Among the pirates at sea, only Wang Zhi is alert and difficult to control. The others are only insignificant fellows, and there is no need to about them."[133]

胡宗宪派人到日本"宣谕"，向王直传递自己的善意：王直的老母和妻儿已经从金华的监狱中释放，安置在杭州，生活过得十分不错；王直如果能够回国，则可以保证他的生命安全。[134]

Hu Zongxian dispatched his people to "declare the imperial edict" in Japan and convey his goodwill to Wang Zhi, "Your mother, wife, and children have been released from the prison in Jinhua and resettled in Hangzhou, living a good life; if you can come back to China, your life safety can be guaranteed."[134]

嘉靖三十六年十一月，王直带着叶宗满、汪汝贤，入军门谒见胡宗宪。胡宗宪也确曾力保汪直，但在以巡按御史王本固为代表的顽固派力主之下，王直还是没能逃过一劫，先被下狱，两年后被斩于杭州官巷口。[135]

In November of the 36th Year of Emperor Jiajing's Reign, Wang Zhi, accompanied by Ye Zongman and Wang Ruxian, entered the military headquarters to have an audience with Hu Zongxian. Hu Zongxian did try his best to protect him. However, under the strong insistence of the die-hard faction represented by Wang Bengu, the Imperial Censor of Inspection, Wang Zhi failed to escape his fate. He was first imprisoned and then was beheaded two years later at Guanxiangkou in Hangzhou.[135]

自嘉靖三十一年至嘉靖三十八年王直被杀，东南海上各海商集团基本上都以王直为公认首领，对明廷进行或明或暗的反抗斗争。

134　同上

135　逄文昱撰《称雄一时的"海上帝王"——汪直》，来源《中国海事》，2011 年 5 期自王直死后至嘉靖四十五年隆庆帝继位，各大海商集团已没有公认的领袖，他们时分时合，继续与明廷对抗。隆庆帝继位后部分开放海禁，随之"海宇宴如"，海商集团的大规模反抗活动基本结束。[136]

From the 31st Year of Emperor Jiajing's Reign to the 38th Year when Wang Zhi was killed, almost all the maritime merchant groups in the southeast seas recognized him as their leader and carried out open or covert resistance struggles against the Ming court. After Wang Zhi died and before Emperor Longqing ascended the throne in the 45th Year of Emperor Jiajing's Reign, there was no recognized leader among the major maritime merchant groups. They separated and reunited from time to time, continuing to resist the Ming court. After Emperor Longqing ascended the throne, he partially lifted the sea ban. Subsequently, "peace prevailed over the seas and the land", and the large-scale resistance activities of the maritime merchant groups almost disappeared.[136]

明末清初的史学家谈迁（1594—1567）在《国榷》中也批评了嘉靖当局的错误决策，指出"胡宗宪许汪直以不死，其后异论汹汹，遂不敢坚请。假看汪直，便宜制海上，则岑港、柯梅之师可无经岁，而闽广、江北亦不至顿甲苦战也"。谈迁的这段史评提示了一个重要的问题，就是如果嘉靖当局当时能接受汪直的归顺受抚，妥善处理好开市通商问题，就能避免之后又蔓延十年的历史悲剧。[137]

In *Records of the Ming Dynasty*, Tan Qian (1594-1657), a historian in the late Ming and early Qing Dynasties, criticized the wrong decision of Emperor Jiajing, pointing out, "Hu Zongxian promised Wang Zhi that he would not be put to death. Later, there were so many dissenting voices that he did not dare to stick firmly to his own proposition. If Wang

---

136　尹晓盛撰《明代私人海上贸易研究》，来源《山东大学》，2007 年

137　胡晨撰《明朝嘉靖时代的"海上王国"—汪直及其东亚海上贸易网络研究（1540—1560)》，来源《海洋大学》，2010 年

Zhi could have been forgiven at that time and allowed to play a certain balancing role on the sea, then the battles at Cengang and Kemei would not have lasted so long, and regions such as Fujian, Guangdong, and provinces north of the Yangtze River would not have been plunged into a long and arduous war." The historical comment by Tan Qian reveals an important problem, that is, if Emperor Jiajing had accepted Wang Zhi's surrender, pacified him and properly handled the issue of opening markets for trade, the historical tragedy that spread for another ten years could have been avoided.[137]

在中国社会历史之中，一旦经政关系涉及军事史，如果走私者是为了生存进行不法活动，可以获得喘息的机会。反之，如果走私者为了生计进行不法活动，那就是死不足惜。

In the history of Chinese society, once the relationship between economy and politics involved military history, smugglers who engaged in illegal activities for the sake of survival might get a chance to take a breather. On the contrary, if they engaged in illegal activities for a livelihood, they deserved to die.

天地对待任何人都一样，都是同时兼顾有情和无情，从而得出"大自然没有必要特意照顾人类"的结论。人类不是想怎么过日子就怎么过日子，人类迁就生存，才能有迁就生活。

God treats everyone equally, taking both sentiment and ruthlessness into account at the same time. This leads to the conclusion that "nature needn't specifically take care of human beings". Humans cannot live their lives as they please. Only by adapting to survival can they adapt to life.

人在社会早晚无所遁形，任何事物都能体现最低价值，越不自量力的人群，就越不安于本分。人想拥抱安全，需要杜绝危险，这是世人反恐能够接受的普遍意义。就像在 21 世纪，中日领土争端冲突升级，有些中国人不学无术，有利敌行为，实际上是从爱国行为迈向恐怖行为。

People will be exposed in society sooner or later, and everything can embody the lowest value. The more a person overestimates his own strength, the less he will be content with his lot. If people want to embrace safety, they need to eliminate dangers. This is a common view acceptable to people in the fight against terrorism. For example, in the 21st century, when the territorial disputes between China and Japan escalated, some ill-informed and inept Chinese people engaged in acts that benefited the enemy, and their patriotic acts were actually turning into terrorist ones.

钓鱼岛列岛位于福建正东，距中国台湾基隆市东北约 92 海里处。该群岛由钓鱼岛、黄尾屿、赤尾屿等岛屿组成，总面积约 6.5 平方公里。日本称其为"尖阁列岛"。[138]

The Diaoyu Archipelago is located to the due east of Fujian Province, approximately 92 nautical miles northeast of Keelung City, Taiwan, China. It consists of Diaoyu Island, Huangwei Islet, Chiwei Islet, and so on, with a total area of about 6.5 square kilometers. Japan refers to them as the "Senkaku Islands."[138]

2004 年，70 岁的鞠德源先生研究钓鱼岛问题数十载，虽然，网上有关这个话题炒得热热闹闹，但他的家里却时常冷清。[139]

By 2004, Mr. Ju Deyuan, who was then 70 years old, had studied the Diaoyu Islands issue for decades. Although the topic was widely debated online, his home had few visitors.[139]

2004 年 3 月 24 日，中国的 7 位民间人士登上钓鱼岛并遭到日本有关当局的非法拘禁，中日两国在钓鱼岛问题上的冲突达到了高

---

138 张爱军撰《日本在钓鱼岛问题上的图谋》，来源《党政干部学刊》，2004 年 7 期

139 《受冷落的钓鱼岛著作》新浪新闻（新浪网），新浪新闻（新浪网）www.sina.com. cn，2004 年 07 月 14 日

潮。那时，才有人来电来访，跟鞠先生讨论或向他请教关于钓鱼岛的学术问题。[140]

On March 24, 2004, seven Chinese civilians landed on Diaoyu Island and were illegally detained by Japanese authorities. This event pushed the conflict concerning the Diaoyu Islands between China and Japan to a climax. It was then that people began to call and visit Mr. Ju, and discuss or seek his advice on academic issues related to the Diaoyu Islands.[140]

其实早在 2003 年，他就在网上公布了自己的电话并售卖自己关于钓鱼岛的专著，可是，家里的电话只是偶尔才会响起。[141]

In fact, as early as 2003, he made his phone number public on the internet and sold his monographs on the Diaoyu Islands, but the phone in his home rang only occasionally.[141]

2004 年 7 月，伴随中日海底资源之争的日趋激烈，网上有关新闻的点击率又一次上升，只是鞠先生的售书电话还是不热闹。[142]

In July 2004, as the dispute regarding undersea resources between China and Japan intensified, the click-through rate of related online news once again increased. However, Mr. Ju's phone for book sales was still rarely rung.[142]

中日围绕钓鱼岛争端开始升级，从 2012 年 4 月 16 日正在美国华盛顿访问的日本东京都知事石原慎太郎发表演讲称，"东京都计划在年内'购买'钓鱼岛"的言论开始，日本首先就钓鱼岛事件发难，9 月 11 日日本内阁会议决定拨 20.5 亿日元来"购岛"，至 21

140　同上

141　同上

142　同上

日日本数十名警察登上了钓鱼岛，全然不顾中方的强烈抗议[143]。

The dispute regarding the Diaoyu Islands between China and Japan began to escalate from April 16, 2012, when Shintaro Ishihara, then Governor of Tokyo, who was visiting Washington in the United States, announced in a speech that "the Tokyo Metropolitan Government planed to 'purchase' the Diaoyu Islands" within the year. Japan was the first to make provocations in the Diaoyu Islands incident. On September 11, the Japanese Cabinet decided to allocate 2.05 billion yen to "purchase the islands." On September 21, dozens of Japanese policemen landed on Diaoyu Island, completely ignoring China's strong protests.[143]

在钓鱼岛争端不断升级的过程中，中国的民意也不断地沸腾，特别是一些保钓人士的出海举动，更是成为公众的视线和舆论的焦点。在民意不断发酵之后，围绕有关钓鱼岛出现的民众反日示威游行呈遍地开花之势，从 15 日开始的示威活动已经涉及北京、上海、广州、西安等至少 52 个城市，因而这些自发形成的游行活动是民意在钓鱼岛事件上最为直观和集中的表达方式。汇集起来的人群如潮水般涌上街头，民意在短时间内集中体现了爱国主义的巨大号召力，也体现了公众对于公共事件强烈的参与意识。但是，在这次自发的群体性游行中，出现了一些非理性行为，如严重的打砸伤人行为以及过激的言论，使得爱国主义的形象在公众心目中被扭曲为暴力的、非理性的情绪释放口。这些非理性行为突出表现在网络环境中一些极端的做法，以及现实环境中打砸抢伤人事件[144]。

As the dispute regarding the Diaoyu Islands continued to escalate, public sentiment in China kept boiling over. In particular, the sea-going actions of some defenders of the Diaoyu Islands became the focus

---

143　蒋万胜、张芝龙撰《钓鱼岛事件中的群体非理性行为透视》，来源《东南传播》，2013 年第 3 期

144　同上

of public attention and media coverage. As public sentiment kept on fermenting, anti-Japanese demonstrations related to the Diaoyu Islands sprang up everywhere. The demonstrations that began on September 15 involved at least 52 cities, including Beijing, Shanghai, Guangzhou, and Xi'an. These spontaneous marches manifested public sentiment on the Diaoyu Islands issue in the most direct and concentrated manner. The assembled crowds surged onto the streets like waves. The public sentiment vividly demonstrated the great appeal of patriotism within a short time and reflected people's strong awareness of participation in public affairs. However, during these spontaneous mass marches, some irrational behaviors emerged, such as serious acts of smashing, looting, and injuring others, as well as radical slogans, which distorted the image of patriotism in people's mind into a vent for violent and irrational emotions. These irrational behaviors were prominently manifested as extreme actions on the internet and incidents of smashing, looting, and injuring others in real life.[144]

2012 年 9 月 15—18 日期间，游行队伍中不断出现冲击日本在华公司，抢劫纵火与日本概念相关的实体经营店，打砸日本品牌车辆的非理性行为，更有甚者，西安市一位日系车车主被打穿颅骨，现场惨不忍睹。9 月 15—18 日北京出现了游行队伍冲击日本驻华大使馆的举动，愤怒的群众与现场维持秩序的武警发生冲突并用矿泉水瓶打砸武警人员。9 月 16 日成都一批大呼"美国是日本狗的主人"口号的示威者冲击了美国领事馆，并现场高唱国歌。9 月 15 日青岛一家日本投资的购物中心被砸，激愤的青年不断地毁坏超市的财物，场面十分混乱。9 月 16 日深圳游行群众与武警发生冲突，现场矿泉水瓶飞舞。一家名为"西武百货"的日本店窗户遭到了砸毁。同时在游行中，不断有人向武警投掷气体瓶，焚烧日本国旗。9 月 18 日香港正值纪念"九一八事变"纪念日，游行群众焚烧日本国旗和美国国旗。9 月 15 日西安游行群众打砸日系车辆，造成车主重伤等极端行为。而这些非理性的极端行为与游行所倡导的爱国主义诉求产生了强烈的反差，并引发了各界的强烈关注与思考 [145]。

From September 15 to 18, 2012, irrational behaviors such as storming Japanese companies in China, looting and arson of physical stores related to Japanese concepts, and smashing Japanese-brand vehicles kept on emerging among the marching crowds. In an extreme case, the owner of a Japanese-brand car in Xi'an had his skull fractured, causing a scene very dreadful to behold. From September 15 to 18, in Beijing, the marching crowds stormed the Japanese embassy in China. Clashing with the policemen maintaining order on the spot, the angry protesters threw mineral water bottles at them. On September 16, in Chengdu, a group of protesters shouting slogans like "The United States is the master of the Japanese dog" stormed the U.S. Consulate and sang the national anthem on the spot. On September 15, in Qingdao, a Japanese-invested shopping center was smashed. The agitated youths continuously destroyed the properties of the supermarket, creating a very chaotic scene. On September 16, in Shenzhen, the marching crowds clashed with the policemen and threw mineral water bottles everywhere. The windows of a Japanese "Seibu Department Store" were smashed. At the same time, in the marches, people continuously threw gas bottles at the policemen and burned Japanese flags. On September 18, in Hong Kong, where the "September 18 Incident" was being commemorated, the marching crowds burned Japanese and American flags. On September 15, in Xi'an, the marching crowds smashed Japanese-brand vehicles, causing serious injuries to the owners and other extreme behaviors.

145 　同上

These irrational extreme behaviors contrasted sharply with the patriotic demands advocated by the marches, and aroused strong attention and reflection in all sectors of society.[145]

在 2015 年 10 月，有资讯显示，反对日本拒买日货和狂购日本商品一样来得如此猛烈，一些国人的爱国天平既可以快速失衡也可以立刻淡忘。就在中日钓鱼岛纷争未卜的前提下，很多中国人把去日本旅游当作最新的选择目的地。虽然日本一切都太贵了，物价基本上是比利时的 1.5 倍，比起中国来高 8 倍以上，可这丝毫阻止不了一些中国人的狂购热情[146]。

In October 2015, it was reported that the boycott of Japanese goods and the frenzy of buying Japanese products came with equal intensity. Some people's patriotic sentiment could either quickly lose control or immediately fade. When the dispute regarding the Diaoyu Islands between China and Japan remained unsolved, many Chinese chose Japan as their latest travel destination. Although everything in Japan was too expensive, with prices about 1.5 times as high as those in Belgium and more than eight times higher than those in China, this did not hinder some Chinese people's enthusiasm for shopping.[146]

"爆买"一词频繁出现在中日媒体与公众视野，成为官方和民间关注的焦点。中国人的"爆买"为日本旅游业的发展注入了活力，为低迷的日本经济起了提振作用，这也是日本政府长期以来倡导和制定旅游发展战略，振兴国内经济所带来的正面效应。[147]

The term "explosive buying" frequently appeared in the Chinese and Japanese media and public view, becoming a focal point of concern for the government and the public. The "explosive buying" by Chinese

---

146　《日媒：中国人正在疯狂拯救日本 只是用嘴巴抗日》，新浪军事（新浪网），www.sina.com.cn，2015 年 10 月 8 日

147　韩勇撰《"爆买"现象下的日本旅游发展战略》，来源《中国商论》，2016 年 32 期

people injected vitality into the development of Japan's tourism industry and boosted its sluggish economy. This reflected a positive effect caused by the long-term acts of the Japanese government to advocate and formulate tourism development strategies and revitalize the domestic economy.[147]

战争是对一个国家综合国力的考量，并非个人逞强的舞台，只有负责任的人才能成为国家英雄。在 21 世纪，人民大喊"国家兴亡，匹夫有责"是建立在此人是否有偷税漏税的基础上，而不是一个人文韬武略有多么优秀。

War is a test of a country's comprehensive strength, not a stage for individuals to show off their false bravado. Only those who are responsible can become national heroes. In the 21st century, when someone shouts "Everyone is responsible for the rise and fall of the country", it should be based on whether he has committed tax evasion or not, rather than how remarkable he is in civil and military strategies.

因为，如果国家遭受侵略，爱国人士不去捐款，就难免会主动或被动，与不爱国人士为伍。甚至，还要与他们做生意，朝夕相对。所以，为国家捐钱捐物，比人民群众进行游行示威更实用。

When a country is invaded, if patriotic people do not donate money, they will inevitably associate with those who are not patriotic, either actively or passively. They may even make a deal with them and stay in each other's company all day long. Therefore, donating money or goods to the country is more practical than holding demonstrations.

一旦中日开战，中国人既反日又亲日是一种资助敌人的行为。如果中国人真心抗日，需要或捐款纳税，或从事写作，或发明创造，或宁死不屈，需要以对日战果来说话。

Once a war breaks out between China and Japan, it is an act of aiding the enemy for Chinese people to hold an anti-Japanese and pro-

Japanese stance at the same time. If Chinese people really want to resist Japan, they need to donate money and pay taxes, or engage in writing, or make inventions, or remain unyielding in the face of death. They need to prove themselves with the results of the fight against Japan.

在 21 世纪，恐怖主义危害社会。全球人口几十亿，有道有德者，能让技不如人者彻底心服口服。笨鸟先飞也能鸡群鹤立，先经过勤能补拙，有了熟能生巧的一技之长，继而技压群雄，造就一鸣惊人，投入保家卫国的洪流之中。

In the 21st century, terrorism does harm to society. Among billions of people in the world, those who are moral and virtuous can truly convince those who are less skilled. Even a slow bird that starts flying early can stand out among a flock of chickens. First, one should work hard to make up for his deficiencies, and master a unique skill through repeated practice. Then, he should outshine the competitors, achieve a stunning feat that amazes everyone, and plunge into the mighty torrent of defending his country.

第二章　中国兵道思想的内涵和外延

Chapter 2: Connotation and Denotation of Chinese Military Thought

中国兵道思想致力于东学西渐，继承明清时期的实学路线，注重解决实际问题，家事国情道家化，杂糅兵家作战思想，充分发挥历史作用处理与恐怖主义有关系的各种东西方事件，使中国古近代历史能够作用于现代社会。

The Chinese military thought is committed to the dissemination of Eastern learning to the West. It inherits the practical learning route of the Ming and Qing Dynasties, focuses on solving practical problems, makes domestic and national affairs conform to Taoist thought, blends operational concepts of military strategists, and plays a historical role in dealing with various Eastern and Western events related to terrorism, so that modern society can benefit from the ancient and modern history of China.

16—18 世纪的中西文化交流与以往相比出现了新的特点：西方文化东传与中国文化西传同时进行，西方的基督教文明和古老的中华文明，进入到第一次大规模和平等的交流时期。并通过交流，彼此取长补短，共同进步。[148]

Compared with previous periods, the cultural exchanges between China and the West from the 16th to the 18th century demonstrated new features: The dissemination of Western culture to the East and the spread of Chinese culture to the West occurred simultaneously. For the first time,

---

148　王军、孟宪凤撰《西学东渐与东学西渐——16—18 世纪中西文化交流特点论略》，来源《北方论丛》，2009 年 4 期

the Western Christian civilization and the ancient Chinese civilization interacted on a large scale and on an equal basis, learned from each other's strengths and made progress together.[148]

　　"东学西渐"的过程，是与欧洲的社会变革过程相统一的。并不是所有的欧洲人都愿意接受中国的文化、哲学和社会制度。在文化、哲学和社会制度方面，封建统治者（包括教会）对中国是采取排斥、抵制的态度，他们知道若引进这些势必危及其利益。主张引进并改造、吸收中国文化、哲学和社会制度的，主要是代表新兴资本势力的变革者。也正是随着社会变革的进行，他们才逐步完成了对中国文化、哲学和社会制度的引进和改造，这同时也就变革了欧洲本身的文化、哲学和社会制度。欧洲也由此而发达。[149]

The spread of Eastern learning to the West was unified with the social transformation in Europe. Not all Europeans were willing to accept Chinese culture, philosophy, and social systems. In terms of culture, philosophy, and social systems, feudal rulers (including the church) adopted an attitude of repulsion and resistance towards China, for they knew that the introduction of these concepts would inevitably threaten their interests. Those who advocated the introduction, transformation, and absorption of Chinese culture, philosophy, and social systems were mainly the reformers representing the emerging capitalist forces. Along with the social transformation, the introduction and transformation of Chinese culture, philosophy, and social systems were gradually completed. At the same time, this process led to the transformation of the European culture, philosophy, and social systems, making Europe prosperous.[149]

　　在西学东渐的历程中既有成功的一面，也有失败的一面。西学

149　刘永佶撰《"东学西渐"与"西学东渐"》，来源《乡音》，2002 年 8 期

中的精华，诸如科学和民主观念已融入东方文化，并与东方古典文化相结合，形成指导人们的价值观和方法论。现代技术落后的民族在西学东渐中学习了现代西方科学技术，快速提高了生产效率。然而，在西学东渐中，东方民族亦饱尝西方文化殖民的苦果和屈辱。此外，西学中的糟粕，诸如极端个人主义、欧洲中心主义、霸权主义、强权政治等作风和观念则与东方文化格格不入，并时常成为文化冲突的祸根。[150]

The spread of Western learning to the East contained both successful and failed elements. The essence of Western learning, like the concepts of science and democracy, was integrated into Eastern culture and combined with classical Eastern culture, serving as values and methodologies that guide people. During the process which saw the spread of Western learning to the East, ethnic groups lagging behind in modern technology learned modern Western science and technology, and improved their production efficiency rapidly. However, also in this process, Eastern ethnic groups suffered the bitter fruits and humiliation of Western cultural colonialism. In addition, the cross in Western learning, manifested as practices and concepts such as extreme individualism, Eurocentrism, hegemonism, and power politics, is incompatible with Eastern culture and often becomes the root cause of cultural conflicts.[150]

古希腊是形而上学的发源地。西方近代的科学、艺术、政治、哲学等等皆源于古希腊，形而上学不过是璀璨的学术之林中的一支。[151]

Ancient Greece was the birthplace of metaphysics. Modern Western science, art, politics and philosophy all originated from Ancient Greece, and metaphysics is only one branch in the splendid academic system.[151]

---

150 王林、缪晓静撰《西学东渐与东学西渐——兼论西方文化教育与民族文化的对外传播》，来源《中国成人教育》，2011 年 7 期

151 李晓峰、杜春峰撰《古希腊形而上学之思》，来源《理论学习》，2008 年 6 期

亚里士多德的"第一哲学"也就是形而上学。在《形而上学》这部论著中，亚里士多德把自哲学诞生之日起哲学家们就从不同角度以不同视点探索着的世界的本原问题归结为形而上学的对象，即作为"存在的存在"或者说是"存在本身"。由于实体是存在的核心，形而上学也就是关于实体的学说。[152]

Aristotle's "First Philosophy" is metaphysics. In his masterpiece *Metaphysics*, he summarized the problem of the origin of the world, which philosophers had been exploring from different angles and perspectives since the birth of philosophy, as the object of metaphysics, that is, as "the being of being" or "being itself". As substance is the core of being, metaphysics is a theory about substance.[152]

古希腊名人亚里士多德所著写的"形而上学"的哲学思想是一种实学。如果将东西方人士为什么要学习西方这种"形而上学"进行口语化，即能翻译为"形而上学，我去学习这种哲学思想，要能够保证我向上爬才行"。

The philosophical thought of "metaphysics" proposed by the famous ancient Greek Aristotle is a kind of authentic and beneficial knowledge. If we explain why Eastern and Western people intend to learn Western "metaphysics" in colloquial terms, it can be interpreted as "The study of the philosophical thought of metaphysics should guarantee that I can move up the social ladder."

自古以来，中国人就有"上为尊，下为贱，为上不为下"的传统陋习。如此，现代中国人对待西方哲学的"形而上学"，乃是重视"上"字，轻视"形"字，甚至"只学上，不习形"。

Since ancient times, the Chinese have had the traditional bad habit

---

152　王新莹撰《形而上学的内在意蕴——以亚里士多德、康德、海德格尔哲学为例》，来源《河南社会科学》，2004 年 6 期

of "esteeming the upper and despising the lower, and preferring to be in the upper rather than in the lower". Therefore, regarding the attitude of modern Chinese towards "metaphysics" in Western philosophy, they attach importance to "meta" and look down upon "physics", even only learning about "meta" while ignoring "physics".

在现代社会，"厕所取代书房"是一个社会现象，它能够上升为社会派的国家高度，既体现了养家糊口的艰辛，也体现了知识改变命运的艰难，这是一种实学的表现。

In modern society, the so-called "toilets replacing studies" is a social phenomenon that can be elevated to the national level of the social school. It reflects the hardship of making a living, as well as the difficulty of changing a person's destiny through knowledge. It is a manifestation of practical learning.

16 世纪至 18 世纪正是中国明清时期。在这两个世纪内，中国和外国的交流往来日益密切，中国实学也是在这两个世纪内逐步得到了切实的应用。明朝亡于内部势力，清朝亡于外国介入，如何处理"内忧外患"是现代国家也没有成功解决的难题。这使明朝清代既成为东西文化互相碰撞的时代，也成为现代外国人研究中国历史的必备朝代。

The period from the 16th to the 18th centuries coincided with the Ming and Qing Dynasties in China. During these two centuries, the exchanges between China and foreign countries became increasingly frequent, and Chinese practical learning was gradually and effectively applied. The Ming Dynasty perished due to internal forces while the Qing Dynasty perished due to foreign intervention. How to deal with "internal troubles and external threats" is a difficult problem that modern countries have failed to solve. Therefore, the Ming and Qing Dynasties not only witnessed the collision between Eastern and Western cultures, but also became a period that modern foreigners who study Chinese history must examine.

明清之际在中国历史上是一段重要时期，无论在政治、经济领域还是在思想、文化领域，旧的传统的思想观念与新的先进的价值理念在这一时期发生了激烈的冲击和碰撞，社会面临着一系列令人瞩目的价值冲突和社会转向。实学思潮和西学东渐就是产生于这一时期的两个有着重大影响的事件，它们之间相互联系、相互影响，初步实现了中西方文化的结合。[153]

The Ming and Qing Dynasties are an important stage in Chinese history. Whether in politics, economics, ideology or culture, old traditional ideas clashed violently with new advanced values. Society was faced with a series of remarkable value conflicts and social transformations. The ideological trend of practical learning and the spread of Western learning to the East were two significant events during this period. Through interconnection and mutual influence, they led to the preliminary integration of Chinese and Western cultures.[153]

明清时期，实学与史学在学术理念上的一致，首先表现在"经世致用"的文化精神上。实学的基本特征是崇实黜虚，崇尚"实功""实行"，侧重于治国平天下的外王之道，要求学术经世致用，为现实服务。而经世致用一向是中国史学的重要传统。史著除了要担当一代王朝、一个民族的集体记忆功能外，还要为当世提供劝诫、借鉴，使统治者"知兴替""正得失"，明治国安邦之理。从《史记》到《资治通鉴》，史学经世致用的功能一直受到高度重视。[154]

During the Ming and Qing Dynasties, the consistency in academic

---

153 覃小放撰《明清实学与西学东渐的相互影响》，来源《赤峰学院学报（汉文哲学社会科学版）》，2009 年 6 期

154 于瑞桓撰《明清时期的实学思潮与史学的繁荣》，来源《孔子研究》，2002 年 3 期

concepts between practical learning and historiography was first manifested in the cultural spirit of "applying learning to practical affairs". The basic feature of practical learning is to advocate the practical and reject the superficial. That is, it advocates "practical achievements" and "practical actions", and focuses on the way of external kingship for governing the state and bringing peace to all under heaven. It also requires that academic theories should be applied to practical affairs and serve the reality. Applying learning to practical affairs has been an important tradition of Chinese historiography. Apart from serving as the collective memory of a dynasty and a nation, historical works should provide admonitions and references for the contemporary era, enabling rulers to "know the laws of the rise and fall of dynasties" and "figure out the pros and cons of their own policies", that is, to understand the principles of governing the country and maintaining social stability. From *Records of the Grand Historian* to *Comprehensive Mirror to Aid in Government*, the function of historiography in applying learning to practical affairs has been highly valued.[154]

经世致用就是关注社会现实，面对社会矛盾，并用所学解决社会问题，以求达到国治民安的实效。经世致用源远流长，但作为一种时代风潮的时期是明清两代。明清之际，中国社会处于从传统社会向近代社会转变的关键时期，无论是在政治领域、经济领域还是在思想文化领域，旧的传统的思想观念和新的先进的价值理念在这个时期发生了激烈的冲突、碰撞，社会面临着一系列引人注目的价值冲突与社会转向。[155]

Applying learning to practical affairs means paying attention to social reality, facing social contradictions, and solving social problems

---

155　刘浩撰《黄宗羲政治伦理思想研究》，来源《湖南师范大学》，2012 年

with what one has learned, so as to achieve the actual effect that the country is well-governed and the people live in peace. Although the doctrine dates back to ancient times, it was during the Ming and Qing Dynasties that it became a prevailing trend of the era. During this period, Chinese society was in a crucial stage of turning from tradition to modernity. Whether in politics, economics, ideology or culture, old traditional ideas clashed violently with new advanced values, and society was faced with a series of remarkable value conflicts and social transformations.[155]

在全世界，不管贤者愚者学历是高是低，都是先有"十年寒窗苦读"，后有"十年读经，十年解经"，才能"尽信书，不如无书"。学习者通过长时间的沉道浸德，旁门左道可以过渡为玄门正宗，从而破茧成蝶。

In the world, whether a person is wise or foolish, whether his level of education is high or low, he must first undergo "ten years of arduous study in seclusion", and then spend "ten years studying the classics and another ten years interpreting them" before being able to understand that "it is better to have no books than to believe everything in the books". Through a long period of immersion in morality and Taoism, a learner can transform an unorthodox school into an orthodox one, thus truly making a breakthrough.

兵道思想崇尚唯物论。在 21 世纪，全球有 200 多个国家与地区，每个国家都有自己独特的文化。全世界有各种各样的语言，很多人根本不擅长翻译，却知晓唯物主义所代表的文化含义。

Chinese military thought advocates materialism. In the 21st century, there are more than 200 countries and regions around the world, with each country having its own unique culture. There are different languages in the world. Many people are not good at translation at all, but they can understand the cultural connotations represented by materialism.

中国古代哲学源远流长，绵延数千年。自先秦始，历经秦、汉、三国、两晋、南北朝、汉唐、宋明直至清代。在中国古代哲学的发展过程中，一些学者和学派比较重视客观实际，并以自然界的客观存在物为其根本，对此我们用现行词语可称之为唯物论[156]。

Ancient Chinese philosophy has a long history, extending over thousands of years. It began in the Pre-Qin period and spanned through the Qin Dynasty, the Han Dynasty, the Three Kingdoms period, the Two Jin Dynasties, the Northern and Southern Dynasties, the Han and Tang Dynasties, the Song and Ming Dynasties, until the Qing Dynasty. In the development process of ancient Chinese philosophy, some scholars and schools attached great importance to objective reality, and took objective natural entities as their foundation. In modern terms, it can be called materialism.[156]

以一个越南重大刑事案件为例子。2024 年 4 月，据越南媒体消息，越南法院正式判处越南房地产商、女首富张美兰死刑。越南女富商张美兰案件，就不仅仅扩射出越南政商界的经济生态。

Take a major criminal case in Vietnam as an example. In April 2024, according to Vietnamese media, the Vietnamese court officially sentenced Truong My Lan, a Vietnamese real estate developer and the richest woman in Vietnam, to death. This case not only reflects the economic ecology of the political and business circles in Vietnam.

据新华社 2024 年 4 月报道，万盛发集团金融犯罪案与原"越南女首富"张美兰有关。张美兰 1956 年 10 月生于越南南部西贡市（今胡志明市），其一手创办的万盛发集团系越南最大的房地产集团

156　谢娟撰《试述中国古代唯物主义》，来源《绵阳师范学院学报》，2009 年第 9 期

之一，其家族被视为越南最富裕的家族之一。[157]

According to a report from Xinhua News Agency in April 2024, the financial crime case of Van Thinh Phat Group was related to Truong My Lan, the former "richest woman in Vietnam". In October 1956, she was born in Saigon (now Ho Chi Minh City) in the southern part of Vietnam. The Van Thinh Phat Group, which was solely founded by her, is one of the largest real estate groups in Vietnam, and her family is regarded as one of the wealthiest in Vietnam.[157]

2024年4月11日，胡志明市人民法院一审判决张美兰死刑。胡志明市人民法院表示，张美兰犯贪污罪，判处死刑；犯行贿罪，判处20年有期徒刑；违反银行经营活动有关规定，判处20年有期徒刑。数罪并罚，判处死刑。越南最高人民检察院递交的公诉书说，张美兰利用行贿等违法手段，获取西贡商业银行85%至91.5%的股份，给该行造成了约498万亿越南盾（约合199亿美元）的损失。[158]

On April 11, 2024, the People's Court of Ho Chi Minh City sentenced Truong My Lan to death in the first instance. The court stated that she was sentenced to death for the crime of embezzlement; was sentenced to 20 years in prison for the crime of bribery; and was sentenced to 20 years in prison for violating regulations related to bank operations. For the combined punishment of multiple crimes, she was sentenced to death. The public prosecution statement submitted by the Supreme People's Procuratorate of Vietnam said that Truong My Lan used bribery and other illegal means to obtain 85% to 91.5% of the shares of Saigon Commercial Bank, causing a loss of approximately 498 trillion

---

157 《涉万盛发集团案，越共又一高官辞职》，澎湃新闻·全球速报（澎湃新闻），www.thepaper.cn，2024年06月20日

158 同上

Vietnamese dong (about 19.9 billion US dollars) to the bank.[158]

越通社更早的报道提到，万盛发集团有关案件中的被告人至少有 86 人，他们 2023 年 12 月被公诉；被告人中，除张美兰外还有 41 名西贡商业银行领导和干部，15 名原国家银行干部，3 名原政府监察总署干部等。[159]

An earlier report from the Vietnam News Agency mentioned that there were at least 86 defendants in the cases associated with Van Thinh Phat Group, and they were prosecuted in December 2023. Among the defendants, apart from Truong My Lan, there were 41 leaders and cadres of Saigon Commercial Bank, 15 former cadres of the State Bank of Vietnam, and 3 former cadres of General Administration of Government Supervision.[159]

不管这次越南女首富张美兰的犯罪性质，是否会诱发民怨沸腾的恐怖主义，有一点可以确定，暴利产业之下没有单打独斗，越南女商人张美兰是陷入"团队合作变成团伙作案"的商业犯罪模式，沦落为一名死刑犯。越南张美兰案件对很多国家与地区高速发展经济敲响了警钟，侧面反映出中小企业对国家还是有用处的。

No matter what is the nature of the crimes committed by Truong My Lan, the richest woman in Vietnam, and no matter whether her crimes may trigger terrorism that leads to rampant public grievances, one thing is certain: In the context of highly profitable industries, there is no solo action. It was because she was trapped in a business crime pattern where "team cooperation turned into gang crime" that the Vietnamese businesswoman Truong My Lan became a condemned prisoner. This case has sounded the alarm for many countries and regions with rapidly developing economies, and indirectly shows that small and medium-sized

---

159　同上

enterprises are useful to a country.

兵道思想还是一种带有朴素辩证法的唯物主义论，力求在对立统一的事物中，依旧能够一统对立，使事物富有冲击感，又不敏感。

Chinese military thought is a form of materialism with primitive dialectics. It strives to unify the opposites among things in a state of unity of opposites, making things impactful but not sensitive.

放眼全世界，人类生活的地球是多海洋，少陆地，可用资源比较少，这是法律和制度都没有办法解决的根本问题。为此，主张不把事情敏感化的朴素辩证法既能成为主角，也能成为配角。就像明清两个朝代是互为敌对的关系，这前后两朝的官方关系剑拔弩张，波及邻近国。然而，清朝取代明朝来统治中国以后，清朝仍然使用明朝的八股科举制度来选择官场人才，这就在客观程度上削弱了中国汉人"排满"思想。明朝有明朝的好与坏，清朝有清朝的好与坏，这使得中国海内外的各方势力看清楚清朝时期的中国人有一定的理由不去"反清复明"。

From the global perspective, the earth on which people live has more oceans than land, and only a few available resources. This is a fundamental problem that cannot be solved by laws and systems. Therefore, the primitive dialectics that advocates not making things overly sensitive can either play a dominating role or a supporting one. For example, the Ming and Qing Dynasties were hostile to each other. The official relationship between these two successive dynasties was so tense that it affected neighboring countries. However, after the Qing Dynasty replaced the Ming Dynasty to rule China, it still used the imperial examination system based on the eight-legged essay to select officials. Objectively, this weakened the "anti-Manchu" sentiment among the Han people. The Ming Dynasty had its own advantages and disadvantages, so did the Qing Dynasty. This made various forces at home and abroad see clearly that the Chinese people during the Qing Dynasty had certain reasons not to "restore the Ming Dynasty and oppose the Qing Dynasty."

朴素唯物主义又称"素朴唯物主义"，是用某种或某几种具体物质形态来解释世界的本原的哲学学说，是唯物主义发展的最初历史形态。它否认世界是神创造的，把世界的本原归根为某种或某几种具体的物质形态，试图从中找到具有无限多样性的自然现象的统一。[160]

Primitive materialism, also known as "simple materialism," is a philosophical theory that uses one or certain specific material forms to explain the origin of the world. It is the initial historical form of materialism. It denies the Creation theory, attributes the origin of the world to one or certain specific material forms, and attempts to find the unity of natural phenomena with infinite diversity.[160]

"对立的统一是辩证法的核心"，中国古代文论的朴素辩证法思想，也有能够体现这个"核心"的。值得注意的是，这方面的思想，强调统一的多，强调对立的少。[161]

"The unity of opposites is the core of dialectics." The primitive dialectical thoughts in ancient Chinese literary theory can also embody this "core." It is worth noting that such thoughts emphasize unity more than opposition.[161]

朝鲜半岛自古就与中国联系密切。朝鲜王朝在 1392 年建立之后一直与明朝保持着牢固的宗藩关系，这种状况一直持续到 1616 年努尔哈赤建立后金。后金建立以后，朝鲜王朝与明朝的关系逐步转变为朝鲜王朝、明朝、后金之间的三角关系。丙子之役之后，朝鲜王朝被迫与后金签订了君臣之盟，朝鲜王朝、明朝、后金之间的三角关系转化为朝鲜王朝对后金的朝贡关系，东部三角关系消亡。

160　郑红峰编《中国哲学史》北京：北京燕山出版社 2011 年 4 月

161　陈祥耀撰《我国古代文论的朴素辩证法》，来源《文艺理论研究》，1985 年 4 期后金建立之初，除了东边的朝鲜王朝，西部还有蒙古。是时，明朝为了与后金的战略决战，一改往日对蒙古的限制与打击政策，采取了拉拢蒙古林丹汗共同打击后金的政策。与明朝相反，后金采取的是联合除了林丹汗的察哈尔部以外的其他蒙古部落的政策。因为后金统治者敏锐地发现了林丹汗以元朝直系后裔自居，对其他蒙古部落进行压迫的弱点。于是，明朝、后金、蒙古三者之间的西部三角关系逐步形成。在明朝与后金这两种截然不同的政策的较量当中，后金占据了上风。经过三征察哈尔以及对其他蒙古部落的和亲、征服，后金将蒙古完全纳入自己的统治当中，将明朝的势力彻底驱逐出蒙古地区。明朝、后金、蒙古之间的西部三角关系也转化为后金与蒙古之间的双边关系，西部三角关系消亡。[162]

Since ancient times, the Korean Peninsula has had close ties with China. After the Joseon Dynasty was established in 1392, it maintained a firm suzerain-vassal relationship with the Ming Dynasty, and this situation continued until 1616 when Nurhaci established the Later Jin Dynasty. After that, the relationship between the Joseon Dynasty and the Ming Dynasty gradually turned into a triangular relationship among the Joseon Dynasty, the Ming Dynasty, and the Later Jin Dynasty. After the Later Jin army invaded Korea in 1636 (the year of Bingzi), the Joseon Dynasty was forced to sign a vassal-master alliance with the Later Jin Dynasty. As a result, the triangular relationship among the Joseon Dynasty, the Ming Dynasty, and the Later Jin Dynasty turned into a relationship featuring the tribute of the Joseon Dynasty to the Later Jin Dynasty, and the triangular relationship in the east disappeared. In the early years of the Later Jin Dynasty, in addition to the Joseon Dynasty in

---

162　唐烈撰《论明清交替之际东北亚政局的变化 ————以后金、明朝、蒙古、朝鲜间的关系为中心》，来源《延安大学》，2015 年 5 月

the east, there were Mongolian tribes in the west. At that time, in order to fight a strategic decisive battle with the Later Jin Dynasty, the Ming Dynasty changed its previous policy of restricting and attacking Mongolia and adopted a policy of winning over Ligdan Khan of Mongolia to jointly attack the Later Jin Dynasty. Contrary to the Ming Dynasty, the Later Jin Dynasty adopted a policy of uniting with other Mongolian tribes except the Chahar tribe of Ligdan Khan. This was because the rulers of the Later Jin Dynasty acutely discovered the weakness of Ligdan Khan, who regarded himself as a direct descendant of the Yuan Dynasty and oppressed other Mongolian tribes. Therefore, a triangular relationship among the Ming Dynasty, the Later Jin Dynasty, and the Mongols gradually came into being in the west. In the contest between the two distinctive policies of the Ming Dynasty and the Later Jin Dynasty, the Later Jin Dynasty gained the upper hand. After three expeditions against the Chahar tribe and through marriage alliances and conquests of other Mongolian tribes, the Later Jin Dynasty brought Mongolia completely under its rule and completely expelled the forces of the Ming Dynasty from the Mongolian region. As a result, the triangular relationship among the Ming Dynasty, the Later Jin Dynasty, and the Mongols turned into a bilateral relationship between the Later Jin Dynasty and the Mongols, and the triangular relationship in the west disappeared.[162]

随着东部与西部两个三角关系的消亡，原本在东北亚地区存在的四方势力构建起的两个三角关系最终演化成明朝与后金（清）之间的双边关系。最终，后金（清）入关，将明朝灭亡建立起中国历史上最后一个统一的封建王朝——清朝，东北亚地区进入了一个新的历史发展时期。[163]

---

163 同上

As the two triangular relationships in the east and the west disappeared, the two triangular relationships originally established by the four parties in Northeast Asia eventually became a bilateral relationship between the Ming Dynasty and the Later Jin Dynasty (Qing Dynasty). In the end, the Later Jin (Qing) army entered the Shanhai Pass, overthrew the Ming Dynasty, and established the Qing Dynasty, which was the last unified feudal dynasty in Chinese history. Consequently, Northeast Asia ushered in a new period of historical development.[163]

八股取士是明代科举考试的主要手段，明代后期甚至成为科举取录士人的唯一途径。正如明代进士一科一样，专以八股文取士作为衡文标准的树立，既有从考试学角度完善和规范全国范围的大规模统一考试的需要，同时也是明朝政府专制皇权政治的需要，形式上的八股文为实质上的思想专制提供了有效的手段，八股文与科举考试关系的最实质特征也正在于此。[164]

Selecting officials through eight-legged essays was a major form of the imperial examination in the Ming Dynasty. In the late Ming Dynasty, it even became the only way to select officials. Just like the Jinshi Discipline, the establishment of the eight-legged essay as the sole standard for evaluating papers reflected not only the need to improve and standardize large-scale unified examinations across China from the perspective of examination science, but also the need of the Ming government in implementing autocratic imperial power politics. The eight-legged essay in form provided an effective means for the ideological autocracy in essence, and this was exactly the most essential feature of the relationship between the eight-legged essay and the imperial examination.[164]

164　王凯旋撰《明代科举制度研究》，来源《吉林大学》，2005 年 4 月

1635 年，后金汗皇太极改女真族号为满洲，女真历史正式结束，开始进入新的统治时期。翌年，后金汗皇太极称帝，改国号为大清。[165]

In 1635, Hong Taiji, the Khan of the Later Jin Dynasty, changed the ethnic name of the Jurchen people to Manchu. The history of the Jurchen people officially ended, marking the beginning of a new ruling period. The next year, Hong Taiji, the Khan of the Later Jin Dynasty, proclaimed himself emperor and changed the name of the state to Great Qing.[165]

明代科举制度是封建专制集权发展到一定程度的产物，在统一测试，人才选拔，笼络人心，稳定政权等方面发挥着重要的作用。中国古代封建科举制度发展至明代可谓成熟且稳定。科举选拔人才开始走向统一与标准化，既方便统治者操作，也提高了行政效率，保证了相对公平。基于此清军入关后在科举的制度、内容、方式等方面基本沿用了明代的科举制度。随后，清统治者对科举制度的改革都是在此基础上做的修改与补充。[166]

As the product of the development of feudal autocratic centralization to a certain extent, the imperial examination system in the Ming Dynasty played an important role in unified testing, talent selection, gaining people's support, and stabilizing the regime. The ancient feudal imperial examination system became mature and stable in the Ming Dynasty. The unity and standardization of the imperial examination for selecting talents not only made it convenient for the rulers to operate, but also improved administrative efficiency and ensured relative fairness. Therefore, after the Qing army entered the Shanhai Pass, it basically adopted the Ming

---

165　陈放撰《朝鲜与女真、满族诸政权关系变迁研究》，来源《延安大学》，2012 年
　　　4 月

166　江艳撰《举业金针——清代八股文读本研究》，来源《华东师范大学》，2014 年
　　　4 月

Dynasty's imperial examination system in terms of system, content, and method. The reforms made by the Qing rulers subsequently were only modifications and supplements on this basis.[166]

随着晚清的衰败，思图新变的学者纷纷将国家贫弱归因于八股取士制度，认为八股文禁锢了士子的思想。八股文读本的泛滥更是成了学风败坏的指责中心，屡有人上奏革疏八股文读本。1902年，光绪帝废除科举考试的八股文以后，八股文读本自然就失去了存在的价值。八股文读本随着八股取士的终结终究沦为一堆废纸，零落不存。[167]

With the decline of the late Qing Dynasty, scholars who were eager for innovation attributed the poverty and weakness of the country to the imperial examination system based on the eight-legged essay, believing that the eight-legged essay shackled the mind of scholars. The widespread reading materials on the eight-legged essay became a focus of criticism for the deterioration of the academic atmosphere, and many people presented memorials to abolish them. In 1902, after Emperor Guangxu abolished the eight-legged essay in the imperial examination, the reading materials on the eight-legged essay lost their value of existence as a matter of course. With the end of the imperial examination system based on the eight-legged essay, these materials eventually became a pile of waste paper, scattered and lost.[167]

实用主义是中国文化的传统之一。科举自实行八股取士以后，便遭致了广泛的批评。明末清初的启蒙思想家顾炎武、黄宗羲等人都有改革科举之论，清初统治集团内部也围绕是否应该废除八股文而发生了多次争论，但结果八股取士仍得以延续。近代中国的内忧外患引发了实用主义思潮，地主阶级改革派、洋务派、早期改良

167　同上

派、维新派以及来华传教士，从救亡图存、人才强国的切实愿望出发，对八股文的保守、禁锢、空疏提出了强烈的批评，并从中国的国情出发，各自提出了渐进式的科举改革方案。鸦片战争后，清代的科举制度在近代中国经济基础遽变的基础上，在中西法律文化交流的时代背景下，由于其以八股文取士，考试内容空疏不切实际，不足以有效应世事，不得不走上了改革并最终被废除的变迁之路。科举在清末的革、废有着历史的必然性，而实用主义是促使清代科举法律文化变迁的思想基础。科举制度的废除，学校制度的建立，体现了文化转型期的进步，而新的学校制度又由法律来保证依法实施，这是清代科举法律文化新的升华。[168]

Pragmatism is a tradition of Chinese culture. Since the imperial examination system based on the eight-legged essay was implemented , it aroused extensive criticism. Enlightenment thinkers such as Gu Yanwu and Huang Zongxi in the late Ming and early Qing Dynasties put forward theories on reforming the imperial examination system. In the early Qing Dynasty, several debates about whether the eight-legged essay should be abolished took place within the ruling group, but in the end, the imperial examination system based on the eight-legged essay still continued. The internal and external troubles in modern China triggered the trend of pragmatism. The reformist faction of the landlord class, the Westernization Faction, the early reformist faction, the Reformists in the Reform Movement, and the Western missionaries in China, starting from the practical desire to save the country from subjugation and strengthen it through talents, strongly criticized the imperial examination system based on conservative, restrictive and impractical eight-legged essays. In addition, starting from China's national conditions, they proposed

---

168　叶晓川撰《清代科举法律文化研究》，来源《中国政法大学》，2006 年 4 月

progressive plans for reforming the imperial examination system. After the Opium War, dramatic changes took place in the economic foundation of modern China in the era context of the exchange between Chinese and Western laws and cultures. As a result, the imperial examination system of the Qing Dynasty had to be reformed and ultimately abolished because eight-legged essays were impractical and empty in terms of content, failing to effectively deal with worldly affairs. The reform and abolition of the imperial examination system in the late Qing Dynasty were inevitable in the context of history, while pragmatism was the ideological foundation that promoted the reform of the laws and cultures related to the imperial examination system. The abolition of the imperial examination system and the establishment of the school system reflected the progress of the cultural transformation period, and the implementation of the new school system was guaranteed in accordance with the law. It was a new sublimation of laws and cultures related to the imperial examination system in the Qing Dynasty.[168]

明清两个朝代爆发政权战争。即使是从亡国灭种的角度出发，清朝就有足够的理由不采用明朝的八股取士制度，也能够大兴文字狱，去迫害汉族。然而，清朝却在统治中国期间，长时间用明代的八股取士制度来选拔官员。站在后来人的立场上来看，在客观上，既能成为清统治阶级对得起明朱皇室的一个历史性做法，也是明朝皇室对付清朝的一种文化能量。在主观上，当朝采用前朝的一种国家政策，能够有取代联合政府的作用。

Regime wars broke out between the Ming and Qing Dynasties. Even from the perspective of the life and death of the country, the Qing Dynasty had sufficient reasons to reject the Ming Dynasty's imperial examination system based on the eight-legged essay, and refuse to launch the literary inquisitions to persecute the Han people. However, during its rule, the Qing Dynasty used this system for a long time to select officials. From the standpoint of later generations, objectively speaking, this was not only a historical practice that relieved the ruling class of the Qing Dynasty of its sense of guilt towards the imperial Zhu family of the Ming Dynasty, but also a kind of cultural influence that the imperial family of the Ming Dynasty had exerted on the Qing Dynasty. Subjectively speaking, when the current dynasty adopts a national policy of the previous dynasty, it plays a role similar to that of a coalition government.

在中国现代史，中国照样有被傀儡政府和外来民族奴役的风险。在商品经济的时代洪流之下，每个中国人如何取舍前朝文化，是在对本朝政府表明自己的态度，更是中国人一种安身立命的本事，以此保证自己怎么在社会上生存和生活。

In modern Chinese history, China still faces the risk of being enslaved by puppet governments and alien ethnic groups. In the torrent of the commodity economy era, how each Chinese person selectively accepts or rejects cultural elements of the previous dynasty not only shows his attitude towards the current government but also represents a kind of survival ability, which ensures his survival and life in society.

大道至简，活路和死路是相对与绝对的。有人能够将活路走成死路，有人则能够将死路走成活路，这都是社会对个人的综合能力的考验。国家软实力和硬实力的发挥，与哲学和兵法密切相联。哲学贵在正，兵法贵在奇，正为主，奇为辅，正带奇，奇显正，正奇结合，天下皆可破。

The greatest truth is the simplest. The chance of living and the dead end embody relativity and absoluteness. Some people can turn a chance of living into a dead end, while others can turn a dead end into a chance of living. This is a test of a person's comprehensive abilities by society. The exertion of a country's soft and hard strengths has a close tie with philosophy and the art of war. Philosophy stresses uprightness, while the art of war puts emphasis on extraordinary strategies. Uprightness is the foundation, while extraordinary strategies serve as a supplement. Uprightness guides extraordinary strategies, while extraordinary strategies manifest uprightness. When uprightness and extraordinary strategies are combined together, everything in the world can be overcome.

早在先秦时期，兵家故事就有道家思想，道家故事就有兵家思想，兵家和道家思想进行互融互补，成为个人解决恐怖主义的尝试。

As early as the pre-Qin period, stories of military strategists contained Taoist thought, while Taoist stories contained the thought of military strategists. The integration and complementation of the thoughts of military strategists and Taoists became an attempt for people to deal with terrorism.

先举一个兵家的例子，这个例子是中国成语故事——"田忌赛马"。

Let's first take an example from the realm of military strategists. It is a Chinese idiom story - "Tian Ji's Horse Racing".

《史记·孙子吴起列传》中记载着这样一个故事：春秋战国时期，齐国的大将军田忌经常与国王及诸公子赛马，并设重金赌注。他们将各自的马分为上、中、下三等，比赛时，上等马对上等马，中等马对中等马，下等马对下等马。由于田忌每个等级的马都比齐威王相应等级的马略逊一筹，所以，每次比赛，田忌都以失败而告终。孙膑仔细观察后发现，田忌每个等级的马和齐威王相应等级的马相差并不远，便告诉田忌，尽管设重金赌注，自己有办法让他获胜。田忌遂以千金做赌注约请国王与他赛马。比赛即将开始，孙膑说："现在用您的下等马对付他们的上等马，拿您的上等马对付他们的中等马，拿您的中等马对付他们的下等马。"三场比赛完后，田忌一场不胜而两场胜，最终赢得齐威王的千金赌注[169]。

The following story is recorded in *Biographies of Sun Tzu and Wu Qi, Records of the Grand Historian*: During the Spring and Autumn Period and the Warring States Period, Tian Ji, a great general of the State of Qi, often raced horses with the king and the princes and placed heavy bets. They divided their horses into three grades: upper, middle, and lower. In a competition, the upper-grade horse raced against the upper-grade horse, the middle-grade horse raced against the middle-grade horse, and the lower-grade horse raced against the lower-grade horse. As Tian Ji's horse of each grade was slightly inferior to that of King Wei of Qi of each corresponding grade, Tian Ji was defeated every time. Through a careful observation, Sun Bin found that the difference between Tian Ji's horse of each grade and that of King Wei of Qi of each corresponding grade was not significant. He told Tian Ji to place heavy bets boldly, and he had a way to make him win. So Tian Ji wagered a thousand pieces of gold and invited the king to race horses with him. Just before the competition, Sun Bin said, "Now use your lower-grade horse to deal with their upper-grade horse, use your upper-grade horse to deal with their middle-grade horse, and use your middle-grade horse to deal with their lower-grade horse." After the competition, Tian Ji lost one race but won the other two, and finally got a bet of one thousand pieces from King Wei of Qi.[169]

田忌赛马的故事主角是田忌、孙膑和齐威王，是中国历史上著名的揭示如何利用自己的长处去对付对手的短处的例子，当事物的内部结构有了变化，便引发了事物的量变，这种量变达到一定的积

169　张学会撰《从"田忌赛马"看人力资源的优化配置》，来源《人才资源开发》2010 年第 1 期

累后转化为质变，这就是事物扩大自己的优势以弱胜强的原因 [170]。

The main characters in Tian Ji's Horse Racing are Tian Ji, Sun Bin, and King Wei of Qi. It is a famous example in Chinese history that reveals how to use a person's own strengths to deal with the opponent's weaknesses. When there is a change in the internal structure of a thing, it will lead to a quantitative change. When the quantitative change is accumulated to a certain extent, it will cause a qualitative change. This is the reason why the weak can expand their own advantages and defeat the strong.[170]

长短互补，方能长短。"田忌赛马"这个故事是配角比主角还主角，有"坏事变好事，验证了世事无常"的定律。

By complementing each other's strengths and weaknesses, the overall optimization can be achieved. In the story of "Tian Ji's Horse Racing", the supporting characters are more prominent than the main characters. It manifests the truth that "a bad thing can turn into a good thing, and the affairs of the world are unpredictable".

在逆水行舟的年代，人要事情结果重于其过程。《道德经》有云："祸兮，福之所倚；福兮，祸之所伏。孰知其极：其无正也。正复为奇，善复为妖。人之迷，其日固久。"将道家思想注入兵家故事"田忌赛马"之中，得出"事情好坏，在一定条件下能够转变"这个原理浑然天成。

In the era in which people strive hard against difficulties, they should value the result of a thing more than the process. As is said in *Tao Te Ching*: "Misfortune is the fundamental basis for the existence of fortune, while fortune is lurking within misfortune. Who knows whether

---

170　徐木子撰《由"田忌赛马"评战国时期的赛马活动》，来源《高中生学习》，2018年第 2 期

it will ultimately turn into fortune or misfortune? The result is uncertain. What is right can turn into what is wrong, and what is good can turn into what is evil. People have been confused about this for a long time." If we inject Taoist thought into the military strategist story of "Tian Ji's Horse Racing", it is very natural to derive the principle that "good things and bad things can be transformed into each other under certain conditions."

"田忌赛马"这个兵家故事的寓意能够注入道家思想，同样，"庄周梦蝶"这个道家故事的寓意则能够注入兵家思想。

The moral of the military strategist story of "Tian Ji's Horse Racing" can be injected into Taoist thought. Similarly, the moral of the Taoist story of "Zhuang Zhou's Dream of the Butterfly" can be injected into the military strategist thought.

庄子，姓庄，名周，字子休，宋国蒙人，约生于公元前 369 年（周烈王七年），卒于公元前 286 年（周赧王二九年），与孟子同时而稍晚。他的生平知之甚少。只知他可能做过蒙地的漆园吏，在那里过着隐士般的生活，可是他的思想和著作当时就很出名。[171]

Zhuangzi, with the surname Zhuang, the given name Zhou, and the courtesy name Zixiu, was a native of Meng in the State of Song. He was born around 369 BC (the 7th Year of King Lie of Zhou) and died in 286 BC (the 29th Year of King Nan of Zhou). He was a contemporary of Mencius, though he was born slightly later. Little is known about his life. It is only known that he might have served as an official in charge of the lacquer garden in Meng, and lived a life like a hermit. However, his thought and works were already well-known at that time.[171]

庄子是中国先秦道家学派的创始人之一。到了汉代道教出现以后，《庄子》一书便成为了道家经典，被尊称为《南华经》，并与

171　卢柏林撰《< 庄子 > 略说》，来源《电大教学》，1998 年 4 期

《老子》《周易》合称"三玄"。作为中华民族的源头性经典作品之一，《庄子》不仅是哲学与文化的重要载体，而且凝结了古代圣哲在诸多领域的智慧精华。[172]

Zhuangzi was one of the founders of the Taoist School in the pre-Qin period of China. After Taoism emerged in the Han Dynasty, the book *Zhuangzi* became a Taoist classic and was respectfully called *Nanhua Jing*. *Zhuangzi*, *Laozi* and *Book of Changes* were collectively referred to as "Three Mysteries". As one of the source classics of the Chinese nation, *Zhuangzi* is not only an important carrier of philosophy and culture but also a collection of the wisdom essence of ancient sages in many fields.[172]

据说大哲学家庄子有一次梦见自己变成了一只蝴蝶，一般人醒来以后知道是做梦也就罢了，但大哲学家的脑袋毕竟与众不同，他竟然想到"万一我并不是庄周，而只不过是蝴蝶做梦变成了我呢？或者更有甚者，是蝴蝶做梦变成了庄周，庄周又做梦变成了蝴蝶？还是反过来，我梦见了蝴蝶，蝴蝶又梦见了我？到底我是在蝴蝶的梦中，还是蝴蝶在我的梦中？"[173]

It is said that the great philosopher Zhuangzi once dreamed that he had turned into a butterfly. An ordinary person would just think it was a dream and let it go after waking up. However, the mind of a great philosopher is really different. He even thought, "What if I'm not Zhuang Zhou, but a butterfly that dreamed of turning into me? Or furthermore, the butterfly dreamed of turning into Zhuang Zhou, and Zhuang Zhou then dreamed of turning into a butterfly? Or vice versa, I dreamed of the butterfly, and the butterfly dreamed of me? Am I in the butterfly's dream, or is the butterfly in my dream?"[173]

172　高钰涵撰《＜庄子＞：一场似梦又本真的求索》，来源《前线》，2018 年 5 期

173　石坚撰《科幻作品的庄周梦蝶模式》，来源《中国青年科技》，1999 年 2 期

"庄周梦蝶"故事有"以蝶化谍，真假难辨"的定律。

The story of "Zhuang Zhou's Dream of the Butterfly" embodies the concept that "a butterfly can be transformed into a spy, making it difficult to distinguish the true from the false".

在中国，那本名气最大的兵书《孙子兵法》的作者孙武就专门辟出一个篇章，来讲述他眼里的世界观与间谍观该怎么成暗明之理。

In China, Sun Wu, the author of the most famous military book *The Art of War*, dedicated a chapter to expounding how his worldview and view on the employment of spies correspond with the principle of light and darkness.

《孙子·用间篇》中有一段精彩的论述："故明君贤将，所以动而胜人，成功出于众者，先知也。先知者不可取于鬼神，不可象于事，不可验于度，必取于人，知敌之情者也。"说的是开明的君主，贤良明智的将帅，所以能取得战争的胜利，在于事先了解情况。要事先了解情况，不能靠祈求鬼神，不能用相似的事情做类比推测，不可以天象星辰运转的度数云验证，而必须能任用有智谋的人做间谍，从敌人那里了解情况[174]。

There is a wonderful passage in *Using Spies, The Art of War*: "Therefore, the reason why enlightened rulers and wise commanders can act and defeat the enemy and achieve success beyond the ordinary lies in the fact that they know information beforehand. Such information cannot be obtained from ghosts and deities, nor can it be inferred from analogies of similar events, nor can it be verified by the measurement of celestial phenomena. It must be obtained from people who know the enemy's situation." It attributes the reason why enlightened rulers and wise commanders can win a war to their knowledge of the situation in

---

174　苏灿杰撰《漫话"用间"》，来源《军事历史》，1985 年第 4 期

advance. To understand the situation in advance, one cannot pray to ghosts and deities, nor can he make analogical speculations based on similar things, nor can he verify it based on the movement of celestial bodies. Instead, one must appoint resourceful people as spies to obtain information from the enemy.[174]

有的间谍见不得光，确实会有些龌龊的举动出现。然而，间谍有时招人误解，需要沉冤昭雪。间谍功与过剪不断，理还乱。不过，高收益高风险，无利不起早，金钱是衡量间谍的"杠杆"。

Some spies are furtive and may perform certain despicable acts. However, spies are sometimes misunderstood and need to be vindicated. The merits and demerits of spies are intertwined and it is difficult to sort them out. However, considering "high returns come from high risks" as well as "no one is willing to get up early without the lure of profit", we can say that money serves as a "lever" for measuring spies.

传统上，情报机构主要靠金钱利诱，以情色或经济问题要挟，许诺未来和个人成就，以及通过冷战时期相当管用的意识形态诉求等手段勾连策反，被发展的本地情报员负责搜集、刺探、窃取、分析信息，其中部分人负责前方人员和后方总部间的信息传递，术语称"交通"。情报员也会策反他人，拓展情报来源[175]。

Traditionally, intelligence agencies mainly rely on enticement with money, coercion with pornographic or economic problems, promises regarding the future and personal achievements, as well as ideological appeals that were quite effective during the Cold War to establish connections and instigate defections. The employed local intelligence agents are responsible for collecting, prying into, stealing, and analyzing

---

175 《境外间谍靠金钱情色策反学生 防间谍手册受热捧》，搜狐军事（搜狐网）www. sohu.com，2014 年 5 月 7 日

information. Some of them are responsible for the transmission of information between the front-line personnel and the rear headquarters, which is called "liaison". Intelligence agents will also instigate others to defect and expand the sources of intelligence.[175]

2007 年 12 月出版的德国《明镜》周刊刊登了文章《德皇陛下的革命家》，副题则是《被收买的革命》。文章披露，俄共布尔什维克领导人列宁与德皇串联，获得皇家政府暗中大量资助，成功地制造了十月革命。没有威廉二世出钱出枪，扩大革命喉舌《真理报》，列宁的武装政变绝无成功的可能。文章说，列宁想要颠覆沙皇，而威廉二世皇帝则要取得在东线的胜利。德意志帝国接连数年以千万计的马克和后勤援助支持了俄国布尔什维克党人[176]。

In December 2007, the German magazine *Der Spiegel* presented an article titled *The Revolutionist of His Majesty the German Emperor*, with the subtitle *The Bribed Revolution*. According to the article, Lenin, the leader of Russian Social-Democratic Labor Party (Bolsheviks), colluded with the German Emperor and received a large amount of secret funds from the royal government, which paved the way for the successful launch of the October Revolution. Without the money and arms provided by Wilhelm II, the influence of the revolutionary mouthpiece "Pravda" would not have been expanded, and Lenin's armed coup would have had failed inevitably. The article stated that Lenin intended to overthrow the Tsar, while Emperor Wilhelm II intended to achieve victory on the Eastern Front. The German Empire supported the Russian Bolsheviks with tens of millions of marks and logistical supplies for several consecutive years.[176]

176　周涵撰《列宁靠德皇资助发动"十月革命"》，来源《国家人文历史》，2010 年第 8 期

针尖对麦芒，间谍战足以造成此消彼长的态势。《孙子兵法》有云："故用间有五：有因间，有内间，有反间，有死间，有生间。五间俱起，莫知其道，是谓神纪，人君之宝也。"

Tit for tat, a spy war suffices to create a situation where one side declines while the other side rises. As is stated in *The Art of War*: "Therefore, there are five methods of using spies, which are recruiting local people from the enemy's territory, bribing enemy officials to work for our side, turning spies dispatched by the enemy into ones working for our side, using our spies to deliberately spread false intelligence to the enemy, and appointing intelligent and eloquent people to gather information from the enemy's territory, respectively. When all the five methods of using spies are employed simultaneously, no one can identify accurate laws. This can be called the divine principle, serving as s magic weapon for all the participants in the war and the monarch."

兵道思想把兵家思想注入道家故事"庄周梦蝶"之中，得出"蝴蝶"可变为"间谍"的思维：蝴蝶和间谍都有引导世人的能力，皆为帮助的大道。

Injecting the military strategist thought into the Taoist story of "Zhuang Zhou's Dream of the Butterfly", we can derive the concept that a "butterfly" can be transformed into a "spy": Both the butterfly and the spy have the ability to guide people, and both can be of great aid.

学习者能够将知识点进行整理、总结、归纳，多思考、注重记忆。知识沉淀能变质，也能质变，学习者要耐得住寂寞，喜欢大器晚成，以免少年得志，反而误入歧途。

Learners should be able to organize, summarize, and generalize knowledge points, think more, and pay attention to memory. The deposited knowledge can either degenerate or undergo a qualitative change. Learners should be able to endure loneliness and prefer to achieve success late in life, so as to avoid going astray from early success.

反思可以成为一种独立的强大力量，看清楚"黑灰白，黑色是黑色，灰色是灰色，白色是白色"，从而牢牢明白是自己没有本事要社会，而不是社会没有本事要自己。

Reflection can become an independent and powerful strength, making us see clearly that "black is black, gray is gray, and white is white", thus firmly understanding that we lack the ability to be accepted by society, rather than society lacks the ability to accept us.

人一定要靠自己，蒸蒸日上不分好事和坏事。学习者要么在家多写论文，要么出门多做考察，反复充实自己，增加自己判断力，能够使"拦路虎"变成"纸老虎"。

One must rely on himself. The process of making progress pays no heed to whether things are good or bad. Learners should enhance their judgment and constantly enrich themselves either by writing more papers at home or by conducting more investigations outside and constantly enriching themselves. In this way, the "stumbling block" can be turned into a "paper tiger".

恐怖主义再可怕，也有规律遵循。人类对世界观、价值观、人生观、宇宙观等认识足够，对预测恐怖主义就有一定的判断力。例如，亚洲中东地区的巴以冲突引发恐怖主义，只要巴以冲突不停止，从自身实际力量出发，巴以两国为了应对恐怖主义，用"人肉炸弹"的巴勒斯坦小学生会苦练军事技能，有"科技强国"之称的以色列，用大数据反恐将会名闻遐迩，这都是必然的事情。

No matter how terrible terrorism is, it follows certain rules. If humans have a sufficient understanding of worldviews, values, life philosophies, and cosmological views, they will have a certain ability to predict terrorism. Take the terrorism in the Palestine-Israel conflict in the Middle East as an example. As long as the conflict continues, Palestine and Israel will deal with terrorism based on their own actual strengths. It is inevitable that Palestinian primary school students who use "human bombs" will practice military skills assiduously, while Israel, known as a "technologically powerful country", will become renowned for its anti-terrorism efforts based on big data.

巴勒斯坦问题作为中东问题的核心，涉及大国争夺、历史恩怨、宗教信仰、民族感情、领土争端、阿以冲突、各国利益等错综复杂的问题，使这一问题的解决变得异常困难[177]。

As the core of the Middle East issue, the Palestinian issue involves scrambles among major powers, historical grudges, religious beliefs, ethnic sentiments, territorial disputes, Arab-Israeli conflicts, interest conflicts between countries, and other complicated problems. Therefore, it is very difficult to solve it.[177]

巴勒斯坦位于亚洲的西部，濒临地中海和红海，被认为是阿拉伯的"腹地"，但居住于此的两个主要民族——巴勒斯坦阿拉伯人和犹太人，都声称自己是巴勒斯坦的真正主人，矛盾由此产生[178]。

Located in the west of Asia, adjacent to the Mediterranean Sea and the Red Sea, Palestine is considered the "heartland" of the Arab world. However, both the Palestinian Arabs and the Jews, who are two main ethnic groups living there, claim to be the authentic masters. This is the root cause of the contradictions.[178]

自第二次世界大战结束以来，以民族问题和宗教矛盾为背景的区域性冲突此起彼伏，有些甚至酿成国家之间的战争，如科索沃战争。但自后冷战时代以来，特别是 20 世纪 90 年代末至 21 世纪，国际以民族问题和宗教矛盾为背景的热点冲突明显趋于缓和。但

177　李国富撰《巴以冲突的历史由来、原因与前景》，来源《前线》，2002 年第 6 期

178　马守途撰《巴以民族冲突研究》，来源《中央民族大学》，2006 年

是，巴以民族冲突以来，已酿成无数次冲突和 5 次中东战争，其间打打谈谈，所蕴积的恩恩怨怨和所经历的艰难曲折说不完道不尽[179]。

Since the Second World War ended, regional conflicts caused by ethnic and religious contradictions have emerged one after another, and some have even escalated into wars between countries, for example, the Kosovo War. However, since the post-Cold War era, especially from the late 1990s to the 21st century, international hot conflicts arising from ethnic and religious contradictions have significantly tended to ease. However, the Palestine-Israel conflict has led to countless conflicts and five Middle East wars. During this period, confrontations and negotiations alternate, with too numerous accumulated grudges, hardships and complications to mention one by one.[179]

2018 年 6 月初前后，位于巴勒斯坦加沙地区的 Al—Hoda 幼儿园组织了一场别开生面的"儿童会演"，5 名打扮成特种部队营救小组成员的少儿以舞台为演习场地，围绕着舞台中央一座临时搭建起来的简易建筑，在数十名家长的围观下，上演了一场迷你真人剧场版的 CS 人质营救大戏[180]。

Around the beginning of June 2018, the Al-Hoda Kindergarten in the Gaza Strip of Palestine organized a unique "children's performance." In the presence of dozens of parents, five children dressed as members of a special forces rescue team used a stage as their training ground, and performed a mini live-action CS hostage rescue drama around a simple building temporarily erected in the center of the stage.[180]

和大多数不针对特定目标的军事演习不同，这场由一群几岁孩子所演绎的舞台剧打一开始就把矛头指向了以色列。不管是那面飘

179　同上
180　《培养特种兵从娃娃抓起？巴勒斯坦幼儿园上演"反以色列"大戏》，腾讯网 www.qq.com，2018 年 6 月 4 日

扬在建筑物上方的六芒星旗，还是"敌军"所身着的那套特殊制服，无一不在向观众传递着"以色列正是恶人"的讯息[181]。

Unlike most military exercises that do not target specific objects, this stage play performed by a group of little kids targeted Israel from the very beginning. From the Star of David flag fluttering above the building to the special uniforms worn by the "enemy forces," everything was conveying the message that "Israel is the villain"[181]

这样一场别开生面的舞台剧显然不是随便什么人都能组织得起来的。这家幼儿园之所以特立独行，是因为它的背后资助方正是大名鼎鼎的巴勒斯坦解放组织（PLO）。这并非这种舞台剧在 Al—Hoda 幼儿园的首次上演，组织方在 2016 和 2017 年也曾动员过小朋友出演战争舞台剧，表演节目均与时下热点局势紧密相关，不是掩埋反坦克雷，就是操作迫击炮。因为"指导老师"大多是来自巴解组织的历战老兵，所以这群"童子军"的表演自然也就展现了超乎一般水平的专业性[182]。

Obviously, this unique stage play was organized by ordinary people. The kindergarten behaved so distinctively because it was funded by the famous Palestine Liberation Organization (PLO). It was not the first time that such a stage play had been performed in Al-Hoda Kindergarten. In 2016 and 2017, the organizers mobilized children to perform war stage plays as well. The programs on show, either burying anti-tank mines or operating mortars, were closely related to the current hot situations. As most "instructors" were battle-hardened veterans from the PLO, this group of "children soldiers" naturally exhibited a kind of professionalism that was beyond the ordinary in their performance.[182]

181　同上
182　同上

以色列是最早在反恐中使用大数据技术的国家之一，这得益于以军的 8200 部门。8200 是以军最精英的电子情报机构，专门从事电子侦察活动，也是以色列大数据技术的领军者。他们搜集网络信息、监听电话以及截获政府、组织甚至个人的电子邮件，经大数据技术处理用于反恐。8200 同时还成为以色列高科技的推手，大量 8200 退伍的技术人才成为高科技公司创始人，继续开发大数据的新技术和软件。有赖于 8200 情报搜集经验，以色列在大数据管理和应用领域至少领先世界 10 年 [183]。

Benefiting from Unit 8200 of Israel Defense Forces, Israel became one of the earliest countries to use big data technology in counter-terrorism. Unit 8200 is the most crucial electronic intelligence agency of the Israel Defense Forces, specializing in electronic reconnaissance activities, as well as the leader of Israel's big data technology. They collect network information, monitor phone calls, and intercept the emails of governments, organizations, and even individuals, and then handle them with big data technology for the purpose of counter-terrorism. At the same time, Unit 8200 has become a driving force for Israel's high-tech industry. A large number of technical talents who have retired from Unit 8200 have become the founders of high-tech companies, continuing to develop new technologies and software regarding big data. Thanks to the intelligence collection experience of Unit 8200, Israel outstrips the world in big data management and application by at least 10 years.[183]

以色列的情报机构运用大数据技术，还得益于以色列蓬勃发展的高技术产业和民用数据分析产品 [184]。

The application of big data technology by Israel's intelligence

---

183　范小林撰《以色列：把大数据变成反恐利器》，来源《军事文摘》，2017 年第 7 期

184　同上

agencies also benefits from the country's prosperous high-tech industry and civilian data analysis products.[184]

以色列自建国至今，一直在对付各种各样的恐怖主义浪潮。2017 年前后的 10 年以来，随着第二次巴勒斯坦人起义的结束和针对巴勒斯坦人的隔离墙的修建，以色列境内恐怖袭击数量大幅减少，主要威胁来自邻国反以武装如真主党和哈马斯的袭击，以及"基地"组织、"伊斯兰国"等国际恐怖主义分子的威胁[185]。

Since its founding, Israel has been dealing with various waves of terrorism. Since about 2017, for the past 10 years, with the end of the Second Palestinian Uprising and the construction of the separation wall against the Palestinians, the number of terrorist attacks within Israel has significantly decreased. The main threats come from anti-Israel armed groups in neighboring countries such as Hezbollah and Hamas, as well as from international terrorists such as Al-Qaeda and the Islamic State.[185]

同样是保家卫国，弱小国家和强大国家所采取的方式却大有不同。不过，任何一种国家都有可能涉嫌恐怖主义，每个国家都有损人利己的历史，这使得国家支恐的风险大大提高。

For the same purpose of safeguarding national security, weak and powerful countries will adopt quite different approaches. However, any country may be suspected of terrorism, and every country has a history of harming others for its own benefit. This remarkably increases the risk of county support for terrorism.

兵道思想既看"正面教材"，也看"反面教材"。一个人去不去反恐都能成为英雄人物。即为英雄人物不反恐照样是英雄人物，英雄人物去反恐也照样是英雄人物。自古以来，由于政府"有黑色，有白色，有灰色"是世界历史的一部分，所以英雄人物反恐只是英

185　同上

雄人物的一种。反恐的英雄人物并未是国家英雄，可能只是社会英雄。例如在明清交替时期，明清两朝都有杰出的代表人物为本国排忧解难，他们却都不是反恐式的英雄人物，还在一定程度上加剧了社会的恐怖与苦难。

Chinese military thought considers not only "positive examples" but also "negative ones." Whether a person engages in counter-terrorism or not, he can become a heroic figure. That is to say, a heroic figure that does not engage in counter-terrorism is still a heroic figure, and a heroic figure that engages in counter-terrorism is also a heroic figure. Since ancient times, it has been a part of world history that the government "has black, white, and gray aspects", so a heroic figure engaging in counter-terrorism is only one type of heroic figure. A heroic figure engaging in counter-terrorism is not necessarily a national hero, but may be only a social hero. For example, during the transition between the Ming and Qing Dynasties, both dynasties generated outstanding representatives who solved problems for their own countries, but they were not counter-terrorism heroes. On the contrary, they increased the terror and misery in society to a certain extent.

李定国与郑成功，是支撑起南明后期政权的抗清将领和民族英雄。他们一个奔波在云贵川地区，一个坐镇东南沿海地带，都在自己的兵力范围内尽心竭力地抵抗清军的虎狼之师，双方不乏书信往来和战略联系。由于战事上和交通联络上的限制等因素，最终没有实现会师，亦被卷入历史的洪流，无力拯救风雨飘摇的永历小朝廷。[186]

Li Dingguo and Zheng Chenggong were anti-Qing generals and national heroes who supported the Southern Ming regime in its later

---

186　李震撰《李定国与郑成功抗清事迹考》，来源《文教资料》，2020 年 36 期

period. Li Dingguo was active in Yunnan, Guizhou, and Sichuan, while Zheng Chenggong was in charge of the southeastern coastal areas. Both spared no effort within their respective military jurisdictions to resist the fierce Qing forces. They had frequent correspondence and strategic contact. However, due to restrictions in military affairs and communication, they failed to join forces in the end. Instead, they were swept away by the tide of history, unable to save the tottering Yongli regime.[186]

张煌言（1620—1664），字玄著，号苍水，浙江鄞县人，明末诗人、将领、著名的抗清民族英雄。张煌言文武兼资，在战斗生涯中留下了大量诗篇。其诗质朴悲壮，反映了一位刚直忠贞的孤臣在艰难动荡的时局里的理想和追求，抒写了一位百折不回的抗清义士的豪迈慷慨，具有很高的文学和历史价值。[187]

Zhang Huangyan (1620-1664), also known as Xuanzhu by courtesy name and Cangshui by literary name, was a native of Yin County, Zhejiang Province. He was a poet, military general, and famous anti-Qing national hero during the late Ming period. He excelled in both literary and martial arts, leaving behind a large number of poems in his military career. His poems, unadorned and glorious, reflect the ideals and pursuits of a loyal and upright minister in a turbulent and difficult era, and express the magnanimity and unyielding spirit of a determined anti-Qing fighter. Therefore, they hold significant literary and historical values.[187]

辛丑（1661）年，郑成功攻克澎湖后进军台湾，郑成功经略台湾的动机遭到很多将领的质疑，煌言便是最突出的一位，煌言深知一旦郑成功抛弃沿海反攻光复大陆的计划转而经略台湾，那么沿海乃至滇中抗清武装将失去依靠和响应，中原抗清志士也将无法得到声援，而台湾远离大陆，从战略上看并无价值，而此时虏廷用暴力

187　曹楷撰《张煌言生平及诗歌考论》，来源《江西师范大学》，2011 年 6 月

手段推行迁海措施以隔绝沿海居民和抗清武装的联系，无数居民家破人亡，人心浮动，此时若能有大军前来接应必能成大事。[188]

In the year of Xinchou (1661), after Zheng Chenggong captured the Penghu Islands, he advanced to Taiwan. His intention for governing Taiwan was questioned by many generals, among whom Zhang Huangyan was the most prominent. He knew clearly that once Zheng Chenggong abandoned the plan of recovering the mainland from along the coastal and turned to governing Taiwan, the anti-Qing forces along the coast and even in Central Yunnan would lose their support and response, and the anti-Qing patriots in the Central Plains would be cut off from aid. On the other hand, Taiwan, being far removed from the mainland, seemed to have no strategic value. At that time, the Qing court resorted to violent means to enforce the maritime relocation policy to sever the connections between the coastal residents and the anti-Qing forces, leading to family disintegration of countless residents and unsettled public sentiment. Under such circumstances, if a large army could come to their aid, they would surely succeed in great undertakings.[188]

张煌言等人所考虑的更多是人心所向问题，而郑成功却很明白此时决定双方形势优劣的不仅是人和，更加需要天时、地利等因素的综合权衡。若仅固守闽南而不救台湾，必将给郑氏集团造成前所未有的打击。因而，郑成功对张煌言等人的意见都是一笑置之的。[189]

People like Zhang Huangyan were more concerned with the matter of popular support, while Zheng Chenggong knew clearly that at that time, the decisive factors for the superiority or inferiority of the two sides were not only human harmony but also a comprehensive integration

---

188 同上

189 吴承祖撰《浅析郑成功收复台湾之历史背景》，来源《内蒙古农业大学学报（社会科学版）》，2013 年 5 期

of timing, geographical advantages and other elements. If the Zheng Faction had defended Southern Fujian tenaciously without rescuing Taiwan, it would have suffered an unprecedented blow. Therefore, Zheng Chenggong dismissed Zhang Huangyan's opinions with a smile.[189]

明亡入清，郑芝龙的儿子郑成功立志抗清复明。郑成功于公元 1659 年以招讨大元帅的名义，率 17 万水陆大军，北上伐清，结果失败。为了继续反清大业，郑成功于公元 1661 年率大军在台湾登陆，彻底赶走了盘据台湾的荷兰殖民者后，在台湾建立了反清根据地。郑成功在光复台湾后的第二年即病逝。[190]

After the downfall of the Ming Dynasty and the establishment of the Qing Dynasty, Zheng Chenggong, the son of Zheng Zhilong, was determined to resist the Qing and restore the Ming. In 1659, Zheng Chenggong, as Grand Marshal of Pacification and Subjugation, led marine and ground forces of 170,000 soldiers to march northward against the Qing Dynasty, but failed. In order to continue the anti-Qing cause, in 1661, he led his troops to land in Taiwan, completely drove out the Dutch colonists from the island they had occupied, and established a base for the anti-Qing movement there. He died of illness the year after the recovery of Taiwan.[190]

康熙元年（1662 年）五月，郑成功病逝，世子郑经承嗣其位，继续经营台湾。时清朝已统一了中国大陆，一个多民族国家的新政权已稳固下来，只有台湾尚独据一隅。为了实现国家的统一，清郑双方曾进行了多次谈判。[191]

In May of the First Year of Emperor Kangxi's Reign (1662), Zheng Chenggong died of illness. His eldest son, Zheng Jing, succeeded him and

---

190　李占才撰《清朝统一台湾的曲折历程》，来源《文史天地》，2012 年 2 期
191　郑以灵撰《试论清朝统一台湾的谈判》，来源《史学集刊》，1991 年 4 期

continued to govern Taiwan. At that time, the Qing Dynasty had unified the mainland, and consolidated the new multi-ethnic regime, with only Taiwan remaining isolated. In order to achieve national unification, the Qing government carried out several negotiations with Zheng Jing's side[191]

郑成功父子孙三代在闽台抗清三十余年，固有助于台湾的开化，却对闽南的自然与人文生态造成了严重的破坏，付出了惨重的代价。除了郑军在闽海不断征讨，征兵搜粮，民众生活困苦，战火所及，民更不聊生，清军为堵绝郑军生路，不惜下极其残酷的迁界令，强迫闽海居民内迁，沿岸城镇成为废墟，百姓之苦难，罄竹难书。直到 1683 年施琅平定台湾后，才解除东南沿海的迁界令。在郑氏抗清英勇事迹的背后，则是闽南及其附近地区的生态环境受到严重的破坏。[192]

For over thirty years, three generations of Zheng's family resisted the Qing in Fujian and Taiwan. Though it contributed to the development of Taiwan, it caused severe damage to the natural and cultural ecology of Southern Fujian. The cost was very heavy. The Zheng army kept on launching military campaigns, conscripting soldiers and searching for grain in the coastal area of Fujian, leading to a miserable life of the local people. Wherever the war raged, the people were plunged into a deeper abyss of misery and hardship. On the other hand, the Qing army, in an effort to cut off the livelihood of the Zheng army, issued an extremely cruel border relocation order, forcing coastal residents to move inland. As a result, the coastal towns were reduced to ruins, and the suffering of the people was beyond measure. It was not until 1683, when Shi Lang pacified Taiwan, that the border relocation order along the southeast

---

192　汪荣祖撰《闽南生态环境与郑成功的复明活动》，来源《闽台文化研究》，2013 年 1 期

coast was lifted. Due to the Zheng family's heroic struggle against the Qing Dynasty, the ecological environment of Southern Fujian and its surrounding areas was severely damaged.[192]

福建简称闽，闽字最早出现于周朝，"闽"是最原始的名称。[193]

Fujian is abbreviated as Min. The Chinese character "Min" first appeared in the Zhou Dynasty. It was the earliest name.[193]

康熙帝统一台湾的政举能够取得胜利，同他唯才是举，能用人，会用人是分不开的。他一贯重视用人之道，善于选用"德才兼备"的官员。在与沿海各种势力的长期斗争中，康熙帝逐渐认识到惯于陆战的清军将领和士兵已不能胜任新的任务，要想平定海疆，收复台湾，就要重用熟悉海疆作战技术的闽浙人。1678年，康熙帝首先擢升屡立战功的福建布政使姚启圣为福建总督，命他担当起恢复地方统一台湾的重任。姚启圣，浙江会稽县人，是个能文能武的将才。康熙帝在看到他接任总督后第一个陈述战略的奏折时，满意地说："闽督今得人，贼且平矣。"在进攻台湾指挥员的人选方面，康熙帝采纳了姚启圣的建议，任命精通海战，熟知台湾郑氏集团内情又有谋略的施琅为指挥官。施琅，福建晋江人，有勇略，在福建与郑氏作战多年，了解台湾情况，熟悉水师机宜及海上风涛之变幻。他一贯主张攻取台湾，统一立场坚定。但因其原是郑氏部下，当康熙帝决定启用施琅时，"举朝大臣以为不可遣，去必叛"。但康熙帝任人唯贤，认为要统一台湾必用施琅，施琅不去，"台湾断不能定"。郑氏集团所畏惧的只有施琅一人，因此，康熙力排众议，特加擢用，授施琅以水师提督官职，并"赋予独任专征"大权，要他相机自行进剿。事实证明，姚、施在实现康熙帝统一台湾决策过程中都做出了巨大贡献。[194]

193　高汝武撰《八闽特色县域地名赏析》，来源《中国地名》，2015年10期

194　石小俭撰《略论康熙帝统一台湾》，来源《牡丹江教育学院学报》，2013年2期

The success of Emperor Kangxi's political initiative to unify Taiwan was inseparable from his practice of appointing people based on their talents, and his ability to employ people and make the best use of them. He always attached great importance to the art of employing people, and was good at selecting officials with both "ability and integrity". In the long-term struggle against coastal forces, he gradually realized that the generals and soldiers of the Qing army had been accustomed to land battles, and so were no longer qualified for new tasks. To pacify the coastal areas and recover Taiwan, he must attach great importance to the inhabitants of Fujian and Zhejiang who were familiar with maritime combat technology. In 1678, he first promoted Yao Qisheng, Chief Administrative Commissioner of Fujian who had made numerous military achievements, to be Governor-General of Fujian, and assigned him with the important task of restoring local order and unifying Taiwan. Yao Qisheng, a native of Kuaiji County, Zhejiang Province, was a talented general who was proficient in both literature and martial arts. When Emperor Kangxi read the first memorial regarding strategies that Yao Qisheng submitted during his tenure as Governor-General, he said with satisfaction, "Now that a capable person has been appointed as Governor-General of Fujian, the rebels will soon be pacified." When selecting the commander for attacking Taiwan, Emperor Kangxi adopted Yao Qisheng's suggestion, appointing Shi Lang, who was proficient in naval battles, familiar with the inside information of Taiwan's Zheng Faction and full of tactic, as the commander. Shi Lang, a native of Jinjiang, Fujian Province, was brave and resourceful. He had fought against the Zheng Faction in Fujian for many years, knowing Taiwan's situation very well, and being familiar with naval tactics and the changes of the sea winds and waves. He had been advocating the capture of Taiwan and holding a firm stance on unification. However, he was originally a subordinate of the Zheng Faction. So when Emperor Kangxi decided to appoint him, "All the ministers in the court were against dispatching him, thinking that he must rebel if dispatched." However, Emperor Kangxi, who appointed people based on their virtues and talents, believed that to unify Taiwan, Shi Lang must be employed. Without Shi Lang, "Taiwan could never be pacified." The only one that the Zheng Faction feared was Shi Lang. Therefore, Emperor Kangxi defied public opinions, specially promoted and appointed him as Naval Admiral, "entrusted him with the exclusive power of leading the expedition", and ordered him to launch an attack at an appropriate time on his own initiative. It turns out that both Yao Qisheng and Shi Lang made great contributions to the realization of Emperor Kangxi's decision to unify Taiwan.[194]

康熙统一台湾不仅是清代历史上的大事，而且也是中国历史上影响深远的重大事件。施琅在康熙皇帝统一台湾的过程中，起了重大作用，虽然其在平台后占有不少的田产，给自身留下污点，但不能因此而将其历史功绩全盘否定。[195]

The unification of Taiwan by Emperor Kangxi was not only a major event in the history of the Qing Dynasty but also a significant event with far-reaching influence in Chinese history. In this process, Shi Lang played a significant role. Although he occupied a large amount of farmland after the pacification of Taiwan, which left a stain on his reputation, his historical achievements should not be completely denied.[195]

康熙六十年（1721 年），台湾爆发了朱一贵起义。朱一贵，原籍福建漳州，在台湾以养鸭为生，平素与下层民众接触甚广。四

---

195 李祖基撰《论施琅＜台湾弃留利弊疏＞的背景与动机——兼谈清初台湾的官庄及武职占垦问题》，来源《史学月刊》，2014 年 1 期

月，因反对台湾知府王廷珍次子之暴政，一贵乃与黄殿、李勇等人削竹为枪，率众起义。凤山下淡水的客家人杜君英揭旗响应。阴历五月初一日，朱一贵与杜君英会师台南，进占台湾府城和凤山、诸罗二县，全台落入起义者手中。为镇压起义，清廷派南澳总兵蓝廷珍、水师提督施世标率兵入台。起义军虽奋勇抵抗，但终因寡不敌众，朱一贵被俘，杜君英与其子自首，起义失败。[196]

In the 60th Year of Emperor Kangxi's Reign (1721), the Zhu Yigui Uprising broke out in Taiwan. Zhu Yigui, originally from Zhangzhou, Fujian Province, made a living by raising ducks in Taiwan and had extensive contacts with the lower-class people. In April, due to his opposition to the tyranny of the second son of Wang Tingzhen, the Magistrate of Taiwan, he, together with Huang Dian and Li Yong, shaved bamboo into spears and initiated a rebellion. Du Junying, a Hakka from Xiadan Shui in Fengshan, raised a banner of rebellion in response. On the first day of the fifth lunar month, Zhu Yigui and Du Junying joined forces in Tainan, and occupied the municipal seat of Taiwan Prefecture, Fengshan County and Zhuluo County, making the whole region of Taiwan fall into the hands of the rebels. To suppress the uprising, the Qing government dispatched the troops led by the Nan'ao General Lan Tingzhen and the Navy Admiral Shi Shibiao into Taiwan. Although the rebel troops resisted bravely, they were outmatched in numbers. Zhu Yigui was captured, and Du Junying and his son surrendered themselves. Hence, the uprising failed.[196]

　　清军崛起于东北满洲的白山黑水之间，虽弓马骑射娴熟，但缺乏海上作战的经验。满族是一个马背上的民族，虽热衷于在大陆

196　王尊旺撰《清代台湾理番政策初探（1683—1874）》，来源《福建师范大学》，2001
　　年4月

上开疆扩土，但天生对海洋缺乏热情。一个对海洋缺乏热情的游牧民族是不可能投入大量的人力、物力和财力建立一支强大的海军舰队，掌握制海权的。在清王朝入主中原的初期不敌郑氏的海军是如此，在清王朝的后期无法抵御西方列强的坚船利炮也是如此。[197]

The Qing army emerged from the white mountains and black waters in Manchuria in Northeast China. Although they were proficient in archery on horseback, they lacked experience in naval battles. The Manchu people were an ethnic group on horseback. Although they were enthusiastic about expanding the territory on the mainland, they had little interest in the sea by nature. It was impossible for the nomadic tribes who had little interest in the sea to invest a large amount of manpower, material resources and financial resources to build a powerful naval fleet and obtain the command of the sea. It was the case when the Qing Dynasty failed to defeat the navy of the Zheng Faction in the early years of its rule in the Central Plains. It was also the case when the Qing Dynasty failed to resist the powerful warships and cannons of the Western powers in the later period.[197]

清王朝和明朝政权之间的陆海战争，既是一场统一中国的归属之战，也是一场"祖宗技艺"的较量之争。明清战争将"兴百姓苦，亡百姓苦"演绎得淋漓尽致。

The land and sea wars between the Qing Dynasty and the Ming Dynasty were not only a fight for the sovereignty of the unified China but also a contest of the "ancestral skills". These wars vividly demonstrated the saying that "when the dynasty thrives, the people suffer; when the dynasty falls, the people also suffer."

197　叶俊杰撰《明末清初台湾海峡地区的军事地理研究》，来源《陕西师范大学》，2013 年 11 月

人民不能是政府的奴隶，政府总要为人民服务。这是再凶狠的恐怖主义也没有办法改变的国家事实。恃强凌弱的最终结果都会伴随着否极泰来，刺激多元化社会也会有思想的统一。

People should not be slaves of the government, and the government must serve the people. This is a national truth that even the most ruthless terrorism cannot change. The ultimate result of bullying the weak by relying on one's strength is accompanied by a turning point from extreme misfortune to good fortune. Even in a pluralistic society, there can be a unification of thoughts .

兵道思想赞同世人面对事物应该多计算和少算计。多算多胜，少算少胜，不算不胜，市场调查能够升级为战前部署，是不战而胜的先决条件。从亚洲有科举制度开始，日本科举折服在本国世袭制之下，中国则不然，这也注定了中日教育制度有着诸多的不同。各国教育模式不同，所造成的社会问题也不尽相同，所面临的恐怖主义也不一样。

The Chinese military thought advocates that people should make more comprehensive calculations and employ fewer treacherous tactics when confronted with something. The more you calculate, the greater the chance of victory; the less you calculate, the smaller the chance of victory; without any calculations, you will gain no victory. The upgrading of market investigation to pre-war deployment is a prerequisite for winning without a fight. After the imperial examination system emerged in Asia, the imperial examination system in Japan was subject to a hereditary system, but it was not the case in China. This determined that there were many differences between the education systems of the two countries. Different education models in different countries will cause different social problems, and make people face different types of terrorism.

所谓世袭，据《广辞苑》（第 6 版）的解释，指嫡系子孙代代继承其家族的地位（爵位或官位）、职业和财产等。在日本古代封建幕藩体制下，法律严格规定了"士农工商"等不同的世袭阶层，其中武士阶层作为统治阶级，以将军、大名为首的各大家族垄断着政治特权，世袭着爵位、职业、俸禄和财产。在近代君主立宪体制下，身份的世袭依然被延续，天皇的重要辅弼机构——贵族院中就有不少世袭的华族、皇族议员。战后日本经过民主化改革，实行西方代议制民主，然而，经过半个多世纪的民主实践，政治家族不但没有消亡，反而在全国各地规模不等地成批滋生出来，相当程度上出现了政治权力"家族化"的现象。这些政治家，虽然是通过所谓"民主选举"产生的，但其在形式上继承了父辈职业，更重要的是继承了父辈留下的选举地盘、遗产（包括政治资金）和名声（影响力），依托当地选区长期当选，表现了相对稳定的代际传承性和地区性特征。因其形式上有不少类似于封建时代传统世袭制的地方，故不妨称之为日本的"政治返祖"。日本媒体和学界将这种政治现象称为"世袭政治"，将这些来自政治家族的成员称为"世袭议员""二代议员""三代议员"等[198]。

According to Kōjien (6th edition), a renowned Japanese-language dictionary, the so-called hereditary system refers to a system in which the direct descendants inherit the status (noble titles or official positions), occupations and properties of their families from generation to generation. Under the ancient Japanese feudal Bakuhan system, the laws strictly defined different hereditary classes such as "samurai, farmer, craftsman, and merchant". The samurai class was the ruling class. Families headed by the shogun and daimyo monopolized political privileges, and inherited

---

198 乔林生撰《当代日本"世袭政治"的文化解读》，来源《廉政文化研究》，2015 年第 4 期

noble titles, occupations, salaries, and properties. Under the modern constitutional monarchy system, the inheritance of status still persisted. There were quite a number of hereditary Peerage MPs and Imperial Family MPs in the House of Nobles, an important advisory institution to the emperor. After the Second World War, through a democratic reform, Japan implemented the Western representative democracy. However, after more than half a century of democratic practice, political families have not disappeared. Instead, they are emerging in batches on different scales across the country, leading to the "familialization" of political power to a considerable extent. Although these politicians are produced through the so-called "democratic elections", they inherit their fathers' occupations in formality. More importantly, they inherit the electoral bases, legacies (including political funds), and reputations (influence) left by their fathers, and take advantage of the local electoral districts to remain in power for a long period, exhibiting relatively stable inter-generational inheritance and regional characteristics. As far as the form is concerned, there are many aspects similar to the traditional hereditary system in the feudal era. Therefore, it can be called Japan's "political atavism". The Japanese media and academic circles call this political phenomenon "hereditary politics",and refer to the members from political families as "hereditary parliamentarians", "second-generation parliamentarians", "third-generation parliamentarians"...[198]

中国的科举制度持续千年，曾经影响到许多国家，其辐射力和影响力巨大。周边的韩国、朝鲜、越南等国都曾是科举制度的忠实拥趸，朝鲜在日本殖民统治下，于 1895 年被强迫废除科举考试，越南则直到 1919 年才取消科举制，此时距科举考试原产地中国废除科举制已经过去了十几年。这之中，日本是个例外。历史上日本没有学习的古代中国的重要制度，恐怕除了宦官制度，再就是科举制度了。[199]

China's imperial examination system lasted for a thousand years. With enormous radiation and influence, it once influenced many countries. Neighboring countries such as South Korea, North Korea and Vietnam were once loyal supporters of the imperial examination system. Under Japanese colonial rule, Korea was forced to abolish the imperial examination in 1895. However, Vietnam did not abolish it until 1919. By that time, more than a decade had passed since the abolition of the imperial examination system in China, the birthplace of this system. Among them, Japan is an exception. In history, among the important systems of ancient China that Japan did not learn, apart from the eunuch system, it was probably the imperial examination system.[199]

古代日本积极模仿唐朝的科举制，选择性地施行了考试选拔的贡举制，它的根本目的在于巩固以天皇为中心的封建体制。但是，随着贡举制的贵族化与高等教育的私家化，贡举制也蜕化为一种"科名世袭制"，逐渐走向消亡。到了日本封建体制趋于成熟的江户时代，日本没有施行大量选拔人才的科举制，而是提出倡导学问、普及教育、推动出版的文教政策，从而为日本高等教育近代化打下了一个连续性的思想与文化基础。[200]

In ancient times, on the basis of actively imitating the imperial examination system of the Tang Dynasty, Japan selectively implemented a system of talent selection through examinations, which was called the tribute-recommendation system. The fundamental purpose was to consolidate the feudal system centered around the emperor. However,

---

199   王璞、石佳丽撰《科举制与日本的福祚和祸患》，来源《教育与考试》，2019 年第 1 期

200   吴光辉撰《日本科举制的兴亡》，来源《厦门大学学报（哲学社会科学版）》，2003 年 5 期

with the aristocratization of the tribute-recommendation system and the privatization of higher education, it degenerated into a kind of "hereditary system of academic titles", and gradually declined into oblivion. In the Edo period when the feudal system became mature, Japan did not implement the imperial examination system to select talents on a large scale, but formulated cultural and educational policies that advocated learning, popularized education, and promoted publishing, thus laying a continuous ideological and cultural foundation for the modernization of its higher education.[200]

做生意有赚有赔天经地义，做生意只赚不赔不切实际。然而，照样有人为了逐利降本，不惜去做诈骗等违法行为。为此，善恶有道，人心向善，出现平等制，人心向恶，出现世袭制。人心向善，接受世袭制，人心向恶，接受平等制。如同盛名之下，有好有坏。有的人好的不学学坏的，于是有了排行榜。有的人学好不学坏，则是排名不分先后，这是老生常谈的实战经验。

As far as doing business is concerned, it is a matter of course that one makes profits and incurs losses at times, and it is unrealistic that one always makes profits without suffering losses. However, in order to pursue profits and reduce costs, some people do not stint their efforts to engage in fraud and other illegal activities. Therefore, there is a way of good and evil. When people's hearts incline towards goodness, the equality system emerges; when people's hearts incline towards evil, the hereditary system appears. When people's hearts incline towards goodness, they can accept the hereditary system; when people's hearts incline towards evil, they can accept the equality system. Under the shadow of great reputation, there are goodness and evil. Some people learn the bad and avoid the good, so a ranking list emerges. Some people learn the good and avoid the bad, and in this case, there is no need to distinguish the order of rankings. This is well-established practical experience.

在当代社会，各国人民所接受的教育是不一样的，再加上，社会在很多方面没有得到统一的共识，成为个人迷茫时期的社会诱因。恐袭和反恐都是不分穷人和富人，国家教育成败决定国家政治走向何方。就像 20 世纪的日本恐怖组织赤军成员，有很多就是高学历分子，家境未必一贫如洗，也照样做了冲动杀人的恐怖政治行为。

In contemporary society, people in different countries have different levels of education. Moreover, society has not reached consensus in many aspects. This has become a social incentive for personal confusion. Terrorism and counter-terrorism do not distinguish between the poor and the rich, while the success or failure of a country's education determines the orientation of national politics. For example, many members of the Japanese Red Army as a terrorist organization in the 20th century were highly educated people, and their families were not necessarily in extreme poverty, but they still carried out impulsive and murderous terrorist political acts.

20 世纪六七十年代，随着极"左"风潮在世界各地的出现，1969 年，一批激进的极"左"大学生组成的"赤军"组织在日本产生了，这支年轻的队伍的恐怖袭击方式以劫机、机场爆炸等为主。据相关资料显示，在 20 世纪 60 至 80 年代的大约 30 年间，共发生 700 多起劫机事件，而日本开展的劫机行动则是其中的重要的且影响极大的组成部分，日本赤军的恐怖主义活动行动于国际层面，对国际社会公共安全产生一定威胁，在其活动了近 30 年后，随着该组织主要领导人的被擒拿，组织也随之消失。[201]

In the 1960s and 1970s, the extreme "leftist" trends emerged around

---

201　朱瑾华撰《消失的"恐惧"—恐怖组织消亡的若干个案分析》，来源《上海师范大学》，2016 年

the world. In 1969, the "Red Army" organization composed of radical extreme "leftist" university students emerged in Japan. This young group mainly resorted to hijacking, airport bombings and other terrorist means. According to relevant data, during the about 30 years from the 1960s to the 1980s, there were altogether more than 700 hijacking incidents, with those carried out by Japan's terrorist organizations being a major and highly influential part. The terrorist activities of the Japanese Red Army were rampant internationally, thus threatening the international public security. After being active for nearly 30 years, the organization perished with the capture of its main leaders.[201]

赤军的成员，不是疯子或暴徒，而是当时名牌大学的学生，堪称那一代年轻人的精英。有人回忆，除了几个赤军头目，大部分赤军成员都是思想单纯、怀有理想的中产阶级青年，他们大部分人都痛恨当时的日本社会，仇恨既得利益团体，同情底层民众。"他们甚至可以说是无私的、高尚的人。"重信房子当然是里面最为杰出的一个。投身于革命的女子，显然是怀有大爱的。"赤军的纲领是建立所谓平均主义的工人世界，打到帝国主义和资本主义。他们相信，实现革命的途径就是进行恐怖主义暴力活动。"[202]

The members of the Red Army were not lunatics or ruffians, but students from prestigious universities, who could be regarded as the elite of the young people of that generation. According to the memory of some people, except for a few leaders, most of the Red Army members were middle-class young people with naive minds and noble aspirations. Most of them hated the Japanese society at that time, hated the groups with vested interests, and sympathized with the lower-class people. "They can

202 《日本"赤军"如何变为"恐怖分子"》腾讯文化（腾讯网）www.qq.com，2015年12月7日

even be regarded as selfless and noble people." Of course, Shigenobu Fusako was one of the most outstanding among them. A woman who devoted herself to revolution obviously had great love. "The Red Army aimed to establish a so-called egalitarian workers' world, and overthrow imperialism and capitalism. They believed that the way to achieve the victory of the revolution was to carry out terrorist violent activities."[202]

重信高中毕业之后先在日本一家公司上班，1965 年进入明治大学文学部地理专业夜大部学习。她的大学时代正处于全球学生运动风起云涌，"革命""斗争"成为部分热血激进学生热衷的字眼，许多学校都成立了"革命"组织。东京大学、日本大学、京都大学等学校的学生纷纷走上街头"闹革命"，并同警察发生了激烈冲突。重信也成了日本"共产主义同盟赤军派"的主要成员之一，是日本学生运动的推动者和组织者。不过，所谓"暴力革命"并不适合日本的国情，许多激进组织学生领袖先后被捕。[203]

After graduating from high school, Shigenobu Fusako first worked in a Japanese company. In 1965, she studied in the night department of geography major of Meiji University's Faculty of Literature. Her university years coincided with the surge of global student movements. As "revolution" and "struggle" became words that some passionate and radical students were obsessed with, many schools established "revolutionary" organizations. Students from the University of Tokyo, Nippon University, and Kyoto University "made a revolution" in the streets, and clashed violently with the police. Shigenobu Fusako also became one of the main members of the "Communist Alliance Red Army Faction" in Japan, playing the role of promoting and organizing the

---

203 《日本赤军"女皇"作为国际恐怖分子沦为阶下囚》搜狐新闻（搜狐网），www.sohu.com，2006 年 3 月 6 日

Japanese student movement. However, the so-called "violent revolution" was not suitable for Japan's national conditions, and many student leaders of radical organizations were arrested successively.[203]

随着中美建交，日本赤军运动受到极大震撼，许多成员在绝望中自杀，此后日本赤军也逐渐走向低谷。80 年代，日本赤军又制造了几起恐怖事件，但影响有限，赤军成员也不复当年盛况。90 年代，苏联崩溃，国际共产主义运动完全陷入低谷。就是在 90 年代，重信房子潜回日本，2000 年身份暴露被抓捕，被判处有期徒刑 20 年。2001 年，在狱中重信房子发布了解散赤军宣言。日本赤军运动至此终结。[204]

With the establishment of diplomatic relations between China and the United States, the Japanese Red Army movement was severely impacted, and many members committed suicide in despair. After that, the Japanese Red Army gradually declined. In the 1980s, it again carried out several terrorist attacks, but the impact was limited, and the members were no longer as powerful as before. In the 1990s, the Soviet Union disintegrated, and the international communist movement completely fell into a trough. In the 1990s, Shigenobu Fusako sneaked back to Japan. In 2000, her identity was exposed, and she was arrested and sentenced to 20 years in prison. In 2001, she issued a declaration to dissolve the Red Army while in prison. By then, the Japanese Red Army movement had come to an end.[204]

2022 年，重信房子 5 月 28 日获释后，女儿前来迎接她出狱，当场约 20 名支持者手持"我们爱房子"的标语到场迎接。重信房子获释后接受采访，先为给不相识的人们带来了伤害道歉，并称

204 《赤军领导重信房子出狱，日本赤军运动是怎么回事？》澎拜新闻 www.thepaper. cn，2022 年 5 月 31 日

"半世纪前，因为优先考虑我们的战斗，例如劫持人质等，我们对素昧平生的无辜民众造成伤害"[205]。

When Shigenobu Fusako was released on May 28, 2022, her daughter came to meet her, and about 20 supporters greeted her on the spot, holding signs that read "We Love Shigenobu Fusako". After her release, she apologized for the harm caused to the people she had not met before in an interview, saying, "Half a century ago, we gave priority to our struggle, like hostage-taking, and caused harm to those innocent people I had not met before."[205]

由于国家制度都是有缺陷的，政治风波总是连绵不绝，恐怖主义的历史伤害又是难以愈合的，因此，政府先以身作则，再教育人民长期做好自己，比人与人互帮互助来得更为重要。

Any national system has flaws, political turmoils break out from time to time, and the historical harm of terrorism can hardly be completely eliminated. Therefore, the government should act as an example first, and then educate people to live up to themselves in the long term, which is more important than people helping each other.

兵道思想认可道理是圆的，起点也有可能是终点，鼓励人要有逆向思维。恐怖主义对哪方面破坏最大，每个人想法都不一样，只要该想法能被社会印证就有被注目的理由。比如，恐怖主义会对国民教育产生了消极的影响。民粹主义"过火"也能成为政治恐怖主义。在中国清末民初，中国革命党人暗杀清朝要员，也能被列为恐怖主义。

The Chinese military thought recognizes that the truth is a circle, so the starting point may also be the endpoint. It encourages people to

---

205 《"日本赤军"前领袖重信房子出狱》观察者网 www.guancha.cn，2022 年 5 月 29 日

have reverse thinking. Regarding the aspect upon which terrorism has the greatest destructive impact, everyone has different ideas. As long as an idea can be verified by society, it deserves attention. For example, terrorism can have a negative impact on national education. Excessive populism can also become political terrorism. In the late Qing Dynasty and early Republic of China, the assassination of Qing officials by Chinese revolutionaries can also be regarded as terrorism.

就辛亥革命的前10年而言，革命党人才是政治暗杀的主角。主其事者多为官宦和富家子弟，或是受教育程度比较高的热血青年。这与俄国近似，俄国贵族青年就是暗杀权贵的主力。怀揣炸弹准备炸死出国考察宪政五大臣的吴樾出身商人家庭，其父先官后商。刺杀恩铭的徐锡麟，其家更是富甲一方，自己还捐了个道员。参与谋杀铁良、亲身行刺王之春的万福华虽说家境不算富裕，但后来也学医经商，还是个候补知县。万福华、章士钊、俞大纯、吴樾、徐锡麟再加上袭击摄政王载沣的汪精卫，都是学养深厚之士[206]。

During the 10 years before the Xinhai Revolution, revolutionaries were main players in carrying out political assassinations. Those in charge were mostly children of officials and rich families, or fervent well-educated young people. This is also the case in Russia, where young nobles were the main force in assassinating powerful and wealthy people. Wu Yue, who attempted to use a bomb to kill the five ministers who went abroad to examine the constitutional government system, came from a family of businessmen. His father was first an official and then a businessman. Xu Xilin, who assassinated Enming, came from a super wealthy family. He even bought the title of circuit intendant. Wan Fuhua, who participated in the plot to kill Tie Liang and personally assassinated

206　齐风撰《暗杀，革命党人绝望中的冲动》，来源《文史博览》，2013 年第 10 期

Wang Zhichun, was not from a rich family, but he later studied medicine, engaged in business, and also served as a reserve county magistrate. Wan Fuhua, Zhang Shizhao, Yu Dachun, Wu Yue, Xu Xilin, and Wang Jingwei, who attacked Prince Regent Zaifeng, were all well-educated scholars.[206]

　　清末革命党人的暗杀活动，不仅仅在当时具有重要的影响，对辛亥革命的成功具有很大的促进作用，而且其余风流变也对民初的政局震动颇深。暗杀的兴起，源于对俄国虚无党人的艳羡与模仿，而其与无政府主义的接榫乃是清末已有的"破坏主义"思想。中国传统的"任侠"文化，为暗杀活动提供了文化基础和思想与行动上的规范。革命党人的暗杀理念还与"文明革命""自杀""流血崇拜"等一度在当时新知识分子中广泛流传的思想纠缠，并产生暗杀"公理"。在武昌起义成功，临时政府成立，满洲贵族退位之后，失去了"公理"的暗杀变得"名不正而言不顺"。在民国初年，暗杀失去了"公理"的制约，完全蜕变为政治权谋的工具，对民初的政治及以后的历史都产生了深远的影响[207]。

The assassination activities of the revolutionaries at the end of the Qing Dynasty had an important influence at that time, and contributed greatly to the success of the Xinhai Revolution. In addition, the influence left over caused a deep shock to the political situation in the early Republic of China. The emergence of assassination originated from the admiration and imitation of Russian Nihilists, and its connection with anarchism was based on the "destructivism" ideology that already existed at the end of the Qing Dynasty. The traditional Chinese "martial arts" culture provided a cultural basis and thought and action norms for assassination activities. The assassination concept of the revolutionaries

---

207　黄滔撰《原杀：清末革命派暗杀研究》，来源《华东师范大学》，2013 年

was also intertwined with ideas such as "civil revolution", "suicide", and "worship of bloodshed", which were widely spread among new intellectuals at that time, and produced the "axiom" for assassination After the success of the Wuchang Uprising, the establishment of the provisional government, and the abdication of the Manchu nobility, assassination lost the "axiomatic nature" and became "unrighteous". In the early years of the Republic of China, without the constraint of "axiomatic nature", assassination completely became a tool of political intrigue. This had a far-reaching influence on the politics of the early Republic of China and the history thereafter.[207]

国家政权对付反革命势力不一定要用以暴制暴的手段才能收到成效。有时，政府对付异议人士也可以换一种思路。例如在一个做生意发不了财的年代，有人去当诈骗犯是为了生存，有人去当反革命分子是为了生活。如此思绪，国家机器给诈骗犯判刑，比给反革命判刑还要重，在很大程度上就促使"揭竿而起"式的人民反抗是一跌再跌。

To deal with counter-revolutionary forces, a national regime does not necessarily rely on violent means. Sometimes, the government can take another approach when dealing with dissenters. For example, in an era when it's hard to get rich through business, some people become fraudsters for survival, and some people become counterrevolutionaries for making a living. In this situation, if the government gives fraudsters heavier sentences than counterrevolutionaries, it will remarkably reduce the possibility of people's resistance manifested as "rising in rebellion".

在中国历代人民思想领域内，只要自己有饭吃，就对反压迫和反迫害不热衷。而且，只要改府打着"为国为民"的旗号，那么，民粹主义以"人民"为话题就无可厚非。只是，由于人民是先有生存才有生活，如此，人民的问题在一定时期内能够以"生存为主，生活为次"。

In the minds of the Chinese people across different historical dynasties, as long as they have food to eat, they are not keen on resisting oppression and persecution. Moreover, as long as the government uses the banner of "for the country and the people", populism shouldn't be blamed for taking "the people" as a topic. However, people have to survive before making a living, so people's problems can be described as "survival is the primary concern, while making a living takes a secondary place" in a certain period.

就业优先于民主、工资优先于民主、环保优先于民主、版图大小优先于民主、安定优先于民主、无党派优先于民主。只要政府部署得当，这六大物质条件即能刺激人民的精神世界。

Employment is prior to democracy, the pay is prior to democracy, environmental protection is prior to democracy, the size of a territory is prior to democracy, stability is prior to democracy, and non-partisan is prior to democracy. As long as the government makes proper arrangements, these six material conditions can stimulate the spiritual world of the people.

兵道思想否定他人连累无辜，排斥为达目的不择手段，主张罪恶行径得到曝光，才有基本的良性社会可言。比如同样的灾难到来，社会同病相怜不在少数，白人把非洲黑人当"黑奴"贩卖到北美，受害者既是非洲奴隶，也让一部分生活在美洲的当地人遭罪。

The Chinese military thought rejects implicating the innocent, rejects employing all means to achieve one's goal, and advocates exposing criminal acts. Only in this way can a basic benign society be formed. For instance, when a similar disaster occurs, many people in society commiserate with the sufferers. When white people sold African blacks as "slaves" to North America, the victims were not only the

African slaves but also some of the local people living in the Americas.

　　贸易往来也是外来传染病在北美大陆传播的重要途径。自从英国人踏上北美大陆，殖民者与印第安人之间以及印第安人各群体之间的贸易往来变得越来越频繁。印第安人用毛皮、土地乃至土著奴隶换来欧洲的酒类、日用品、生产工具等制成品。在这个过程中，北美大陆的印第安人自觉不自觉地参与到大西洋贸易体系中，成为世界经济的一个组成部分。随着贸易的开展，欧洲人、黑人与印第安人之间的餐饮和聚会逐渐增多，白人与黑人身上所携带的天花、麻疹、鼠疫、流感、痢疾和黄热病等外来传染病病菌、病毒不断传播到北美各地。在大西洋贸易网络中，黑奴贸易很快成为"旧世界"疾病传播到北美大陆的重要渠道。在近代早期的非洲，天花肆虐。当奴隶船在运送过程中发现天花或者疾病尚处于潜伏期，疾病才会最终传播到目的地。这些带有天花病毒的黑人与印第安人混合在一起后，就将天花带到了印第安人中间。从16世纪末到17世纪，英国人将利比里亚黑人变成奴隶，从尼日尔河流域、刚果河流域输出黑奴，以取代日益减少的印第安人。1671年，卡罗来纳输入第一批黑人奴隶。1738年在南卡罗来纳发生的天花瘟疫，实际上就是由一艘非洲奴隶船引入的。其他疾病如疟疾、黄热病等，也和天花类似，通过黑奴运输船只从非洲或欧洲传播到北美大陆。有学者称，从事非洲奴隶贸易的船只在疾病网络中编织了结实的绳索，不断地把天花等疾病传播到美洲人口中 [208]。

　　Trade exchanges also significantly contributed to the spread of exotic infectious diseases in North America. After the British entered North America, trade interactions between the colonists and the Native Americans, as well as among different Native American groups, became

---

208　丁见民撰《外来传染病与美国历史早期印第安人人口的削减》，来源《世界历史》，2018年第1期

increasingly frequent. The Native Americans exchanged furs, land, and even indigenous slaves for European finished products such as wine, daily necessities, and production tools. In this process, the Native Americans were consciously or unconsciously involved in the Atlantic trade system, becoming a participant of the world economy. With the development of trade, meals and social gatherings among Europeans, black people, and Native Americans became more and more frequent. Pathogens and viruses of exotic infectious diseases carried by white and black people, such as smallpox, measles, plague, influenza, dysentery, and yellow fever, continuously spread to different areas of North America. In the Atlantic trade network, the slave trade immediately became an important channel for the spread of diseases from the "Old World" to North America. In early modern Africa, smallpox raged. When smallpox was detected on slave ships during transportation or the disease was still in its incubation period, it would eventually spread to the destination. After the black people carrying smallpox viruses mixed with the Native Americans, smallpox was brought to the Native Americans. From the late 16th century to the 17th century, the British turned the Liberian black people into slaves, and trafficked slaves from the Niger River Basin and the Congo River Basin to replace the Native Americans, whose numbers gradually decreased. In 1671, the first batch of black slaves were brought to Carolina. The smallpox epidemic that occurred in South Carolina in 1738 was actually introduced by an African slave ship. Similar to smallpox, other diseases such as malaria and yellow fever were also spread from Africa or Europe to North America via slave transport ships. Some scholars claim that the ships engaged in the African slave trade wove a tight web of diseases, and constantly spread smallpox and other diseases to people in the Americas.[208]

从实在角度来说，奴隶贸易产生了病毒传播。治病救人找医生。医疗质量是医护人员能够战胜病魔，让病患起死回生的切实工具。医疗质量要有三样东西做保证——"医德、论文、资金"。

From a practical perspective, the slave trade led to the spread of viruses. When people are ill, they consult a doctor. Medical quality is a practical tool that enables medical staffs to defeat diseases and bring patients back to life. Medical quality is guaranteed by three things: "medical ethics, academic papers, and funds."

医德为上，论文为中，资金为下，这是理论。100 颗医德为基础、1000 篇论文为理论、1 人捐款 1 万元，这是实践。这些"医德、论文、资金"的明暗关系，能够无中生有。

In theory, medical ethics are of the highest importance, academic papers are in the middle, and funds are of relatively lower importance. In practice, 100 medical ethics serve as the foundation, 1000 academic papers constitute a theoretical framework, and each person donates 10,000 yuan. The implicit and explicit relationships among "medical ethics, academic papers, and funds" can generate something out of nothing.

医德、论文、资金进行每每结合，能够提高医疗质量，是将疾病打成魂飞魄散的催化剂，更是驱散世态炎凉的解药。

The combination of medical ethics, academic papers, and funds can improve medical quality. It is not only a catalyst that can completely vanquish diseases but also a remedy that dispels the coldness of the world.

从虚有角度来说，奴隶贸易产生对立行径。爱恨情仇消磨时间，时间既可以消磨爱，也可以消磨恨。"黑白战"可以变成"黑白和"，这是不分肤色的。只要经过天长地久的磨合，满足必要的条件，这世界上任何不愉快的过去都能成为过去，反而能够成为友谊的见证。

From a virtual aspect, the slave trade gave rise to acts of opposition. Love, hatred, resentment and affection can consume time. Time can consume not only love but also hatred. Regardless of skin color, the "conflict between the black and the white" can be turned into a "reconciliation between the black and the white". As long as the necessary conditions are met through a long-term process of accommodation, any past unpleasantness in the world can be left behind. On the contrary, it can become a testament to friendship.

不过，"病向浅中医"。要是政府办事不力，随着事件的恶化，那么，这些大事小情就不是政治方面、经济方面、军事方面、外交方面等症状，而是，逐渐演变成政府行为与无政府主义之间的对决，继而还能发展为唯物主义和唯心主义的较量，后来还能化为阴阳对立的两点。

However, as the saying goes, "A disease should be treated in its early stage." If the government fails to act effectively and the situation continuously deteriorates, then these issues, whether major or minor, will reveal more symptoms than just those at the political, economic, military and diplomatic levels. Instead, they will gradually evolve into a confrontation between government actions and anarchism, then into a contest between materialism and idealism, and eventually into the antithesis of Yin and Yang.

唯物主义之上的唯心主义能够拨云见日。有道是："人在屋檐下，不得不低头。"不管是个人还是国家，以及社会，这些事物各式各样的价值观都要经得住历史长河的风吹雨打，才能够成为人类的行为准则。

Idealism, when based on materialism, can provide clarity. As the old saying goes, "When under another person's roof, bow your head." Whether for an individual, a country, or society, all kinds of values must withstand the tests of history before becoming guiding principles for human behaviors.

道德能够作用于唯物主义和唯心主义，恐怖主义同属于唯物主义和唯心主义领域，道德和恐怖主义是一对相生相克的事物。道德对付恐怖主义，会害怕的永远是做贼心虚分子，就算没有人觉得自己是恐怖分子，可丝毫也不能改变既定事实。哪怕事实残酷、血腥、具有迷惑性，道德力量却一直激励人类自强不息，直到解决恐怖主义为止。

Morality can act on both materialism and idealism. Terrorism falls within the realm of both materialism and idealism. Morality and terrorism are things of mutual generation and mutual restriction. If morality is used to deal with terrorism, those with a guilty conscience will feel afraid in the end. Even if no one admits to being a terrorist, the established facts cannot be changed in the slightest. Even if the facts are cruel, bloody, and misleading, the power of morality has been inspiring people to strive constantly for self-improvement until the eradication of terrorism.

第三章　中国兵道思想主张用反恐三大派系内不出兵反恐

Chapter 3: Chinese Military Thought Advocating Non-Dispatch of Troops against Terrorism within the Three Major Anti-Terrorism Factions

在中国，各种各样的文化都在分党分派，却又彼倡此和，构造了博大精深的中国文化。文化人"读书啃面包也分三六九等"，能直观发现"歧路亡羊"。就比如说中国道家思想能被划分为多门多派，其代表人物就各有不同。这些道家流派对解决恐怖主义皆有贡献，其中的创立和发展都与政治无常多是密不可分。然而，不同的道家人物却因对"道"和"无为"理解有别，这些道家学派思想观点也是同中有异，异能看同。

In China, different cultures belong to different factions, yet they echo and support each other. This shows that Chinese culture is profound and extensive. Among cultural people, even things like "reading books and eating bread" can be classified into different tiers, and the principle behind idioms like "a lost sheep on a forked road" (meaning that things are complex and changeable, and without a correct direction, one will go astray) can be intuitively discerned. For example, the Taoist thought can be divided into different schools, each having its own representative figures. All these Taoist schools have made contributions to solving the issue of terrorism, and their establishment and development are usually closely related to the impermanence of politics. However, due to different understandings of the "Tao" and "inaction" among Taoist figures, the ideological viewpoints of these Taoist schools present both similarities amid differences, as well as differences within similarities.

道家学派在《老子》一书的基础上，又发展成两个支派。一是"老庄学派"，偏重于从哲学层面阐述《老子》"道"之精神；另一个是"黄老学派"，偏重于从政治层面发挥《老子》"君人南面之术"。而他们的起源都与巫史传统有关。《汉书·艺文志》说："道家者流，盖出于史官。"道家人物之所以独盛于楚国，道家学派起源及其发展之所以也在楚国，原因即在于楚国浓厚的史官学术环境[209]。

Based on the book *Laozi*, the Taoist school has developed into two branches. One is the "Lao-Zhuang School", which focuses more on expounding the spirit of the "Tao" from the philosophical perspective; the other is the "Huang-Lao School", which places more emphasis on how to apply the "the art of a ruler governing" from the political perspective. Their origins are related to the historical tradition of witchcraft. *The Treatise on Literature, The History of the Han Dynasty* states, "The Taoist school probably originated from historians." The State of Chu boasted a strong academic atmosphere among historians, thus it produced many particularly prominent Taoist figures, and the Taoist school also originated and developed there.[209]

黄老学派的"老"是老子，"黄"指的是炎黄民族奉信的始祖黄帝。在春秋战国时期诸子百家争鸣，未发现"黄老学派"，它要想在思想界争得一席之地，才抬出黄帝以壮声势。黄帝是中华民族公认的领袖。古代思想家为了增加本学派的声望，儒家孔子尊周公，墨家尊禹，孟子尊尧舜。"黄老学派"自称继承黄帝、老子的思想，实质上是老子加秦朝的法家。汉初人对秦朝的暴政记忆犹新，对法家抱有反感，但是，为了全国统一的有效管理，又必须树立一种强制型的治国理论。汉朝有意回避它与秦朝的继承关系，于是出现了"黄老学派"[210]。

209　江林昌撰《出土文献所见楚国的史官学术与"老庄学派""黄老学派"》，来源《江汉论坛》，2006 年第 9 期

210　任继愈撰《寿命最短的黄老学派，效应长久的黄老思想》，来源《齐鲁学刊》，2006 年第 1 期

The "Lao" in the Huang-Lao School refers to Lao Tzu, and the "Huang" refers to the Yellow Emperor, the ancestor revered by the Yan-Huang people. The "Huang-Lao School" was not among the "Hundred Schools of Thought" that contended with each other in the Spring and Autumn Period and the Warring States Period. In order to gain a foothold in the realm of thought, it leveraged the name of the Yellow Emperor to enhance its influence. The Yellow Emperor is a recognized leader of the Chinese nation. Among ancient thinkers, in order to enhance the prestige of their own schools, the Confucian School revered the Duke of Zhou, the Mohist School revered Yu, and the Mencius School revered Yao and Shun. The "Huang-Lao School" claimed to have inherited the thoughts of the Yellow Emperor and Lao Tzu, but in essence, its thought was a combination of that of Lao Tzu and that of the Legalist School of the Qin Dynasty. In the early Han Dynasty, people still had fresh memories of the tyranny of the Qin Dynasty, so they loathed the Legalist school. However, in order to achieve an effective and unified management of the country, the rulers had to establish a coercive country-governance theory. The Han Dynasty deliberately shunned any mention of its inheritance from the Qin Dynasty. Hence, the "Huang-Lao School" emerged.[210]

老庄道家，又简称为老庄，是先秦道家主要学派之一。老庄道家是以道家思想的创始人老子和集大成者庄子及其门人后学为主的思想学派。道家最早原是先秦诸子百家中的一家，因此通常将这一时期的道家思想和代表学者称为先秦道家，而先秦道家更是在整个道家思想文化史上占据主流地位。[211]

The Lao-Zhuang School, briefly referred to as Lao-Zhuang, is one

---

211 张明初撰《老庄道家德育思想及其当代价值研究》，来源《四川农业大学》，2014年6月

of the main Taoist schools in the pre-Qin period. Its thought is mainly a combination of that of Lao Tzu, the founder of Taoist thought, and that of Zhuangzi, a master who synthesized and developed Taoist thought, and his disciples and later followers. Taoism was among the various schools of thought in the pre-Qin period. Therefore, the Taoist thought and representative scholars of this period are usually called pre-Qin Taoism, which occupies a dominant position in the entire history of Taoist thought and culture.[211]

老庄思想以其超越自我、解构主体、追求自由、逍遥不羁的思想风格和尊重自然、顺道"无为"、消极避世的处世哲学，对以儒学为主体的传统文化形成了一种反思和救济，使中国传统文化刚健有为、自强不息的同时又具有圆润和谐、柔中带刚的文化风格。[212]

Featuring an ideological style of transcending the self, deconstructing the subject, pursuing freedom, and being unrestrained, and a life philosophy of respecting nature, practicing "inaction" according to the Tao, and passively withdrawing from society, the Lao-Zhuang thought embodies a reflection on and relief of the traditional culture that highlights Confucianism. It endows traditional Chinese culture with the characteristics of being vigorous and striving constantly for self-improvement, as well as the styles of mellowness, harmony, and a hint of firmness within its softness.[212]

杨朱是道家学派的早期人物，战国时期其思想成为显学，盛行一时。作为最早的个人主义的思想者之一，杨朱提出了"为我""贵己""全性保真，不以外物累形"等主张，确立生命最为人的终极价值，并且坚持个体生命的主宰性。当然，杨朱的思想面临

---

212 杨川林、杨英法撰《西方后现代主义思潮与老庄思想的关系探析》，来源《兰州学刊》，2014 年 5 期

着巨大的挑战，最终衰落下去，被更为成熟的老庄思想所替代[213]。

Yang Zhu was a figure in the early stage of the Taoist School. During the Warring States Period, his thought became prominent and popular. As one of the earliest thinkers of individualism, he put forward propositions such as "for myself", "valuing oneself", and "preserving one's true nature and integrity, without being restricted by the external environment", established life as the ultimate value of human beings, and insisted on the dominance of individual life. Of course, in the face of enormous challenges, his thought finally declined and was replaced by the more mature Lao-Zhuang thought.[213]

列子名御寇，郑人，是先秦道家学派代表人物。文献中称其"子列子""列御寇""列子圄寇""列圉寇"。《庄子》《吕氏春秋》《淮南子》《尸子》《战国策》《韩非子》等载有列子之事。[214]

Liezi, whose given name was Yukou, was a native of the State of Zheng and a representative figure of the pre-Qin Taoist school. In the documents, he is referred to as "Master Liezi", "Lie Yukou", "Liezi Yukou" or "Lie Yukou". His deeds are recorded in works such as *Zhuangzi, Lu's Spring and Autumn Annals, Huainanzi, Shizi, Strategies of the Warring States*, and *Hanfeizi*.[214]

通过对于生化论及等同万物的思考，列子最终走向了贵虚。在他看来，道产生了万物，而万物又随顺道的生化而不停运作。万物的终极特性即是生化，任何物体均不能逃脱生化的约束。天地虽然包容万物，但天地也是由道产生，也必须遵循道的规律，最终也会如万物一样归于宇宙。贵虚即是一无所求，将一切看透。因为万物都会消亡，所以人应当努力探寻道的真谛，不应再为无谓的

213　于蕾撰《杨朱思想简论》，来源《文艺生活·文艺理论》，2016 年第 6 期

214　吴芬芬撰《< 列子 > 与 < 列子 > 人生哲学 ———以 < 天瑞 >、< 黄帝 >、< 力命 > 为中心》，来源《郑州大学》，2015 年 5 月

纷争而浪费时光。列子曾向壶子、关尹子、伯昏无人问学，他们先后教导列子要等同物我、纯朴无为，从道的高度来看待生死问题，这些最终都被列子所消化吸收，成为他贵虚论中等同物我思想的组成部分。列子思想虽然也属于老庄道家的范畴，但与老子从大处着眼不同，列子更加倾向于对人自身的探寻。列子对宇宙论的探寻没有如老子一样为生化之源命名，而是通过对万物转化的描述阐释自己的观点，使人切身感到自我与万物没有区别。同时，又强调人应当"雕琢复朴，块然独以其形立"，这便将自我从宇宙论中解放出来，使得人成为一个个体，而不是宇宙的附属。[215]

Through contemplation on the theory of generation and transformation as well as the equivalence between the self and all things, Liezi ultimately established the idea of valuing emptiness. In his view, the Tao gave rise to all things, and all things evolve continuously in accordance with the law of generation and transformation under the Tao. The ultimate characteristic of all things is generation and transformation, and nothing can be free from generation and transformation. Although heaven and earth encompass all things, they were also produced by the Tao and must follow the laws of generation and transformation. Eventually, they will return to the universe like all other things. Valuing emptiness means having no desires and seeing through everything. Since all things will perish, people should strive to explore the essence of the Tao instead of wasting time on meaningless disputes. Liezi once learned from Huzi, Guanyinzi, and Bohun Wuren, and they successively taught him to equate the self with all things, to be simple and inactive, and to view the issue of life and death from the perspective of the Tao. These teachings were eventually absorbed by him and became an integral

---

215　刘佩德撰《列子学研究》，来源《华东师范大学》，2013 年 3 月

part of his thought of equating the self with all things within the theory of valuing emptiness. Liezi's thought can be classified as a part of the Taoism of Laozi and Zhuangzi, but unlike Laozi who took a broad perspective, he was more inclined to explore human beings themselves. Liezi did not name the source of generation and transformation as Laozi did in his exploration of cosmology. Instead, he expounded his views through descriptions of the transformation between all things, making people keenly aware that there is no distinction between the self and all things. At the same time, he emphasized that people should "get rid of external decorations, and return to their authentic and original state", thereby liberating the self from cosmology, and making the individual an independent entity rather than an appendage of the universe.[215]

"无为"作为道家最鲜明的特征，说法不一。总体来看，有消极无为、随波逐流、冷眼旁观、顺其自然、宽刑简政、休养生息等几种观点[216]。

"Non-action" is the most distinctive feature of Taoism, and there are different interpretations of it. Generally, it can be interpreted as follows: passive non-action, going with the flow, being a cold bystander, following the course of nature, implementing lenient punishments and simple governance, and promoting recuperation and revitalization.[216]

道家"无为"既是在顺其自然，也是在屈从环境。"无为"是中国文化的一部分，本身带有自己的利弊。不过，由于浪费时间不可取，无论东西方文化差异无大，任何一个人要想有所作为，就要了解"无为"能够如何节约自己宝贵的时间。

The "non-action" of Taoism means following the course of nature

---

216 李吉春撰《顺其自然的道家》，来源《中华活页文选（高二、高三年级）》，2013 年第 10 期

and submitting to the environment. As one part of Chinese culture, "non-action" has its own advantages and disadvantages. However, wasting time is inadvisable. No matter how big the gap is between the Eastern culture and the Western one, anyone who wants to achieve something must understand how "non-action" can help save his precious time.

无论是战时还是平时，"无为"能退而生、能下而生、能柔而生、能软而生、能弱而生、能输而生，这是无为有所作为的时间条件，以免自己筋疲力尽，还是一事无成，白白做无用功。

Whether in times of war or peace, "non-action" enables one to survive by retreating, by being humble, by being flexible, by being soft, by being weak, and by conceding defeat. These are the temporal conditions for achieving something through non-action, lest one exhaust himself without accomplishing anything and doing useless work in vain.

思想总是背靠时代，面向人类，能找到相似的同类，能够产生无中生有。同理可推，反恐从"动"与"静"层面来说，反恐能分为三大派系：出兵反恐，不出兵反恐，屯兵反恐。

Thoughts always rely on the times and face humanity. They can have counterparts and generate something from nothing. Similarly, from the perspective of the "dynamic" and the "static", counter-terrorism can be divided into three major factions: dispatch of troops, non-dispatch of troops, and stationing troops.

社会瑕瑜互见，出兵反恐强在动，弱也在动；不出兵反恐强在静，弱也在静；屯兵反恐强在不战不和，弱也在不战不和。

Society has both merits and demerits. The advantage of dispatch of troops against terrorism lies in dynamism but its disadvantage also lies in dynamism; the advantage of non-dispatch of troops lies in statism but its disadvantage also lies in statism; the advantage of stationing troops lies in neither war nor peace but its disadvantage also lies in neither war nor peace.

反恐三大派系都有自己的"性格"，这些反恐派系各有自己的长处和短处，却都可以大行其道。就像在21世纪，即便俄联邦的俄式反恐只适合苏联，不过，由于20世纪组建起来的苏联是超级大国，俄式反恐照样有令人研究的价值。

Each counter-terrorism faction has a "character" and each has its own advantage and disadvantage. However, all of them can become dominant. For example, in the 21st century, even though the Russian-style counter-terrorism of the Russian Federation is only suitable for the Soviet Union, given that the Soviet Union, established in the 20th century, was a superpower, Russian-style counter-terrorism still has its research value.

无论世人采取反恐三大派系哪一种派系进行反恐，都要有十足的把握，不能便宜他人，才能放心进行反恐。充足的物质基础，是反恐三大派系必须备好的必需品。就像明朝万历年间，中国朝鲜两国联合数年抗击日本侵略者，取得了战争最后的胜利。这场发生在东北亚朝鲜半岛的战争，后勤补给始终扮演着重要角色。

No matter which faction is adopted for counter-terrorism, full confidence is indispensable. If one lets others gain an unearned advantage, one cannot engage in counter-terrorism at ease. For any of the three major counter-terrorism factions, an adequate material foundation is a must. For example, during Emperor Wanli's Reign of the Ming Dynasty, China and Korea jointly resisted the Japanese invaders for several years and achieved the ultimate victory. In this war that took place on the Korean Peninsula in Northeast Asia, logistical support played an important role all the time.

壬辰倭乱是中国明万历朝时期日本侵略朝鲜的战争，韩国和朝鲜称之为壬辰倭乱。此时的朝鲜处于李氏王朝时期，国内长期和平，武备松弛，"人不知兵二百余年"。而朝堂上又党争不断，互相倾轧，政治日趋腐败[217]。

The Imjin War was a war in which Japan invaded Korea during Emperor Wanli's Reign of the Ming Dynasty. It is referred to as the Ren Chen Japanese Turmoil in South Korea and North Korea. At that time, Korea was under the Joseon Dynasty. Due to long-term domestic peace, Korea was lax in military preparedness. "People haven't known about war for more than two hundred years." Moreover, there were constant factional struggles and mutual attacks in the court, and the politics was becoming increasingly corrupt.[217]

1590 年，丰臣写信给朝鲜国王，"吾欲假道贵国，超越山海，直入于明，使其四百州皆入我俗"。1592 年，日本首次侵朝初期进展顺利，丰臣秀吉就开始筹划迁都于北京，自己"居守宁波府"，以便"尊圣意，占领天竺印度"[218]。

In 1590, Toyotomi Hideyoshi wrote to the King of Korea, "I request permission to pass through your country, cross the Shanhai Pass, and directly enter the Ming Empire, so that all its four hundred prefectures will be under my rule." In 1592, Japan made smooth progress in its first invasion of the Korea, and Toyotomi Hideyoshi schemed to move Japan's capital to Beijing, and he himself would "reside in Ningbo Prefecture" so that he could "obey the imperial will and occupy Tianzhu (ancient name for India)."[218]

丰臣秀吉发动的这场战争中朝日三国有不同的叫法：中国史书上称之为"万历朝鲜役"或"万历日本役"；朝鲜史书称之为"壬辰、丁酉倭乱"或"壬辰、丁酉之役"，也叫作"壬辰卫国战争"；

217　金美兰撰《朝鲜时期战争小说中的异国形象研究——以〈崔陟传〉为中心》，来源《青年文学家》，2011 年第 19 期

218　《16 世纪日本丰臣秀吉如何打算迁都北京进军印度?》，凤凰读书（凤凰网）www. ifeng.com，2010 年 4 月 9 日

日本方面称之为"文禄、庆长之役"。这是一场在古代东亚国际关系史上重要的历史事件，它历时 7 年，丰臣秀吉共纠集兵力达到 33 万，其中约 20 万出征朝鲜，名古屋驻兵约 10 万，京都守卫兵力约为 3 万。其军用物资，包括粮食、战船、军备早在 1590 年就开始准备。1592 年 3 月，丰臣秀吉下令 17 万陆军和 3 万余海军出征朝鲜半岛，并亲自坐镇于名古屋。宇喜多秀家为前总指挥，下辖 9 个战斗队，兵分三路向朝鲜进军。[219]

The war launched by Tcyotomi Hideyoshi has different names in China, Korea and Japan. The Chinese historical records refer to it as the "Wanli Korean Campaign" or the "Wanli Japanese Campaign"; the Korean historical records refer to it as the "Ren Chen and Ding You Japanese Invasions" or the "Ren Chen and Dingyou Campaigns," also known as the "Ren Chen and Ding You War of Defense of the Motherland"; the Japanese side refers to it as the "Bunroku and Keichc Campaigns." It was an important historical event in the history of ancient East Asian international relations, and lasted for 7 years. Toyotomi Hideyoshi mobilized a total of 330,000 soldiers, of which about 200,000 were dispatched to invade Korea, about 100,000 were stationed in Nagoya, and about 30,000 were for the defense of Kyoto. As early as 1590, they began to prepare military supplies, including food, warships, and armaments. In March 1592, Toyotomi Hideyoshi ordered 170,000 army soldiers and more than 30,000 naval soldiers to march towards the Korean Peninsula. He himself was in command in Nagoya. Ukita Hideie was the frontline commander-in-chief. He commanded nine combat teams, which advanced towards Korea in three routes.[219]

1592 年 4 月 13 日，丰臣秀吉向集结在九州的日军下达出发命

219　潘慧撰《试论丰臣秀吉及其朝鲜政策》，来源《延边大学》，2009 年

令。侵朝日军先头部队小西行长第一军团 18000 人分乘 400 余艘舰船跨过对马海峡，于 4 月 14 日在釜山登陆，仅用两小时即攻克釜山。随后日军主力部队陆续在朝鲜登陆，以小西行长、加藤清正和黑田长政三个军团为主要突击集团，向汉城迅速推进。5 月 2 日，小西行长军团进入空无一人的汉城。此前两天，朝鲜宣宗李昖已与文武百官一起逃往平壤。6 月 11 日，李昖放弃平壤，再次向中朝边境的义州出逃，并遣使向中国求援[220]。

On April 13, 1592, Toyotomi Hideyoshi ordered the Japanese troops that had been assembled in Kyushu to set out. 18,000 people from Konishi Yukinaga's first legion, as the vanguard of the Japanese army, crossed the Tsushima Strait on more than 400 ships. On April 14, they landed in Busan, and captured it in only two hours. Subsequently, the main forces of the Japanese army landed in Korea successively. With Konishi Yukinaga's legion, Kato Kiyomasa's legion and Kuroda Nagamasa's legion as the main assault groups, they advanced rapidly towards Seoul. On May 2, Konishi Yukinaga's legion entered the deserted Seoul. Two days before that, Yi Yeon, King Seonjo of Joseon, had fled to Pyongyang with all the civil and military officials. On June 11, Yi Yeon abandoned Pyongyang, fled to Yizhou on the China-Korea border, and dispatched envoys to China for aid.[220]

朝鲜国王遣使向明朝告急，要求出兵援助。明朝廷认为，"倭寇之图朝鲜，意实在中国，而我兵之救朝鲜实所以保中国"，故决定援朝抗倭[221]。

The King of Korea dispatched envoys to the Ming Dynasty to

---

220 《借道朝鲜征服中国：丰成秀吉梦碎露梁海战》，海外网财经（海外网）www.haiwainet.cn，2015 年 10 月 21 日

221 《丰臣秀吉野心勃勃入侵朝鲜 万历遣军大胜倭寇》，新浪军事（新浪网）www.sina.com.cn，2014 年 11 月 27 日

report the emergency and request military assistance. "The Japanese pirates invade Korea with the actual intention of invading China. The dispatch of troops by our dynasty to aid Korea is actually a move to safeguard us." Considering this situation, the Ming court decided to aid Korea and resist Japan.[221]

第一次交战以中日议和告终。1597 年，战端重开，丰臣秀吉意外病逝，日军全线撤退，中朝联军趁机追击，最终结束了这场持续数年的战争[222]。

The first engagement ended with peace negotiations between China and Japan. In 1597, the war broke out again. However, Toyotomi Hideyoshi died unexpectedly, and the Japanese army retreated in full force. The Sino-Korean allied forces took this opportunity to pursue the retreating Japanese troops. Eventually, this war that had lasted for several years came to an end.[222]

自战争爆发伊始，明朝不断向朝鲜调兵转饷，为其投入了大量的人力物力和财力，致使国力疲敝。同时，北方还面临着蒙古、女真的军事威胁，明朝必须面对军事和经济上的双重压力。考虑到本国的困境，明廷面对援朝所耗巨额粮饷时，必然有所考量。[223]

From the very beginning of the war, the Ming Dynasty continuously dispatched troops and transported supplies to Korea, and invested a large amount of manpower, material resources, and financial resources. These actions exhausted its national strength. At the same time, the Ming Dynasty faced military threats from the Mongols and the Jurchens in the north. Therefore, it had both military and economic pressures. Considering its own difficulties, the Ming court had to exercise some

---

222　《中韩将如何还原"万历朝鲜战争"》，新华网 www.news.cn，2014 年 7 月 17 日

223　李壮撰《壬辰战争时期明朝与朝鲜的粮饷矛盾》，来源《辽宁大学》，2019 年

restraint in the huge military provisions and funds spent on aiding Korea.[223]

日本的侵略，打破了朝鲜二百余年的和平环境。为了适应卫国战争的需要，李朝政府采取了一些措施，把军事后勤由平时转为战时体制。[224]

Japan's invasion shattered the more than two-hundred-year peaceful environment in Korea. In order to meet the needs of the war of national defense, the Joseon government took some measures to transform the military logistics from a peacetime system to a wartime system.[224]

从国家贡献来看，保家卫国通常都是少数人的历史行为。如此一来，后勤补给可以使主角成配角，配角成主角，波及国家的军事战略和军事战术。一旦国家的军事战略变成军事战术，军事战术变成军事战略，则会使敌人有机可乘，侵略战争会再度打响，恐怖主义容易重新崛起。

From the perspective of national contributions, defending the country is usually a historical action of a few people. As a result, logistical support can turn the leading role into a supporting one, and the supporting role into a leading one. It involves a country's military strategy and military tactics. Once the military strategy turns into military tactics, and the military tactics turn into a military strategy, the enemy will have an opportunity to exploit this situation, the war of aggression may break out again, and terrorism tends to emerge again.

从古至今，国家间爆发战争都会涉及恐怖主义，兵饷粮草的供给问题决定了敌我双方乃至第三国家的安定和稳定程度。在 21 世纪，陆地战提供后勤保障容易，海洋战提供后勤保障困难。于此，

224　徐德源主编《世界军事后勤史—中世纪部分（公元 479—1640）》，金盾出版社 1993 年 10 月

若国家战争是在陆地上打仗，则有长期作战的可能。反之，若国家战争是在海洋上打仗，则有短期作战的可能。

Since ancient times, wars between countries are associated with terrorism. The issue of the supply of military pay, provisions, and supplies determines the level of stability and security of the warring parties as well as third countries. In the 21st century, it is relatively easy to provide logistical support in land wars, while it is more difficult to do so in naval wars. Therefore, if a war between countries takes place on land, there is a possibility of a long-term conflict. On the contrary, if a war occurs at sea, there is a great likelihood of a short-term conflict.

国家间互相作战越长，恐怖主义相应就会越多越强。同理，国家间互相作战越短，恐怖主义相应就会越少越弱。在新世纪，国家与地区的恐怖主义越多，干涉就越多。相反的，恐怖主义越少，干涉就越少。这是综合国力无法改变的战争史实，迫使现代战争也只能短期作战，不能长期作战，将利敌一面压制到最低程度。

The longer a war between countries lasts, the more terrorist incidents there will be and the higher the intensity of terrorism will become. On the contrary, the shorter a war between countries lasts, the fewer terrorist incidents there will be and the lower the intensity of terrorism will become. In the new century, the more terrorist incidents there are in a country or region, the more external interventions there will be. Conversely, the fewer terrorist incidents there are, the fewer external interventions there will be. This is an established fact of war that cannot be changed by national comprehensive strength, forcing modern wars to be short-term rather than long-term, so as to minimize the negative impact on the enemy.

恐怖主义危害国家安全，解决恐怖主义是国家要完成的作业。反恐最终目的是相同的，反恐使用手段却能不同，道和德成为反恐的观察工具。

Terrorism poses a threat to national security, so a country must resolve the issue of terrorism. Counter-terrorism efforts should have the same ultimate goal, yet they can involve different methods. Morality is a tool for evaluating counter-terrorism efforts.

出兵反恐是一场战争。战争会消耗大量金钱，使经济滞后，汇率波动，造成国家动荡，社会不安，政权交替，人民流离失所。就像早在 2007 年时，西方国家以解决恐怖主义的名义发动各种各样的"反恐战争"，就已经成为一种战争灾难。

Dispatch of troops against terrorism is a war, which consumes a large amount of money, leading to economic slowdowns, fluctuations in exchange rates, national unrest, social instability, regime changes, and people becoming homeless. For example, in 2007, Western countries launched various "anti-terrorism wars" in the name of solving the issue of terrorism, but these actions led to disasters.

2007 年 10 月 8 日，英国智库"牛津研究团体"发表报告警告，美国领导的反恐战争已成为"灾难"，布什政府及其盟友必须改变目前在伊拉克和阿富汗的政策，才能击败"基地"组织[225]。

On October 8, 2007, the British think tank "Oxford Research Group" issued a report, warning that the anti-terrorism wars led by the United States had become a "disaster," and that the Bush administration and its allies were unable to defeat al-Qaeda unless they changed their current policies on Iraq and Afghanistan.[225]

据香港《大公报》报道，自从 2001 年 9 月 11 日美国遭到恐怖袭击以来，西方国家的战略不但无法消除伊斯兰极端主义的威胁，

---

225 《英国智库称反恐战争已成灾难》，新浪新闻（新浪网）www.sina.com，2007 年 10 月 9 日

反而火上浇油[226]。

According to Hong Kong's *Ta Kung Pao*, since the September 11, 2001 terrorist attacks in the United States, the strategies of Western countries have not only failed to eliminate the threat of Islamic extremism but also added fuel to the fire.[225]

美国人犯了一个错误，即试图以军事手段寻求解决方案。使用武力是必须的，但武力只能解决表面问题。杀掉恐怖分子，你只是杀掉了工蜂，蜂王是那些传教士，他们在学校和清真寺里宣扬扭曲的伊斯兰教教义，污染并俘虏了年轻人的心灵……恐怖分子说："我乐于献身，之后还会有千千万万的后来人。"[227]

The Americans have made a mistake, as they attempt to find a solution through military measures. The use of force is necessary, but it can only address superficial problems. Killing terrorists is like killing worker bees. However, the real queen bees are those preachers who spread distorted Islamic teachings in schools and mosques. By doing so, they pollute and capture the minds of young people... The terrorists say, "I am willing to sacrifice myself, and there will be thousands of successors."[227]

社会现实是残酷的。反恐武装力量解决恐怖主义就算真的是相对正义，也不能否认政府武装反恐会改变国家或地区，乃至全球的现有秩序。

The social reality is harsh. Even if using counter-terrorism armed forces to solve the issue of terrorism is relatively just, it cannot be denied that counter-terrorism based on government troops can change the existing order of a country, a region, or even the whole world.

226　同上

227　《李光耀：我们靠什么战胜伊斯兰极端主义》，凤凰财经（凤凰网）www.ifeng. com，2015 年 11 月 16 日屯兵反恐有阴谋诡计。"君子不立危墙之下"。反恐没有绝对的对错，是是非非令人唯恐避之不及，害群之马败坏国家形象，见利忘义不是解决恐怖主义的态度。就像在 2019 年，曾经为国争光的俄罗斯特种部队，居然在国内卷入违法乱纪的罪案之中，实在是给国家抹黑。

Stationing troops for counter-terrorism involves intrigues. "A noble man does not stand under a dangerous wall." There is no absolute right or wrong in counter-terrorism, and the complex issues of right and wrong make people eager to keep away from it. Troublemakers will damage a country's image. Being greedy for profit is not the right attitude towards solving the issue of terrorism. For example, in 2019, the Russian special forces that once brought glory to the country were involved in illegal acts and disciplinary violations. This event really tarnished the national reputation.

2019 年，俄媒报道称，6 月 10 日 16 时左右，一名在莫斯科"萨达沃"市场工作的中国公民持有的 1.4 亿卢布（约人民币 1600 万）在位于 Ivana Babushkina 街的一间银行办公室内被劫走。当时一伙俄联邦安全局成员得到银行工作人员报信赶到现场，随后以这笔钱是"黑钱"为由对该商人实施抢劫后分赃[228]。

According to Russian media, at around 16:00 on June 10, 2019, the 140 million rubles (approximately RMB 16 million yuan) held by a Chinese citizen working in the "Sadovaya" market in Moscow was robbed in a bank office on Ivana Babushkina Street. At that time, a group of members of the Federal Security Service of the Russian Federation (FSB) arrived at the spot after being informed by the bank staff. But they

---

228　《俄特种部队指挥官离职 部下曾涉嫌抢劫中国商人》，新浪新闻（新浪网）www.sina.com.cn，2019 年 7 月 16 日

robbed the businessman on the pretext that the money was "dirty money" and divided the spoils.[228]

7 月 5 日，俄罗斯军事法庭以涉嫌抢劫罪名下令批捕 5 名俄罗斯联邦安全局成员，另有 2 名嫌犯被处软禁。据国际文传电讯社此前报道，嫌犯中有 3 人来自阿尔法特种部队，1 人来自信号旗特种部队（Vympel）。此外，曾在俄罗斯联邦安全局特别用途中心 K 科工作过的经济安全处工作人员也有涉案嫌疑[229]。

On July 5, the Russian Military Court ordered the arrest of five FSB members on suspicion of robbery, and two other suspects were placed under house arrest. According to previous reports by the Interfax News Agency, three of the suspects were from the Alpha Special Forces, and one was from the Vympel Special Forces. In addition, some staff members of the Economic Security Department who had worked in the K Department of the FSB's Special Purpose Center were suspected of being involved in the case.[229]

阿尔法特种部队是苏联国家安全委员会（克格勃）所属的特种部队，于 1974 年 7 月 28 日在苏联克格勃主席尤里·安德罗波夫的倡议下成立，主要负责反恐任务，曾先后参与过车臣战争、1993 年俄罗斯宪政危机、2002 年莫斯科轴承厂文化宫大楼剧院人质事件及 2004 年别斯兰人质事件等[230]。

Subordinate to the Committee for State Security of the Soviet Union (KGB), the Alpha Special Forces were established at the initiative of Yuri Andropov, the KGB Chairman on July 28, 1974. Mainly responsible for counter-terrorism tasks, they were involved in the Chechen Wars, the 1993 Russian constitutional crisis, the 2002 Moscow Bearing Factory

---

229　同上

230　同上

Cultural Palace Building Theatre hostage crisis, and the 2004 Beslan school hostage crisis successively.[230]

从实际利益角度出发，屯兵反恐能够更好地做到"有好处就前进，有坏处就后退，是战是和自主选择"。然而，一旦屯兵反恐只知道见风使舵，忽略对内对外的自身形象，早晚沦为跟无恶不作的土匪一般。

From the perspective of practical interests, through stationing troops for counter-terrorism, one will perform better in "advancing in the face of advantages, retreating in the face of disadvantages, and choosing freely between war and peace". However, once the troops stationed for counter-terrorism only know how to trim their sails to the wind and neglect their own internal and external images, they will eventually degenerate into vicious bandits.

和平不代表不需要战争，人类要会以退为进，才能进行铸剑为犁，无忧无虑只能徒增烦恼。比如，20 世纪 70 年代，日本没有反恐武装力量，恶化了日本多个层面的能力。

Peace does not mean that war is unnecessary. Only through strategic withdrawal for advancement can humans beat swords into plowshares. Simply pursuing carefree living will bring more troubles. For example, in the 1970s, Japan had no counter-terrorism armed forces. As a result, its capabilities at different levels worsened.

和世界上其他国家不同，日本的特种部队不占用军事编制，最初的特种部队是从警察建制中开始组建的。1977 年 9 月，恐怖组织日本赤军在孟加拉国的达卡劫持了日本航空公司的客机，由于事先没有处置该类突发事件的任何经验，日本政府非常被动，被迫答应恐怖分子提出的释放在押的 6 名赤军成员，并提供 16 亿日元的要求才使危机得以化解，但是作为一个国家的政府向恐怖分子屈服使得日本政府在世界上非常丢脸，同时也招致国内的一片嘘声。事后，日本政府接受该次事件的教训，迅速于 1977 年在东京警视厅和大阪府警察本部内按照美国、德国、英国等国家的特种部队样式秘密组建特种部队[23]。

Unlike other countries, Japan excludes special forces from the military system. The initial special forces were established within the police system. In September 1977, the terrorist organization Japanese Red Army hijacked a passenger plane of Japan Airlines in Dhaka, Bangladesh. Due to the lack of any experience in handling such emergencies, the Japanese government fell into a very passive position. To resolve the crisis, the government was forced to accede to the terrorists' demands of releasing six members of the Red Army in custody and providing 1.6 billion yen. However, the Japanese government, as a national government, was completely disgraced in the world and caused boos at home due to its submission to the terrorists. After the incident, the Japanese government drew lessons from it, and immediately and secretly established special forces within the Tokyo Metropolitan Police Department and the Osaka Prefectural Police Headquarters in 1977, following the models of the special forces of the United States, Germany, and the United Kingdom.[231]

人命关天。反恐确实需要未雨绸缪，各国组建反恐部队运用武力至上打击恐怖主义，却未必是一条可持续发展道路。由此得出一个道理，军事手段解决恐怖主义是"必须"还是"必需"也是莫衷一是。

Human life is of paramount importance. Advanced preparations are really needed in counter-terrorism, but it may not be sustainable for countries to form counter-terrorism forces and use the principle of the

---

231 《新闻背景：反恐精英之日本警察厅特种突击队》，人民网军事（人民网）www.people.com.cn，2004 年 12 月 13 日

supremacy of force to combat terrorism. Therefore, we can conclude that there is still no consensus on whether the use of military means to solve the issue of terrorism is a "must" or a "requisite".

反恐能力比较弱的人认为"军事手段解决恐怖主义是必须的"，即一定得要，一定要使用出来，不能只作为反恐后备力量。

Those with weaker counter-terrorism capabilities believe that "using military means to solve the issue of terrorism is a must", that is, military means must be employed and cannot serve only as a backup force for counter-terrorism.

反恐能力比较强的人认为"军事手段解决恐怖主义是必需的"，即一定得有，可以只作为反恐后备力量，未必要使用出来。

Those with stronger counter-terrorism capabilities believe that "using military means to solve the issue of terrorism is a requisite", that is, military means must exist and can only be used as a backup force for counter-terrorism. However, whether to use it or not is not necessary.

在"军事手段解决恐怖主义有不确定性"的大浪潮下，各国武力反恐人员早晚要顺应时局擅长口才。武装反恐人员说服能力高超，或能为进攻恐怖分子服务，或能为包围恐怖分子服务，或能为化解恐怖袭击服务，或能为跳出恐怖分子包围圈服务，或能为斩断恐怖分子"左膀右臂"服务。

Under the great trend that "using military means to solve the issue of terrorism involves uncertainty", people engaged in counter-terrorism by force in each country will eventually have to adapt to the current situation and be proficient in eloquence. The excellent persuasive ability of the armed counter-terrorism operatives can serve to attack terrorists, or to encircle terrorists, or to resolve terrorist attacks, or to escape from the terrorists' encirclement, or to sever the terrorists' "close assistants".

报道称，尽管美国当局不断宣称其"绝不与恐怖分子谈判"，但这并非事实。最典型的例证就是当时名噪一时的"伊朗售武事件"。里根政府为了解救美国在黎巴嫩的人质，答应向伊朗秘密出售武器。[232]

According to reports, although the US authorities keep on claiming that they "will never negotiate with terrorists", this is not the truth. The most typical example is the "Incident of Selling Arms to Iran", which became widely-known overnight. In order to rescue the American hostages in Lebanon, the Reagan administration promised to secretly sell weapons to Iran.[232]

此外，其他国家也曾有过类似举动。2011 年，以色列用 1027 名巴勒斯坦人交换吉拉德·沙利特 (Gilad Shalit)，这一事件为以后的和谈打开大门。2013 年 7 月，以色列总理内塔尼亚胡也为囚犯交换大开绿灯。此外，西班牙政府也曾于 1989 年流露出与巴斯克分裂组织"埃塔"（ETA ）谈判的意愿，而这也促成双方于 2011 年最终举行和平会谈。除此之外，最著名的例子是英国政府曾与爱尔兰共和军就结束北爱尔兰动乱进行谈判。[233]

In addition, there were once similar actions in other countries. In 2011, Israel exchanged 1,027 Palestinians for Gilad Shalit. This event opened the door for future peace negotiations. In July 2013, Israeli Prime Minister Benjamin Netanyahu gave the green light to prisoner exchanges. In addition, the Spanish government showed its willingness to negotiate with the Basque separatist organization ETA in 1989. This eventually led to peace negotiations in 2011. In addition, the most famous example is that the British government once negotiated with the Irish Republican Army to end the unrest in Northern Ireland.[233]

---

232 《外媒：美国曾多次与恐怖分子谈判"自食其言"》人民网国际（人民网）www. people.com.cn，2014 年 6 月 5 日

233 同上

反恐武装人员有"三寸不烂之舌"，其作用不下于使用冷热兵器作战，反恐谈判实为一门"多喷口水，少流鲜血"的变化学问。而且，反恐武装人员擅长谈判，能够为出兵反恐、不出兵反恐、屯兵反恐"如虎添翼"。反恐人员有深厚的信息知识量才能多技多艺，文武双全。

The persuasive tongue of an armed counter-terrorism operative is no less effective than using cold and hot weapons in combat. Counter-terrorism negotiation is an art of transformation that involves "shedding more words and less blood". Moreover, the proficiency of the armed counter-terrorism operative in negotiation can be of great help to dispatch of troops for counter-terrorism, non-dispatch of troops for counter-terrorism, and stationing troops for counter-terrorism. Only with a large amount of information and knowledge can the counter-terrorism operative be versatile and proficient in both civil and military affairs.

战争时期，国家开支会比平常加剧增多。打一个比方，在战场对决，5万人消耗5万人粮食，20万人消耗60万人粮食，60万人消耗80万人粮食，80万人消耗120万人粮食……以此类推，反恐战争在战争前后，会增加人民的生活负担。

During a war, the national expenditure will increase dramatically. For example, in a battlefield confrontation, 50,000 people may consume as much food as is usually consumed by 50,000 people, 200,000 people may consume as much food as is usually consumed by 600,000 people, 600,000 people may consume as much food as is usually consumed by 800,000 people, and 800,000 people may consume as much food as is usually consumed by 1.2 million people...... Before and after a counter-terrorism war, the living burden of the people will increase.

"三军未动，粮草先行"。打仗不能投机取巧，其中很直接一的点，就是作战双方在后勤补给上宁愿多投入物质基础，也不能缺衣少食进行攻防战。相比出兵和屯兵反恐，不出兵反恐的确会让恐怖分子得到更多调整恢复的时间。但是，动用经济手段杀伤恐怖分子却也是一种行之有效的手段。

"Before the troops move, provisions should be made earlier." One cannot resort to tricks in fighting. A very straightforward point is that both sides in a battle would rather invest more in material resources for logistical support than conduct offensive and defensive battles while suffering from shortages of food and clothing. Compared with dispatch of troops and stationing troops, non-dispatch of troops for counter-terrorism will indeed give terrorists more time to adjust and recover. However, employing economic measures against terrorists can also be effective.

"兵马未动，粮草先行"这一古训是前人对历次战争的经验总结，它反映了后勤保障在军事行动中的特殊地位和作用。早在春秋时期，军事家孙武就断言"军无辎重则亡，无粮食则亡，无委积则亡"，阐明了后勤补给与军队存亡的关系。虽然现在"兵马"与"粮草"的含义发生了很大的变化，但其原理对现代战役仍然具有十分积极的指导意义[234]。

From the experience of previous wars, our predecessors summarized the old saying "Food and fodder should go ahead of troops and horses." It reflects the special position and role of logistical support in military operations. As early as the Spring and Autumn Period, the military strategist Sun Wu asserted that "An army will perish without weapons, food or accumulated supplies", expounding the relationship between logistical support and the survival of the army. Although "troops and horses" and "food and fodder" have quite different meanings nowadays,

---

234 王加文、黄光华撰《从"兵马未动，粮草先行"看现代战役后勤保障》，来源《军事经济研究》，1992 年第 6 期

this principle is still of great positive guiding significance to modern battles.[234]

2006 年，为打击日益猖獗的恐怖主义，欧盟执行委员会草拟一项新法案，将对企业课处"反恐税"，预估小型企业每年约缴交 2000 英镑，中型企业则是 91400 英镑，一旦实施将对企业经营造成沉重负担。[235]

In 2006, in order to combat the increasingly rampant terrorism, the European Commission drafted a bill to impose a "counter - terrorism tax" on enterprises. It is estimated that small enterprises would pay about £2,000 per year, and medium-sized enterprises would pay £91,400 per year. Once implemented, it would impose a heavy burden on business operations.[235]

英国小型企业协会警告，一旦欧盟强制施行反恐新规定，将有许多会员因此破产，"如此一来反而让恐怖主义获得胜利"。[236]

The Association of Small Businesses in the UK warned that if the European Union enforced the new counter-terrorism regulations, many of its members would go bankrupt as a result, "This will actually lead to the victory of terrorism"[236]

据外媒报道，英国警察和犯罪事务专员协会称，到 2020 年前，英格兰和威尔士警方需新增逾 13 亿英镑用以有效的安全保障行动。[237]

According to foreign media, the Association of Police and Crime Commissioners in the UK said that by 2020, the police in England and Wales would have to spend an additional more than £1.3 billion on

---

235 《欧盟计划向企业征收"反恐税"料造成企业重负》，中国新闻网国际新闻（中国新闻网）www.chinanews.com.cn，2006 年 11 月 20 日

236 同上

237 《英国警方需新增逾 13 亿英镑拨款 以打击恐怖主义》新浪军事（新浪网）www.sina.com.cn，2017 年 10 月 31 日

effective security operations.[237]

据悉，该款项将用于新增 5000 名打击新型犯罪的专员以及 1100 名武装警察（特种部队）。[238]

It was reported that the fund would be used to employ 5,000 more commissioners who would combat new types of crimes, and 1,100 more armed policemen (special forces).[238]

新的拨款需求与这些地区犯罪环境的恶化有关，其中包括恐怖主义等新型犯罪的出现以及移民数量的日趋增长。[239]

The new funding requirements were related to the deterioration of the crime environment in these areas, including the emergence of terrorism and other new types of crimes, as well as the increasing number of immigrants.[239]

在峰回路转的社会，无论是古代、近代、现代，解决恐怖主义未必要以经济指导为主力。虽然，经济反恐会形成物欲横流的社会局面，不过，政治反恐却是阴暗丛生，军事反恐必是杀戮过重，外交反恐总是虚情假意。即使经济反恐不是最佳的选择，却也不是最差的选择。说到底，人要穿衣吃饭才能生存，人可以不需要政治、军事、外交，却离不开经济。

In a society full of twists and turns, whether in ancient, modern or contemporary times, economic guidance does not necessarily have to play a dominant role in solving the issue of terrorism. Counter-terrorism through economic means may cause a social situation in which people are indulged in their material desires. However, counter-terrorism through political means is full of evil, counter-terrorism through military means leads to excessive killing, and counter-terrorism through diplomatic

---

238 同上
239 同上

means involves hypocrisy. Even though counter-terrorism through economic means is not the best choice, it is not the worst either. After all, people need food and clothes to survive. They can do without politics, military and diplomacy, but they cannot do without the economy.

自古以来，安身立命与经济实力就是一对难舍难离的关系。物质基础决定一个人乃至每个人子孙后代的祸福荣辱，也是国泰民安的经济保障。

Since ancient times, making a living and economic strength have formed an inseparable relationship. The material foundation determines the fortune, misfortune, honor and shame of people and even their descendants, and it is also the economic guarantee for national stability and people's well-being.

既然解决恐怖主义需要拨出反恐经费，才能有的放矢，那么，"物质押金"就很有可能成为国际合作反恐的一部分，甚至"反恐有物质抵押"可能比多国合作出兵打击恐怖主义，更加深入人心。就像从 20 世纪开始，美国就时常对古巴实施不友好的国家政策，导致有的古巴人就对美国不友好。在 21 世纪，美国要改善本国和古巴的关系，依靠反复无常的政策，就是一纸空谈。

Solving the issue of terrorism in a targeted manner requires counter-terrorism funds, Therefore, "material deposits" may become part of international cooperation in counter-terrorism, and even "material collateral for counter-terrorism" may gain more popularity than multinational cooperation in dispatching troops to combat terrorism. Since the 20th century, the United States has often implemented unfriendly national policies towards Cuba, making some Cubans unfriendly to the United States. In the 21st century, relying on capricious policies for the United States to improve its relations with Cuba is just empty talk.

美国在 1982 年把古巴列为支持恐怖主义国家。当时的古巴被美国指控为"支持非洲、拉丁美洲的武装叛乱和西班牙恐怖组织埃塔"。但实际上美国此举更多的是政治考虑，是对古巴经济封锁的一部分。将古巴列为恐怖主义国家后，国际金融机构与古巴的任何资金往来和合作都会受到制裁，因此古巴事实上无法进入国际金融市场。就连古巴设在华盛顿的行使一部分大使馆功能的办事处，也因为美国政府这个决定无法在任何银行开设账户 [240]。

In 1982, the United States listed Cuba as a country that supported terrorism. At that time, Cuba was accused by the United States of "supporting armed rebellions in Africa and Latin America, as well as backing the Spanish terrorist organization ETA." However, this act was actually more out of political considerations, serving as part of its policy of economic blockade against Cuba. After Cuba was listed as a terrorist country, any financial transactions and cooperation between international financial institutions and Cuba were subject to sanctions, making Cuba unable to enter the international financial market. Even the office of Cuba in Washington, which performed some embassy functions, was unable to open an account in any bank due to this decision of the US government.[240]

在 2015 年，当时的美国总统巴拉克·奥巴马宣布恢复与古巴的外交关系。奥巴马放松了贸易禁运，取消了对旅行、资金转移和海军管制的一些限制 [241]。

In 2015, the then US President Barack Obama announced the restoration of diplomatic relations with Cuba. He relaxed the trade embargo and lifted some restrictions on tourism, fund transfer and naval

---

240 《奥巴马决定将古巴移出"支恐名单"迟来 4 天的宣布背后有玄机》，环球国际（环球网）www.huanqiu.com，2015 年 4 月 16 日

241 《古巴总统抨击美国制裁是一种"种族灭绝"政策》，腾讯网 www.qq.com，2019 年 9 月 25 日

control.[241]

2015 年，很多古巴人以平常心态面对这一变化，因为他们清楚美国人不会轻易放弃对古巴数十年的禁运。还有分析人士认为，美国放下"架子"与古巴改善关系，但最终改变古巴社会主义政权的图谋不会变，且在形式上将使古巴政府更难以对付，古巴处理与美国关系所涉及的因素更多了，更复杂了[242]。

In 2015, many Cubans faced this change with a normal state of mind, for they knew that the American government would not easily give up the decades-long embargo against Cuba. Some analysts believed that although the United States "lowered its stance" to improve relations with Cuba, its attempt to ultimately change Cuba's socialist regime would not change. And in form, it would add more difficulties for the Cuban government to deal with. The factors involved in Cuba's handling of its relations with the United States increased and became more complicated.[242]

2015 年的古巴，还有部分人对美国保持警惕。哈瓦那市民胡利奥对《环球时报》记者说，古美关系变化，不应损害古巴人的利益，包括古巴的独立和自由。普通人从古巴革命中获得的经济和社会实惠也不应被剥夺。古巴有良好的教育和医疗，是古巴制度的成就。古巴不应该改变这一切，我们仍应像过去一样生活。我们现在居住的房子很多是革命后分配给穷人的。美国人如果有什么想法，如归还，古巴人不会答应。古巴革命不会允许复辟的。他认为，古巴革命不会让古巴人民失望，相信政府会以聪明的方式处理古美关系，与美国人打了这么多年，古巴人有自由的方式去应对古美新型关系[243]。

---

242 《古巴民众平和看待古美解冻 部分人仍对美保持警惕》，环球国际（环球网）www.huanqiu.com，2015 年 4 月 13 日

243 同上

In 2015, some Cubans still remained vigilant against the United States. Julio, a citizen of Havana, told a reporter from *Global Times* that changes in Cuba-US relations should not harm the interests of Cubans, including Cuba's independence and freedom. "The economic and social benefits that ordinary people have obtained from the Cuban revolution should not be deprived. Cuba boasts good education and medical care, which are achieved through the Cuban system. All these should not be changed. We should live a life as we did in the past. Many of the houses we live in were allocated to the poor after the revolution. If the Americans intend to return the houses to landlords or have similar ideas, Cubans will not agree. The Cuban revolution will not allow a restoration." He believed that the Cuban revolution would not let down the Cubans, and that the government could handle Cuba-US relations in a clever way. "After fighting against the United States for so many years, Cubans can deal with the new Cuba-US relations freely."[243]

特朗普政府上台后，美国再次收紧对古巴的政策，试图结束奥巴马执政时对古巴开放的局面[244]。

After the Donald John Trump assumed office, the United States again tightened its policies towards Cuba, attempting to end the situation of opening up towards Cuba during Obama's tenure.[244]

2018 年 9 月 10 日，特朗普签署法令，将 1962 年对古巴实施的贸易禁运措施延长一年，美国公司和旅客被禁止与制裁名单上的古巴实体进行任何业务往来。11 月 1 日，联合国大会以压倒性多数通过决议，敦促美国解除对古巴的禁运[245]。

On September 10, 2018, Trump signed a decree, which extended the

---

244 《特朗普政府对古巴制裁加大 古巴外交部：侵略升级》，新浪新闻（新浪网）www.sina.com.cn，2019 年 3 月 6 日

245 同上

trade embargo against Cuba implemented in 1962 for another year, and prohibited US companies and travelers from engaging in any businesses with Cuban entities on the sanctions list. On November 1, the United Nations General Assembly adopted a resolution by an overwhelming majority, urging the United States to lift the embargo against Cuba.[245]

礼多人不怪。美国要想真心实意和古巴正常交往，美国政府就需要给古巴支付"诚意金"，来证明美国对古巴友好的诚意，以防风险。

More gifts, no offense. If the US government really intends to have normal interaction with Cuba, it should pay a "good-faith deposit" to Cuba to prove its sincerity in being friendly to Cuba and prevent risks.

政府打击恐怖主义需要国家的市场手段，恐怖分子兴风作浪也利用国家的市场手段。政府可以遵循市场规律，主要用经济手段，并辅助政治、军事、外交等手段来进攻恐怖分子。只要政府部署得当，统筹规划，协调发展，对恐怖分子绝水断粮，必能指日可待恐怖分子水米不进而死。这样，哪怕恐怖分子富可敌国，最后也只能用金钱来陪葬，长埋冢下。

The government needs to make use of national market-based means to combat terrorism. Terrorists also leverage national market-based means to create trouble. The government can attack terrorists by following market rules, mainly employing economic means, supplemented by political, military, and diplomatic means. As long as the government makes appropriate and comprehensive deployment, insists on coordinated development, and deprives terrorists of basic necessities, they will surely be subdued due to lack of resources in the near future. In this way, even if terrorists are extremely wealthy, they will ultimately be doomed along with their wealth and meet their downfall.

只是人在具体行动上怎么"活活渴死饿死恐怖分子"，没有绝对的答案。只要对反恐有效. 成果大小都不要介意。就像可口可乐既能被恐怖分子利用，沦为恐怖主义的附属品，也能破格为反恐牵线搭桥。如此，如何预防、斩断、杜绝歹人对有经济价值的东西下黑手，是有必要的。

However, in terms of specific actions, there is no standard answer to the question how to "make the terrorists run out of ammunition and provisions." As long as an action is effective in counter-terrorism, the size of the achievements is not important. For example, Coca-Cola can be used by terrorists as an accessory of terrorism, but it can also serve as a go-between for counter-terrorism. Therefore, it is necessary to prevent terrorists from playing dirty tricks on things of economic value.

"基地"组织的触角还伸向了各个不同的产业，利用多种经营活动赚钱。美国情报部门甚至发出警报："世界上每卖出一听可口可乐，也许就会给本·拉登的口袋增加一笔收入。"这话听起来夸张，却有事实依据，因为生产可乐要使用阿拉伯树胶，而这种树胶多来自苏丹的树胶厂，其幕后老板很可能就是拉登本人。2002 年美国公布的《恐怖组织金融体系》报告称，"基地"组织就像一家能量巨大的控股公司，跟随拉登左右的"基地"高层人员中不乏金融学家[246]。

Al-Qaeda also extended its influence to various industries, making money through different business activities. The US intelligence community even warned: "The selling of every Coca-Cola in the world may add a sum of money to Osama bin Laden's pocket." This statement sounds exaggerated, but it is based on facts. The reason is that the production of cola requires gum arabic, most of which comes from gum

---

246 《偷渡卖毒品洗黑钱，"基地"组织为钱啥都干》，人民网国际（人民网）www people.com.cn，2003 年 9 月 10 日

factories in Sudan, and the behind-the-scenes boss may well be bin Laden. According to *The Financial System of Terrorist Organizations*, a report released in the United States in 2002, Al-Qaeda was like a powerful holding company, and among the senior personnel around bin Laden, there were many financial experts.[246]

"基地"组织还掌握着一张金融大网，为其洗黑钱和进行资金周转。因此"基地"组织完全有可能应付各国政府针对它的联合金融封锁。据悉，拉登在全球 50 个国家的几百家银行、公司以及慈善机构都有户头。为防止资产被西方国家冻结，拉登还一直利用活跃于中亚一带的地下钱庄。而全球电子货币卡的普及，也增加了追查恐怖分子洗钱的难度[247]。

Al-Qaeda also mastered a gigantic financial network for money-laundering and capital turnover. Therefore, it was fully capable of coping with the joint financial blockade imposed by governments of different countries. It was reported that bin Laden had opened accounts in hundreds of banks, companies and charitable organizations in 50 countries around the world. To prevent his assets from being frozen by Western countries, bin Laden leveraged underground banks active in Central Asia. Moreover, the popularization of electronic money cards in the world also increased the difficulty of investigating money-laundering of terrorists.[247]

此外，走私军火、地下投资和制假贩假都是"基地"组织的生财之道[248]。

In addition, arms smuggling, underground investment, and production and sales of fakes were all ways for Al-Qaeda to make money.[248]

247　同上

248　同上

违法犯罪组织在社会上权力寻租司空见惯，充足的资金保障是恐怖组织 ISIS 的招募活动如此成功的原因之一。2015 年开始，ISIS 被多个国家用各种手段打击，ISIS 开始走"下坡路"，其中该组织由于资金不足，加剧了"祸起萧墙"接连不断。

It is very common for criminal organizations to seek rent by leveraging power in society. Sufficient financial support was one of the reasons why the recruitment of the terrorist organization ISIS was so successful. From 2015, attacked by various means by different countries, ISIS started to decline. In particular, insufficient funds led to more and fiercer internal conflicts within the organization.

ISIS或减薪或发不起薪水使得爆发内讧和械斗[249]、ISIS成员"辞职跳槽"[250]、ISIS成员有人临阵脱逃[251]、打击恐怖组织ISIS士气，ISIS成员忠诚度和参与度受到了影响[252]，为了填补资金缺口，ISIS居然从组织成员身上摘取器官到黑市贩卖[253]……

Internal conflicts and armed fights occurred within ISIS due to reduction of salaries or inability to pay salaries;[249] some ISIS members "resigned and changed jobs";[250] some ISIS members deserted in the face of battle;[251] the morale, loyalty and participation level of ISIS members were impacted due to combats against terrorist organizations;[252] in order

---

249　《ISIS 或已发不起工资 深夜内讧爆发武装冲突》，界面新闻（界面网）www.jiemian.com，2016 年 4 月 6 日

250　《工资缩水 75% 数百名 ISIS 武装分子辞职跳槽》，新浪财经（新浪网）www.sina.com.cn，2015 年 10 月 2 日

251　《ISIS 将魔爪伸向自己人 冻死活埋叛逃者》，界面新闻（界面网）www.jiemian.com，2016 年 5 月 13 日

252　《ISIS 财政危机？奥巴马的目标近了》，新浪财经（新浪网）www.sina.com.cn，2016 年 4 月 6 日

253　《ISIS 势力范围锐减超 1/4》，和讯新闻（和讯网）www.hexun.com，2016 年 10 月 10 日

to fill the fund gap, ISIS should extract organs from its members and sell them on the black market[253]...

确实，政府不出兵反恐也是有缺陷的，但是出兵反恐和屯兵反恐也有不妥之处。例如，出兵反恐会误杀误伤平民；不出兵反恐会干扰商品贸易，让人饱饿不定；屯兵反恐容易上演政府角力博弈的"戏码"，引酿出国家级别的危机。

Indeed, non-dispatch of troops against terrorism has its drawbacks, but dispatch of troops and stationing troops also have defects. For example, dispatch of troops may lead to accidental killing and injury of civilians; non-dispatch of troops may disturb commodity trade and affect people's livelihood; stationing troops may cause government power play, leading to a national crisis.

2017 年 4 月，美国国防部 1 日发表声明说，由美国主导的打击极端组织"伊斯兰国"（ISIS）军事行动"内在决心"自 2014 年开始以来，已"无意"中造成至少 229 名平民死亡 [254]。

According to a statement issued by the U.S. Department of Defense on April 1, 2017, since the launch of the U.S.-led military operation "Operation Inherent Resolve" against the extremist organization Islamic State of Iraq and Syria (ISIS) in 2014, it had "unintentionally" caused the deaths of at least 229 civilians.[254]

美国有线电视新闻网（CNN）报道称，这一统计并不包含上个月疑似由国际联盟对伊拉克北部重镇摩苏尔展开的空袭致死情况，因此平民死亡人数可能还会大幅上升 [255]。

According to a report by Cable News Network (CNN), this statistic did not include the suspected civilian deaths caused by the air strikes

---

254 《美军承认打击 ISIS 行动已致 229 名平民丧生》，界面新闻天下（界面新闻）www. jiemian.com，2017 年 4 月 3 日

255 同上

carried out by the international coalition on Mosul, a major city in northern Iraq, last month. Therefore, the number of civilian deaths was likely to rise significantly.[255]

2014 年 12 月，IS 的财政主管 Sheikh Abu Saad 公布的 IS 年度预算为 20 亿美元，这还不包括 2.5 亿美元的毒品收入。但更多反恐专家表示，该组织的年收入远不止 20 亿美元。2015 年，该组织以各种非法手段大肆敛财，被美国官员称为已知的最富有恐怖组织[256]。

In December 2014, the annual budget announced by Sheikh Abu Saad, the financial director of ISIS, was $2 billion, which did not include the drug income of $250 million. However, more anti-terrorism experts said that the annual income of the organization was far more than $2 billion. In 2015, it was regarded by U.S. officials as the wealthiest known terrorist organization, which had amassed a large amount of wealth through various illegal means.[256]

《华尔街日报》曾指出，西方国家和阿拉伯世界希望切断 IS 的金融资源，但他们面对的是一个棘手的问题：打击有助于 IS 融资的经济活动可能使 IS 控制地区发生人道主义危机[257]。

The Wall Street Journal once pointed out that Western countries and the Arab world hoped to cut off the financial resources of the IS, but they faced a thorny problem: Cracking down on the economic activities that contribute to IS financing may lead to humanitarian crises in the areas controlled by IS.[257]

一名西方的反恐官员就表示："能制止 IS 获取财产吗？实际上不能，因为他们已经拥有大量财富。你必须干扰贸易网。可如果你

256　《制造巴黎恐怖主义袭击的 IS 是从哪里获得钱财的?》，搜狐财经（搜狐网）www.sohu.com，2015 年 11 月 16 日

257　同上

干扰商品贸易，比如，食品，几千平民都有饿死的危险。"[258]

A Western counter-terrorism official said, "Can we stop the Islamic State (IS) from acquiring property? In fact, we can't, because they already have a large amount of wealth. You have to disrupt the trade network. But if you disrupt the trade of goods, for example, food, there is a risk that thousands of civilians will starve to death."[258]

2014 年，在叙利亚和伊拉克这两个打击极端组织"伊斯兰国"的主要战场上，形势日趋严峻。土叙边境重镇科巴尼，库尔德人与极端组织的对抗持续胶着。在伊拉克西部，与叙利亚相连的安巴尔省 80% 已经失守，极端组织的触角甚至延伸到距伊拉克首都巴格达西北仅 29 公里的阿布格莱布。虽然美国及其领导的"国际联盟"在持续对极端组织进行空中打击，但就连美国人自己也承认，仅靠空袭难以阻止极端组织攻势[259]。

In 2014, the situation became increasingly severe on the main battlefields against the extremist organization "Islamic State" in Syria and Iraq. In Kobani, a key town on the Turkish-Syrian border, the confrontation between the Kurds and the extremist organization remained in a stalemate. In western Iraq, 80% of the territory of Anbar Province, which was connected to Syria, was lost, and the extremist organization even extended its influence to Abu Ghraib, which was only 29 kilometers northwest of Baghdad, the capital of Iraq. Although the United States and the "Global Coalition to Defeat ISIS" led by it continuously carried out air strikes against the extremist organization, even the Americans admitted that they could hardly stop the offensive of the extremist organization by relying on air strikes alone.[259]

---

258 同上

259 《军报：美打造反恐联盟力不从心 空袭 IS 更像闹剧》，搜狐军事（搜狐网）www. sohu.com，2014 年 10 月 15 日综合来说，此次中东局势深陷动荡，除了叙利亚和伊拉克自身不稳定因素外，也是各国出于各自地缘政治利益的考虑，暗地勾结、火上浇油，做出了一系列灾难性选择的结果[260]。

Generally speaking, this turbulent situation in the Middle East was not only caused by the internal instability of Syria and Iraq, but also the result of a series of disastrous choices made by various countries, which secretly colluded and added fuel to the fire out of considerations for their respective geopolitical interests.[260]

解决恐怖主义是需要充分的时间的，幻想一步登天解决恐怖主义是给恐怖主义喘息的机会。恐怖主义有上千年的历史，用几千年时间来解决恐怖主义是正常思路。

It will take ample time to solve the problem of terrorism. The illusion of solving terrorism in one step actually gives terrorism a chance to catch its breath. Terrorism has a history of over a thousand years, and it is common sense to take several thousand years to address it.

所以，沉浸在短时间内能让全世界没有恐怖主义，使全世界"越反越恐"成了必然，而非偶然。由此，遵道循德的以慢打快，也能成为一种反恐的主流思想。

Therefore, it is not occasional but inevitable that being immersed in the fantasy of eliminating terrorism worldwide within a short period of time will lead to a situation described as "the higher the intensity of counter-terrorism is, the more rampant terrorism becomes". Therefore, the concept of using a slow approach to deal with a fast-moving threat in accordance with moral principles can become a mainstream ideology in counter-terrorism.

"9·11"事件前，美国的国际地位可以说达到了有史以来的最

260　同上

高点。当时苏联解体，两极格局消失，美国的经济、政治、军事地位空前突出。这时美国试图按照自己的意志构筑新的国际秩序，建立一极世界。特别是，小布什政府上台伊始，便坚持部署 NMD 和 TMD，增加国防预算，拒不执行《京都议定书》，加强对伊拉克的制裁，暂缓改善美朝关系，对俄罗斯与中国的政策都趋于强硬。美国人从来没有这样自信和霸道，更想不到有人会在此时主动对美国本土发动袭击。然而就在 2001 年 9 月 11 日，恐怖分子通过劫持民航飞机，对美国发动了史无前例的攻击。纽约的标志性建筑——世界贸易中心双子大厦倒塌，美国国防部所在地五角大楼遭到重创，几千名在那里工作的无辜人员瞬间被夺去了生命。历史如此相似，很多美国人，包括美国总统小布什在内，都惊呼这天发生了"21 世纪的珍珠港事件"[261]。

Before the September 11 terrorist attacks, it can be said that the international status of the United States had reached the highest point in its history. At that time, the disintegration of the Soviet Union led to the disappearance of the bipolar pattern, and the economic, political, and military status of the United States became unprecedentedly prominent. Then, the United States attempted to build a new international order according to its own will and create a unipolar world. In particular, shortly after George W. Bush assumed office, the government insisted on deploying the National Missile Defense (NMD) and the Theater Missile Defense (TMD), increased the defense budget, refused to implement *Kyoto Protocol*, strengthened sanctions against Iraq, suspended the improvement of US-North Korea relations, and adopted tougher policies towards Russia and China. Americans were so confident and overbearing

---

261 吕建刚撰《"9·11"事件与"珍珠港事件"之比较》，来源《首都师范大学学报（社会科学版）》，2004 年第 S2 期

that they never imagined that someone would launch an attack on the American mainland. However, on September 11, 2001, terrorists launched an unprecedented attack on the United States by hijacking civilian airliners. The Twin Towers of the World Trade Center, the iconic buildings in New York, collapsed, and the Pentagon, the headquarters of the United States Department of Defense, was severely damaged. Thousands of innocent people working there lost their lives in an instant. History was so similar. Many Americans, including President George W. Bush, exclaimed that the "Pearl Harbor Incident of the 21st century" had occurred on that day.[261]

2011 年 5 月 1 日，美国总统奥巴马宣布，"基地"组织领导人乌萨马·本·拉登死于美军当天的军事行动。本·拉登之死结束了美国从 20 世纪 90 年代即对他展开的追捕，自然是美国反恐战争的一大胜利。但是，2011 年的前几年，本·拉登只作为"基地"组织精神领袖存在，很少直接指挥恐怖袭击。他的死难以使美国走出"反恐战争越反越恐"的怪圈[262]。

On May 1, 2011, US President Barack Obama announced that Osama bin Laden, the leader of al-Qaeda, had been killed in a military operation carried out by the US military on that day. The death of bin Laden put an end to the pursuit that the United States had launched against him since the 1990s. Of course, it was a major victory in the US war on terror. However, in the few years before 2011, bin Laden only existed as the spiritual leader of al-Qaeda and seldom directly commanded terrorist attacks. His death could hardly help the United States get out of the vicious circle described as "the higher the intensity

---

262 《本·拉登之死难解"越反越恐"怪圈》，腾讯新闻（腾讯网）www.qq.com，2011 年 5 月 2 日

of counter-terrorism is, the more rampant terrorism becomes".[262]

自古以来，任何人要养家糊口都要有合法收入。社会各个方面竞争都很激烈，就是在切断安身立命的经济来源。在中国历史长河中，从国家角度来说，官逼民反通常并非军事问题，乃是经济问题，其区别在于政府所下达的经济政策是直接原因，还是主要原因，以及重要原因的不同。

Since ancient times, anyone must have a legitimate income to make a living. Excessively fierce competition in all aspects of society is tantamount to cutting off people's sources of income for making a living. In the long history of China, from the national perspective, it was usually not due to military reasons but due to economic reasons that the people were compelled to rise up against the government. The difference lies in whether the economic policies formulated by the government are the direct cause, the main cause, or an important cause.

"安定"是民生的，"稳定"是政治的；"安定"是"民本位"的，"稳定"是"官本位"的；"安定"是百姓要求，"稳定"是官员要求。"安定"的本质是老百姓的幸福安宁、"心安神定"，在此基础上带来社会秩序的安定有序，所以其重要性不言而喻。相比"稳定"来说，"安定"是形而下的，与百姓更贴心，不会成为"帽子"；用"安定"来衡量社会现象，有着充分的暖色调。求"稳定"，往往可动用高压手段，压出"稳"来；而求"安定"，则必须解决民生疾苦、调和民众矛盾，抚慰百姓情绪，是真正的以人为本、以民为先[263]。

"Peace" is about people's livelihood, while "stability" is about politics; "peace" is "people-oriented", while "stability" is "official-oriented"; "peace" is common people's demand, while "stability" is

---

263　徐迅雷撰《用"安定"超越"稳定"》，来源《学习月刊》，2008 年第 1 期

officials' demand. The essence of "peace" is happiness and mental tranquility of common people, along with the resultant stability of social order, so its importance is self-evident. Compared with "stability," "peace" is more tangible and closer to common people, and will not be used as a "label." Measuring social phenomena with "peace" reveals a full warm tone. To seek "stability," high-pressure means can often be used. However, to seek "peace", it is necessary to address the daily hardships of the people, reconcile public disputes, and soothe the emotions of the people. It really manifests the principle of putting people first and prioritizing them.[263]

没有对比就没有伤害。出兵反恐和屯兵反恐未必能够不战而屈人之兵，不出兵反恐赢在不战而胜的起跑线上。比如说如果证明斩首行动和傀儡政策都是反恐的"败笔"，那么，经济反恐将会水涨船高。

There is no harm without comparison. Dispatch of troops against terrorism or stationing troops against terrorism may not necessarily lead to a bloodless victory over the enemy. Non-dispatch of troops against terrorism may lead to a bloodless victory at the starting line. For example, if the decapitation operation and the puppet policy can both be proven to be "failures" in the fight against terrorism, then counter-terrorism through economic means will become more important.

1988 年，以色列特工暗杀了巴勒斯坦解放运动领导人阿布·杰哈德，从此，一个"新名词"逐渐为各国舆论所熟悉，这就是所谓的"斩首行动"。然而，巴勒斯坦民众的起义并没有因为阿布·杰哈德以及其他重要领导人（比如哈马斯精神领袖亚辛等关键性人物）的遇难而销声匿迹或者呈现出弱势。结果，以色列方面遭受的人员和财产损失反而变得越来越大。无独有偶，以色列最重要的盟友美国在遭受了"9·11"恐怖袭击后，有几年也颇为青睐"斩首行动"。尽管美国在类似的行动中先后炸死了"基地"组织的诸多主要头目，比如本·拉登的军事顾问阿提夫，但并没有从根本上遏制住前者在很多国家发动袭击。[264]

In 1988, Israeli agents assassinated Abu Jihad, the leader of the Palestine Liberation Movement. After that, "decapitation operation", as a "new term", gradually spread to people around the world. However, the uprisings of the Palestinian people did not disappear or weaken because of the deaths of Abu Jihad and other important leaders (for example, Sheikh Ahmed Yassin, the spiritual leader of Hamas, and other key figures). On the contrary, the losses of personnel and property suffered by Israel became increasingly larger. Coincidentally, the United States, Israel's most important ally, was enthusiastic about the "decapitation operation" for several years after the September 11 terrorist attacks. Although the United States successively killed many main leaders of al-Qaeda, such as Osama bin Laden's military advisor Atif, in similar operations, it did not fundamentally curb the organization's attacks in many countries.[264]

一些研究人员在调查后发现，历史上诸多成功结束的"斩首"行动只让大约20%的恐怖目标或者极端组织垮掉，其他的反而成为对手进一步成长的"催化剂"。因此，所谓的"斩首"行动绝不是解决恐怖主义问题泛滥的"万能钥匙"。在2006年，由于"基地"组织缺乏统一的领导机构，因此越来越多打着该组织名号的"分支"在搞自杀性袭击活动，比如约旦人扎卡维在伊拉克创立的"支部"等等。[265]

Through investigations, some researchers found that the numerous

---

264 《专家："斩首"行动不能清除恐怖主义》新浪新闻（新浪网）www.sina.com.cn，
    2006年1月22日

265 同上

"decapitation" operations that were successfully carried out in history only destroyed about 20% of the terrorist targets or extremist organizations, and that some even became a "catalyst" for the further growth of the opponents. Therefore, the so-called "decapitation" operation is by no means a "master key" to solving the issue of rampant terrorism. Due to the lack of a unified leadership structure within al-Qaeda, in 2006, more and more organizations carried out suicide attacks in the name of al-Qaeda "branches". For example, the "branch" established by the Jordanian Abu Musab al-Zarqawi in Iraq was one of such organizations.[265]

同时，如果国家放弃斩首行动反恐，而且采取傀儡政策对付恐怖组织，就代表国家需要扶持恐怖组织。要知道，政府扶持恐怖组织等于与虎谋皮，自身很容易遭受反噬，也会丧失民心，酿成其他类型的社会问题。所以，在更大程度上，斩首行动和傀儡政策是用来证明国家反恐的方向和力度，而非用来炫耀本国反恐的成果的。

At the same time, if a country abandons the decapitation operation in its fight against terrorism and adopts a puppet policy towards terrorist organizations, it means that the country needs to support these terrorist organizations. It should be known that a government's support for terrorist organizations is like making an alliance with the devil. The government will easily be consumed by this policy and lose the people's support, causing social problems of different types. Therefore, to a greater extent, the decapitation operation and the puppet policy should be used to demonstrate a country's orientation and intensity in its fight against terrorism, rather than to show off its anti-terrorism achievements.

在 21 世纪，和平与发展是主流思想，不出兵反恐比起出兵反恐和屯兵反恐赢在了起跑线上。就如同金融风暴可以瓦解政治制度，经济危机可以促进平民化。一场大型的世界经济灾难的破坏力就不低于局部战争，不出兵反恐也能保卫家国。

In the 21st century, peace and development are the mainstream thought. Non-patch of troops against terrorism has an advantage over dispatch of troops or stationing troops right from the start. Just as a financial crisis can disintegrate a political system, an economic crisis can promote the process of democratization. The destructive power of a large-scale global economic disaster is no less than that of a local war, and non-dispatch of troops against terrorism can also be employed to defend the country.

1997 年下半年，一场金融风暴席卷亚洲，导致这一地区发生严重经济危机，进而波及全球。其发生之突然，扩展之迅猛，动荡之剧烈，危害之严重，举世瞩目，举世震惊 [266]。

In the second half of 1997, a financial turmoil swept across Asia, leading to a severe economic crisis in this region. Then, the crisis spread globally, astonishing the whole world for its sudden occurrence, rapid expansion, intense turbulence, and serious harm.[266]

亚洲金融危机暴露美日之间在亚太政治、经济和安全领域方面存在的歧义，日美关系的复杂化和日本对自身利益的追求，尤其是对日本自身安全政策的考虑，会使日本外交更注重加强自身的色彩。由于美日同盟关系的限定使日本在接近中国的道路上不可能走得太远，在这种情势下，日本有可能把加强自身色彩的这种努力，转向日台关系的发展 [267]。

The Asian financial crisis revealed the discrepancies between the United States and Japan in politics, economics, and security within the Asia-Pacific region. The complexity of the Japan-US relationship and

---

266 韩文高主编《世纪末金融风暴》，北京：经济日报出版社，2001 年 1 月第 1 版

267 周忠菲撰《亚洲金融危机对台湾的政治影响》，来源《台湾研究集刊》，1998 年第 4 期

Japan's pursuit of its own interests, especially its considerations regarding its own security policies, will make Japan's diplomacy focus more on strengthening its own characteristics. Due to the limitations of the Japan-US alliance, Japan cannot go too far in embracing China. In such a situation, Japan may shift its efforts to strengthen its own characteristics towards the development of the Japan-Taiwan relationship.[267]

不仅如此，1997 年的金融危机也成为了一个加剧韩国社会阶级两极分化的导火索，使得韩国社会学界、政界以及韩国国民开始意识到阶级分化问题的严重性与迫切性。[268]

In addition, the financial crisis in 1997 was a trigger that exacerbated the polarization between the social classes in South Korea,making the sociological community, the political circle, and the Korean people realize the seriousness and urgency of class polarization.[268]

1929 年 10 月 4 日被称为黑色星期四的那天，美国股市崩盘，5000 多亿顷刻间化为乌有。接着银行破产、工厂倒闭、工人失业，最多时失业人口达四分之一。存货堆积如山，流民充斥街头。究其原因，就是因为资本主义国家社会生产上的无政府状态，导致了宏观失控。为拯救经济危机，西方各国采取了一系列加强宏观控制的措施，加大国家对经济的干预力度。著名的"罗斯福新政"就是在这时推出的。1933 年就任美国第 32 任总统的罗斯福，从金融业、工业、农业、社会福利和公共设施等多方面推行新政策。一方面是从国家层面实施了泰罗制的一些措施，如统一建设公共设施、控制金融、调整税率等；另一方面是推行更加人性化的管理。如缩短工作时间、提高最低工资、禁止使用童工、增加劳保福利等。实际就是推行凯恩斯主义。许多政策一直延续至 21 世纪。新政取得了巨大成功，经济迅速复苏，使美国很快重振雄风，为二战中同盟国最终

268　李洵撰《1997 年金融危机对韩国社会分层影响研究》，来源《辽宁大学》，2017 年

战胜法西斯主义提供了雄厚的物质保证[269]。

October 24, 1929, known as Black Thursday, saw the US stock market crash, in which more than 500 billion dollars vanished in an instant. Subsequently, banks went bankrupt, factories closed down, and workers lost their jobs. At the worst stage, the number of unemployed people accounted for a quarter of the total workforce. Inventories piled up, and homeless people filled the streets. The root cause was that the anarchic state of social production in capitalist countries had led to a lack of macro-control. To resolve the economic crisis, Western countries adopted a series of measures to strengthen macro-control, and strengthened the national intervention in the economy. The famous "Roosevelt's New Deal" was launched at that time. Roosevelt, who assumed office as the 32nd President of the United States in 1933, implemented new policies in finance, industry, agriculture, social welfare, public facility, and many other aspects. On the one hand, some measures of the Taylor system such as unified construction of public facilities, control of finance, and adjustment of tax rates were implemented at the national level. On the other hand, more human-oriented management measures such as shortening working hours, raising the minimum wage, banning the use of child labor, and increasing labor protection and welfare were adopted. In essence, it was the implementation of Keynesianism. Many of these policies have continued into the 21st century. As the New Deal achieved great success, the economy recovered rapidly, making the United States quickly regain its strength, and providing a solid material guarantee for the Allied forces to ultimately defeat fascism in the Second World War.[269]

269　朱永涛撰《经济大萧条助推行为科学》，来源《化工管理》，2015 年第 13 期

商场如战场。经济战线兴衰成败关乎国民幸福指数，昭示政府执政能力。在 21 世纪，国企和民企都有从事内销和外贸的生意。如果是政府做亏本生意，是一种自上而下的国家灾难。反之，如果是人民做亏本生意，是一种自下而上的国家灾难。

The marketplace is like a battlefield. The rise and fall of the economic front are related to the national happiness index and demonstrate the government's governance ability. In the 21st century, both state-owned and private enterprises are engaged in domestic sales and foreign trade. If the government engages in unprofitable businesses, it is a top-down national disaster. Conversely, if ordinary people engage in unprofitable businesses, it is a bottom-up national disaster.

国家先有从事生产劳动，才有人民丰衣足食。恐怖主义破坏生产劳作。尽管，反恐三大派系对付恐怖主义的主要手段并不一样，却都要充分保障社会生产力得到有效的正常运转。其中一个具体表现，就是反恐三大派系都要立足于恐怖分子是"过街老鼠，人人喊打"，方能发挥反恐最大能量。就像分裂中国北方疆土的"东突"恐怖组织，如果在维吾尔族心中被认为是坏人，新疆人才会对"东突"分子不予支持。

Only when the country engages in productive labor can the people enjoy ample food and clothing. Terrorism does harm to productive labor. Although the main measures adopted by the three major anti-terrorism factions to deal with terrorism are different, they should fully guarantee the effective and normal operation of social productive forces. One of the specific manifestations is that none of the three major anti-terrorism factions can exert the utmost energy in the fight against terrorism unless they follow the principle that terrorists are "rats crossing the street". For example, only when the "East Turkestan" terrorist organization that attempts to divide the northern territory from China is regarded as evil by the Uygurs will it lose the support from the people of Xinjiang.

"东突厥斯坦"（简称"东突"）这一名词确切地讲出现于 19 世纪末期。"斯坦"原为"地方""区域"之意。就在"泛突厥主义思想"开始产生影响的同时，19 世纪下半叶，俄、英帝国主义列强在推行殖民主义政策的极端民族主义过程中，为肢解和瓜分中国，将"东突厥斯坦"纯地理称谓引申为政治概念。国内外一些图谋不轨者利用这一概念，伪造新疆历史，把新疆说成是"独立"于中华民族大家庭之外的"东突厥斯坦"。因此，这个概念一出笼就体现着帝国主义势力明显的侵略意图和民族分裂主义势力将新疆分裂出去的企图。[270]

The term "East Turkestan" (abbreviated as "ET") precisely emerged in the late 19th century. The word "stan" originally means "place" or "region". In the second half of the 19th century when the ideology of pan-Turkism began to exert influence, the imperialist powers like Russia and Britain, attempted to dismember and carve up China, so they expanded the purely geographical term "East Turkestan" to the political category while implementing extreme nationalist and colonialist policies. Some malicious people at home and abroad exploited this concept to fabricate the history of Xinjiang and refer to Xinjiang as "East Turkestan", which they claimed to be "independent" from the big family of the Chinese nation. Therefore, from the very beginning, this concept embodies the evident aggressive intentions of imperialist forces and the attempts of ethnic separatist forces to split Xinjiang from China.[270]

"东突"势力严重侵害新疆各族人民生存和发展的基本人权。20 世纪 90 年代以来，"东突"势力大量组织实施暴力恐怖活动，严重侵害新疆各族人民的生命财产安全。据不完全统计，1990—2001

---

270 《突厥、东突厥与新疆问题》，观察网，www.guancha.cn，2014 年 6 月 16 日

年，境内外"东突"势力采取爆炸、暗杀、投毒、纵火、袭击、骚乱及暴乱等方式，在我国新疆境内制造了 200 余起暴力恐怖事件，造成各民族群众、基层干部、宗教人士等 162 人丧生，440 多人受伤[271]。

The "East Turkestan" forces seriously violated the basic human rights of all ethnic groups in Xinjiang to survive and develop. After the 1990s, they carried out a large number of violent terrorist activities, seriously endangering the lives and property of all ethnic groups in Xinjiang. According to incomplete statistics, from 1990 to 2001, the "East Turkestan" forces at home and abroad, created more than 200 violent terrorist events in Xinjiang, China by means of bombing, assassination, poisoning, arson, attack, riot and uprising, resulting in the deaths of 162 people, including people of all ethnic groups, primary-level cadres, and religious personnel, and injuries of more than 440 people.[271]

政府在反恐前后，总会遇到涉嫌恐怖主义的组织成员否认自己是恐怖分子，或者指责他人才是真正的恐怖分子。为此，反恐者需要拥有自己的真知灼见，不热爱反恐事业的人去解决恐怖主义，是不能消灭恐怖主义的。

Before and during a campaign against terrorism, the government may often encounter a situation in which organizations suspected of terrorism deny being terrorists or accuse others of being the real terrorists. As a result, those who fight against terrorism should have penetrating insights. If people who do not love the anti-terrorism cause are employed to deal with the issue of terrorism, terrorism cannot be eliminated.

反恐三大派系思想并无高低、强弱、上下、贵贱之分，亦无

271　《"东突"暴行 20 年：仅新疆一地共残杀 359 人》，搜狐历史（搜狐网），www.sohu.com，2014 年 3 月 3 日

男女、阴阳、雄雌、贫富之别。世人做事情都是有利有弊的。反恐三大派系遵循做事情利大于弊就会付诸行动，弊大于利则放弃不做的原则。就像大明王朝有特务机构锦衣卫和东厂西厂，被人合称为"厂卫"。对于明朝特务制度，受益者称赞，受害者批评，个中利弊自有人知。

Among the ideological concepts of the three major anti-terrorism factions, there is no distinction between the higher and the lower, between the stronger and the weaker, between the upper and the lower, between the noble and the humble, nor is there any distinction between man and woman, between Yin and Yang, between male and female, between the poor and the rich. Anything that people do has advantages and disadvantages. The three major anti-terrorism factions should follow the principle that an action with more advantages than disadvantages will be carried out, and an action with more disadvantages than advantages will be discarded. For example, Jinyiwei (Imperial Guard of the Brocade Uniforms), Dongchang (Eastern Bureau of Investigation) and Xichang (Western Bureau of Investigation), the spy agencies of the Ming Dynasty, were collectively referred to as "Changwei". This system was praised by those who benefited from it, and criticized by those who suffered from it. The advantages and disadvantages were known to those involved.

"厂卫"是东厂、西厂、内行厂和锦衣卫的合称，是明代最具特色也最臭名昭著的政治创设，作为皇帝的耳目和爪牙，这两套机构大多数时间掌控在宦官手里，和"特务政治""宦官政治"紧密联系在一起。明末学者沈起堂曾说："明不亡于流寇，而亡于厂卫"。这样总结明代灭亡的原因虽然流于简单化，但厂卫横行、宦官专权却也是明亡的主要原因之一。像一把双刃剑一样，厂卫在维护专制皇权的同时却不断损害着大明王朝的肌体，成为后世引以为戒的镜鉴。而这把双刃剑的铸成，还要追溯到明太祖朱元璋和他的儿子朱棣。[272]

As a collective term for Dongchang (Eastern Bureau of Investigation), Xichang (Western Bureau of Investigation), Neixingchang (Inner Bureau of Investigation), and Jinyiwei (Imperial Guard of the Brocade Uniforms), "Changwei" was the most distinctive and notorious political creation in the Ming Dynasty. Serving the function of informants and henchmen for the emperor, the two sets of institutions were mastered by eunuchs for most of the time, thus closely associated with "special agent politics" and "eunuch politics". Shen Qitang, a scholar in the late Ming Dynasty, pointed out, "The Ming Dynasty perished not due to rebel forces, but due to the Changwei system." Although this summary is simplistic, the rampant actions of Changwei and the eunuchs' monopolization of power were indeed major factors for the downfall of the Ming Dynasty. Like a double-edged sword, Changwei safeguarded the autocratic imperial power, but kept on damaging the fabric of the Ming Dynasty. Therefore, it became a mirror for future generations to draw lessons from. The forging of this double-edged sword can be traced back to Zhu Yuanzhang, the founding emperor of the Ming Dynasty, and his son Zhu Di.[272]

厂卫制度从建立起就与明朝共存续，其原因是它确实起到了肃清朝廷不正之风、打击结党营私、惩治官员腐败的作用。明朝前100多年官员作风比较清明，人民生活也相对安定。不得不说有厂卫的功劳。但最终明又是亡于厂卫，其原因，也在于厂卫偏离了它的本职工作。[273]

Since its establishment, the Changwei system coexisted with the

---

272　熊崧策撰《厂卫诞生记 皇帝该依靠谁?》，来源《文史参考》，2012 年 4 期

273　张疏桐撰《论明代厂卫制度与社会政治秩序维护》，来源《西南政法大学》，2014 年

Ming Dynasty, because it actually had a positive effect on rectifying the unhealthy tendencies in the court, cracking down on cliques, and punishing official corruption. During the first more than a century of the dynasty, the work style of officials was relatively upright, and the people's lives were relatively stable. It can be said that the Changwei system deserves the credit for this. However, the Ming Dynasty ultimately perished due to the Changwei system, and the reason is that it had deviated from its original function.[273]

很明显，由于厂卫制度是替皇帝君主"看天下"，才严密成长起来的惩治工具。倘若是明君执掌天下，锦衣卫和东厂西厂的利弊就算是"有功有过也是功"，民心不一无心计较。然而，如果昏君当道，那么其中厂卫的利弊就是"无功无过也是过"，民怨沸腾有意计较。如此，一旦"上梁不正下梁歪"的情况愈发猖獗，在贪污腐败和恐怖主义的催动下，朝野逐渐爆发出战争演义。

It is obvious that the Changwei system was a punishment tool that developed rigorously for "supervising the country" for the emperor. If a wise emperor was in power, the advantages and disadvantages of Jinyiwei, Dongchang and Xichang could be described as "even with both merits and demerits, the merits prevail", and the people, with divided opinions, would not care too much. However, if a fatuous emperor was in power, the advantages and disadvantages of Changwei could be described as "even with no merits or demerits, the demerits prevail", and the people, with boiling grievances, would care about it. In this context, once the situation of "if the upper beam is not straight, the lower beam will be crooked" worsened, driven by corruption and terrorism, wars and upheavals would gradually emerge in the court and among the commonalty.

由于解决恐怖主义要根据国力和民情以及社会环境进行反恐，

第三章　中国兵道思想主张用反恐三大派系内不出兵反恐

Chapter 3: Chinese Military Thought Advocating Non-Dispatch of Troops against Terrorism within the Three Major Anti-Terrorism Factions

故此，不同的国家与地区，将会对反恐三大派系进行有目的性的选择。在将来，反恐三大派系中哪一派系更受人欢迎，只能证明这一反恐派系是目前的潮流，并不能因此将其他反恐派系否定。反恐思路、思维、思想保持新鲜很有必要，拥有旺盛生命力的反恐思想，是对付恐怖分子的一把利器。

To resolve the issue of terrorism, we must take into account national strength, public sentiment, and social environment. Therefore, different countries and regions will make choices purposefully among the three major anti-terrorism factions. In the future, the popularity of a certain faction can only prove that it is currently in vogue, but it cannot be used to deny the other factions. It is necessary to maintain fresh anti-terrorism ideas, thinking, and concepts. An anti-terrorism ideology with strong vitality is a sharp weapon against terrorists.

第四章　腐败助推恐怖主义

Chapter 4: Corruption Fueling Terrorism

在 21 世纪，只要还有人认为这世界还有明显的恐怖主义，那么，在很长的一段时间里，人民相信政府腐败有多无少。

In the 21st century, as long as some people still believe that there is obvious terrorism in the world, then, for a long period of time, people will believe that there is no shortage of government corruption.

在汉语中，腐败一词最初源于《汉书·食货志上》："太仓之粟，陈陈相因，充溢露积于外，腐败不可食。"意思是指（谷物）发霉、腐烂。这是腐败的原意。《辞海》将"腐败"解释为"腐烂。也泛指败坏、堕落"。《辞源》将"腐败"解释为"腐烂发臭、陈旧迂陋、腐朽败坏，一般用于对食物的描绘"[274]。

In Chinese, the word "corruption" first appeared in *Records of Food and Goods (Part I), The Book of Han*, "In the royal warehouses, grain was stacked year after year, with new grain piling on top of the old. The grain was so much that it overflowed and was piled outside. Over a long period, it rotted and became inedible." This means that (the grain) becomes moldy and rotten, which is the original meaning of "corruption". In *Cihai*, "corruption" is interpreted as "to rot. It also generally refers to deterioration and depravity." In *Ciyuan*, "corruption"is interpreted as "to rot and give off a foul smell, to be outdated and pedantic, to be decadent and corrupt, and it is generally used to describe food."[274]

腐败和恐怖主义有直接的联系，很多人解决腐败和恐怖主义往

274　李晓明、张长梅撰《腐败概念的泛化与界定》，来源《河北法学》，2008 年第 9 期

往要用道德和法制及法治。

There is a direct connection between corruption and terrorism. Many people often resort to morality, the legal system, and the rule of law to fight against corruption and terrorism.

从词源意义上看。"法制"一词历史悠久。"如《管子·君臣上》中有'法制有常，则民不偷'；《左传·文公六年》中有'策之法制，告之训典'；《国语·周语》中有'是弃先王之法制'，……。因此，从词义上看，古代'法制'即有制作法典，创立制度之义"。在汉语中，法制就是法律制度的简称。在英文中，法制则为 legal system（法律的体系），legal in—situation（法律的制度），legality（合法性）。因此，从字面上可以看出，"法制"一词主要是有关法律的制度、法律条文、法律体系等，强调的主要是静态的法。而"法治"一词"在中文中有'法治主义'，'以法治国，法治天下'等。在英文中有'rule of law，（法的统治），rule by law'（以法统治），'government by law'（依法治理），'government through law'（通过法律的治理）等"。因此，字面意义上的法治具有以法律治理国家，管理人民的意思，强调的是动态的法律运行，即依法而治，以法而治。[275]

From the etymological perspective, the term "the legal system" has a long history. For example, *On the Ruler and the Ministers (Part I), Guanzi* mentions that "If the legal system is stable and consistent, the people will not be dishonest"; *The Sixth Year of Duke Wen, Zuo Zhuan* mentions that "Regulate people's behaviors by formulating clear legal systems, and guide them with teachings of the ancient sovereigns"; *Discourses of the Zhou State, Discourses of the States* mentions that "This is to abandon the legal system of the ancient sovereigns"; ... Therefore, from the perspective of word meaning, in ancient times,

---

275　李寿荣撰《论法制与法治的关系》，来源《西部法学评论》，2006 年第 2 期

"the legal system" meant compiling a code of laws and establishing systems. In Chinese, fǎ zhì is an abbreviation for fǎ lǜ zhì dù (the legal system). In English, it is described as legal system, legal in-situation, and legality. Therefore, literally speaking, the term "the legal system" is mainly about legal institutions, legal provisions, and legal systems, with emphasis on the static aspect of the law. As for the term "the rule of law", in Chinese, it includes meanings such as "legalism", "governing the country by law, governing the world by law", and so on. In English, it includes meanings such as "rule of law", "rule by law" , "government by law", "government through law", and so on. Therefore, literally, the rule of law means governing the country and managing the people with the law, emphasizing the dynamic operation of the law, that is, governing in accordance with the law.[275]

在《万历十五年》中，黄仁宇教授认为："中国两千年来，以道德代替法制，至明代而极，这就是明朝一切问题的症结。"[276]

In *1587, A Year of No Significance: The Ming Dynasty in Decline*, Professor Huang Renyu believed that "For the two thousand years in China, morality was used to replace the legal system, and this reached its extreme during the Ming Dynasty. This is the crux of all the problems of the Ming Dynasty."[276]

黄仁宇，美籍华人，历史学家，曾在美国南伊利诺大学及纽约州立大学任教，又曾任哥伦比亚大学访问副教授及哈佛大学东亚研究所研究员。生于湖南长沙，参加过抗日战争，曾与廖沫沙一同起居办报，与田汉、范长江等人过从颇密。中年之后赴美，在餐店洗碗碟做小工，整日劳动后退居斗室研习历史，感受过失业、经济危

276　高骊撰《浅谈明代道德与制度——〈万历十五年〉读后》，来源《宁夏师范学院学报》，2011 年第 1 期

机以及被人歧视的种种景况[277]。

Huang Renyu, a Chinese-American historian, worked as a teacher at Southern Illinois University and the State University of New York in the United States. He also served as a visiting associate professor at Columbia University and a research fellow at the East Asian Research Institute of Harvard University. He was born in Changsha, Hunan Province. He participated in the War of Resistance against Japanese Aggression. He once lived and ran a newspaper with Liao Mosha, and had close interactions with Tian Han and Fan Changjiang. In his middle age, he went to the United States, working as a dishwasher and a laborer in restaurants. After a day's work, he often studied history in a small room. He had experiences such as unemployment, economic crises, and being discriminated against.[277]

曾以《万历十五年》等著作名世的历史学家黄仁宇于 2000 年 1 月 8 日晚心脏病发不治，在纽约去世，享年 82 岁[278]。

Huang Renyu, the historian renowned for works such as *1587, A Year of No Significance: The Ming Dynasty in Decline*, died of a heart attack in New York on the evening of January 8, 2000, at the age of 82.[278]

法律有灰色和真空地带，以至于惩恶扬善鞭长莫及，这使得道德理国尤为宝贵。犹如"三人成虎"和"罗生门"都能"曾参杀人"，反而照耀"曾参杀猪"。

There are gray and vacuum areas in the law. Therefore, it is difficult to punish evil and promote good, which makes governing the country with morality particularly valuable. For example, the situations similar to "three men make a tiger" and "Rashomon", like the rumor of "Zeng Shen

---

277　白峰撰《黄仁宇的〈赫逊河畔谈中国历史〉》，来源《青年记者》，1996 年第 4 期

278　徐明撰《历史学家黄仁宇去世》，来源《天涯》，2000 年第 2 期

kills a man", can distort reality. In contrast, the integrity shown in "Zeng Shen kills a pig" shines even brighter.

法制和法治比道德优秀在哪里无法确定，不过，在古代、近代、现代，各个国家与地区都不缺不要脸的士农工商，这是确定的。

It is uncertain in which aspects the legal system and the rule of law are superior to morality. However, it is certain that throughout ancient, modern, and contemporary times, there is no lack of shameless people among scholars, farmers, artisans, and merchants in different countries and regions.

然而，在中国官场历史之中，中国古代有清官和好官。这些中国官吏能够成为廉洁奉公的官员，是与他们自身的高素质分不开的。

However, in ancient Chinese officialdom, there was no lack honest and good officials. Their honesty and dedication to public service stemmed from their own high qualities.

南宋官员宋慈能够著写《洗冤集录》一书，首要条件是他有百姓父母官的责任心，其次才是宋慈有时间、有精力、有能力写出这本检尸书籍。这个道理是贪腐者和罪恶者可能自己也明白，本身却做不到的事情。

Song Ci, an official in the Southern Song Dynasty, wrote the book *Collected Records of Washing Away Injustices*. The primary cause was that he had a sense of responsibility as a parent official of the people. The secondary cause was that he had the time, energy, and ability to write this book about autopsy. Even corrupt officials can understand the principle of serving the people wholeheartedly, yet they fail to live up to it.

宋慈（1186 年—1249 年），字惠父，福建建阳童游里人，中国古代著名法医学家，是中国古代法医学的开创者。[279]

279　杨维、徐锐撰《宋慈＜洗冤集录＞的成就与缺憾》，来源《长沙铁道学院学报（社会科学版）》，2007 年 4 期

Song Ci (1186-1249), known as Huifu by courtesy name, was a native of Tongyouli, Jianyang, Fujian Province. He was a famous forensic scientist as well as a pioneer of forensic science in ancient China.[279]

宋慈撰写的《洗冤集录》是中外学者公认的世界上最早的、系统的法医学专著，比意大利巴列尔摩（Palermo）大学费德罗教授（FortunatoFedle）的《医生的报告》（《DeRelationbusMedicorum》）要早350多年，是宝贵的世界文化遗产，在中国和世界法医学史上占有非常重要的地位，其科学研究价值和影响力在法医科学发展史上是罕见的。《洗冤集录》作为中国古代法医检验必备书籍，各种版本达39种，被传至亚、欧、美的各种译本达21种，内容既涉及了现代法医学的大部分内容，还有关于检验的条令与职业道德；不但记载了一些案例和验尸的方法及注意事项，而且还较全面地阐述了检验原理和经验；反映了当时法学、法医学和有关科技的水平和社会发展状况，是研究当时法律和检案的重要历史材料。[280]

The *Collected Records of Washing Away Injustices* written by Song Ci is recognized by Chinese and foreign scholars as the earliest and most systematic forensic science monograph in the world. It is more than 350 years earlier than *De Relationbus Medicorum* written by Professor Fortunato Fedle from the University of Palermo in Italy. As a precious cultural heritage in the world, it occupies a very important position in the history of forensic science both in China and globally, and reveals extraordinary scientific research values and influences in the history of the development of forensic science. As an essential book for forensic inspection in ancient China, the *Collected Records of Washing Away Injustices* has 39 versions, among which up to 21 translated versions have

---

280 陈新山、黄瑞亭撰《＜洗冤集录＞的现代价值》，来源《中国法医学杂志》，2009年5期

been spread to Asia, Europe, and the United States. It not only involves most of the content of modern forensic science but also includes decrees on inspection and professional ethics. It has not only recorded some cases, methods of corpse inspection, and matters needing attention but also comprehensively expounded the principles and experience of inspection. Reflecting the level of jurisprudence, forensic science, and related science and technology at that time, as well as the social development status, it is considered an important historical record for studying the laws and case inspections at that time.[280]

《洗冤集录》是宋慈在长期担任提点刑狱的监司重任中，大量纠正冤假错案的真实记录和宝贵治狱断案经验的科学总结，体现了他"雪冤禁暴"的法治思想。[281]

The *Collected Records of Washing Away Injustices* incorporates authentic records of correcting a large number of unjust, false and wrong cases during Song Ci's long tenure as the supervisor in charge of judicial affairs, as well as a scientific summary of his precious experience in handling cases and administering justice. It reflects his legal thought of "clearing up grievances and suppressing violence".[281]

抽丝剥茧需要时间，公仆精神鞭挞声色犬马使其无所遁形，丰功伟绩不随喜怒哀乐此消彼长，再多的丰碑都经得住时间的风吹雨打，更不用世人来吹捧。

It takes time to analyze things in a meticulous way. The spirit of public service lashes out at debauchery and makes it have nowhere to hide. Great achievements do not ebb and flow with people's emotions. No matter how many great monuments there are, they can withstand the test of time, without the need to be flattered by the people.

281　黄丽云撰《宋慈＜洗冤集录＞的法治思想》，来源《海峡通讯》，2017 年 2 期

品德低下的人总是喜欢去连累他人，行损人利己或损人不利己的事情，就算是丢人现眼和触犯法律也在所不惜，这延续了官逼民反存在于世的必要性。

People with a low moral character tend to implicate others and do things that benefit themselves at the expense of others or harm others without benefiting themselves. They may even take the risk of making an exhibition of themselves and breaking the law. This can well account for why the situation where the people are driven to rebellion by officials' oppression exists continuously.

在世界现代史，弱国小国和强国大国都有天灾人祸，弱国小国面对天灾人祸总是"多天灾，少人祸"，强国大国面对天灾人祸总是"少天灾，多人祸"，这是工业革命时代也遵循的灾难路线。这让人只相信人治不相信法治。故此，道德能够速战速决战胜法学，给人以解决腐败和恐怖主义的曙光。

In modern world history, no matter whether a country is weak or strong, small or large, it will face natural and human-caused disasters. When weak and small countries face natural and human-caused disasters, the situation is "more natural disasters than human-caused disasters"; when strong and large countries face them, the situation is "fewer natural disasters than human-caused disasters". It is a pattern of disasters that was followed even in the era of the Industrial Revolution. This makes people only believe in rule by man rather than rule by law. Therefore, morality can quickly defeat the science of law and give people hope of resolving the issue of corruption and terrorism.

腐败既能够亡国灭种，也能够颠倒黑白，就算是发生过工业革命的现代社会也是如此。甚至，一旦贪腐行为屡剿不灭，借助工业革命还能让恐怖主义变得更加强大。

Corruption can lead not only to the subjugation of a country, but also to reversion of right and wrong. This is the case even in modern societies that have experienced the Industrial Revolution. More seriously, once corruption cannot be eradicated despite repeated crackdowns, terrorism, with the help of the Industrial Revolution, can become more powerful.

恐怖主义最大力量是建立在社会不公平、不公正、不公义之上。在 21 世纪，政府和恐怖分子的行为都有不公平、不公正、不公义的地方。为此，无论是政府还是恐怖分子，都有无良无德的丑陋行为。

The greatest power of terrorism is based on social unfairness, injustice and lack of righteousness. In the 21st century, both the behaviors of governments and terrorists involve aspects of unfairness, injustice and lack of righteousness. Therefore, both governments and terrorists have immoral and unethical ugly behaviors.

2012 年，针对驻阿富汗美军士兵焚烧《古兰经》的亵渎行为，美国方面 2 月 24 日表示对于事态的不断扩散严重关切，并再次表达最有诚意的道歉。阿富汗国内的抗议活动进入第 4 天，丝毫没有停止的迹象。不仅如此，巴基斯坦、利比亚国内也掀起了新一轮的反美高潮 [282]。

On February 24, 2012, in response to the blasphemous act of American soldiers stationed in Afghanistan burning the Quran, the United States expressed serious concern about the continuous escalation of the situation, and once again expressed its most sincere apology. The protest activities in Afghanistan continued to the fourth day without the slightest sign of stopping. Moreover, new rounds of anti-American upsurges also broke out in Pakistan and Libya.[282]

---

282 《美军士兵焚烧古兰经事件掀起多国反美高潮》，腾讯新闻（腾讯网），www.qq.com，2012 年 2 月 26 日

2015 年 3 月，极端组织伊斯兰国（ISIS）烧毁了伊拉克境内摩苏尔市的一个公共图书馆，一同遭殃的是馆内 8000 余册珍贵的旧书和手稿。在伊拉克西部的安巴尔省，ISIS 已经焚毁了超过 10 万本书[283]。

In March 2015, the extremist organization ISIS burned a public library in Mosul City, Iraq. More than 8,000 precious ancient books and manuscripts in the library were destroyed. In Anbar Province, western Iraq, ISIS had burned more than 100,000 books.[283]

2015 年，继焚书毁寺之后，极端组织 ISIS（伊斯兰国）又将目光对准了伊拉克的珍贵文物。在 ISIS 于 2 月 26 日发布的一段 5 分钟的视频中，该组织洗劫了摩苏尔中央博物馆，挥动铁锤和电钻，砸毁具有上千年历史的古文物和雕像，还威胁要推翻中东几千年的和平共处，试图镇压一切与伊斯兰圣战思想不符的力量[284]。

In 2015, following the burning of books and destruction of temples, the extremist organization ISIS turned its attention to the precious cultural relics in Iraq. In a 5-minute video released by ISIS on February 26, the organization looted the Mosul Central Museum. They wielded hammers and power drills to smash ancient cultural relics and statues with a history of more than a thousand years, threatening to destroy the situation of peaceful coexistence that had lasted for thousands of years in the Middle East, and attempting to suppress all forces that did not conform to the Islamic Jihadist ideology.[284]

从有古物记载开始，到现代互联网时代为止，叙写个人、集体、组织等贪污腐败行为数不胜数，花样层出不穷，令人眼花缭

---

283 《人类焚书史：纳粹不是开始，伊斯兰国恐怕也不是结束》，腾讯文化（腾讯网），www.qq.com，2015 年 3 月 11 日

284 《ISIS 疯狂破坏伊拉克两千多年前古珍贵文物》，搜狐文化（搜狐网），www.sohu.com，2015 年 2 月 27 日

乱，难以得到扼杀。诸如大贪大腐有十二种手段：

From the time when records of ancient artifacts emerged to the modern Internet era, there have been countless descriptions of the corrupt behaviors of individuals, collectives, and organizations. These corrupt behaviors involve various patterns, which are bewildering and can hardly be eliminated. For example, there are twelve major means of severe corruption:

在东方西方，东方十二生肖和西方十二星座有异曲同工之妙。大贪大腐十二种手段暗合东方十二生肖和西方十二星座的数量规律，即意思为这十二种贪腐手段是东西方共有的不法手段。

The twelve Chinese zodiac signs in the East and the twelve constellations in the West share the same subtlety despite differences. The twelve major means of severe corruption coincide with the number twelve of the Chinese zodiac signs in the East as well as the constellations in the West. In other words, these twelve illegal way of corruption are common in both the East and the West.

一、美人计。心慈未必貌美，貌美未必心慈。心慈貌美照样有联系。

I The beauty trap. Being kind-hearted does not necessarily mean being beautiful, and being beautiful does not necessarily mean being kind-hearted. However, there is a certain connection between being kind-hearted and being beautiful.

2014 年 12 月初，伊朗战机对伊拉克境内的极端分子发动空袭，表明伊朗开始公开在境外打击"伊斯兰国"的军事行动。而此前，虽然伊朗明确表达过对"伊斯兰国"的态度，但在具体行动时往往通过"代理人"的形式秘密进行 [285]。

285　周戎撰《中东"谍王"苏莱曼尼》，来源《环球人物》，2014 年第 34 期

At the beginning of December 2014, Iranian fighter jets launched air strikes against extremists in Iraq, indicating that Iran began to publicly carry out military operations against the "Islamic State" outside its territory. Previously, although Iran had clearly expressed its attitude towards the "Islamic State", when it came to specific actions, it usually carried out secret operations through "agents".[285]

伊朗这一战略转变，是由一个关键人物促成的，他就是伊朗特种部队"圣城旅"的缔造者、最高领袖哈梅内伊的高级军事顾问和政策顾问——卡西姆·苏莱曼尼[286]。

The strategic shift in Iran was brought about by a key figure, namely Qasem Soleimani, the founder of Iran's special forces "Quds Force", a senior military advisor and policy advisor to the Supreme Leader Ali Khamenei.[286]

2020 年 1 月 3 日，美国动用无人机，对伊朗高级将领苏莱曼尼发起斩首行动，苏莱曼尼当场身亡。事发后，本已趋于缓和的美伊关系迅速激化至前所未有的地步，伊朗甚至不惜动用数十枚导弹对驻伊拉克美军基地展开攻击。同时，伊朗民众也自发组成游行队伍，对苏莱曼尼进行悼念。但据《环球时报》报道，1 月，美国国防部公布了更多关于苏莱曼尼死亡的细节，其中来自伊朗方面的"内部因素"更是在美军开始行动前便将苏莱曼尼"宣告死亡"[287]。

On January 3, 2020, the United States used a drone to launch a decapitation operation against Iranian senior general Qasem Soleimani. He was killed on the spot. After the incident, the tensions between the United States and Iran, which had been somewhat relieved, rapidly escalated to an unprecedented level, and Iran even attacked the U.S.

---

286 同上

287 《苏莱曼尼死亡真相：女内奸为其贴身服务，被杀前 36 小时已注定死亡》，腾讯网 www.qq.com，2020 年 1 月 13 日

military bases in Iraq with dozens of missiles. At the same time, the Iranian people spontaneously held a demonstration to mourn Soleimani. However, according to a report by *Global Times*, in January, the US Department of Defense released more details about Soleimani's death, among which the "internal factors" on the Iranian side had made Soleimani's death an inevitable event before the US military began its operation.[287]

据美方透露，在针对苏莱曼尼的暗杀行动中，除了负责执行最终打击任务的无人机外，美军还投入了大量情报人员和特种作战人员，并且得到了伊朗"内鬼"的有力支持。作为伊朗军方知名度最高的"战将"，苏莱曼尼有着丰富的实际作战经验，更是深谙反情报作战之道。有消息显示，苏莱曼尼甚至很少使用手机等现代化电子设备，出行更是要缜密规划出行方式和行程，也正是因此，在美国"要犯名单"上盘踞多年的苏莱曼尼才得以长期活跃于伊朗军界。然而，面对美国无孔不入的情报网络，苏莱曼尼最终还是没能逃过一劫。消息人士表示，早在苏莱曼尼启程前往巴格达前，美国就已经通过买通伊朗政府内部人员掌握了苏莱曼尼的详细行程安排，美国联邦政府国安顾问奥布莱恩更是表示苏莱曼尼在死前的36小时内受到了美军的"严密监控"[288]。

According to US sources, in the assassination operation against Soleimani, in addition to the drone that carried out the final strike, the US military also deployed a large number of intelligence agents and special forces operators, and received strong support from "inside traitors" in Iran. As the most well-known "warrior" in the Iranian military, Soleimani had rich practical combat experience and had a profound understanding of anti-intelligence operations. According to some sources, Soleimani

---

288　同上

rarely used mobile phones or other modern electronic devices, and he would meticulously plan his travel methods and schedules. As a result, Soleimani, who had been on the US "most-wanted list" for many years, was able to remain active in the Iranian military for a long time. However, in the face of the all-pervasive US intelligence network, he ultimately failed to escape his fate. An informant said that long before Soleimani set off for Baghdad, the United States had obtained the detailed information about his schedule by bribing insiders within the Iranian government. O'Brien, the US National Security Advisor, even said that Soleimani was under the "close surveillance" of the US military within 36 hours before his death.[288]

奥布莱恩此言当然不是空口无凭。据媒体报道，1 月，伊朗方面宣布，其已经抓获了一名与苏莱曼尼死亡密切相关的美国间谍，而这名间谍正是苏莱曼尼搭乘航班上的空姐。据报道，为了能够对苏莱曼尼进行严密监视，这名空姐甚至为苏莱曼尼提供了"贴身服务"。此外，苏莱曼尼降落的巴格达机场也有着多名美国间谍人员，这些间谍人员使美军能够及时获得有关苏莱曼尼位置的实时信息，并最终在苏莱曼尼刚刚抵达巴格达便将其斩首。而且，为了能够确保行动成功，美军同时还派出了特种部队士兵对苏莱曼尼进行跟踪。据悉，在苏莱曼尼身亡不到两分钟后，就已经有美军特种部队士兵抵达事发地点进行成果确认。在美国近乎天罗地网的密切监视以及身边"战友"的出卖下，苏莱曼尼纵有三头六臂也实在无法逃出生天[289]。

Of course, O'Brien's remarks were not groundless. According to media reports, in January, Iran announced that it had captured a US spy closely associated with Soleimani's death. The spy was actually a flight

---

289　同上

attendant on the plane that Soleimani took. It is reported that in order to closely monitor Soleimani, the flight attendant even provided "close service" to him. In addition, there were several US spies at Baghdad Airport where Soleimani landed. These spies enabled the US military to obtain real-time information about Soleimani's location, and ultimately decapitate him as soon as he arrived in Baghdad. Moreover, to ensure the success of the operation, the US military also dispatched special forces soldiers to track Soleimani. It is reported that within two minutes after Soleimani's death, some US special forces soldiers had arrived at the scene to confirm the result. Due to the extremely close surveillance of the United States and the betrayal of his "comrades" around him, even if Soleimani had extraordinary abilities, he had no way to escape.[289]

二、裙带关系，贪污腐败和反贪反腐，都是连绵不绝。

II Endless nepotism, corruption, and anti-corruption efforts.

1948 年，中国国家元首蒋介石的儿子蒋经国在上海反腐，结果以失败告终。蒋经国反腐失败其中一个重要原因就是，统治中国大陆的是国民政府。这个政府是靠蒋宋孔陈四大家族来保持经济命脉的，蒋宋孔陈四大家族本身就是中国的"大老虎"，还与祸害老百姓的中国黑社会有关联。

In 1948, Chiang Ching-kuo, the son of Chiang Kai-shek, the head of China at that time, carried out an anti-corruption campaign in Shanghai, but it ended in failure. One important factor that led to his failure can be attributed to the Nationalist government that ruled China's mainland. The government relied on the four major families of Chiang, Soong, Kung, and Chen to maintain its economic lifeline. The four families themselves were "big tigers" in China. Moreover, they were associated with the Chinese underworld that brought disaster to the common people.

孔宋家族成员孔令侃在上海经营一家扬子公司，从事进出口贸易，孔令侃在商界的诨号是"南京老虎"，他和青帮首脑杜月笙关系不错。杜月笙的绰号是"大耳杜"，有时候被称为"经济老虎"[290]。

Kong Lingkan, a member of the Kung and Soong families, ran the Yangtze Industrial Company in Shanghai, which was engaged in import and export trade. Nicknamed "Nanjing Tiger" in the business community, Kong Lingkan had a good relationship with Du Yuesheng, the leader of the Green Gang. Du Yuesheng was nicknamed "Big Ear Du", and was sometimes called "Economic Tiger".[290]

杜月笙不但是黑社会头子，在中国银行、交通银行和上海证券交易所也位居要职。他长久以来和宋子文、孔祥熙有密切往来，传说跟蒋介石还是拜把兄弟。当蒋经国抵达上海时，杜月笙请他吃饭，小蒋婉谢。杜月笙可不习惯被人这样谢绝[291]。

Du Yuesheng was not only the leader of the underworld but also held important positions in the Bank of China, the Bank of Communications, and the Shanghai Stock Exchange. He had close contact with T. V. Soong and H. H. Kung for a long time, and it was rumored that he was even a sworn brother with Chiang Kai-shek. When Chiang Ching-kuo arrived in Shanghai, Du Yuesheng invited him to dinner, but Chiang Ching-kuo politely declined. Du Yuesheng was not used to being declined like that.[291]

另一只"老虎"是杜月笙的"外甥"万墨林，因为日本占领时期从米粮上赚得大钱，绰号"米粮老虎"。蒋经国的检查小组一开始就逮捕了万墨林，罪名是非法囤积稻米，迫使米价上扬，不当侵占政府米谷贷款。蒋经国更放胆逮捕了杜月笙的儿子杜维屏，理由是投机炒作、囤积居奇，非法在股市交易。同一天（9月3日），他逮捕了一家棉纺厂和一家香烟公司经理，宋子文投资的永安棉纺厂

290　《蒋经国上海"打虎"：与杜月笙对垒始末》，腾讯评论（腾讯网）www.qq.com，
　　　2013 年 8 月 2 日

291　同上

经理也不能幸免，甚至棉布商公会、纸商公会、食用油商公会以及米商公会会长，通通抓起来。戡建大队喊出"我们只打老虎，不拍苍蝇"的口号，赢得"打虎队"的美誉[292]。

Another "tiger" was Wan Molin, Du Yuesheng's "nephew". He was nicknamed the "Rice Tiger" because he made a fortune from rice during the Japanese occupation. At first, Chiang Ching-kuo's inspection team arrested Wan Molin on the charge of illegally hoarding rice, pushing up the rice price, and illegally embezzling the government's rice loan. Chiang Ching-kuo was even summoned up his courage to arrest Du Yuesheng's son Du Weiping on the grounds of speculation, hoarding, and illegal stock trading. On the same day (September 3), he arrested the managers of a cotton spinning factory and a cigarette company. Even the manager of the Yong'an Cotton Mill, in which T. V. Soong had invested, could not escape his fate. Even the chairmen of the Cotton Merchants Association, the Paper Merchants Association, the Edible Oil Merchants Association, and the Rice Merchants Association were arrested. The Pacification and Construction Brigade shouted the slogan "We only fight tigers, not swat flies", thus winning the reputation of the "Tiger-fighting Team".[292]

孔令侃仗着"皇亲国戚"的地位在上海横行霸道，明火执仗地投机倒把，大发国难财。据说蒋经国事先还向蒋介石打了招呼，蒋介石也同意牺牲这个浑蛋外甥。孔令侃得知这一消息后很是紧张，便想请蒋经国吃饭疏通，结果小蒋不买他的账。孔一看苗头不对，连夜跑到南京向宋美龄哭诉。宋便向蒋介石表示坚决不能拿她这个外甥开刀，蒋介石只好要求蒋经国作罢。于是便有了蒋经国转而逮

292　同上

捕杜月笙儿子杜维屏的事情[293]。

Kong Lingkan, relying on his status as a "relative of the imperial family", acted recklessly in Shanghai. He openly engaged in speculation and profiteering, making a fortune from national crisis. It is said that Chiang Ching-kuo had informed Chiang Kai-shek in advance, and Chiang Kai-shek agreed to sacrifice this despicable nephew. When Kong Lingkan learned of that, he became nervous and attempted to invite Chiang Ching-kuo to dinner to pull some strings. However, Chiang Ching-kuo refused to show him any favor. Feeling that something was wrong, Kong Lingkan rushed to Nanjing overnight and sobbed out the story to Soong Mei-ling. Soong Mei-ling told Chiang Kai-shek that she firmly opposed taking action against her nephew. Chiang Kai-shek had no choice but to ask Chiang Ching-kuo to give up. As a result, Chiang Ching-kuo turned to arrest Du Yuesheng's son, Du Weiping.[293]

然而杜月笙处理此事，表面公道仗义，实则抓住蒋经国不能制裁孔令侃的软肋当众向他发难。结果是法院终审判刑6个月，杜象征性地交了一点罚金，以罚代刑，放人了事[294]。

However, when Du Yuesheng dealt with this matter in a seemingly fair and just manner, he actually publicly challenged Chiang Ching-kuo by exploiting Chiang Ching-kuo's weakness of being unable to punish Kong Lingkan. In the end, the court sentenced Du Weiping to six months in prison. Du Yuesheng symbolically paid a small amount of fine, using it as a substitute for the penalty and securing his son's release.[294]

但是，蒋介石顾全国民政府和孔氏家族的体面，担心"夜长梦多，授人口实"，最终还是只能以大事化小、后台结案的方式了

---

293 《蒋经国上海整顿经济：最终扳不倒"皇亲国戚"》，搜狐历史（搜狐网）www.sohu.com，2013年5月19日

294 同上

断。到了扬子公司问题上，蒋介石碍于宋美龄和孔令侃之间的关系，压制调查，窒息言论，徇私包庇，终于毁灭了国民党和政府拥戴者的最后一点希望，陷入人心尽失的严重局面[295]。

However, out of the consideration of the dignity of the Nationalist Government and the Kong family, and out of the concern that "the longer it drags on, the more likely something will go wrong, and it will give others a chance to gossip", Chiang Kai-shek ultimately resolved the matter by playing it down and closed the case secretly. When it came to the issue of the Yangtze Industrial Company, Chiang Kai-shek, due to the relationship between Soong Mei-ling and Kong Lingkan, suppressed the investigation, silenced public opinions, practiced favouritism, and engaged in malpractice, leading to the loss of the last hope of the supporters of the Kuomintang and the Nationalist Government and causing a serious situation of completely losing the people's trust.[295]

三、先来后到，随机应变，积少成多，吃喝不愁。

III First come, first benefit. Be flexible in response to circumstances. Build up bit by bit. No worry about food and drink.

2014 年 2 月，国家预防腐败局原专职副局长崔海容，在纪检监察系统工作整整 30 年后卸任身退[296]。

In February 2014, Cui Hairong, the former full-time deputy director of the National Bureau of Corruption Prevention, stepped down after working in the discipline inspection and supervision system for 30 years.[296]

2015 年，崔海容对《南方都市报》记者说过："关于推进政务公

295　《蒋经国上海滩打虎记：因蒋介石包庇孔氏家族而失败》，腾讯文化（腾讯网）www.qq.com，2014 年 7 月 31 日

296　《国家预防腐败局原副局长：有打字员受贿 400 余万》，腾讯新闻（腾讯网）www.qq.com，2015 年 3 月 24 日

开，去年两会期间我接受人民网采访，已经谈过。行政许可审批，前些年确实较烦琐，比如，房地产项目，从征地到房子盖起来，要盖近百个章子，每个章子加盖过程中都可能存在寻租的空间[297]。"

In 2015, Cui Hairong told a reporter from *Southern Metropolis Daily*: "Regarding promoting government affairs transparency, I talked about it when I was interviewed by People's Daily during the Two Sessions last year. In previous years, the administrative approval procedures were indeed cumbersome. For example, for a real estate project, from land acquisition to the completion of the building, nearly a hundred official seals were needed, and there may be room for power rent-seeking behind each official seal."[297]

"有个最典型的案例，南方某省会城市土地房产部门的一个打字员受贿 400 余万元。她非官也非吏，审批签章都轮不到她，为何受贿这么多钱？原因是需要到她那里打印材料的人太多，要排队等候。搞房地产的老板不差钱，早一天审批过关，就早一天回收银子，打字员就有了谁先谁后打印的选择权。"[298]

"The most typical case is that a typist in the land and real estate department of a provincial capital city in the South took bribes of more than 4 million yuan. She was neither an official nor a clerk, and had no approval power or signature and seal power at all. Why was she bribed with so much money? The reason was that many people had to print materials in her office and they had to queue up. Real estate bosses didn't care about money. If they got the approval earlier, they could get their money back earlier. So the typist had the right to choose whom she would serve first."[298]

---

297 同上
298 同上

四、钱财不可漏眼，钱财藏地道，升级为钱财藏"暗处"。网络在暗中，暗中有网络。

IV. The principle of not leaking money and hiding money in tunnels has been upgraded to the principle of hiding money in a "dark place". The network is in the dark, and there is a network in the dark.

洗钱，主要是指将毒品犯罪、黑社会性质的组织犯罪、恐怖活动犯罪、走私犯罪或者其他犯罪的违法所得及其产生的收益，通过各种手段掩饰、隐瞒其来源和性质，使其在形式上合法化的行为[299]。

Money laundering mainly refers to the act of concealing and disguising the sources and natures of the illegal gains from drug-related crimes, crimes committed by organizations with the nature of the underworld, terrorist crimes, smuggling crimes, or other crimes, as well as the proceeds generated therefrom, through various means, so as to make them legitimate in form.[299]

根据一张不具来源的图表，贪污贿赂犯罪占据破获洗钱案件的5.6%。官员贪污贿赂的黑钱洗白之后，就等于毁灭了腐败分子的证据。法律专家指出："今后几年将是中国黑钱加紧洗钱的年代，如果中国听之任之，再过10年，所有中国腐败贪污分子都将堂而皇之地成为合法资本家。"[300]

According to a chart without a source, crimes of corruption and bribery account for 5.6% of the cracked money laundering cases. After the black money from officials' corruption and bribery is laundered, it is equivalent to destroying the evidence against the corrupt officials. Legal experts pointed out: "In the next few years, money laundering in China will be intensified. If the government turns a blind eye to it, in another

---

299　《侠客岛：普通官员、文艺官员和二逼官员都咋洗钱》，网易新闻（网易网）www.163.com，2014年5月26日

300　同上

10 years, all corrupt officials in China will openly become legitimate capitalists."[299]

五、混乱时期，逃过一劫，身后留名，祸福与共。

V Escape a disaster during the chaotic period, leave a good name behind after one's death, and share both fortune and misfortune.

1972 年，5 名男子潜入华盛顿水门饭店民主党总部办公室，安装窃听器并偷拍文件。调查发现，5 人为尼克松所属共和党"间谍"，尼克松政府事后试图遮掩。在众议院准备启动弹劾程序后，尼克松 1974 年 8 月宣布辞职，他政府内不少高官受到起诉、审理、定罪，甚至服刑[301]。

In 1972, five men broke into the Democratic National Committee headquarters office in the Watergate Hotel in Washington, D.C., installed wiretaps, and secretly photographed documents. An investigation revealed that the five men were "spies" of the Republican Party to which Richard Nixon belonged, and the Nixon administration tried to conceal the incident afterwards. When the House of Representatives was about to initiate impeachment proceedings, Nixon announced his resignation in August 1974. Many high-ranking officials in his administration were indicted, tried, convicted, and even served prison terms.[301]

以最著名的尼克松总统特赦案为例，福特总统上任才 30 天，在无预警也未告知任何党内大佬情况下，直接透过记者会宣布予尼克松特赦，其后果是一夕之间，福特的民调支持度由 71% 滑落到 49%，"特赦宣布的方式有如珍珠港空袭"。事后白宫也无法提出说服人心、具有法律依据的公共论述，从此以后福特陷入政治泥沼，期中选举一路输，甚至在 1976 年总统大选时败给寂寂无闻的卡特。

---

301 《"水门事件"中尼克松证词被公开》，台海中心（台海网）www.taihainet.com，2011 年 11 月 13 日

福特的政治代价是牺牲了自己的政治生涯，成就了尼克松免于牢狱之灾，而尼克松终其一生，也未对水门事件道歉、认错[302]。

Take the most famous amnesty of President Nixon as an example. Having been in office for only 30 days, President Gerald Ford, without any prior warning and without informing any of the bigwigs in his party, directly announced the amnesty of Nixon at a press conference. This led to Ford's approval rating in polls dropping from 71% to 49% overnight. "The way the amnesty was announced is comparable to the attack on Pearl Harbor." Afterwards, the White House was unable to put forward a convincing public discourse with legal basis. This incident plunged Ford into a political quagmire. He was defeated continuously in the midterm elections, and was even defeated by the relatively unknown Jimmy Carter in the 1976 presidential election. Ford's political cost was sacrificing his own political career to spare Nixon from imprisonment. Throughout his life, Nixon never apologized or admitted his fault for the Watergate incident.[302]

六、捞够钱财，逃往海外，成败与否，一起丢脸。

VI Rake in enough money and flee overseas. Regardless of success or failure, lose face together.

有人对级别的认定到了要命的程度。在机关，在行政伦理上，在会议席位先后上，在花名册排列上，排列不对有人就窝火。这倒情有可原。在机关里，在单位里，这叫行政，我们可以无条件承认和接受它的级别，你说一就是一，你说二就是二，官大一级压死人。级别就是真理，级别就是有理，机关里、单位里，全是级别说话，级别才有发言权，没级别别说话。凡事论级别。[303]

Some people care about ranks to an extreme degree. In government

---

302　《台湾时事评论员：马英九不会碰陈水扁问题》，中国新闻（中国网）www.china.com.cn，2012 年 7 月 20 日

303　马蹄撰《要命的级别》，来源《杂文月刊：原创版》，2012 年第 5 期

institutions, in terms of administrative ethics, regarding the order of seats at meetings and the sequence of names in rosters, if the arrangement is wrong, some people will feel irritated. Well, this is somewhat understandable. In government institutions and work units, this is called administration, and we have to unconditionally recognize and accept the ranks. If you say it's number one, then it's number one; if you say it's number two, then it's number two. The higher-ranking official crushes those beneath him. Rank is regarded as truth, and rank means being justified. In government institutions and work units, everything is decided by rank. Only those with a certain rank have the right to speak, and those not high enough in rank should keep silent. Everything is determined by rank.[303]

2011 年央行披露的数据显示，20 世纪 90 年代以来，外逃贪官携款超过人民币 8000 亿，导致中国大量资金外流。这同时带来跨境追逃追赃这一反腐难题[304]。

According to the data disclosed by the People's Bank of China in 2011, since the 1990s, corrupt officials who fled abroad have taken away more than 800 billion yuan in funds, resulting in a large amount of capital outflows from China. This has also led to the anti-corruption challenge of pursuing fugitives and recovering embezzled funds across borders.[304]

红色通缉令，又被称为红色通报，是国际刑警组织发出的最高级别通缉令，通缉对象是有关国家法律部门已发出逮捕令、要求成员国引渡的在逃犯。2015 年 4 月 22 日，中国集中公开了通过国际刑警组织发布的红色通缉令，曝光 100 名外逃人员，并表示要加大追缉力度[305]。

---

304 《外逃贪官携款超 8000 亿 中国已与 38 国签引渡条约》，腾讯新闻（腾讯网）www. qq.com，2014 年 8 月 25 日

305 《"百名红通"归案 40 人：多人被减刑 一人获无期》，中国青年网 www.youth.cn，2017 年 4 月 23 日

The Red Notice, also known as the Red Bulletin, is the highest-level arrest warrant issued by the International Criminal Police Organization (INTERPOL). It targets the fugitives for whom relevant national legal departments have issued arrest warrants, and whom the member states are requested to extradite. On April 22, 2015, in a concentrated manner, China made public the Red Notices issued through INTERPOL, exposing 100 fugitives who had fled abroad, and stated that it would strengthen its efforts in hunting them down.[305]

七、陆海结合，官商勾结，钱权交易，飘忽不定。

VII Combination of land-sea approaches, collusion between officials and businessmen, power-money deal, and capriciousness.

深圳与香港山水相依，历史上本为一体。近代以来，随着西方资本主义发达国家的坚船利炮轰开了闭关自守的中国国门，香港首当其冲，被分离出来租借给了英国。其后的深港两地，几经变迁，历尽沧桑。中华人民共和国的成立，标志着中国开始走上社会主义道路，对于香港问题，中共中央从长计议，采取了"维持现状"的政策，人民解放军止步于深圳河畔的罗湖桥，没有乘势收复香港。深港边境成为联系香港与祖国内地的纽带，并且在反对美国等西方国家对华禁运的斗争中，成为中国抢运战略物资的重要通道，发挥了独特的作用。另一方面，在冷战的国际背景下，深港边境也成为中英两个国家、两种社会制度较量与对峙的前沿阵地。新中国成立后，港英政府改变了长期以来粤港人民可以自由往来的传统，限制中国人自由出入香港；中国政府也开始实行出入境管理，深港边境地区的偷渡外逃现象开始出现并由此蔓延开来[306]。

Shenzhen and Hong Kong are two adjacent cities, interconnected

---

306　周华撰《试论建国初期的深圳与香港边境态势》，来源《广东党史》，2010年第4期

by mountains and rivers. They have formed a relationship of being part of each other throughout history. In modern times, as the powerful warships and cannons of developed Western capitalist countries forced open the gate of China, which had adopted a seclusion policy, Hong Kong was the first to be separated and leased to the United Kingdom. After that, Shenzhen and Hong Kong witnessed numerous vicissitudes. The founding of the People's Republic of China marked that China had embarked on the socialist path. Regarding the Hong Kong issue, the Central Committee of the Communist Party of China took a long-term view and adopted the policy of "maintaining the status quo". The People's Liberation Army stopped at Luohu Bridge on the bank of the Shenzhen River instead of taking this opportunity to recover Hong Kong. The Shenzhen-Hong Kong border became a bond between Hong Kong and China's mainland. Moreover, it played a unique role in the struggle against the embargo imposed by the United States and other Western countries, serving as an important channel for China to transport strategic materials. On the other hand, in the international background of the Cold War, the Shenzhen-Hong Kong border became the front line of the contest and confrontation between China and the United Kingdom, between two different social systems. After the founding of new China, the Hong Kong British government changed the long-standing tradition that people in Guangdong and Hong Kong could move freely between the two places, and curbed the Chinese people's free entry and exit to Hong Kong. The Chinese government also implemented exit and entry management. As a result, illegal immigration and fleeing in the Shenzhen-Hong Kong border area emerged and spread.[306]

自 1997 年 7 月 1 日香港回归中国后，香港问题就完全属于中国内政问题了。香港在"一国两制"的政策下，不仅保留了资本主义制度，与美欧等西方资本主义国家有着密切的联系，而且香港在中国的统一主权下拥有特殊的国内地位，是中国对外开放的门户，对中国的改革开放和稳定发展具有重大的意义。因此，不论是在国际还是国内，香港的地位都是十分之特殊的。国际社会对香港问题的关注也是有增无减，尤其是美国，成为继英国人走后香港问题的最大干预者[307]。

Since Hong Kong's return to China on July 1, 1997, the Hong Kong issue has thoroughly become an internal affair of China. Under the policy of "one country, two systems", Hong Kong has not only retained the capitalist system, having close ties with the United States, European countries, and other Western capitalist countries, but also enjoys a special domestic status under China's unified sovereignty, serving as the gateway for China's opening up, and playing a significant role in promoting China's reform and opening up, and maintaining stable development. Therefore, whether internationally or domestically, Hong Kong enjoys a very special status. The international community's attention to the Hong Kong issue is increasing instead of decreasing. Especially, the United States interferes most deeply in the Hong Kong issue after the withdrawal of the British government.[307]

改革开放初，深圳经济特区甫一创办，便融入邓小平倡导的实现四个现代化、实现中国统一这两大历史任务中。在香港回归谈判前后，深圳特区政治、经济内涵有明显发展。中国政府在与英国政府谈判中圆满实现了目标，在对深圳特区这个棋子的运用上也颇具匠心。深圳特区在国家全局战略中的位置由此奠定[308]。

When the Shenzhen Special Economic Zone was established at the

---

307 郝文娟撰《1997—2007 年美国对香港政策研究》，来源《广东外语外贸大学》，2008 年

308 王硕撰《深圳经济特区与香港回归谈判》，来源《百年潮》，2012 年第 10 期

beginning of China's reform and opening up, it immediately assumed the two historical assignments advocated by Deng Xiaoping: achieving the four modernizations and realizing China's reunification. Before and after the negotiations on Hong Kong's return, the political and economic connotations of the Shenzhen Special Economic Zone underwent significant development. The Chinese government not only successfully achieved its goals in the negotiations with the British government, but also showed great ingenuity in employing the Shenzhen Special Economic Zone as a chess piece. Thus, the position of the Shenzhen Special Economic Zone in the overall national strategy was established.[308]

在 2015 年，廉政公署历时 3 年调查，香港前特首曾荫权被指接受富豪款待（乘搭私人飞机及游艇外游）、接受红酒等礼物、在深圳租住商人豪宅，涉嫌利益输送的事件[309]。

In 2015, after a three-year investigation by the Independent Commission Against Corruption, Donald Tsang Yam-kuen, the former Chief Executive of Hong Kong, was accused of accepting the hospitality of wealthy people (including traveling by private jet and yacht), accepting red wine and other gifts, and renting a luxury mansion owned by a businessman in Shenzhen, and was suspected of interest transfer.[309]

2018 年 7 月，据港媒报道，现年 73 岁的曾荫权，被裁定于 2010 年 1 月 1 日至 2012 年 6 月 30 日期间，以特首及行会主席的身份，参与处理雄涛广播的牌照等 3 项申请时，没有向行会申报他与雄涛股东黄楚标之间就深圳豪宅居所商谈租约，当时被陪审团以 8 比 1 裁定罪成，被判入狱 20 个月，他服刑约两个月后获准保释。[310]

---

309 《曾荫权被指涉嫌利益输送 港廉署已完成调查》，腾讯新闻（腾讯网），www.qq.com，2015 年 1 月 27 日

310 《前港首曾荫权定罪上诉被驳回 减刑至 12 个月》，海外网资讯（海外网），www.haiwainet.cn，2019 年 1 月 15 日

In July 2018, according to Hong Kong media, Donald Tsang Yam-kuen, who was 73 years old at that time, was ruled guilty. During the period from January 1, 2010, to June 30, 2012, when Donald Tsang Yam-kuen, in his capacity as the Chief Executive and Chairman of the Executive Council, handled three applications, one of which concerned the license of Wave Media Limited, he didn't declare to the Executive Council the negotiated lease regarding the luxury residence in Shenzhen between him and Wong Cho-bau, a shareholder of Wave Media Limited. At that time, he was ruled guilty by the jury by a majority vote of 8 to 1, and was sentenced to 20 months in prison. Then, after serving about two months in prison, he was granted bail.[310]

曾荫权后向终审法院提出终极上诉。2019 年 6 月，终审法院 5 位法官 26 日一致裁定其上诉成功，定罪和刑期一并撤销。终审法院下令此案不作重审[311]。

Later, Donald Tsang Yam-kuen lodged a final appeal with the Court of Final Appeal. On June 26, 2019, the five judges of the Court of Final Appeal unanimously ruled that his appeal was successful, and both the conviction and the sentence were canceled. The Court of Final Appeal ordered that the case should not be retried.[311]

八、政治商人屈服暴利和暴力，利用政策优势，顺水推舟，漂洋过海。

VIII Political merchants yield to the lure of huge profits and violence, take advantage of policies, act in accordance with the trend, and venture across the sea.

在香港的腾飞期，李嘉诚白手起家创立了一个庞大商业帝国，

311　《香港特区前行政长官曾荫权获撤销定罪和刑期》，东方网国内（东方网），www.eastday.com，2019 年 6 月 26 日

成为凭借自己的奋斗实现"香港梦"的典型代表，深受敬仰。但随着香港社会贫富差距日益拉大，掌控着港岛经济命脉并且深深影响公共政策的财团广受抨击，李嘉诚首当其冲[312]。

During the booming period of Hong Kong, Li Ka-shing started from scratch and established a huge business empire. As a representative who realized the "Hong Kong Dream" through his own hard work, he was widely respected. However, as the gap between the rich and the poor in Hong Kong society widened increasingly, the financial groups that controlled the economic lifeline of Hong Kong and had a profound influence on public policies were widely criticized, and Li Ka-shing was the first to be affected.[312]

然而，李嘉诚对自己的垄断行为却几无反思。2013 年 3 月，在面对多个社会团体的抗议，要求政府创设"李嘉诚税"（资产增值税、股息税和累进利得税），通过财富再分配解决香港贫富悬殊的问题时，李嘉诚一笑置之，称这正是他多年来加大海外投资的原因，树大招风，引起社会仇富很正常。既然大家不愿意看到他垄断香港，那他就去欧洲、去北美、去内地投资[313]。

However, Li Ka-shing hardly reflected on his monopolistic behavior. In March 2013, in the face of protests from multiple social groups, which called on the government to establish the "Li Ka-shing Tax" (asset value-added tax, dividend tax, and progressive profit tax) to address the issue of the huge gap between the rich and the poor in Hong Kong through wealth redistribution, Li Ka-shing dismissed them with a laugh, saying that this was exactly the reason why he had increased his overseas investments

---

312 《李嘉诚，从"超人"到"万恶的资本家"》，搜狐财经（搜狐网）www.sohu.com，2013 年 11 月 7 日

313 《宗庆后：李嘉诚垄断香港多个行业损害港人利益》，搜狐财经（搜狐网）www.sohu.com，2013 年 8 月 16 日

over the years. As tall trees catch much wind, the wealthy tend to be hated by others. Since no one was willing to see his monopoly position in Hong Kong, he would turn to investing in Europe, North America, and China's mainland.[313]

从 20 世纪 70 年代末开始，受回归预期的影响，英资集团开始部署撤离，李嘉诚被他们选中为"接盘侠"，1979 年 9 月，汇丰银行将总市值 28.6 亿港元的和记洋行以 6.39 亿港元出售予李嘉诚，使之一跃而入港商超级俱乐部。1984 年中英谈判，李嘉诚积极向中方靠拢，高调入资荣毅仁的中信信托。此后 30 年，他成为北京最信任和依靠的首席商人领袖，长袖善舞间，硬生生地让香港成为"李家城"[314]。

From the late 1970s, influenced by the expected return of Hong Kong, British capital groups began to make arrangements for withdrawal, and Li Ka-shing was chosen by them as a "fall guy". In September 1979, the Hongkong and Shanghai Banking Corporation sold Hutchison Whampoa, whose total market value was HK$2.86 billion, to Li Ka-shing for HK$639 million, making him a member of the Hong Kong entrepreneurs super club. During the Sino-British negotiations in 1984, Li Ka-shing actively aligned with the Chinese side and made a high-profile investment in CITIC Trust led by Rong Yiren. In the following 30 years, he became the most trusted and reliable chief business leader in Beijing Through his skillful maneuvering, he virtually turned Hong Kong into the "City of the Li Family".[314]

李嘉诚对大陆的勇猛进击，则是 90 年代之后的事情，1992 年年底，北京召开中共十四大，确立了"建设社会主义市场经济体

---

314 《在这个即将来临的周末，长江和记开启后李嘉诚时代》，腾讯网 www.qq.com，2018 年 3 月 17 日

制"的国家新战略，李嘉诚扮演了一个热烈响应的重要角色[315]。

It was not until the 1990s that Li Ka-shing started his bold actions toward China's mainland. At the end of 1992, the 14th National Congress of the Communist Party of China was held to establish the new national strategy of "building socialist market economic system". Li Ka-shing played an important role of active response.[315]

李嘉诚与英国有着长期的关系，2000 年被英女王授予 KBE 爵士勋位。他在英国的投资遍布众多公用事业，从法国电力公司（EDF）在英国的分销业务到天然气公司 Wales West Utilities，以及 Northumbrian 水务公司，这些全部是他过去 5 年收购的[316]。

Li Ka-shing had a long-term relationship with the UK. In 2000, he was conferred the title of Knight Commander of the Order of the British Empire (KBE) by Queen Elizabeth II. His investments in the UK covered many public utilities, ranging from the distribution business of Électricité de France (EDF) in the UK to the gas company Wales West Utilities and Northumbrian Water Group. All these had been acquired by him over the past five years.[316]

九、以权谋私，必有好处；遗臭万年，在所不惜。

IX Abusing power can inevitably bring about benefits. Feel no regret even if it means leaving a bad name for posterity.

李鸿章（1823—1901），安徽合肥人，世人多尊称李中堂，亦称李合肥，本名章桐，字渐甫或子黻，号少荃（泉），晚年自号仪叟，别号省心，谥文忠。作为淮军创始人和统帅、洋务运动的主要倡导者之一、晚清重臣，他官至直隶总督兼北洋通商大臣，授文华

315　同上

316　《李嘉诚近乎买下英国 控制三大行业》，搜狐财经（搜狐网）www.sohu.com，2015 年 10 月 23 日

殿大学士[317]。

Li Hongzhang (1823-1901), a native of Hefei, Anhui Province, was usually respectfully addressed as Li Zhongtang. He was also known as Li Hefei. His original name was Zhangtong, with the courtesy names Jianfu or Zifu, and the style name Shaoquan. In his later years, he called himself Yisou, with the alternative name Shengxin, and was posthumously titled Wenzhong. As the founder and commander-in-chief of the Huai Army, one of the main advocates of the Westernization Movement, and a high-ranking official in the late Qing Dynasty, he held the positions of Governor-General of Zhili and Minister of Commerce for the Northern Ports, and was conferred the title of Grand Secretary of the Wenhua Hall.[317]

李鸿章去世时，留给子孙 4000 万两白银，当时全国财政收入不过 8000 万两。这些钱，主要是办洋务贪污，还有徒子徒孙孝敬的。[318]

When Li Hongzhang died, he left his descendants 40 million taels of silver. At that time, the national fiscal revenue was only 80 million taels. This money mainly came from embezzlement during the Westernization Movement and offerings from his disciples and followers.[318]

对李鸿章的评价，世人历来观点都是多元的，也常常是极端的。在有的人看来，李鸿章是晚清的"中兴之臣"，只是苦于没有理想的施政环境，埋没了自身的才华，如果把伊藤博文和李鸿章换个位，日本会更强大，清朝会更无能。也有的人认为李鸿章是宰相合肥天下瘦，不过是晚清时代众多中饱私囊的权臣中的一个而已。而在有的人看来，没有李鸿章，晚清会加速灭亡，国家甚至会被列强瓜分，认为李鸿章甚至可以上升到民族英雄的地位。不过也有一些人直到现在依旧认为李鸿章是替清朝镇压汉人的汉奸，是个专门

317　《李鸿章：功过一生》，腾讯新闻（腾讯网）www.qq.com，2019 年 3 月 6 日

318　《客观评价李鸿章：贪官还是忠臣?》，腾讯新闻（腾讯网）www.qq.com，2018 年 12 月 8 日

签订不平等条约的卖国贼，正是因为他的一些举措，让中国在中法战争中不败而败，甲午战争遭遇惨败，改变了国家的命运[319]。

People's evaluations of Li Hongzhang are diverse and often extreme throughout history. In the eyes of some people, he was a "minister of rejuvenation" in the late Qing Dynasty; however, due to the lack of an ideal governing environment, his talents were stifled; if Ito Hirobumi and Li Hongzhang had switched positions, Japan would have become even more powerful, and the Qing Dynasty would have become even weaker. In the eyes of some people, Li Hongzhang was a "prime minister from Hefei who made the whole country poor", and he was only one of the many powerful officials in the late Qing Dynasty who lined their own pockets. In the eyes of some people, without Li Hongzhang, the late Qing Dynasty would have perished more quickly, and the country might even have been carved up by the Western powers; therefore, he can be regarded as a national hero. However, even today, some people still think that Li Hongzhang was a traitor who suppressed the Han people on behalf of the Qing Dynasty and signed unequal treaties specially. It was due to some of his measures that although China achieved military victory in the Sino-French War, it still suffered humiliation. These measures also caused China to suffer a crushing defeat in the First Sino-Japanese War. As a result, the fate of the country was changed.[319]

十、破罐破摔，虚情假意，图谋不轨，东山再起。

X Abandon oneself to despair, be hypocritical, have ulterior motives, and make a comeback.

南明（1644—1662）是指农民军李自成攻进北京，明朝崇祯帝

---

319 《颇具争议的李鸿章，功过该如何评价?》，腾讯新闻（腾讯网）www.qq.com，2018年10月15日

自缢殉国后，吴三桂开关迎清军，清朝趁机夺取了胜利果实，福临（顺治）登上帝座，东南各省明军将领不服，拥戴明裔，纷纷起兵勤王抵抗，力图复明的这段历史 [320]。

The Southern Ming Dynasty (1644-1662) refers to the historical period after Li Zicheng, the leader of the peasant army, captured Beijing and Emperor Chongzhen of the Ming Dynasty hanged himself for his country. During this period, Wu Sangui opened the Shanhai Pass to welcome the Qing army, the Qing Dynasty took this opportunity to seize the fruits of victory, and Emperor Fulin (Shunzhi) ascended the throne. However, the Ming generals in southeastern provinces refused to accept this situation. They supported the imperial descendants of the Ming Dynasty, and raised troops successively to rescue the throne and fight against the Qing Dynasty, attempting to restore the Ming Dynasty.[320]

吴三桂是影响明末清初历史进程的重要人物，同时也被许多正统史家视为十恶不赦的反面人物。作为明末辽东总兵，吴三桂因为勤王不力，导致京城被李自成起义军攻陷、崇祯皇帝自杀，被视为不忠。作为汉人，吴三桂因引清军入关，消灭了李自成起义军，被视为汉奸。降清之后，吴三桂对南明政权穷追不舍，斩尽杀绝，被视为无情。清人统一中国后，吴三桂作为镇守云南的平西王，又起兵叛清，被视为逆臣。这样一个没有原则、反复无常的人，自然与儒家文化所倡导的忠义格格不入 [321]。

Wu Sangui was an important person who influenced the historical process in the late Ming and early Qing Dynasties, but he was regarded by many orthodox historians as an extremely heinous negative figure. As the

---

320 顾峰撰《论大西军与永历朝的联明抗清》，来源《楚雄师范学院学报》，1996 年第1 期

321 《吴三桂的无奈人生：从降清到反清，都是逼上梁山》，腾讯新闻（腾讯网）www.qq.com，2019 年 10 月 6 日

General of Liaodong at the end of the Ming Dynasty, he failed to make a sufficient effort to rescue the throne, which led to the capital being captured by Li Zicheng's peasant army and Emperor Chongzhen's suicide, so he was regarded as disloyal. As a member of the Han ethnic group, he led the Qing army into the Shanhai Pass and eliminated Li Zicheng's peasant army, so he was regarded as a traitor. After surrendering to the Qing Dynasty, he fiercely attacked the Southern Ming regime and exterminated its royal members, so he was regarded as merciless. After the Qing forces unified China, as Prince Pingxi who garrisoned Yunnan, he rebelled against the Qing Dynasty, so he was regarded as a rebellious minister. Such an unprincipled and capricious person was naturally incompatible with the loyalty and righteousness advocated by Confucian culture.[321]

十一、利用契约，利用一高一低，利用时间沉淀，运用"三合一"造成差价，从中聚敛钱财。

XI Mass wealth by leveraging contracts, high-low differences, time deposits, and price differences caused by the "three-in-one".

台湾检方特侦组成立于 2007 年，全称为"最高法院检察署特别侦查组"。其主要任务是侦办比较重大的经济犯罪或高官大案，特侦组的检察官直接对台"检察总长"负责，办案过程回避性强、守密性高，特别是在侦办大案和高官要案时，其独立层次是台湾地区侦办机构中最高的。[322]

Taiwan Prosecutorial Special Investigation Panel was established in 2007, with the full name being "Special Investigation Panel of the Supreme Prosecutors Office". Its main task is to investigate major economic crimes or crimes related to high-level officials. The prosecutors

---

322 《台湾检方特侦组新增 6 名检察官》搜狐新闻（搜狐网），www.sohu.com，2009 年 3 月 25 日

of the special investigation panel are directly responsible to the "Prosecutor-General" of Taiwan, and the case-handling process is highly avoidance-oriented and confidential. Especially when investigating major cases and cases related to high-level officials, it holds the highest independence among the investigative institutions in the Taiwan region.[322]

2009 年 12 月，台湾检方特侦组 24 日宣布，陈水扁等涉及"二次金改"衍生弊案侦查结束，依贪污、洗钱等罪起诉包括陈水扁一家 4 口在内的 23 人。检方认定，陈水扁夫妇在此案中收受金融企业贿款逾 6 亿元新台币。[323]

On December, 24, 2009, the special investigation panel announced the conclusion of its investigation into the derivative corruption case related to "second financial reform", which involved Chen Shui-bian and his party. 23 people, including Chen Shui-bian's 4 family members, were prosecuted for corruption, money laundering and other crimes. The prosecution determined that Chen Shui-bian and his wife had received bribes of more than 600 million New Taiwan dollars from financial enterprises in this case.[323]

2010 年 6 月，台湾高等法院就陈水扁家族所涉"机要费"贪腐案等多起弊案作出二审判决，判决陈水扁 20 年有期徒刑，判决陈水扁之妻吴淑珍 20 年有期徒刑，均比一审时有所减轻。[324]

In June 2010, the Taiwan High Court made a second-instance judgment on the "confidential expense" case and other corruption cases involving the Chen Shui-bian family, sentencing Chen Shui-bian and his wife Wu Shu-zhen to 20 years of fixed-term imprisonment. This sentence

---

323　《陈水扁一家因涉金改弊案被起诉》《宁波日报 第 A14 版：国内新闻》，2009 年 12 月 25 日

324　《陈水扁家族贪腐弊案二审获轻判》新浪财经（新浪网），www.sina.com.cn，2010 年 6 月 12 日

was lighter than the first-instance judgment.[324]

2014 年，台湾方面对照陈水扁家 7 年前以 1.2 亿多元买下两户宝徕豪宅，北检卖掉 1 户就得款 1.2 亿多元，显示扁家宝徕房价短短 7 年就增值 1 倍[325]。

In 2014, the Taiwan side compared the two Baolai luxury mansions bought by Chen Shui-bian's family seven years ago for more than 120 million yuan. The Taipei District Prosecutors' Office sold one mansion and got more than 120 million yuan. This meant that the value of Chen Shui-bian's Baolai mansions doubled in only seven years.[325]

十二、先苦后甜，站稳脚跟，大捞油水，派头十足。

XII Happiness comes after suffering. Stand firm, make a fortune, and show off.

1952 年 2 月 10 日，星期日，正是正月十五闹红火的日子，而河北省省会城市古城保定，却笼罩在一片激愤冷峻的气氛中，因为这天是枪毙大贪污犯刘青山、张子善的日子[326]。

February 10, 1952, a Sunday, coincided with the Lantern Festival, but the ancient city of Baoding, the capital of Hebei Province, was shrouded in an atmosphere of anger and chill. It was the day when the embezzlers Liu Qingshan and Zhang Zishan were executed.[326]

对于刘、张二人在新中国成立前的历史，中共河北省委在开除二人党籍的决议中，也有一段评价："刘青山、张子善参加革命斗争均已 20 年左右，他们在国民党血腥的白色恐怖下，在艰难的八年抗日战争和三年多的人民解放战争中，都曾奋不顾身地为党和人民群

---

325 《台北检方首次出售陈水扁资产 一豪宅卖出 1.3 亿台币》，中华网新闻（中华网）www.china.com，2014 年 9 月 14 日

326 史云、李新撰《轰动全国的刘青山张子善贪污案》，来源《文史月刊》，2003 年第 4 期

众的解放，进行过英勇的斗争，建立过功绩。"[327]

Regarding the history of Liu Qingshan and Zhang Zishan before the founding of new China, the Hebei Provincial Committee of the Communist Party of China had a comment in its resolution to expel the two from the Party: "Liu Qingshan and Zhang Zishan participated in revolutionary struggles about 20 years ago. Under the bloody white terror of the Kuomintang, during the eight-year arduous War of Resistance Against Japanese Aggression and the three-year-plus People's Liberation War, they fought bravely for the cause of the Party and the liberation of the people, and made great contributions."[327]

1949 年 8 月，张子善任中共天津地委副书记、天津区行政督察专员公署专员。1951 年 6 月，继刘青山任中共天津地委书记[328]。

In August 1949, Zhang Zishan was appointed as the deputy secretary of the Tianjin Municipal Committee of the Communist Party of China and the commissioner of the Tianjin District Administrative Inspectorate. In June 1951, he succeeded Liu Qingshan as the secretary of the Tianjin Municipal Committee of the Communist Party of China.[328]

刘青山、张子善一时间将天津地委、天津专署搞成一个水泼不进、针插不进的独立王国。为了掩饰其罪恶行为，他们压制民主，破坏党的组织原则，建立自己的封建统治秩序[329]。

Liu Qingshan and Zhang Zishan immediately turned the Tianjin Municipal Committee and Tianjin Special Commissioner's Office into an independent kingdom immune to any external influence. In order to

327 《揭秘新中国肃贪首案：刘青山、张子善被判处死刑全过程》，搜狐文化（搜狐网）www.sohu.com，2013 年 1 月 28 日

328 《哪两位中共高官为刘青山张子善向毛泽东求情》，凤凰历史（凤凰网）www.ifeng.com，2012 年 8 月 26 日

329 半戎（整理）撰《重话刘青山与张子善》，来源《文史月刊》，2011 年第 12 期

conceal their crimes, they suppressed democracy, destroyed the Party's organizational principles, and established their feudal ruling order.[329]

这两人居功自傲，贪图享受，革命意志消沉，腐化堕落。他们扬言："天下是老子打下来的，享受一点还不应当吗？"[330]

The two people were arrogant because of their contributions, greedy for pleasure, and weak in their revolutionary will, thus becoming corrupt. They boasted, "Since the regime was established with my efforts, isn't it justifiable to indulge myself a bit?"[330]

当刘青山、张子善将被处决的消息在内部传开之后，在河北省各级干部中引起极大的震动。一些干部特别是当年曾和刘青山、张子善一起出生入死闹革命的干部，感到惋惜，有不少的议论。有的说："他们是有功之臣，不能杀呀！"有的认为："可以判个重刑，让他们劳动改造，重新做人。"有的呼吁："希望中央能刀下留情！"有的感叹："30多岁正是好年华，说杀就杀了，实在可惜，应该给他们一个立功赎罪的机会。"[331]……

When the news that Liu Qingshan and Zhang Zishan would be executed spread within the Party, it caused a great shock among the cadres at all levels in Hebei Province. Some cadres, especially those who had fought with them in the revolutionary cause, felt sorry and talked about it heatedly. Some said, "They are meritorious officials, and shouldn't be killed!" Some thought, "They can be sentenced to heavy punishment, be reformed through labor and start a new life." Some appealed, "I hope that the central government can show some mercy!" Some sighed, "The thirties are truly the golden years. It's a pity that they

---

330　《毛泽东如何惩治腐败分子：先后处死七名贪官》，人民网文史频道（人民网）www.people.com.cn，2013年2月19日

331　《处决刘青山和张子善细节 毛泽东亲批斩杀令》，凤凰历史（凤凰网）www.ifeng.com，2009年7月28日

will be killed like that. They should be given a chance to make up for their mistakes and redeem themselves."...[331]

这些意见和呼声，集中地反映到了当时的天津市委书记那里。他觉得有必要向毛泽东和党中央反映一下，于是他找到了华北局第一书记薄一波。他对薄一波说：刘青山、张子善错误严重，罪有应得，当判重刑。但考虑到他们在战争年代出生入死，有过功劳，在干部中影响较大，是否可以向毛主席说说，不要枪毙了，给他们一个改过的机会[332]。

These opinions and appeals were collected and reported to the then Tianjin Municipal Committee Secretary. He felt it necessary to report them to Mao Zedong and the Central Committee of the Party, so he visited Bo Yibo, the first secretary of the North China Bureau, and said, "Liu Qingshan and Zhang Zishan's mistakes are serious and deserve heavy punishment. However, considering that they risked their lives in the wars, made great contributions and had a significant influence among cadres, can you suggest to Chairman Mao that they should be spared the death penalty and given a chance to reform themselves."[332]

在这种情况下，薄一波如实地向毛泽东转达了"枪下留人"的意见[333]。

In this context, Bo Yibo truthfully conveyed the opinion of "staying the execution" to Mao Zedong.[333]

毛泽东在听了薄一波转述的意见后，抽着烟，沉思了一会儿，对薄一波说了几句话："正因为他们两人的地位高，功劳大，影响大，所以才要下决心处决他们。只有处决他们，才可能挽救 20 个、200 个、2000 个、2 万个犯有各种不同程度错误的干部。"[334]

332　同上
333　同上
334　同上

After listening to the opinions relayed by Bo Yibo, Mao Zedong smoked a cigarette, thought for a while, and said, "It is precisely because of their high status, great contributions, and great influences that we must make up our minds to execute them. Only by executing them can we save 20, 200, 2,000, or even 20,000 cadres who have committed various mistakes of different degrees."[334]

社会天长地久，经济条件决定物质生活，贪欲未泯的凡夫俗子以身试法不惜铤而走险。即便是英雄人物，也能蜕化为祸国殃民的蛀虫。这些都充分证明"人为财死，鸟为食亡"的吸引力。也印证了有些时代是"实则先有享福，才有国家，而非先有国家，才有享福"。

Society is eternal. Economic conditions determine material life. People with unquenched greed tend to defy the law at their own peril. Even heroes can degenerate into pests that bring disasters to the country and the people. These all fully demonstrate the truth of the saying "people die for wealth, and birds die for food". It also reflects that in some eras, "happiness exists before the establishment of a country, rather than coming from the establishment of a country".

预防胜于治疗。反腐人士要敏锐察觉到贪污腐败藏在"好事和坏事"里面。人腐败容易，反腐困难。腐败重可以让国家灭亡，腐败轻是国家起死回生的"种子"。譬如俄国历史是先有沙俄，才有苏联，接下来才是俄联邦。在 20 世纪，沙俄和苏联是敌对关系，俄罗斯人在 1991 年苏联解体后，重造国家之时选择俄罗斯联邦来代表自己。

Prevention is better than cure. Anti-corruption activists should be keenly aware that corruption is hidden in "good and bad things". It's easy for people to be corrupt, but it's difficult to fight against corruption. Serious corruption can lead to the extinction of a country, while light corruption is a "seed" for the rebirth of a country. For example, the

Russian history witnessed the succession of the Tsarist Russia, the Soviet Union, and the Russian Federation. In the 20th century, the Tsarist Russia and the Soviet Union were hostile to each other. After the disintegration of the Soviet Union in 1991, the Russian people chose the Russian Federation to represent themselves.

如果要俄罗斯人"二选一"，选择用苏联来代表自己，而不用俄联邦做最终代表，没有富足财产的苏联领导人斯大林能成为一种旗帜鲜明的化学试剂。

If the Russians were asked to make a decision between the two, i.e. to choose the Soviet Union to represent themselves or to choose the Russian Federation to represent themselves, then Stalin, the Soviet Union leader with no substantial fortune, would become a chemical reagent with distinct features.

"妖魔化斯大林"是西方在冷战的"人心之争"中取得胜利的手段之一。苏联历史上的"去斯大林化"运动导致了历史虚无主义泛滥和社会思想混乱等严重后果，也引发了后来的俄罗斯社会围绕"如何评价斯大林的历史作用和历史地位"这一焦点问题的长期斗争和舆论争议。近年来俄罗斯多家民意调查机构长期持续的数据显示，对斯大林持正面评价的受访者数量在不断增长，特别是年轻人对国家历史有了更全面的认识，俄罗斯民众对斯大林在国家历史中的作用持肯定态度成为一种新的"社会常态"。同时，俄罗斯通过实施国家文化战略和一系列专项文化建设方案，注重发挥国家主流政治价值观的指引作用，以重振国家气质和民族精神 [335]。

"Demonization of Stalin" was a method employed by the West to achieve victory in the "battle for people's hearts" during the Cold War.

---

335 许华撰《俄罗斯社会在斯大林评价问题上的新变化》，来源《世界社会主义研究》，2019 年第 8 期

The "de-Stalinization" movement led to serious consequences such as the rampant spread of historical nihilism and the chaos of social thoughts. It also triggered a long-term struggle and public opinion controversies in Russian society later, with the central issue being "how to evaluate Stalin's historical role and status." In recent years, according to long-term and continuous data from several public opinion polling agencies in Russia, more and more respondents hold a positive view of Stalin. In particular, as young people have gained a more comprehensive understanding of the national history, it has become a new "social norm" for the Russian people to hold a positive attitude towards Stalin's role in the national history. At the same time, Russia has implemented the national cultural strategy and a series of special cultural construction programs, with emphasis on giving play to the guiding role of the national mainstream political values, so as to revitalize the national temperament and the national spirit.[335]

斯大林一生俭朴，不仅得到他身边工作人员的证实，而且连一再指责斯大林的人也说斯大林是个禁欲主义者。苏联党和国家领导人谢列平说："斯大林死后，人们登记总书记的财产时发现，这件工作很简单。没有任何贵重的东西，除了一架公家的钢琴，甚至没有一幅好的、真正的画。摆的是不值钱的家具，沙发椅套着布套。没有一件古董，墙上挂的是普通木框镶的纸印复制品。在客厅的中心部位挂了一幅玛·伊·乌里扬诺娃 1922 年 9 月在哥尔克拍的放大的照片，上面有列宁和斯大林。地板上铺了两块地毯。斯大林睡觉时盖的是战士们用的被子。除一身元帅服之外，穿的东西中有两套普通衣服（一套是帆布服），一双绱了鞋底的毡靴和一件农民穿的皮袄。"[336]

---

336 肖德甫著《世纪悲歌：苏联共产党执政失败的前前后后》，北京：中共党史出版社，2008 年 8 月

Stalin lived simply all his life, which was confirmed by the staff members around him. Even those who repeatedly criticized him described him as an ascetic. Alexander Nikolayevich Shelepin, a leader of the Soviet Union Party and State, said, "After the death of General Secretary Stalin, people found it very easy to register his property. There was nothing valuable. Except for a piano owned by the state, there wasn't even a good, genuine painting. The furniture was of little value, and the sofa was covered with a cloth cover. There were no antiques. The walls were decorated with paper prints in ordinary wooden frames. In the central part of the living room hung an enlarged photo taken by Maria Ilyinichna Ulyanova in Gorki in September 1922, which showed Lenin and Stalin. There were two carpets on the floor. When Stalin slept, he covered himself with a quilt used by soldiers. In addition to a marshal's uniform, his clothes included two ordinary outfits (one was a canvas suit), a pair of felt boots sewed with soles, and a peasant's sheepskin coat."[336]

比起旧朝代，新朝代在各个方面都各胜一筹才是正宗的成功。然而，苏联推翻沙俄，俄国内战前后仍有一定数量的俄罗斯士农工商怀念沙俄，这就是苏联推翻沙俄的不足。

A new dynasty can be considered a genuine success only when it surpasses the old dynasty in all aspects. However, after the Soviet Union overthrew Tsarist Russia, during and after the Russian Civil War, there were still a certain number of Russian people from all walks of life, including scholars, farmers, artisans, and merchants, who missed Tsarist Russia. This shows the weakness of the Soviet Union despite its overthrow of Tsarist Russia.

1917 年十月革命前，俄国的移民主要是逃避沙皇当局迫害，进行革命活动的知识分子。他们大都侨居在日内瓦、巴黎和伦敦等大城市中。另外，还有移居西欧、北美的农民和犹太人。10 年后，情况发生了根本逆转，原来那批革命知识分子陆续回国（他们中有些人对 30 年代的恐怖感到震惊和失望，后来又回到侨居地）。而随着白军的溃退，近百万俄国人离乡背井，移居世界各地 [337]。

Before the October Revolution in 1917, the Russian immigrants were mainly intellectuals who fled the persecution of the Tsarist authorities and participated in revolutionary activities. Most of them lived in big cities such as Geneva, Paris, and London. In addition, there were farmers and Jews who migrated to Western Europe and North America. Ten years later, the situation was completely changed. The original revolutionary intellectuals returned to their homeland successively (some of them were shocked and disappointed by the terror in the 1930s, and later returned to their places of residence abroad). After the White Guards were routed, nearly one million Russians left their hometowns and migrated to all parts of the world.[337]

1917 年，列宁和托洛茨基并肩领导了俄国的十月革命。1924 年列宁死后，斯大林夺取了布尔什维克的最高领导权。1928 年，托洛茨基因反对斯大林再次被流放到西伯利亚，1929 年被驱逐出境，最后在墨西哥被斯大林派遣的特工刺杀身亡 [338]。

In 1917, Lenin and Trotsky jointly led the October Revolution in Russia. After Lenin's death in 1924, Stalin seized the highest leadership of the Bolsheviks. In 1928, Trotsky was again exiled to Siberia due to his opposition to Stalin. In 1929, he was expelled from Russia. In the end, he was assassinated by agents dispatched by Stalin in Mexico.[338]

此后，在苏联大清洗中，数百万人遭到监禁、流放，其中不少人是沙俄时代的老牌政治犯，他们不无怀念地回忆起沙皇时代的监

337　萤窗撰《苏联移民问题今昔》，来源《俄罗斯研究》，1989 年第 3 期
338　《苏联大清洗时期，沙皇的监狱为何让人怀念?》，人民网文史（人民网）www. people.com.cn，2010 年 11 月 22 日

狱生涯。梅利古诺夫说："那是沙皇的监狱，幸福的回忆中的监狱，现在政治犯们几乎怀着欢乐的感情去回忆它。"[339]

Later, during the Great Purge of the Soviet Union, millions of people were imprisoned and exiled, including many veteran political prisoners during the Tsarist era. They recalled their prison life during the Tsarist era with nostalgia. Meligonov said, "It was the Tsar's prison, a prison from happy memories. Now, almost all the political prisoners recall it with happy feelings."[339]

腐败能够决定战争的胜负，对反恐有莫大的阻碍。不过，即使如此，自古以来，许多人将贪腐视为打开富贵之门的必需手段。犹如富贵险中求，腐败是恐怖主义之母，有贪污腐败就能时常看见恐怖主义的身影。

Corruption can determine the outcome of a war and acts as a great obstacle to counter-terrorism. However, since ancient times, many people have regarded corruption as a necessary means to achieve wealth and rank. Just as the saying goes, "Wealth is sought through risks," corruption is the mother of terrorism. Where there is corruption, there is often a shadow of terrorism.

倘若学术界愿意从社会学视角观察，那么，腐败实际上是一种消极的越轨行为。这恰恰是当前腐败问题研究者所忽视的一种思路。社会学认为，任何人行为的动因在于追求满足自身欲望的社会资源，而社会资源的有限必然决定它采取一定的所有权形式，因而个人追求社会资源的行为必然是一种涉及他人利益的社会行为，必须遵循一定的社会规范。除宗教规范以外，社会规范体系主要由两大子系统构成，一是合理性规范，主要由观念规范（世界观、人生观、价值观）和道德规范（道德、风俗习惯等）所构成的观念道德

339　同上

规范；二是广义的合法性规范，主要由纪律规范（党纪政纪）、法律规范（法律法规）和制度规范（政治经济制度及其管理体制）所构成的法纪制度规范。狭义的合法性规范是指符合法律规范。在现实生活中，人们往往企图超越这些社会规范的限制，表现为越轨行为。所谓越轨行为就是指偏离或违反社会行为规范的行为。它兼具好坏两重性，凡是违反落后的反动的社会规范的越轨行为，都是有利于社会公共生活或社会进步的积极的越轨行为；凡是违反合理性和合法性社会规范的越轨行为，都是妨碍社会公共生活或社会进步的消极的越轨行为。唯有这种消极的越轨行为才是腐败。因此，腐败是违反合理性和合法性社会规范且妨碍社会公共生活或社会进步的行为。这个以社会规范为轴心的腐败定义，囊括一切社会腐败行为，指出腐败的一般特性在于它的不合法性和不合理性，强调腐败是妨碍社会公共生活或社会进步的社会问题。但该定义不能指明权力腐败的主体、客体、目的和手段等因素 [340]。

If the academic community is willing to observe corruption from the sociological perspective, it will see that corruption is actually a negative deviant behavior. This is exactly a way of thinking that is often neglected by current researchers on the issue of corruption. Sociology holds that the motivation for anyone's behavior lies in the pursuit of social resources to satisfy his/her own desires. The limitation of social resources inevitably determines that they should take a certain form of ownership. Therefore, the individual pursuit of social resources must be a social behavior that involves the interests of others and must follow certain social norms. Apart from religious norms, the social norm system is mainly composed of two major subsystems. The first is the rationality norms, mainly composed of the conceptual and moral norms, which

---

340 蔡陈聪撰：《腐败定义及其类型》，来源《中国青年政治学院学报》，2001 年第 2 期

include conceptual norms (world outlook, outlook on life, values) and moral norms (morality, customs, etc.). The second is legitimacy norms in a broad sense, mainly composed of the discipline and institutional norms, which include discipline norms (Party discipline and government discipline), legal norms (laws and regulations), and institutional norms (political and economic systems and their management systems). The legitimacy norms in a narrow sense refer to compliance with legal norms. In real life, people often attempt to go beyond the limitations of these social norms, which is manifested as deviant behaviors. The so-called deviant behavior refers to an action that deviates from or violates social norms. It has both positive and negative aspects. Any deviant behavior that violates backward and reactionary social norms is a positive one that is beneficial to social public life or social progress. Any deviant behavior that violates reasonable and legitimate social norms is a negative one that hinders social public life or social progress. Only the negative deviant behavior can be regarded as corruption. Therefore, corruption is a behavior that violates reasonable and legitimate social norms and hinders social public life or social progress. This definition of corruption centered on social norms encompasses all social corruption behaviors. It reveals that the general characteristics of corruption lie in its illegitimacy and unreasonableness, and emphasizes that corruption is a social problem that hinders social public life or social progress. However, this definition has not specified the subject, object, purpose, means and other factors of power corruption.[340]

从地方的恐怖事件到国际的恐怖活动，恐怖主义都与国家存在着密切的联系。在国际学术界，许多研究者都曾发现"国家失败是导致恐怖主义的根源"。在这里，国家失败是指国家无力保障人民的人身安全、贫困、政府腐败无能、政局动荡等状况，正是这样的社会环境成为滋生恐怖主义的温床。比如，美国纽约外交关系委员会Bridget L. Coggin发表在*Journal of Conflict Resolution*杂志上的《国家失败会导致恐怖主义吗?》（2015年第3期）一文就曾表达了这样的观点。他用兰德公司收集的1999—2008年间发生在153个国家的恐怖主义事件数据检验了"国家失败是导致恐怖主义的根源"这一命题。研究发现，国家失败与否并不先天性地与恐怖主义相联系，只有在那些最失败的国家，即在人民极度贫困、腐败严重、战争和政局动荡的国家，恐怖主义的发生率才会比其他国家显著更高[341]。

From local terrorist incidents to international terrorist activities, terrorism is closely related to countries. In the international academic community, many researchers have found that "state failure is the root cause of terrorism." Here, state failure refers to the inability of a country to ensure the safety of the people, the plight of poverty, the corruption and incompetence of the government, political unrest, and so on. This social environment has become a hotbed for the breeding of terrorism. For example, Bridget L. Coggin, a member of the Council on Foreign Relations in New York, the United States once expressed this view in *Will State Failure Lead to Terrorism?*", a paper published in *Journal of Conflict Resolution* (Volume 3, 2015). The writer used the data collected by the RAND Corporation on terrorist incidents in 153 countries that took place from 1999 to 2008 to test the viewpoint that "state failure is the root cause of terrorism." The study found that state failure is not inherently linked to terrorism. Only in those countries with the most serious failure, that is, in countries where people live in extreme poverty,

---

341 《国家失败是恐怖主义的根源?》，腾讯文化（腾讯网），www.qq.com，2015年11月20日

suffer from severe corruption. and are plagued by wars and political upheavals, the incidence of terrorism is significantly higher than that in other countries.[341]

在 21 世纪，腐败和恐怖主义已经互相"挂钩"，牢牢勾搭在一起。就像在 21 世纪，美国和墨西哥边境墙的砖头、瓦片、石块关乎国际化，稍有风吹草动，就很有可能让很多人钱财损失惨重，却无法阻挡恐怖主义的入侵。

In the 21st century, corruption and terrorism are closely intertwined. This resembles the situation that in the 21st century, the bricks, tiles, and stones of the border wall between the United States and Mexico are related to internationalization. Even with the slightest stir, many people will probably suffer heavy financial losses. However, it cannot stop the invasion of terrorism.

美墨边境建墙是特朗普在 2016 年大选中的关键竞选承诺，也是他在 2020 年竞选活动中的核心宣传内容。特朗普认为，需要边境墙来遏制非法移民和贩毒活动[342]。

Building the border wall between the United States and Mexico was a key campaign promise of Donald Trump during the 2016 US presidential election, as well as a core publicity content of his campaign in 2020. Trump believed that the border wall was an essential facility to curb illegal immigration and drug trafficking.[342]

有分析称，特朗普政府一面不断为拉美国家发展制造障碍，一面又妄想用高墙将拉美难民拦在边境之外，也就不可能从根本上解决美墨边境日益严峻的非法移民问题和难民问题，"特朗普墙"也注定成为摆设[343]。

342　《尴尬！一阵大风刮倒了正在修建的"特朗普墙"》，腾讯新闻（腾讯网）www.qq.com，2020 年 2 月 1 日

343　同上

According to a certain analysis, the Trump administration, on the one hand, continuously created obstacles for the development of Latin American countries, and on the other hand, attempted to block Latin American refugees with a high wall. These measures could not fundamentally solve the increasingly severe problems of illegal immigration and refugees at the US-Mexico border, so the "Trump Wall" was doomed to be of no avail.[343]

2020 年 6 月 26 日，美国联邦法院裁定，特朗普政府挪用五角大楼资金建立美国与墨西哥之间的边境墙属于违法行为。裁决认为，特朗普挪用国防、军事和其他数十亿本身并未被指定用于边界墙建设的资金，这一做法违反了美国《宪法》中的拨款条款。"这些资金本有他用，挪用资金属于未经法规授权从财政部提取资金，因此已经违反宪法条款"，裁决显示，政府的资金挪用"不合法"[344]。

On June 26, 2020, the United States Federal Court ruled that the Trump administration's misappropriation of the Pentagon fund to build the border wall between the United States and Mexico was illegal. The ruling held that Trump's diversion of billions of dollars in defense, military, and other fields that were not designated for the border wall construction violated the appropriation clause in the US Constitution. "These funds should have been used for other purposes. Diverting the funds is equivalent to withdrawing money from the Treasury without statutory authorization, thus violating the constitutional clause." According to the ruling, the administration's fund diversion was "illegal".[344]

对恐怖主义有所认识的中外很多人士都意识到，有些政府出于

---

344 《美国联邦法院裁决特朗普挪用资金建边境墙违法》，网易财经（网易网）www.163.com，2020 年 6 月 27 日

私欲，为达成不可告人的目的，不惜利用、资助、扶持恐怖分子。这种违法行为属于腐败，直接助长恐怖主义坐大。

Many Chinese and foreign people with an understanding of terrorism have realized that some governments, driven by selfish desires and in order to achieve ulterior motives, will use, fund, and support terrorists regardless of the consequences. These are illegal and corrupt behaviors that directly contribute to the growth of terrorism.

在腐败的支援下，恐怖分子可以向各个领域进行或单或双、或明或暗、或长或短、或大或小的传播、蛊惑、侦察、渗透、控制、分裂、煽动、颠覆、策反、扶植、窃密、推翻、造谣、传谣等破坏活动，使屡剿不灭的恐怖主义威胁一浪高过一浪。诸如怀抱恐怖主义的组织有特别想法，政府又判断错误，只要有组织犯罪愿意不惜同归于尽，就能拿到武器军火，从而制造惨剧。

With the support of corruption, terrorists can carry out various destructive activities such as spreading, incitement, espionage, infiltration, control, splitting, instigation, subversion, defection, support, theft of secrets, overthrowing, rumoring, and disinformation in different fields, in a single or double mode, in an overt or covert manner, for a long or short time, on a large or small scale. This has led to the increasing threat of terrorism, which can hardly be eradicated. For example, in the case that an terrorist organization has special intentions and the government makes wrong judgments, as long as organized criminals are willing to bring about mutual destruction, they can obtain weapons and ammunition, thus creating tragedies.

1993 年发生一起邪教悲剧，震惊美国社会。加州有一个叫作大卫教派的邪教组织，其头目大卫出身于单亲家庭，九年级退学，一无所长，唯独具有宗教狂热，对《圣经》过目成诵，并随心所欲地进行讲解，吸引了许多信徒。其中以白种中年人为主，许多人是失业者、失恋者、失意者，他们认为自己被社会抛弃，对社会愤愤不平。大卫利用他们的负罪感和压抑感，进行宗教灌输，有一次他连续说教 56 小时，建立了至高无上的权威，使信徒失去独立思维判断的能力，心甘情愿地接受摆布。大卫对他的教徒说，他是基督再生，有权幸临所有女子，他把《圣经》随意做淫秽解释，让男人把妻子奉献给他，父母把女儿向他效忠。他娶了 19 个妻子，其中最小的 12 岁，并在举行宗教仪式时现场性交。他预言世界末日将要到来，"那时将会流血，血是进入天堂的通行证，我将被杀，然后复活，如同耶稣"。显然他是做了血洗的准备[345]。

In 1993, a cult tragedy took place, shocking American society. In California, there was a cult organization called the Davidians, whose leader, David, came from a single-parent family. He dropped out of school in the ninth grade, and had no specific skills. However, he was a religious fanatic, and was able to recite the Bible. As he explained the Bible freely, he attracted many followers, mainly middle-aged white people. Many of them were unemployed, heartbroken, or disappointed. They believed that they had been abandoned by society and became indignant. David conducted religious indoctrination by taking advantage of their sense of guilt and repression. He once preached continuously for 56 hours, thereby establishing supreme authority and causing believers to lose their ability to think independently and willingly submit to being manipulated. David told his followers that he was the reincarnation of Jesus Christ and had the right to have sexual intercourse with all women. He interpreted the Bible in a vulgar manner, inciting men to offer their wives and parents to donate their daughters to him. He had 19 wives, the youngest of whom was only 12 years old. He even had sexual intercourse

---

345　卢汉川、袁颖编著《透视美国》，北京：中国物资出版社，1998 年 12 月第 1 版

on the spot during religious ceremonies. He prophesied that the end of the world would soon come, "At that time, there will be bloodshed, and blood is the passport to heaven. I will be killed and then resurrected, just like Jesus." Obviously, he was well-prepared for a bloodbath.[345]

为此，他准备了武器弹药，共有军用冲锋枪 165 支，子弹 8000 多发，一个榴弹发射器，30 公斤黑色炸药，一架足以穿透钢板门和水泥墙的口径 50 毫米的机枪，割据两个庄园，自立王国，聚集忠实信徒 100 多人。情报飞到联邦政府，1993 年 2 月 28 日，联邦财政部所属烟酒火器局派出 100 名大员，大摇大摆地走向庄园，企图搜查武器。没想到迎面一阵枪声，4 人应声倒地。联邦政府下令联邦调查局并由国防部派出重型坦克封锁庄园达 40 余天，并使用心理战，把营地电源切断，用强光照射，日夜用高音喇叭播送西藏喇嘛沉闷的诵经声、垂死兔子的惨叫声、牙科用电钻的尖叫声。这种愚蠢对策适得其反，使教徒深信世界末日就要到来，坚定了他们斗争的信心。围攻 40 天毫无进展，使联邦调查局丢脸。于是由联邦司法部部长主持讨论，采取施放催泪瓦斯的办法，并经总统克林顿同意，于 4 月 9 日行动。结果庄园起火，一片混乱，持续一个上午，烧死 107 人，其中儿童 17 人，仅活 4 人。美国政府受到各方面的谴责，白宫内外吵吵嚷嚷一阵子，克林顿及其他高级官员连忙认错[346]。

For this purpose, he prepared weapons and ammunition, including 165 military submachine guns, over 8000 bullets, one grenade launcher, 30 kilograms of black explosives, and one machine gun with a caliber of 50 millimeters that was capable of penetrating steel doors and concrete walls. He established a "regime" in two manors, proclaimed himself king, and gathered more than 100 loyal followers. When the news spread

---

346 同上

to the federal government, the Bureau of Alcohol, Tobacco, Firearms and Explosives under the Federal Treasury Department dispatched 100 officials on February 28, 1993. They swaggered to the manors, attempting to search for weapons. Unexpectedly, there came a burst of gunfire head on, and four people fell to the ground. The federal government ordered the Federal Bureau of Investigation to conduct an investigation, and ordered the Department of Defense to dispatch heavy tanks to blockade the manors for more than 40 days. They employed psychological tactics, cut off the power supply of the camp, illuminated it with strong lights, and used high-power loudspeakers to broadcast dull chanting sounds of Tibetan lama, the shrill cries of dying rabbits, and the screeching noises of dental drills day and night. This foolish strategy had the opposite effect, making believers firmly believe that the end of the world was coming, and strengthening their confidence in the struggle. The siege lasted for 40 days without any progress, causing embarrassment to the Federal Bureau of Investigation. Through a discussion chaired by Minister of the Federal Justice Department, the method of using tear gas was adopted. After being approved by President Clinton, the action began on April 9. As a consequence, the manors caught fire, causing chaos that lasted for a morning. 107 people were burned to death, including 17 children, and only 4 survived. The US government was condemned by different parties, and there was a hubbub inside and outside the White House for some time. As a result, Clinton and other senior officials had to apologize.[346]

腐败和恐怖主义都会连累无辜。在任何一个年代，"冤有头，债有主"都是一道不可逾越的红线。任何人一旦"过红线"，就没有正确可言。

Corruption and terrorism will implicate the innocent. In any era, the principle that "the wrong has its owner, and the debt has its debtor" is an insurmountable red line. Once this line is crossed, it will be unjustifiable.

腐败和恐怖主义都是顽疾，它们之间是五十步笑百步的关系。贪污腐败不比恐怖主义优秀，这二者是各国都有的症状，哪个祸害更大，因人而异，无法盖棺论定。

Both corruption and terrorism are intractable problems, and the difference between them is merely a matter of degree.. Corruption is no better than terrorism. Both are symptoms that exist in various countries. As to which one is more harmful, different people have different opinions, and it is difficult to reach a definitive conclusion.

不过，当反腐和反恐不能同时进行的时候，人会因为知识有限为主导因素，产生这样一个疑惑——"国家反恐和反腐的先后战斗序列该怎么排列"。

However, when anti-corruption and anti-terrorism efforts cannot be made simultaneously, due to the dominant factor of limited knowledge, people will have a question - "In what sequence should a country carry out its anti-terrorism and anti-corruption operations?"

政府军反恐要保持军队有强大的战斗力。自古以来，就有国家武装力量混入"混口饭吃入伍参军"与"为了坐办公室入伍参军"的男男女女。

In order to carry out anti-terrorism operations, government forces must maintain strong combat effectiveness. However, since ancient times, national armed forces have been mixed with people who "join the army just to make a living" or to "get an office job".

军队有互为落后和先进的腐败思想，从而滞后了部队发展建设，容易造成"一挺机枪占领一个警察局"，给反恐造成了"投鼠忌器"的局面。所以，由于社会龙蛇混杂，有人认为要"先反腐、后反恐"。比如，在 2014 年，伊拉克政府军难以抵挡 ISIS 攻势就是一个例子。

The armed forces have both backward and advanced ideas regarding corruption. This hinders the development and construction of the military, and tends to cause a situation in which "a police station can be seized with a single machine gun", making the operatives overly cautious when combating terrorism. Considering the mixed-up situation in society, some people believe that "anti-corruption efforts should be made before anti-terrorism operations." This is typically manifested in the case that in 2014, the Iraqi government forces were unable to withstand the offensive of ISIS.

2003 年至 2011 年，美国在伊拉克战场上投入了逾 200 亿美元，美国国防部还要求国会明年为训练伊拉克军队投入 12 亿美元。在伊拉克，初级士兵的薪水是每月 600 美元，"吃空饷"每年会吃掉伊拉克军费 3.8 亿美元，并且这可能只是冰山一角。[347]

From 2003 to 2011, the United States invested over $20 billion in the Iraqi battlefield. The US Department of Defense also requested Congress to allocate $1.2 billion for training the Iraqi army in the following year. In Iraq, the salary of a junior soldier was $600 per month, but "ghost employment" consumed a military budget of $380 million every year. This may only be a tip of the iceberg.[347]

专家称，这些薪水通常是被军官冒领，他们会谎报士兵数量，并把多余的钱收入私囊。据伊拉克议会国防和安全委员会的一名官员称，他们正在组织更深入的调查，"真实情况可能是这个数字的三倍，腐败人员必须被严惩，他们掏空了伊拉克的安全。"[348]

Experts said that these salaries were usually embezzled by officers who would falsify the number of soldiers and pocket the extra money. According to an official from the Defense and Security Committee of

---

347 《伊拉克军队腐败严重 5 万士兵薪水被"吃空饷"》环球国际（环球网）www. huanqiu.com，2014 年 12 月 1 日

348 同上

the Iraqi Parliament, they would organize a further investigation. "The real number may be three times this amount. Corrupt officials must be severely punished. They have threatened Iraq's security."[348]

"反腐和反恐孰轻孰重"，各人都有自己的一套说法，如同文人武夫对"打天下和守天下"的争执。不过，治标不治本不可取，政府"先反恐、后反腐"，才能保证政府反思角度是全方位的，是政府反思力度优于恐怖分子的前提保障。

Everyone has his own opinion on "which is more important, anti-corruption or anti-terrorism efforts". It is similar to the dispute between scholars and warriors over "which is more important, conquering a country or governing a country." However, it is not advisable to merely treat the symptoms without addressing the root cause. Only when the government "carries out anti-terrorism campaigns before anti-corruption operations" can it ensure comprehensive consideration. This is a prerequisite for the government's consideration to be superior to that of terrorists.

政府"先反腐、后反恐"有易安内难攘外的气息，怕出现停滞不前的恶果。世人综合反恐与反腐的种种利弊相比较，"吃亏是福"的心态能决定选择"先反恐、后反腐"为主流思想之一，这种是有缺陷却能独当一面的想法。

If the government adopts the approach of "carrying out anti-corruption operations before anti-terrorism campaigns", it gives the impression that it is easy to stabilize the internal situation, but it is difficult to repel external threats, and may cause the negative consequence of stagnation. When people compare the advantages and disadvantages of anti-terrorism and anti-corruption efforts, influenced by the mindset that "misfortune can be an actual blessing", they may choose "carrying out anti-terrorism campaigns before anti-corruption operations" as a mainstream idea. This idea can work independently despite its flaws.

国家反恐方向应该以"先反恐、后反腐"为指导思想解决世人对反恐和反腐的纠结。因为，政府反恐是对内对外的较量，政府反腐是对内为主的较量。

National anti-terrorism should take "carrying out anti-terrorism campaigns before anti-corruption operations" as a guiding principle to resolve people's indecision between anti-terrorism and anti-corruption. The reason is that the government's anti-terrorism efforts are a contest both at home and abroad, while its anti-corruption efforts are mainly an internal contest.

人对待恐怖主义要泾渭分明，不偏不倚评价恐怖分子也是在反恐。如同恐怖主义到底是破坏力量，公正廉明到底是建设力量，有些恐怖组织比某些政府还要廉洁，例如，把恐怖组织 ISIS 和伊拉克、叙利亚这两个世俗政府进行对比，这两个政府比恐怖组织更腐败就是一个例子。

People should draw a distinct line when dealing with terrorism, and an unbiased evaluation of terrorists is also a part of anti-terrorism efforts. After all, terrorism is a destructive force, while being impartial and incorruptible is a constructive force. Some terrorist organizations are even more honest and clean than some governments. For example, when comparing the terrorist organization ISIS with the Iraqi and Syrian secular governments, we can see that these two governments are more corrupt than the terrorist organization.

"伊斯兰国"大声宣称，他们正在进行一场伊斯兰圣战，但是和被他们所取代的伊拉克和叙利亚世俗政权一样，他们也难以摆脱当地根深蒂固的腐败之风的影响[349]。

---

349 《ISIS 真正危机：自身的逐渐贪腐》，新浪财经（新浪网）www.sina.com.cn，2015年 12 月 21 日

The so-called "Islamic State" loudly proclaims that it is waging an Islamic holy war. However, just like the Iraqi and Syrian secular regimes replaced by it, it is unable to escape the influence of the deeply ingrained corruption in the region.[349]

很多曾经是极端组织旗下军人或者文员的人都说，尽管他们高喊着圣战口号去驱逐伊拉克和叙利亚的世俗政府，但实际上，他们的官员也会模仿那些政府对官僚政治的嗜好——以及腐败[350]。

Many people who were once soldiers or office clerks under the extremist organization said that although they shouted the slogan of a holy war to overthrow the Iraqi and Syrian secular governments, their officials would actually imitate those governments' penchant for bureaucracy and corruption.[350]

从农业管理到食品补贴，"伊斯兰国"任命的官员往往都会采用与叙利亚和伊拉克政府一样的系统，包括文牍主义的风格[351]。

From agricultural management to food subsidies, the officials appointed by the "Islamic State" often adopted the same systems as those of the Iraqi and Syrian governments, including a bureaucratic style.[351]

"毫无疑问，这个政权的做法已经开始让他们在我们眼里变成了一个腐败的，专制的系统。"一位西方情报官员如是说[352]。

"There is no doubt that the practices of this regime have made it a corrupt and autocratic system in our eyes," said a Western intelligence official.[352]

即便如此，情报官员们依然表示，"伊斯兰国"对贪腐的容忍度还是要比前政权们低一些的。在极端组织攻城略地期间，许多人之所以愿意容忍他们的统治，一再被提及的原因之一就是他们做事

350　同上

351　同上

352　同上

更有效率，贪腐更少。这对于盟军而言本身就是一个值得警惕的信号，因为要击败极端组织，他们需要和伊拉克政府这样的伙伴合作[353]。

In spite of that, some intelligence officials still said that the "Islamic State" had a lower tolerance for corruption compared to the previous regimes. During the period when the extremist organization was seizing territory, one of the frequently mentioned reasons why many people were willing to tolerate their rule was that they were more efficient and less corrupt. This is a warning sign for the Allied forces. To defeat the extremist organization, they need to cooperate with partners like the Iraqi government.[353]

然而，即使如此，这也不能改变 ISIS 的邪恶本质，只能说明 ISIS 身上有闪光点，确有进步色彩值得世人学习。例如，2019 年 ISIS 大头目巴格达迪因为美国斩首行动而亡，可是，ISIS 首领接班人出场了。只是，ISIS 领导者就算从"中东恶魔"，升级为"中东狂魔"，恐怖组织 ISIS 仍然是继续展露其丑陋的嘴脸。

However, this cannot change the evil nature of ISIS. It can only be said that ISIS has some shining points, and indeed has some progressive aspects worthy of learning. For example, in 2019, the top leader of ISIS, Abu Bakr al-Baghdadi, was killed in a US decapitation operation, but his successor emerged. However, even if the leader of ISIS was upgraded from a "Middle Eastern devil" to a "Middle Eastern lunatic," the terrorist organization ISIS still showed its ugly face.

2013 年 3 月，"胜利阵线"攻占叙利亚东部城市拉卡，这是第一个被反对派武装攻下的省会城市。拉卡拥有百万人口，是叙伊边境地带的重镇，拥有丰富的石油储备，随后，"胜利阵线"在人员

353　同上

和资金各方面突飞猛进。当年 4 月，"伊拉克和黎凡特伊斯兰国"，即 ISIS 正式成立[354]。

In March 2013, the "Al-Nusra Front" captured Raqqa, a city in eastern Syria, which was the first provincial capital city captured by the opposition armed forces. With a population of one million and abundant oil resources, Raqqa is an important city in the border area between Syria and Iraq. Subsequently, the "Islamic State of Iraq and al-Shams," abbreviated as ISIS, was formally established in April of the same year.[354]

2014 年 1 月，这支宗教极端武装又杀回伊拉克。这时候，伊拉克政府发现，之前总是被轻易击溃的武装分子经过叙利亚内战的"锻炼"，已经能够娴熟地实施地面协同作战，而缺乏训练的政府军已经不是其对手了[355]。

In January 2014, this religious extremist armed group returned to Iraq. At that time, the Iraqi government found that the militants, who had been easily defeated before, had, through the "tempering" of the Syrian civil war, become proficient in implementing ground coordinated operations, and that the ill-trained government forces were no longer a match for them.[355]

2019 年 10 月 31 日，ISIS 宣传机构"阿玛克通讯社"（Amaq News Agency）发布了一段长 7 分半钟的录音，证实巴格达迪已经在美军上周末的突袭行动中身亡，同时丧命的还有该组织发言人穆哈吉尔（Abu Hassan al—Muhajir）[356]。

On October 31, 2019, the propaganda agency of ISIS, the Amaq News Agency, released a seven-and-a-half-minute record, confirming that

---

354　同上

355　同上

356　《ISIS 确认巴格达迪死亡及接班人，警告美国别太得意》，腾讯新闻（腾讯网），www.qq.com，2019 年 11 月 1 日

Abu Bakr al-Baghdadi had been killed in a US military raid the previous weekend, and that the organization's spokesman, Abu Hassan al-Muhajir was also killed.[356]

5 年的全球反恐战让 ISIS 逐渐式微，在叙利亚和伊拉克的占领地大规模丢失，巴格达迪之死更是对该组织的一次重大打击。分析人士指出，巴格达迪之死很可能造成 ISIS 的进一步分裂，新头目的首要任务就是把整个组织重新凝聚起来，形成战斗力。无论如何，ISIS 的意识形态和宗派仇恨对一些人来说依然具有吸引力，因此巴格达迪的死未必会对其战斗力造成大的影响[357]。

Due to the five-year global anti-terrorism war, ISIS was gradually weakened, and lost a large amount of occupied territory in Syria and Iraq. The death of Abu Bakr al-Baghdadi was a more severe blow to the organization. According to some analysts, his death may probably cause further fragmentation of ISIS, and the new leader will give top priority to reuniting the organization so as to form combat effectiveness. In any case, the ideology and sectarian hatred of ISIS still hold some appeal for certain people. Therefore, the death of Abu Bakr al-Baghdadi may not necessarily have a major impact on its combat effectiveness.[357]

ISIS 既是恐怖组织，又是极端组织。ISIS 满足反国家、反社会、反人类这些标准。与全世界一样，ISIS 也要有收入才能开支，只不过，ISIS 是恐怖组织，ISIS 赚的多是"黑心钱"。

With anti-state, anti-society, and anti-human features, ISIS is a terrorist organization as well as an extremist one. Just like the other organizations in the world, ISIS must have income to cover its expenses. However, since it is a terrorist organization, it basically earns "dirty money".

357　同上

在一段时间里 ISIS 成为世界头号恐怖组织，违法、非法、不法的经济手段，ISIS 都有采用。

For a time, ISIS became the number one terrorist organization in the world, resorting to various illegal, unlawful, and criminal economic means.

要说新世纪恐怖组织中谁最成功、又最臭名昭著，当数 2014 年迅速崛起、2017 年年末又迅速败亡的"伊斯兰国"（Islamic State, IS）了。其极盛时期不仅占据着叙利亚和伊拉克的大片领土、统治着大约 1000 万的阿拉伯民众，还拥有雄厚的资金和极具吸引力的宣传方式 [358]。

The most successful and notorious terrorist organization in the new century is undoubtedly the "Islamic State" (IS), which emerged rapidly in 2014 and collapsed quickly at the end of 2017. At its peak, it not only occupied a large amount of land in Syria and Iraq and ruled over approximately 10 million Arabs but also possessed substantial funds and highly seductive propaganda methods.[358]

2014 年成功崛起后，世界各地的大小恐怖组织纷纷对其宣誓效忠，其领土野心也越发膨胀，号称要在整个伊斯兰世界建立庞大的"哈里发国"。但这种扩张的本质，在于掠地收割，将利益做分配，没有钱的"霸业"终究是空中楼阁 [359]。

After the successful rise of the "Islamic State" in 2014, terrorist organizations around the world, large or small, swore allegiance to it successively. As a result, it became increasingly ambitious for territory, and claimed to establish a vast "Caliphate" across the entire Islamic world. However, the essence of this expansion was to seize territory, reap

---

358 《每年收入 3 个亿，'伊斯兰国'是如何抢钱的?》，界面新闻 www.jiemian.com，
　　2019 年 3 月 19 日

359 同上

benefits, and distribute them. A "great cause" without money was just like a castle in the air.[359]

于是随着 2015 年该组织建立起数倍于英国领土面积的控制区域，其最主要的两大赚钱方式也最终形成：石油走私和征收种类繁多的重税[360]。

Therefore, when the organization controlled an area several times the size of the United Kingdom in 2015, it adopted two major approaches to earning money: oil smuggling and imposing a wide variety of heavy taxes.[360]

这两大主要赚钱方式是"伊斯兰国"的根本命脉，但遇到特殊情况，比如，石油产区被政府军重新夺回，或者丧失部分所占领土，那么石油收入和人头税就要大打折扣。所以"伊斯兰国"还有一整套形式多样的补充性次要收入来源，比如，贩卖文物和人口、绑架人质、洗劫银行、控制区域内农业商业等[361]。

These two main sources of income were the fundamental lifelines of the "Islamic State." However, in special circumstances, such as when the oil-producing areas were recaptured by the government forces or when part of its occupied territory was lost, the oil revenue and the poll tax would be significantly reduced. Therefore, the "Islamic State" had diverse secondary sources of income as a supplement, such as profits from cultural relics and human trafficking, hostage kidnapping, bank looting, and control of agriculture and commerce within the area.[361]

这些次要收入来源不可小觑，这在"伊斯兰国"意识形态宣传、人员的全球吸引和招募、组织的稳定和发展方面起着重要的作用[362]。

These secondary sources of income should not be underestimated, as

---

360　同上

361　同上

362　同上

they played an important role in the ideological propaganda of the "Islamic State," the global attraction and recruitment of personnel, and the stability and development of the organization.[362]

仅凭这些ISIS种种违法犯罪的收入，就能一次又一次地证明恐怖分子是"拉大旗作虎皮"。由于ISIS连"君子爱财，取之有道"都做不到，如此，有识之士便知道ISIS绝非好货色。

These illegal incomes of ISIS repeatedly demonstrated that the terrorists were "draping themselves in the flag to frighten people." Since ISIS even failed to abide by the principle that "a gentleman loves wealth but acquires it in a proper way," people of insight could immediately identify its evil nature.

有人更憎恨腐败，有人更憎恨恐怖主义。法学无法给人下达"腐败和恐怖主义，哪一个更可恶"的答案。哲学则告诉世人，腐败和恐怖主义都是坏事，人们都要对它们进行抵制。

Some people hate corruption more, while others hate terrorism more. Jurisprudence cannot answer the question of "which is more hateful, corruption or terrorism." Philosophy, on the other hand, tells people that both corruption and terrorism are bad, and should be fought against.

很多国家都是多事之秋，政府能够治理好国家，使人民安居乐业，已经是难能可贵。事有轻重缓急之分，即使政府不打击恐怖分子，可是政府也不能支持恐怖分子、利用恐怖分子、利于恐怖分子、反恐不力，无人与恐怖分子做任何交易，恐怖分子也会遭遇致命危机。

Many countries are going through troubled times. It is an admirable act for a government to govern the country well and make the people live and work in peace. All things have their priorities. Even if the government does not crack down on terrorists, it cannot support them, exploit them, benefit from them, or be ineffective in counter-terrorism efforts. As long as no one makes any deals with terrorists, terrorists will encounter a fatal crisis.

在全球商品遵循等价交换的原则下，过度消费总有终结的时刻。这样，无论恐怖分子怕不怕死，恐怖分子都能因饥渴死亡。

When commodities across the globe follow the principle of equivalent exchange, excessive consumption will ultimately perish. In this way, whether terrorists fear death or not, they will perish due to depletion of resources.

叙利亚、土耳其与"伊斯兰国"（ISIS）之间的关系错综复杂，但其中核心是石油资源。ISIS 通过战争抢夺叙利亚油田，再经由土耳其等渠道销售，从而成为最富有的恐怖组织[363]。

The relationships among Syria, Turkey and ISIS are intricate, but the core lies in oil resources. ISIS seized Syrian oil fields through warfare and then sold the oil via Turkey and other channels, thus becoming the richest terrorist organization.[363]

2015 年，这些原油除了在当地卖，也通过黑市偷卖到土耳其和其他国家。连与 ISIS 作战的叙利亚反对派也因为 ISIS 的石油便宜而从其中间人手中购买石油[364]。

In 2015, apart from being sold locally, the crude oil was smuggled to Turkey and other countries through the black market. Even the Syrian opposition forces that were fighting against ISIS bought oil from the intermediaries of ISIS because of its low prices.[364]

2015 年，这些石油除用于"伊斯兰国"控制地区外，甚至被卖到与其交战的地区，如叙利亚反对派控制的北部地区。当地医院、

---

363 秦海霞、蓝玉才、刘红色撰《石油会要了 ISIS 的命?》，来源《国企管理》，2016年第 18 期

364 《除了卖石油 ISIS 的钱都从哪儿来的?》，新浪财经（新浪网）www.sina.com.cn，2015 年 11 月 19 日

商店、汽车等都依赖"伊斯兰国"所产石油[365]。

In 2015, apart from being used in the regions controlled by the "Islamic State", the oil was sold to areas at war with it, such as the northern areas controlled by the Syrian opposition. Even local hospitals, stores and vehicles relied on the oil produced by the "Islamic State".[365]

政府消极对待恐怖主义，是政府明里暗地利用恐怖分子，镇压人民起义、镇压黑社会、镇压军事力量的谋划。

If the government deals with terrorism in a passive manner, it actually utilizes terrorists secretly or overtly to suppress people's uprisings, criminal underworld organizations and military forces.

尽管，政府支持恐怖主义的目标是不一样的，却都有转移阶级矛盾的目的。

Although different governments support terrorism for different purposes, they all aim to shift class contradictions.

自 1996 年至 2001 年，塔利班在阿富汗建立全国性政权，正式名称为阿富汗伊斯兰酋长国。由于它在阿富汗实施独裁专制和政教合一政策，因此仅被巴基斯坦、阿拉伯联合酋长国和沙特阿拉伯三个国家承认是代表阿富汗的合法政府，它曾经为奥萨玛·本·拉登提供庇护。[366]

From 1996 to 2001, the Taliban established a national regime in Afghanistan, with the official name being the Islamic Emirate of Afghanistan. Due to its implementation of autocratic and theocratic policies in Afghanistan, it was recognized as the legitimate government representing Afghanistan by only three countries: Pakistan, the United Arab Emirates, and Saudi Arabia. It once provided asylum for Osama bin

---

365 《揭秘 IS 组织的石油黑金链：抢占油田 快速敛财》，环球军事（环球网）www.huanqiu.com，2015 年 12 月 7 日

366 《解密阿富汗塔利班》，网易新闻（网易网），www.163.com，2011 年 5 月 23 日

Laden.[366]

塔利班从 1994 年出现到 2000 年在不到 6 年的时间里控制了阿富汗 90% 以上的国土，决定性地改变了阿富汗内战的进程和方向。塔利班崛起成为阿富汗自 1979 年苏联入侵阿富汗以来最有实质意义和全局影响的事件。[367]

After the emergence of the Taliban in 1994, they spent six years controlling more than 90% of Afghanistan's territory, thus decisively changing the course and direction of the Afghan civil war. The rise of the Taliban became an event of the greatest significance and had the most far-reaching impact in Afghanistan since the Soviet Union invaded Afghanistan in 1979.[367]

1998 年 7 月，塔利班北进大举进攻北方联盟，并于 8 月 8 日夺取了北方重镇马扎里沙里夫。北方联盟各派则四处分散，退守到各自部落的山区，继续以游击战与塔利班对抗。[368]

In July 1998, the Taliban launched a large-scale offensive northward against the Northern Alliance. On August 8, it captured the northern city Mazar-i-Sharif. The factions of the Northern Alliance scattered in all directions and retreated to the mountainous areas of their respective tribes, continuing to resist the Taliban with guerrilla warfare.[368]

2001 年，美军轰炸阿富汗四个星期后，阿富汗首都喀布尔的阿富汗人接受采访时表示，他们希望他们的"客人"本·拉登能够收拾行囊，离开阿富汗。[369]

In 2001, after the United States bombed Afghanistan for four weeks,

---

367　郭建军撰《塔利班崛起和阿富汗地缘政治之争》，来源《中国社会科学院研究生院》，2000 年

368　同上

369　《拉登不再受欢迎 阿富汗人希望其立刻离开》搜狐新闻（搜狐网）www.sohu.com，2001 年 11 月 5 日

Afghans in Kabul, the capital of Afghanistan, said in an interview that they hoped their "guest" Osama bin Laden could pack his bags and leave Afghanistan.[369]

本·拉登 1996 年被沙特阿拉伯驱逐出境后，就来到了阿富汗。由于阿富汗塔利班一再拒绝将其交出，2001 年，美国总统布什于 10 月 7 日下令，开始空袭阿富汗。[370]

After being expelled from Saudi Arabia in 1996, Osama bin Laden came to Afghanistan. Because the Taliban regime in Afghanistan repeatedly refused to hand him over, US President George W. Bush ordered air strikes against Afghanistan on October 7, 2001.[370]

本·拉登基地组织与他的阿拉伯盟友在阿富汗一直就不受欢迎，因为他们态度傲慢，专横。然而，尽管他们冷漠无情而且吝啬，但大部分阿富汗人民好像都接受他们的存在。[371]

Bin Laden's al-Qaeda organization and his Arab allies were never popular in Afghanistan because of their arrogance and high-handedness. However, despite their coldness, ruthlessness and stinginess, most Afghan people seemed to accept their presence.[371]

但是"9·11"恐怖袭击之后，由于害怕美国的报复，这种情况改变了。2001 年，随着美军对阿轰炸进入第五周，一些阿富汗人开始对拉登的存在表示不满。[372]

However, after the September 11 terrorist attacks, due to the fear of US retaliation, the situation changed. In 2001, during the fifth week of the US bombing campaign in Afghanistan, some Afghans began to express their dissatisfaction with the presence of bin Laden.[372]

2021 年，英国国防大臣华莱士 8 月 16 日表示，塔利班已控制

370　同上

371　同上

372　同上

阿富汗，但英国和北约部队不会重返阿富汗打击塔利班武装人员。[373]

On August 16, 2021, British Defense Secretary Wallace said that the Taliban had taken control of Afghanistan, but British and NATO forces would not return to Afghanistan to fight against Taliban militants.[373]

2014 年 10 月 15 日，据俄罗斯 RT 新闻网报道，美国及其盟友正在对极端组织 IS 进行空袭打击。2014 年，一股新的力量亦加入打击 IS 的战队——来自荷兰的摩托车黑帮。据报道，该摩托车黑帮名为"绝不投降"（No Surrender）。据悉，其 3 名成员已于上周前往伊拉克和叙利亚，加入库尔德武装，共同对抗 IS 进攻。当被问及该帮派行为是否合法时，荷兰检察官表示，他们允许那样做。检察官发言人维姆·德·布鲁因（Wim de Bruin）称："以前，荷兰人加入外国武装军队将受到惩罚，但现在已不再被禁止。"[374]

According to the news released by the Russian RT on October 15, 2014, the United States and its allies were conducting air strikes against the extremist organization IS. In 2014, a new force, a motorcycle gang from the Netherlands, joined the battle against IS. It was reported that the motorcycle gang was called "No Surrender". Three of its members had gone to Iraq and Syria the previous week to join the Kurdish armed forces and jointly fight against the offensive of IS. When asked whether the gang's actions were legal, the Dutch prosecutor said that they were allowed to do so. Wim de Bruin, the prosecutor's spokesman, said, "Before, Dutch people who joined foreign armed forces would be punished, but now they are no longer prohibited."[374]

据美国 fortress America 网站透露，该组织可能成立于 2013 年，

---

373 《英国国防大臣承认塔利班已控制阿富汗 但称英军不会返阿》，新浪军事（新浪网），www.sina.com.cn，2021 年 8 月 16 日

374 《荷兰黑社会分子赴伊拉克打击 ISIS》，凤凰军事（凤凰网）www.ifeng.com，2014 年 10 月 17 日

荷兰警方将其定性为非法团伙 [375]。

According to the website Fortress America, the organization was probably established in 2013, and the Dutch police classified it as an illegal gang.[375]

冷战时期，西方宣传苏联—东欧集团根据成本—效益比的实用战略和意识形态倾向支持恐怖主义组织；根据苏联叛逃人员的言辞指责苏联开办恐怖分子训练营地；指责苏联支持国际恐怖主义组织集会和联合；指责苏联支持中东恐怖分子进行国际恐怖主义袭击。而事实上是，西方阵营也支持恐怖活动。以杜鲁门主义为标志，冷战一开始就涉及中东。[376]

During the Cold War, the Western camp accused the Soviet Union and Eastern Europe of supporting terrorist organizations based on a practical strategy of cost-benefit ratio and ideological tendencies; accused the Soviet Union of conducting training camps for terrorists according to the words of defectors from the Soviet Union; accused the Soviet Union of supporting the gatherings and unions of international terrorist organizations; and accused the Soviet Union of supporting Middle Eastern terrorists in carrying out international terrorist attacks. In fact, the Western camp also supported terrorist activities. Marked by the Truman Doctrine, the Cold War involved the Middle East from the very beginning.[376]

支持恐怖主义不是长久的方法，连一时奏效也是后患无穷。在21世纪，管控国家的政府通常拥有强大的力量，各国政府都是反恐中坚力量，政府首先要成为反恐先行者。每个国家都有民族主义，也许他们想让本国能够富饶强大，只是，要想让自己的国家成为大

375　《荷兰黑社会"摩托车帮"分子赴伊拉克打击 IS》，国际在线新闻（国际在线）www.cri.cn，2014 年 10 月 16 日

376　张金平著《中东恐怖主义的历史演进》，昆明：云南大学出版社，2008 年 8 月

国，绝对不能依靠"与虎谋皮"式方法来饮鸩止渴，否则，到头来最终也只能被反噬。

Supporting terrorism is not a sustainable approach. Even if it seems to work temporarily, it will bring about endless troubles. In the 21st century, national governments usually possess great power, and the government of each country is a core force in anti-terrorism operations. The government should first become an anti-terrorism pioneer. Every country has nationalism. Perhaps they hope that their country can become prosperous and powerful. However, to make a country powerful, one must never rely on approaches such as "seeking cooperation with the devil" and "quenching thirst by drinking poison." Otherwise, they will have an adverse effect in the end.

腐败使反恐力量"面和心不和"，"一盘散沙"的反恐力量解决不了恐怖主义。没有贪污腐败的恐怖主义才有起码的人神共愤，反恐是给受害者一种说法。

Corruption makes the anti-terrorism forces "seem united but actually divided." Anti-terrorism forces that are "in disarray" cannot resolve the issue of terrorism. Only terrorism without corruption can arouse the minimum public indignation. Anti-terrorism is an expression for the victims.

贪污腐败随意破坏资源，人不能把西北风当饭菜吃，省吃俭用不会过时。反贪反腐是可以获得最终的胜利，其所走的道路是不一样的。

Corruption will cause wanton damage to resources. People can't live on air. Being thrifty will never be out-dated. The fight against corruption can achieve final victory, yet it will take a different path.

在 21 世纪，人离不腐败的境界还相差甚多。2017 年 2 月 21 日中国界面新闻网站，就刊登了一篇标题为《报告：如果各国不解决腐败问题 ISIS 永远无法被打败》的文章。

In the 21st century, people are still far from the realm of being free from corruption. On February 21, 2017, Jiemian, a Chinese news website, published an article titled *Report - If Countries Fail to Resolve the Issue of Corruption, ISIS Will Never Be Defeated.*

该文章部分内容如下:"透明国际 20 日发布名为'腐败与暴力极端主义崛起'的报告。报告指出国际社会花了很大精力追踪 ISIS 的意识形态问题,但完全忽视了让 ISIS 崛起的'物质条件'。"

Part of this article is as follows: "On February 20, Transparency International released a report titled *Corruption and the Rise of Violent Extremism*. It points out that the international community has devoted a great deal of effort to tracing the ideological issues of ISIS, but has completely ignored the 'material conditions' that led to the rise of ISIS."

其中一个重要条件就是腐败。报告称 ISIS 在招募吸引新兵时,充分利用了民众对滥用职权和腐败的愤怒。

One of the important conditions is corruption. The report claims that when recruiting new members, ISIS has fully exploited the public's anger towards the abuse of power and corruption.

通过分析 ISIS 发布在社交媒体上的宣传文章,报告指出 ISIS 经常提到中东地区政府的腐败、官员擅自挪用国家资金等问题。在指出政府腐败问题的同时,ISIS 将自己描绘为能提供安全、社会公平和福利保障的组织。

By analyzing the propaganda articles released by ISIS on social media, the report points out that ISIS often mentions the corruption of governments in the Middle East and the unauthorized embezzlement of state funds by officials. While pointing out the problem of government corruption, ISIS portrays itself as an organization that can provide security, social justice, and welfare guarantees.

恐怖主义越萎靡不振,利用腐败借题发挥就越凸显关键。在

2012 年 6 月 14 日，中国新闻网刊登了一条题为"财政枯竭人员凋零 基地组织面临困境日渐式微"的新闻。

The more sluggish a terrorist organization becomes, the more it will seize on the issue of corruption to conceal its own problems. On June 14, 2012, China News Service published a news article titled *Financial Exhaustion and Depletion of Personnel: Al-Qaeda Faces Dilemmas and Is Declining.*

在这篇报道当中，中国官媒引用了外媒的评论——"基地组织已今非昔比，据路透社报道，这已是一个财政枯竭、面临困境的组织，连它曾经的崇拜者都怀疑它还能存在多久……'只要还有软弱而腐败的统治，只要还对美国、以色列或是西方国家感到不公正或深深的不满，他们就仍会招募到新成员。'BBC 分析道。"

In this report, Chinese official media quoted remarks from some foreign media outlets: "Al-Qaeda is no longer what it used to be. According to Reuters, it is now an organization facing financial exhaustion and a serious plight. Even its former admirers are skeptical about how long it can continue to exist... 'As long as it has weak and corrupt governance, and a sense of injustice or deep dissatisfaction with the United States, Israel, or Western countries, it will recruit new members,' the BBC analyzed."

2013 年，"我们今天正在目睹基地组织第三代的演变，或者如我所称：基地组织 3.0。第一代是创造基地的那一代人，直至'9·11'事件发生时为止。第二代是从阿富汗塔利班政权倒台，至本·拉登被打死和两年前的'阿拉伯之春'，那时阿拉伯世界政治动荡开始"，反恐专家布鲁斯表示[377]。

---

377 《"基地"组织 3.0 时代已到来?》，腾讯财经（腾讯网）www.qq.com，2013 年 8 月 31 日

In 2013, "We are witnessing the evolution of the third generation of Al-Qaeda, or as I call it, Al-Qaeda 3.0. The first generation established Al-Qaeda. They existed until the occurrence of the September 11 attacks. The second generation existed from the downfall of the Taliban regime in Afghanistan to the killing of Osama bin Laden and the 'Arab Spring' two years ago. At that time, political unrest began in the Arab world," said Bruce, an anti-terrorism expert.[377]

分析认为，当前的"基地"组织，已经不再是"9·11"之前那个单纯的恐怖主义组织实体，而是"脱胎换骨"，变成了一个以"基地"组织为核心、以地区附属组织为外围和活动主力，容纳了大量意识形态相同的合作恐怖组织和恐怖分子个人的全球性恐怖主义网络[378]。

According to analysis, the current "Al-Qaeda" is no longer the terrorist organization it used to be before the September 11 attacks. Instead, it has been "completely transformed" into a global terrorist network with "Al-Qaeda" as the core, regional affiliated organizations as the periphery and the main force of activities, which has absorbed a large number of cooperative terrorist organizations and individual terrorists with the same ideology.[378]

与此同时，新一代"基地"组织，也就是"基地"组织 3.0，开始转向关注身边的敌人，而不仅仅把目光锁在远处的美国和欧洲。美国中东问题专家布鲁斯·里德尔表示[379]。

At the same time, the new generation of "Al-Qaeda" or "Al-Qaeda 3.0" has started to focus on the enemies around them, rather than just fixing their eyes on the distant United States and Europe. Bruce Riedel,

---

378　同上
379　同上

an American expert on Middle East issues, said.[379]

"基地"组织再次"升级"绝非偶然，而是地缘政治和国际局势共同作用的结果[380]。

The second "upgrade" of "Al-Qaeda" is by no means accidental, but is the result of the combined effect of geopolitics and the international situation.[380]

只要人想进步就无法瞒天过海，说话、唱歌、读书、看报、写字、上网、画画是常见的个人进步手段，必有规律可摸索。

As long as one hopes to make progress, he cannot hide his true intentions. Talking, singing, reading books and newspapers, writing, surfing internet, and painting are common means of personal progress. When engaging in these activities, there must be some rules to follow.

社会上总有人爱撒谎，有道有德者，自认知识包装自己是伪装；无道无德者，自认知识伪装自己是包装。人不渴望吃香的喝辣的了，国家没有贪官污吏都有可能，这也是解决腐败的一种变化思维。

Society is not short of people who like to lie. A virtuous person believes that using knowledge to package himself is a guise, while an immoral person believes that using knowledge to disguise himself is a package. If people no longer desire to live a luxurious life, the country may have no corrupt officials. This is a new perspective for resolving the issue of corruption.

在 21 世纪，文明力量既能遏制贪污腐败，也能遏制恐怖主义。许多国家与地区都为反腐和反恐付诸行动，只是效果有大有小。如此，则能说明国家处事正确，邪不胜正的苗头总能浮现其中。

In the 21st century, the power of civilization can not only curb

---

380　同上

corruption but also terrorism. Many countries and regions have taken actions against corruption and terrorism. The only difference lies in the effect. It shows that if a country can handle matters properly, the sign that justice prevails over evil will emerge.

恐怖主义受益于腐败。不过，即使腐败消失于世，恐怖主义也不一定会销声匿迹，最多只是恐怖主义的威胁大幅度降低而已，解决了贪污腐败不等于解决了恐怖主义。

Terrorism benefits from corruption. However, even if corruption vanishes, terrorism may not necessarily vanish. At best, the threat of terrorism will be remarkably reduced. Resolving the issue of corruption does not mean resolving the issue of terrorism.

当官有公仆准则，公仆是要为人民服务的。现实世界的理想公仆并不是什么错误都不犯，而是知错就改，勇于承认自己的错误，不会对自己的错误遮遮掩掩。政府有腐败导致国家有恐怖主义，政府却不能以法不责众为借口，致使腐败让国家陷入恐怖主义深渊之中。

An official should follow principles for being a public servant. A public servant is supposed to serve the people. In the real world, an ideal public servant is not someone who never commits mistakes, but someone who has the courage to acknowledge and correct his mistakes rather than conceal them. If government corruption leads to terrorism in a country, the government should not use the excuse of "the law does not punish the multitude" to let corruption plunge the country into the abyss of terrorism.

第五章　人民在反恐中的位置

Chapter 5: The Position of the People in Anti-terrorism

在世界现代史，晚处理恐怖主义不如早处理恐怖主义。否则，支持恐怖主义的群体不再是高学历的专利，会扩散到整个士农工商，乃至三百六十行之中。

In modern world history, it is better to deal with terrorism early than late. Otherwise, the groups that support terrorism will no longer be restricted to highly educated people, but will be expanded to all social classes, including scholars, farmers, artisans, and merchants, and even covering all occupations.

无忧无虑的人生不存在，强大的经济压力就会让很多人不择手段。功成名就之下，有人犯下恐怖主义，有人没有犯下恐怖主义。即使是历史名人，功成名就以后也可能只有一条正确的道路可以走下去，何况平凡的小人物。

A carefree life does not exist. Intense economic pressure will drive many people to resort to unscrupulous means. When people achieve success and fame, some may commit acts of terrorism while others do not. Even for historical celebrities, there may be only one right path to follow after achieving success and fame, let alone for ordinary people.

政府武装反恐能让恐怖主义陷入一蹶不振的低谷。然而，拥枪和禁枪的国家都要面对政府坐吃山空和人民做生意发不了财的窘境。为了物质钱财支持恐怖主义和发动恐怖袭击的大有人在，因此政府就要解决士农工商为了经济利益而进行涉恐的国家问题。

Armed anti-terrorism operations by the government can push terrorism into a slump. However, whether a country bans guns or not, it has to face the dilemma of resource depletion for the government and business failures for the people. There are many people who support terrorism and launch terrorist attacks for the sake of material wealth. Therefore, the government has to address the national issue of scholars, farmers, artisans, and merchants being involved in terrorism for economic interests.

政府不反恐，人民会支恐。人民不反恐，政府乱反恐。在全球"越反越恐"的时代背景下，人民面对恐怖主义，既是一种弱势群体，有时也扮演了一些不光彩的辅助角色。

If the government does not carry out anti-terrorism operations, the people may support terrorism. If the people do not participate in anti-terrorism operations, the government may conduct anti-terrorism operations in a chaotic manner. In the era when "the higher the intensity of counter-terrorism is, the more rampant terrorism becomes" globally, when faced with terrorism, the people are a vulnerable group, but sometimes play a disgraceful auxiliary role.

不过时间会证明，社会安定才会有安定的社会。当人民夹杂在政府与恐怖分子之间，人民或两不相帮，或偏向恐怖分子，或帮助政府，其最后的结局都是反恐胜利的局面，人民不可能有支恐胜利的能力。

However, time will prove that social stability can lead to a stable society. When people are caught between the government and terrorists, they may choose to help neither side, or be partial to the terrorists, or support the government. The final result will be a victory in counter-terrorism. It's impossible that people have the ability to achieve victory in supporting terrorism.

恐怖主义强弱兴衰，有愚民和刁民在作祟，政府因此进退两难，确实不妥。一方面无道无德的政府是滋生愚民和刁民的病根，恐怖主义才能受益，催动了愚民和刁民不思悔过的本色，也是在尽显政府无良的过错。

The rise and fall of terrorism are influenced by ignorant and unruly people. It's indeed inappropriate that the government is caught in a dilemma. On the one hand, only when an immoral government serves as a hotbed for the breeding of ignorant and unruly people, can terrorism benefit from it. It encourages the unrepentant nature of ignorant and unruly people, and fully reveals the faults of the immoral government.

另一方面，不良人民也可以书写涉恐历史，这就为人们给邪恶的政府增添几分好感，使人对官逼民反的后续发展产生疑问。像在清朝末年，中国产生义和团运动，是由中外联手压迫民间的不安因素催化而成的，可是，"义和团排外"却带有恐怖主义性质，如同暴民作祟。

On the other hand, unruly people can create a history involving terrorism. This makes people have a slight favorable feeling towards an evil government and question the subsequent development of the situation where the tyranny of officials forces the people to rebel. For example, at the end of the Qing Dynasty, the Boxer Rebellion in China was caused by the joint oppression of the Chinese people by both domestic and foreign forces. However, the "Boxers' anti-foreign sentiment" had a terrorist nature, similar to the actions of mobs.

义和团源起于山东，始称义和拳。后在清政府"剿""抚"不定的政策中发展壮大，终于在1900年从山东扩展至直隶，爆发了大规模的锋芒指向帝国主义的农民革命运动。其实，这也同甲午战争有直接关系。战时山东省直接受到日本侵略军的铁蹄践踏，战后日本不仅强索了巨额赔款，而且还割占了中国的台湾及其附属岛屿；沙俄以"干涉还辽"有功，迫使清政府与之签订《中俄密约》，攫取中东路，扩大对东北的侵略；德国亦以同样的理由强占胶州湾，并进而把整个山东划为它的势力范围；法国强租广州湾，英国强租威海卫，中国几被列强瓜分。"外人至此直已视中国如无物，更兼一般教民，假借教会暨领事裁判权之特殊势力，横行乡里，恶印象直接深入民间。大者远者，有国家危亡之惧，小者近者，尤深切肤之痛，排外仇教之感情，因而洋溢全国。"各帝国主义在中国大地上欺凌中国百姓，经济侵略使得农民生活日益困难，长期积压在内心深处的对帝国主义的仇恨，终以义和团运动为载体如火山爆发一样喷射出来[381]。

Originating from Shandong, the Boxers were initially called Yihequan. Later, they grew up under the Qing government's policy of alternating between suppression and conciliation. Finally, in 1900, they spread from Shandong to Zhili, and a large-scale peasant revolutionary movement targeting imperialism broke out. In fact, this was directly related to the First Sino-Japanese War. During the war, Shandong was directly trampled upon by the Japanese aggressive army. After the war, Japan not only claimed a huge amount of compensation but also occupied Taiwan and its affiliated islands. Tsarist Russia, taking credit for "mediating the return of the Liaodong Peninsula", forced the Qing government to sign *Sino-Russian Secret Treaty*, thus seizing the Chinese Eastern Railway and expanding its aggression in Northeast China. Germany occupied Jiaozhou Bay for the same reason and then treated the entire Shandong Province as its sphere of influence. France forcibly leased Guangzhou Bay, and the United Kingdom forcibly leased Weihaiwei. China was almost divided up by the great powers. "By then, foreigners had dismissed China as nothing. Moreover, a handful of local

---

381 陈景彦撰《义和团运动时日俄两国对中国的侵略》，来源《东北亚论坛》，2006 年第 4 期

Christians, taking advantage of the special powers of the church and the consular jurisdiction, domineered over the local people, and left a bad impression among them. On a large and far-reaching scale, people feared the peril of the country. On a small and immediate scale, there was a keenly felt pain. Therefore, an anti-foreign sentiment and hatred towards Christianity spread throughout the country." The imperialist powers bullied the Chinese people within China's territory, and their economic aggression made the farmers live an increasingly difficult life. The long-suppressed hatred for imperialism in the hearts of the people finally erupted like a volcano through the Boxer Rebellion.[381]

义和团把传教士称为"毛子",教民称为"二毛子","通洋学""谙洋语""用洋货"……者依次被称为"三毛子""四毛子"……直到"十毛子",通通在严厉打击之列。他们经常随便找一家大户人家,指其"里通外国",然后冲入家中洗劫一空。因为义和团仇视一切与洋人有关的东西,有用洋物者"必杀无赦,若纸烟,若小眼镜,甚至洋伞、洋袜,用者辄置极刑。曾有学士6人仓皇避乱,因身边随带铅笔一支,洋纸一张,途遇团匪搜出,乱刀并下,皆死非命"。甚至有"一家有一枚火柴,而8口同戮者"……对开明官绅、维新派人士,义和团更是明言打杀,要"拆毁同文馆、大学堂等,所有师徒,均不饶放"[382]。

The Boxers called missionaries "maozi (hairy foreigners)", and called local Christians "secondary maozi". Those who "knew foreign learning", those who "were proficient in foreign languages", and those who "used foreign goods" were called "third-level maozi", "fourth-level maozi" and "fifth-level maozi" respectively. The last one in this naming

---

382 《义和团的荒唐故事:谁带支铅笔都会被砍死》,搜狐文化(搜狐网)www.sohu.com,2008年8月6日

list was the "tenth-level maozi". All of them were among the list to be severely cracked down on. They often randomly selected a wealthy family, accused it of "colluding with foreign countries," and then rushed into the house and looted it. Because the Boxers hated everything related to foreigners, those who used foreign goods would "be killed without mercy. For example, those who used cigarettes, small glasses, and even foreign-made umbrellas and socks would be executed. Once, six scholars fled in a hurry to avoid the turmoil. On the way, the Boxers searched them, found a pencil and a piece of foreign-made paper, and hacked them to death with random slashes of the knife." Even in a case, "all eight members of a family were killed just because there was a match in the house"... As to enlightened officials, gentry, and reformists, the Boxers explicitly claimed to attack and kill them. They also claimed to "demolish institutions such as the Imperial College of Translators and the Imperial University, and not spare any teachers and students."[382]

1900 年 6 月 20 日，德国驻华公使克林德在乘轿前往清总理衙门途中，于东单牌楼被端亲王载漪的虎神营士兵恩海开枪击毙。此事成为八国联军入侵的重要借口。义和团运动失败，八国联军攻占北京，克林德事件遂成为议和谈判中的重要内容之一[383]。

On June 20, 1900, Clemens von Ketteler, the German Minister Plenipotentiary to China, was shot and killed by En Hai, a soldier of the Tiger God Battalion of Prince Duan, Zaiyi, on his way to the General Office of Foreign Affairs in a sedan chair near Dongdan Archway. This incident became an important excuse for the Eight-Nation Alliance's invasion. After the Boxers were defeated and the Eight-Nation Alliance captured Beijing, the Ketteler incident became one of the important

---

383　李学通撰《醇亲王载沣使德史实考》，来源《历史档案》，1990 年第 2 期

contents in the peace negotiations.[383]

八国联军打着"护馆""护教""护侨""营救公使""代剿拳民"的幌子，发动了蓄谋已久的侵华战争。这场战争是以步步进逼的方式展开的。义和团兴起时，列强要求清政府进行镇压[384]。

Under the pretext of "protecting the legations," "protecting the churches," "protecting the overseas Chinese," "rescuing the ministers," and "suppressing the Boxers on behalf of the Qing government," the Eight-Nation Alliance launched a long-premeditated war of aggression against China. The war unfolded in a step-by-step manner. When the Boxers emerged, the great powers demanded that the Qing government suppress them.[384]

义和团运动时期驻外公使们处境尴尬，以他们为主镇压义和团运动，对八国联军入侵一味妥协；同时，也为捍卫国家和民族利益付出了巨大努力。另外，驻外公使们与李鸿章、刘坤一、张之洞等洋务派官员、清朝中央政府以及驻在国的交涉往来中，反映了其间的复杂关系[385]。

During the Boxer Rebellion, the ministers plenipotentiary abroad were in an awkward situation. They became a major force in suppressing the Boxer Rebellion and made concessions to the Eight-Nation Alliance. At the same time, they made great efforts to defend the national and ethnic interests. In addition, they negotiated with Westernization officials such as Li Hongzhang, Liu Kunyi, and Zhang Zhidong, as well as with the central government of the Qing Dynasty, and the host countries. This series of interactions reflected the complex relationships among different parties at that time.[385]

384　徐松荣撰《论己亥建储与义和团运动》，来源《求索》，2001 年第 1 期

385　郭双林撰《晚清驻外公使与义和团运动》，来源《史学月刊》，2001 年第 2 期

无良的士农工商所作所为往往都会利于恐怖主义，成为病态社会的症状之一。这些社会问题在官方和民间，都能像滚雪球一样，越滚越大，成为烫手的山芋。

The actions of unscrupulous scholars, farmers, artisans, and merchants tend to benefit terrorism, thus becoming a symptom of the sick society. These social problems will snowball in the official circle and among common people, and become a hot potato.

天下无道，王纲失序，礼崩乐坏，这三个条件只要满足一个，人心就会不稳。一旦人心涣散，人群中主张"恶为真，善为假，实胜虚，有争胜无争，人为己不为他，坏是永恒不变，好只是暂时的"的相争之论就会蠢蠢欲动。

The lack of justice in the world, the disorder of the royal principles, and the collapse of the social norms and moral principles are three factors, any of which will lead to the uneasiness in people's minds. Once people are demoralized, the arguments which advocate that "evil is real, good is false, the real prevails over the false, competition prevails over non-competition, people act for themselves rather than for others, the bad is eternal, and the good is temporary" will show signs of activity.

一旦社会黑暗，人又怕死，就有人不远离恐怖分子，往恐怖主义靠近。有的人重视自身利益，恐怖分子又肯给足够的好处，那么，人民依靠恐怖分子就是数量多少的问题。

Once society is dark and people are afraid of death, some people will get closer to terrorists rather than stay away from them. Some people put emphasis on their own interests. In this case, if terrorists are willing to offer enough benefits, there will be more or fewer people who rely on terrorists.

人民里面有刁民和愚民。无论是江湖还是庙堂，恐怖主义都能够生根发芽。没有计划的政府直接运用人民反恐，将造成不良人员在国家反恐氛围中茁壮成长。

Unruly and ignorant people are part of society. Terrorism can take root and germinate among the general public or in government agencies. If the government directly employs the people to carry out counter-terrorism operations without a proper plan, it will lead to the proliferation of malicious elements in the context of national counter-terrorism efforts.

在 21 世纪, 多个国家的校园霸凌原本就屡禁不止, 给学生灌输大量反恐知识会增加"校霸"反恐技能, 校园暴力会在恐怖主义的荫蔽下发育, 茁壮成长为成芽、成熟、成型。

In the 21st century, school bullying continues to exist despite repeated bans in many countries. Teaching students a lot of anti-terrorism knowledge may lead to the bullies' increase of anti-terrorism skills. In this case, school violence will take root, grow, and take shape under the shield of terrorism.

2020 年 6 月, 美国教育部和司法部一项研究显示, 过去 5 年, 全美发生暴力事件的公立中小学校从 71% 增加到 81%, 同时校园暴力并不局限于出现在未成年学生群体, 高达 8% 的美国在校中小学教师表示, 他们每月至少在学校受到一次暴力威胁[386]。

According to a study released by the Department of Education and the Department of Justice of the U.S. in June 2020, over the past five years, the number of public primary and secondary schools in the United States where violent incidents occurred increased from 71% to 81%. At the same time, school violence is not limited to underage students. As high as 8% of U.S. primary and secondary school teachers said that they were at least threatened with violence once a month at school.[386]

---

386 《美国每年有 2% 的教职工遭受攻击, 校园暴力何时休?》, 腾讯新闻(腾讯网)
www.qq.com, 2020 年 6 月 8 日

自 1999—2020 年，各种暴力事件如病毒般穿透在美国校园的各个"非管制"的时间点和区域，由此已经造成了被害者身体上的极度重创甚至于夺去了一部分受害者的性命[387]。

From 1999 to 2020, all kinds of violent incidents spread like viruses through each "unregulated" area of U.S. schools at each "unregulated" time interval, causing extremely serious physical injuries to the victims and even taking the lives of some people.[387]

同时，看上去零碎和"无意"的欺凌在校园里亦是无法计数。一系列案件摆在台面上，以及那些看似无足轻重的学生与学生之间的肢体冲突，显然已经将学校的生态氛围推向异化，引起美国社会和法律界极大的关注和担忧[388]。

At the same time, there are countless seemingly sporadic and "inadvertent" acts of bullying in schools. A series of cases on the surface, as well as those seemingly insignificant physical conflicts between students, have obviously pushed the ecological atmosphere of schools towards alienation, causing great concern and worry in American society and the legal community.[388]

校园暴力是美国社会的棘手问题，不禁枪的美国是武器管制不严、枪支泛滥的国家，这增加了美国处理校园暴力的困难程度，甚至校园暴力还演变成为校园枪击。

School violence is a thorny issue in American society. The United States does not ban guns, leading to loose control of guns and a proliferation of firearms, and increasing the difficulty of dealing with school violence, which may even evolve into school shootings.

政府治国治理社会，越俎代庖不是永恒之道，中规中矩方能驶

387　同上

388　同上

入中正之道。如此，"官为民，民卫官，官民无为"，国家自然和谐。

When the government governs the country and society, it should not exceed its authority, as this is not a sustainable way. Only by following the rules can it move on the right path. In this way, "officials serve the people, the people protect officials, and both officials and the people act in accordance with the proper way," and the country will naturally become harmonious.

人天生喜欢无拘无束，自由自在，人民由政府管束，已经存有矛盾，很难消失。人民对国家的最大义务就是纳税，其他都是次要的。人民交税，政府收税，如何让人民心向政府是关键。

People are innately fond of living an unrestrained and free life. There is a natural conflict between the people and the government that governs them. This conflict can hardly disappear. The people's greatest obligation to the country is to pay taxes, and everything else is secondary. The people pay taxes, and the government collects them. The key is how to make the people support the government.

"公仆"是人民对理想政府的蓝图。"正统"不是人民选择政府的标杆，"一沐三捉发，一饭三吐哺，起以待士，犹恐失天下之贤人"才是民心所向的选择。

In people's mind, an ideal government should be "a public servant". "Orthodoxy" is not the people's benchmark for a government. "I often have to lift up my hair three times when washing my head, and have to spit out the food I'm chewing three times during a meal, so that I can stand up at any time to receive the virtuous and talented scholars who come to visit me. I'm always afraid of losing the virtuous and capable people of the world due to negligence." This description truly reflects what the people desire.

谁侵犯人民的利益，人民就会憎恨谁。政府要人民与之站在同一阵线反恐，其轴心并非用众多的法令强制执行，而是人民觉得政府就是自己的家人。

People will hate those who infringe on their interests. If the government hopes that the people can side with it against terrorism, the core is not to force them with numerous decrees but to make them feel that the government is just like their family members.

保护家人是人的天性，人民和政府真能亲如一家，是整个国家之幸。如此，恐怖主义袭扰政府，就等同于向人民开战。政府无须动员人民，人民即会自告奋勇保护。

Protecting one's family is human nature. If the people and the government can truly be as close as a family, it is a blessing for the whole country. In this case, if terrorists harass the government, it is equivalent to declaring war on the people. Without the need to mobilize the people, the people will volunteer to protect the government.

人民不看对他人有害的书籍和视频，不说过激言语，不做网络极端主义的帮凶和主谋，不赚黑心钱……天下不是某个人的，与其多做贡献，不如少做破坏。不触犯他人利益，比帮助他人更加重要，这是人民能够为反恐所做的力所能及的事情。

The people should not read books or watch videos that are harmful to others, nor should they speak extreme words, nor should they be accomplices or masterminds for online extremists, nor should they earn dirty money... The world does not belong to any single person. It is better to do less damage than to make more contributions. Not infringing on the interests of others is more important than helping others. These are the things that the people can do within their power for the anti-terrorism cause.

如果政府一定要动用人民反恐，最多只能让人民配合政府反恐，人民只能做间接反恐的事情，安分守己才是人民的主业，人民直接反恐会把灾难带到家里来。就像在 20 世纪以前，日本近代杰出教育家福泽谕吉，他对民族独立性有自己的见解，对促进官民携手合作有积极向上的一面。

If the government has to mobilize the people to fight against terrorism, it can only let the people play a cooperative role and fight against terrorism indirectly. Being law-abiding is the people's main obligation. If the people are directly involved in anti-terrorism operations, they may bring disasters to their own homes. For example, before the 20th century, Fukuzawa Yukichi, an outstanding modern Japanese educator, had his own views on national independence, and these views were of positive significance for promoting cooperation between officials and the people.

福泽谕吉（1834—1901）大量地吸收基佐（1787—1874）的历史哲学，结合自身的理论持点，从本国实际国情出发，开创了一套具有鲜明日本时代特色的文明史学。福泽在融合基佐优势理论的同时，又保持了西方文明史学强调历史进化论的中心论调，并辩证地将其应用到具体的史学研究中，对日本及近代亚洲各国封建史学的消亡和新史学的诞生，具有划时代的重要意义。[389]

Absorbing many historical-philosophical views of François Guizot (1787-1874) and combining them with the characteristics of his own theories, Fukuzawa Yukichi (1834-1901) created a set of civilization history studies with distinct Japanese era features based on the national conditions. While absorbing Guizot's advantage theory, Fukuzawa maintained the central viewpoint of Western civilization history studies that emphasized historical evolutionism, and applied it to

---

389　朱喆撰《福泽谕吉与基佐的文明史观比较研究》，来源《衡阳师范学院学报》，2012 年 4 期

specific historical studies in a dialectical way. This is of epoch-making significance for the demise of feudal history studies and the birth of new history studies in Japan and other modern Asian countries.[389]

自庆应四年（1868）（也即明治元年）八月从幕府退职后，福泽谕吉再也没有出任过任何官职。在明治年间，他被选为东京府会副议长、东京府参事会员等，他都婉言辞任，并未出仕为官。[390]

Since Fukuzawa Yukichi resigned from the the position of shogunate in the Eighth Month of the Fourth Year of Emperor Keio's Reign (1868) (that is, the First Year of Emperor Meiji's Reign), he no longer held any official position. During Emperor Meiji's Reign, he was elected as the vice speaker of the Tokyo Prefectural Assembly and a member of the Tokyo Prefectural Council, but he politely declined and didn't became an official.[390]

总之，福泽谕吉决心终身不仕的主要原因是：对封建门阀等级制度不满，对所谓的遗臣遗老的轻浮作风厌恶，讨厌盲目的攘夷主义，自身不重功名、不重身份，保持洁身自好、自身独立以及不想身体力行于政治运动等。他在终身不仕的指导思想下不足之处是有的。[391]

In short, the main factors that contribute to Fukuzawa Yukichi's thought of never entering officialdom were: dissatisfaction with the hierarchical system of the feudal aristocracy, disgust for the frivolous behavior of the so-called remnants of the old regime, dislike for blind anti-foreignism, disdain for reputation and status, eagerness for maintaining his integrity and independence, and unwillingness to be

---

390　刘益希撰《张之洞与福泽谕吉德育思想比较研究》，来源《西南政法大学》，2015 年

391　吉家友撰《福泽谕吉终身不仕的原因》，来源《信阳师范学院学报（哲学社会科学版）》，1989 年 4 期

involved in political movements. There were indeed some deficiencies in his guiding ideology of never entering officialdom.[391]

福泽还从具体的角度谈到了培养独立精神的方式，如应当站在个人的立场，或研究学术，或从事贸易，或讨论法律、著书立说、发行报纸，只要不超过人民的本分，就要大胆地去做。他建议，作为知识分子，应当把一切文明事业都引为己任，为前驱，协助政府，增进国力。福泽理想中的政府与人民的关系是：政府保护文明事业，人民兴办文明事业。政府是人民的政府，故人民不应害怕政府，而应当靠拢政府；不应当疑惑政府，而应亲近政府。只有这样，"学术、商业和法律就自然会各得其所，国民与政府的力量亦能平衡，才可以维持全国的独立"。把个人独立与国家独立联系起来加以考虑，这是福泽理论的独特之处。[392]

Fukuzawa Yukichi also discussed the ways of cultivating the spirit of independence from specific perspectives. For example, whether engaging in academic research, conducting trade, discussing laws, writing books, establishing theories, or publishing newspapers, one should proceed from his individual perspective. As long as a thing falls in the scope of what a citizen should do, one should be bold enough to do it. He suggested that intellectuals should assume all civilized undertakings, serve as pioneers, assist the government, and contribute to the enhancement of national strength. In his mind, the ideal relationships between the government and the people can be described as follows: The government protects civilized undertakings, while the people initiate civilized undertakings. The government is for the people, so the people should not be afraid of it but rather get closer to it; the people should not be suspicious of the

---

392 焦润明撰《从＜劝学篇＞看福泽谕吉建构国民新道德之努力》，来源《日本研究》，2000 年第 4 期

government but be friendly with it. Only in this way can "the academic, business and legal communities naturally find their proper positions, the power of the citizens and the government be balanced, and the national independence be maintained." Combining individual independence with national independence is a unique feature of Fukuzawa Yukichi's theory.[392]

身为教育师的福泽谕吉，他的言行举止也是发扬自己思想的一部分。福泽谕吉的思想在国际上也有立足之地，旁观者应该加以选择性的接受，避免自己坐井观天。

As an educator, Fukuzawa Yukichi used his words and deeds to spread his thoughts, which have gained international influence. Therefore, the audience should selectively adopt them to avoid being narrow-minded.

有时候间接反恐的能量不低于直接反恐，也就是说，人可以不去反恐，但更加不能去支持恐怖主义和执行恐怖主义。就像历史风流人物未必自己去反恐，反而自己也曾经犯下恐怖主义。要是有人真想在反恐领域有一番作为，倒不如或保持中立，或不忘初心，或拒绝为五斗米折腰，或威武不能屈，或不要荣华富贵，或做明哲保身的小人物，也照样能反恐，此乃以虚胜实。就像在中国古代时期，汉朝有苏武牧羊，来表示自己不会卖国屈敌。

Sometimes, the power of indirect anti-terrorism efforts is no less than that of direct anti-terrorism operations. That is, one can avoid directly engaging in anti-terrorism operations, but one should never support or carry out terrorist activities. For example, some historical celebrities did not directly participated in anti-terrorism operations. On the contrary, they once committed terrorist actions themselves. If one truly intends to make achievements in anti-terrorism, he should remain neutral, or stay true to his original aspirations, or refuse to compromise for a meager salary, or stand firm in the face of force, or give up the pursuit of glory and wealth, or be a small person who knows how to protect himself. In this way, he can also contribute to the anti-terrorism cause. This is a way of overcoming the substantial with the insubstantial. For example, in ancient China, during the Han Dynasty, Su Wu herded sheep in the north to demonstrate his determination not to betray his country or surrender to the enemy.

据《汉书·苏武传》载：天汉之年（公元前 100 年），苏武奉命赴匈奴被扣，匈奴贵族多方威胁诱降未遂，又将他遣到北海（今贝加尔湖）边牧羊。始元六年（公元前 81 年），因匈奴与汉和好，才被遣回国朝，官典属国，历时 19 年。他不肯背叛祖国的气节流芳百世，传唱千古。[393]

According to *Biography of Su Wu, Book of Han*, during the First Year of Emperor Tianhan's Reign (100 BC), Su Wu was dispatched on a mission to the Xiongnu and was detained. The Xiongnu nobles tried every means to threaten and induce him to surrender, but they failed. Then, they sent him to herd sheep at Beihai (now Lake Baikal). It was not until the Sixth Year of Emperor Shiyuan's Reign (81 BC) that he was able to return to the Han Dynasty due to the reconciliation between the Xiongnu and the Han Dynasty. Then, he was appointed as an official in charge of vassal states. The sheep-herding life had lasted for 19 years. His integrity of not betraying his motherland has been remembered and widely praised by later generations.[393]

从古到今，都是发展个人容易，发展团体困难；分裂个人困难，分裂团体容易；中立个人容易，中立团体困难；融入个人容易，融入团体困难。

393　李惠莉撰《论声乐套曲＜苏武牧羊＞的艺术特色》，来源《安阳师范学院学报》，2007 年 6 期

Since ancient times, it has been easier to cultivate an individual than to cultivate a group; more difficult to divide an individual than to divide a group; easier for an individual to remain neutral than for a group to remain neutral; and easier to be integrated into an individual than to be integrated into a group.

在 21 世纪，每个人都有沉重的经济负担，政府让人民拒绝支持恐怖主义，比让人民反抗恐怖袭击来得更加现实。

In the 21st century, everyone has a heavy economic burden. It is more realistic for the government to make people refuse to support terrorism than to make them resist terrorist attacks.

从情感层面来说，恐怖主义具有欺骗性，往往要博取旁人信任，欺负他人善良。由于男娶女嫁下的成家立业和生儿育女都要有合法的经济收入来源，所以男人不能娶支持恐怖主义的女人，女人不能嫁给支持恐怖主义的男人，这就是一种反恐爱情观，与人民生活是密不可分的。

From an emotional perspective, terrorism is deceptive. It often tries to win the trust of others and take advantage of their kindness. Under the traditional mode of marriage, whether to form a family, establish a career, or have children, one needs a legitimate source of economic income, so men should not marry women who support terrorism, and women should not marry men who support terrorism. This view of love has anti-terrorism features and is closely related to people's lives.

法国国内情报总局前局长卡路易斯·皮奥尼认为，很多西方女性是在"帮助圣战士兄弟""为他们生孩子，以延续圣战力量"念头的驱使下离家出走的。[394]

Carlos Pioni, the former director of the French General Directorate

---

394 《西方女子为何投入ISIS怀抱?》,《青年参考 17 版：新闻故事》(2014 年 10 月 08 日)

of Domestic Intelligence, believes that many Western women left home driven by the idea of "helping the holy warriors" and "giving birth to children for them to continue the power of jihad."[394]

在法国国际和战略关系研究所教授卡里姆·帕扎德看来，西方年轻女性"对战争与战士的浪漫幻想"是她们加入极端组织的原因。[395]

According to Karim Pazard, a professor at the French Institute of International and Strategic Relations, the "romantic fantasies about war and warriors" of Western young women are the reasons for their joining extremist organizations.[395]

"斩首和割喉这种残忍的手段，被她们视为颇有英雄气概的行为，实施这些酷刑的人成了她们眼中的英雄。"帕扎德说。[396]

"Cruel means such as beheading and throat-slitting are regarded by them as heroic acts, and those who carry out these tortures have become heroes in their eyes," Pazard said.[396]

英国穆斯林女性组织执行董事斯威特·戈希尔表示，加入 ISIS 的女性中，"有些人年龄很小，很天真，根本不知道战争与信仰的真正含义"。[397]

Sweet Gohir, the executive director of the British Muslim Women's Organization, said that among the women who joined ISIS, "some are very young and naive, and they have no idea of the true meaning of war and faith."[397]

美国马萨诸塞大学教授、《震撼：女性与恐怖主义》一书的作者米娅·布鲁姆告诉美联社，ISIS 等极端组织在招募西方女性时，将组织成员的生活描述成"迪斯尼乐园般的景象"，有的女性被金

395　同上

396　同上

397　同上

钱诱惑。布鲁姆发现，投身极端组织后，一些女性遭到性侵和虐待，一些被卖到工厂里做奴工，一些被迫嫁给武装分子，为他们生儿育女。[398]

Mia Bloom, a professor at the University of Massachusetts in the United States and the author of the book *Shock: Women and Terrorism*, told the Associated Press that when extremist organizations like ISIS recruited Western women, they described the life of their members as "a Disneyland-like scene," and some women were lured by money. Bloom found that after joining extremist organizations, some women were sexually assaulted and abused, some were sold as slaves working in factories, and some were forced to marry militants and have children for them.[398]

恐怖主义是有组织、有计划、有预谋的，其中就包括欺骗男男女女的纯真感情。年少无知往往伴随不负责任行为和错误情感。一旦成年人步入社会找工作，以前的种种幼稚行为就会得到自己的证明。所以说，爱情是一种建立在材料下的真感情。

Terrorism is organized, planned, and premeditated, which involves playing with the innocent feelings of people. Youth and ignorance are often accompanied by irresponsible behaviors and wrong emotions. Once adults enter society and seek jobs, their previous behaviors will prove naive to themselves. Therefore, love is a true emotion based on materials.

关于爱情，有人可以悟出"朋友妻，死后欺"；有人可以悟出"犯错的感情是要付出代价的"；有人可以悟出"离婚的女人也能收获爱情"；有人可以悟出"好男人远离淫娃荡妇"。

Regarding love, some people think that "a friend's wife can be harassed after the friend's death"; some people think that "wrong feelings

---

398　同上

will lead to consequences"; some people think that "a divorced woman can also find love"; and some people think that "a good man should stay away from flirtatious women."

21 世纪是一个讲究物质基础的社会。综合对比多种爱情观，普通人更加相信富有感情基础的现实爱情。即男男女女谈婚论嫁，要用感情基础创造缘分，而非用缘分创造感情基础。

Society in the 21st century attaches great importance to material foundations. Through a comprehensive comparison of different views of love, ordinary people will have more faith in realistic love with a solid emotional foundation. That is, when men and women consider marriage, they should create a destiny based on emotions, rather than create an emotional foundation based on fate.

一个人面对爱情和面包如何选择，其实，早在世界古代史就有了一些史例作为结论。不论太平时期或者乱世时期，现实生活压力都太大，如果男女双方不能缓解各式各样的恐怖压力，注定不能长相厮守。比如，在翻脸无情的社会，翻脸如翻书。中国明末清初有名妓"秦淮八艳"，这八位美妓在中国改朝换代的浪潮之下，她们有几位的爱情就是以悲剧收场。

An individual's choice between love and bread is actually illustrated by some cases in ancient world history. Whether in times of peace or turmoil, people have to tolerate enormous pressures of real life. If a couple fails to relieve various horrible pressures, they are doomed to separate in the end. For example, in a merciless society, people tend to change their attitude as quickly as turning a page. During the late Ming and early Qing Dynasties, there were eight famous courtesans known as the "Eight Beauties of Qinhuai." Amid the dynastic changes, some of them had tragic love endings.

根据相关历史资料记载，在"江南佳丽地，金陵帝王州"的南京，有八位名妓以其出众的容貌、绝佳的才艺脱颖而出，名扬四方，她们就是"秦淮八艳"，即柳如是、马湘兰、李香君、董小宛、寇白门、卞玉京、顾横波和陈圆圆。"秦淮八艳"都出身卑微，命运的捉弄使她们沦落风尘，但是她们努力学习才艺，坚守操守，绝不做倚门卖笑之流。她们与大夫名士交往密切，仰慕他们的才华和气度，并成为他们的红颜知己，演绎了一段段曲折的爱情传奇。在财富和权势面前，她们往往嗤之以鼻，不屑一顾。在明清江山易主的紧要关头，她们表现出了巾帼不让须眉的极高的民族气节和人格操守，令所有卖国求荣、贪生怕死的男子为之汗颜、羞愧。当时特殊的文化环境给了她们特殊的际遇，秦淮八艳获得了相对宽松的氛围，能够大胆追求爱情、追求幸福。她们的才气、气节以及身处的环境，使她们创造出了不平凡的传奇人生。[399]

According to relevant historical records, in Nanjing, known as "the land of beautiful women in the south of the Yangtze River and the imperial city of Jinling," eight famous courtesans stood out and became widely-known due to their outstanding looks and excellent skills. They were known as the "Eight Beauties of Qinhuai," namely Liu Rushi, Ma Xianglan, Li Xiangjun, Dong Xiaowan, Kou Baimen, Bian Yujing, Gu Hengbo, and Chen Yuanyuan. All of them came from humble families, and were forced into prostitution by the caprices of fate. However, they worked hard to learn skills, adhered to their moral principles, and refused to be ordinary prostitutes. They had close interactions with scholars and celebrities, admired their talents and demeanor, and became their confidantes, creating a series of tortuous love legends. They often showed contempt for wealth and power. At the critical moment when the

---

399 刘倩撰《古代江南佳丽的诗性审美精神阐释》，来源《江南大学学报（人文社会科学版）》，2010 年 2 期

Ming Dynasty was being replaced by the Qing Dynasty, they showed an extraordinary national integrity and moral character that were no less than those of men, making all men who betrayed their country for personal gains and feared death feel ashamed. In the special cultural environment at that time, they captured special opportunities, enjoyed a relatively relaxed atmosphere, and were able to boldly pursue love and happiness. Their talents, integrity, and the environment enabled them to create an extraordinary legendary life.[399]

这些风尘女子之所以后世留名，除却自身之才华技艺之外，推究起来，就是与所结交之人物相互映衬。柳如是之于钱谦益，董小宛之于冒襄，卞玉京之于吴梅村，顾横波之于龚鼎慈，马湘兰之于王稚登，陈圆圆更是引来"冲冠一怒为红颜"，一身系明亡清兴，而李香君所结交的，正是侯方域。[400]

Apart from their own skills, the contrast and complement between them and the people they contacted can well account for why they are remembered by later generations. Liu Rushi and Qian Qianyi, Dong Xiaowan and Mao Xiang, Bian Yujing and Wu Weiye, Gu Hengbo and Gong Dingzi, Ma Xianglan and Wang Zhideng, all of them set off each other perfectly. Chen Yuanyuan even caused the "wrath for the beauty" incident, being closely related to the fall of the Ming Dynasty and the rise of the Qing Dynasty. And the person with whom Li Xiangjun had intimate relations was none other than Hou Fangyu.[400]

崇祯自缢，清军入关后，南京建成了弘光小朝廷，柳如是支持钱谦益当了南明的礼部尚书。不久，清军南下，很快便兵临城下。柳如是劝钱谦益和她一起投水殉国，钱沉思不语，后来在柳如是再三催促下，走下荷花池试了试水，飞快又上来说："水太冷，不能

400　刘春先撰《明末清初时局下的侯方域研究》，来源《广西师范大学》，2012 年

下。"柳如是失望之余，"奋身欲沉池水中"，被钱谦益硬拖住了。后来，钱谦益终还是迎降了清朝廷，去北京做了礼部侍郎兼翰林学士（也有说钱并非贪图富贵，而是曲线救国，为了一展抱负为国为民，这里不表）。柳如是自留在南京不去。[401]

After Emperor Chongzhen hanged himself and the Qing troops entered the Shanhai Pass, the Southern Ming regime headed by Emperor Hongguang was established in Nanjing. Liu Rushi supported Qian Qianyi in becoming the Minister of Rites. Then, the Qing troops advanced southward and soon reached the city walls. Liu Rushi tried to persuade Qian Qianyi to drown himself with her to show loyalty to the country, but he pondered without saying a word. Later, urged by Liu Rushi repeatedly, he stepped into the lotus pond to test the water, but quickly sprang up and said, "The water is too cold to enter." Feeling disappointed, Liu Rushi "tried to throw herself into the pond," but was held back by Qian Qianyi. Later, Qian Qianyi surrendered to the Qing court and went to Beijing to serve as the Minister of Rites and the Hanlin Academy Scholar (Someone argues that Qian Qianyi was not driven by greed for wealth and glory, but aimed to save the country indirectly to fulfill his ambition of serving the country and the people. This viewpoint will not be elaborated here). However, Liu Rushi stayed in Nanjing and refused to go with him.[401]

然而，作为降臣，钱谦益并没有受到清朝廷的信任，再加上他受柳如是影响，半年后便称病辞归。后来又因为其他案件株连，吃了两次官司。柳如是在病中代他贿赂营救出狱，鼓励他与尚在抵抗的郑成功、张煌言、瞿式耜、魏耕等将领联系，并尽全力资助、慰劳抗清义军。钱谦益去世后，乡里族人聚众欲夺其房产，柳如是

---

401 《最好命的风尘女子》，新浪新闻（新浪网），www.sina.com.cn，2023 年 04 月 11 日

为了保护钱家产业，用缕帛结项自尽明志。恶棍们自此被吓走，可是，一代才女柳如是，却也因此结束了传奇而绚丽的一生。[402]

However, as a minister who had surrendered to the Qing Dynasty, Qian Qianyi was not trusted by the imperial court. Moreover, influenced by Liu Rushi, he pleaded illness and resigned half a year later. Later, he was involved in two lawsuits due to other cases. When Liu Rushi was ill, she managed to get him released through bribery, encouraged him to get in touch with generals who were still resisting the Qing Dynasty, such as Zheng Chenggong, Zhang Huangyan, Qu Shisi, and Wei Geng, and spared no efforts to provide financial support and offer consolation to the righteous anti-Qing army. After Qian Qianyi's death, the clan members gathered together, attempting to seize his property. In order to protect his family estate, Liu Rushi hanged herself with silk to show her determination. The villains were scared away, but the legendary and brilliant life of this talented woman also came to an end.[402]

寇白门，原名寇湄，字白门，明末清初"秦淮八艳"之一。崇祯十五年暮春，声势显赫的功臣保国公朱国弼来到钞库街寇家，几次交往后，他给白门留下了良好印象，在朱氏提出婚娶时便一口同意。[403]

Kou Baimen, known as Koumei by original name and Baimen by courtesy name, was one of the "Eight Beauties of Qinhuai". In the late spring of the 15th Year of Emperor Chongzhen's Reign, Zhu Guobi, the prestigious and powerful Duke of Baoguo, a meritorious official, came to Kou Baimen's residence on Chaoku Street. After several interactions, he left a favorable impression on her. When he proposed marriage, she

---

402　同上

403　《青楼大观：中国历史上十大富豪名妓》，凤凰资讯（凤凰网），www.ifeng.com，2008 年 07 月 09 日

immediately agreed.[403]

1645 年清军南下，朱国弼降清，不久被软禁。朱氏欲将连寇白门在内的歌姬婢女一起卖掉，白门对朱说："若卖妾所得不过数百金……若使妾南归，一月之间当得万金以报公。"朱思忖后遂答允。寇白门归返金陵，在旧院姊妹帮助下筹集了 2 万两银子将朱国弼赎释。这时朱氏想重圆好梦，被寇拒绝，她说："当年你用银子赎我脱籍，如今我也用银子将你赎回，我俩就此了结。"[404]

In 1645, when the Qing troops advanced southward, Zhu Guobi surrendered and was soon placed under house arrest. He intended to sell the singing girls and maidservants, among whom was Kou Baimen. Kou Baimen said to him, "If you sell me, you will only get a few hundred taels of silver... If you let me return to the south, I am able to obtain ten thousand taels of silver within a month to repay you." After thinking for a while, Zhu Guobi agreed. Then, Kou Baimen returned to Jinling. With the help of her sisters in the former brothel quarter, she managed to raise 20,000 taels of silver and ransomed Zhu Guobi. At that time, Zhu Guobi wanted to resume their old relationship, but was declined by Kou Baimen. She said, "You once used silver to redeem me and relieve me from being a courtesan. Now, I have also used silver to ransom you, so our relationship should come to an end."[404]

陈圆圆是明清之际的一位颇有"影响"的人物，据说李自成的军队攻入北京城后，给时在山海关抵抗清兵的宁远总兵吴三桂写信招降，吴本拟应允，可意外得知自己的宠妾陈圆圆被李自成（一说为李的大将刘宗敏）所夺，顿时勃然大怒，"大丈夫不能保一女子，何以生为"，于是投降清军，引兵入关。[405]

404　同上

405　王逊撰《文艺传播与历史传奇——论陈圆圆形象塑造的三种模式》，来源《文艺争鸣》，2016 年 04 期

Chen Yuanyuan was a highly "influential" figure during the transition between the Ming and the Qing Dynasties. It is said that after Li Zicheng's army captured Beijing, Li Zicheng sent a letter to persuade Wu Sangui, who was the General-in-Chief of Ningyuan and fighting against the Qing troops at Shanhai Pass, to surrender. At first, Wu Sangui intended to agree. However, when he accidentally learned that his beloved concubine Chen Yuanyuan had been taken away by Li Zicheng (or according to another version, by Liu Zongmin, a general of Li Zicheng), he immediately flew into a rage and said, "A real man who cannot protect a woman has no reason to live." Thus, he surrendered to the Qing troops and led them into Shanhai Pass.[405]

常年的国仇家恨包裹着随之而来的恐怖主义。在恐怖事件之下，很多人是忠是奸的本性就露了出来。有的人选择视死如归，有的人选择变节投敌，有的人左右摇摆，有的人随波逐流……不管这些选择是出于主动，还是出于被动，都能改变同性和异性对其的根本看法，决定其能否收获爱情。

Years of national hatred and family grudges are accompanied by the subsequent terrorism. Under the shadow of terrorist incidents, the true nature of many people, loyal or treacherous, will be revealed. Some face death unflinchingly, some defect to the enemy, some vacillate between two sides, some drift with the tide... Whether these choices are made actively or passively, they can change the fundamental views of both those of the same sex and those of the opposite sex towards them, and determine whether they can obtain love.

恐怖主义不仅使爱情和事业饱受摧残，更是寻常人家的敌人。和其他事物一样，国家对付敌对目标有笔杆子和枪杆子两种方法。有一种对敌策略是官民合作，即一方面政府可以运用枪杆子打击恐怖分子，另一方面人民可以运用笔杆子净化政府毒瘤。笔杆子和枪杆子相结合，才能文武合一，对恐怖主义造成极大杀伤力。就像二战以后，日本著名社会派推理小说家松本清张大获成功，反映了当时日本社会是病态的。这种"有病"的日本社会，在国家"小病小痛"时期，就要去医治，以免成为国家的大灾大难。

Terrorism not only severely damages love and causes but also is an enemy of ordinary families. Just like dealing with other matters, a country has two means to deal with hostile targets: the pen and the gun. Specifically, one strategy against the enemy is the cooperation between the government and the people. That is, on the one hand, the government uses the gun to crack down on terrorists, and on the other hand, the people use the pen to purify the harmful and corrupt aspects within the government. Only by combining the pen with the gun can we integrate the civil and military aspects and cause great damage to terrorism. For example, after the Second World War, Matsumoto Seicho, a famous Japanese mystery novelist of the social school, achieved great success, and his works revealed that Japanese society at that time was in an ill state. It was necessary to treat this "sick" Japanese society during the period of "minor illnesses and pains" of the country lest it bring a severe disaster for the country.

松本清张（1909—1992），日本侦探推理小说家。松本清张与柯南道尔、阿加莎·克里斯蒂并称为"世界推理小说三巨匠"。此外，松本清张、江户川乱步、横沟正史并称为"日本推理文坛三大高峰"。日本有悠久的悬疑推理小说传统，奈良时代的《古事记》《宇津保物语》与日本妖怪物等古典文学作品，都带有早期悬疑推理小说的雏形。到了江户时代，带有侦探意味的作品开始广泛引起读者的兴趣；明治时代出现了著名的推理小说翻译家黑岩泪香，从这时开始具有现实主义色彩，在一定程度上反映了社会现实的日本推理文学成为日本文坛上别有特色的文学形式。大正末期出现的专门刊载日本青年作家推理作品的《新青年》杂志，是日本近代推理小说园地，此后才出现了以江户川乱步、松本清张为代表的现代推理小说名家。[406]

Matsumoto Seicho (1909-1992) was a Japanese detective novelist. Matsumoto Seicho, Arthur Conan Doyle, and Agatha Christie are together known as the "Three Greatest Mystery Novelists in the World." In addition, Matsumoto Seicho, Edogawa Rampo, and Yokomizo Seishi are together known as the "Three Greatest Mystery Novelists in Japan." Suspense and detective novels have a long tradition in Japan. Classical literary works such as *Kojiki* and *Utsubo Monogatari* from the Nara period, as well as works about Japanese monsters and spirits, can be considered the embryonic forms of early suspense and detective novels. In the Edo period, works with detective elements began to arouse the interest of readers nationwide. In the Meiji period, there emerged a famous detective novel translator, Kuroiwa Ruiko. From then on, Japanese detective literature, which took on a realistic color and reflected social reality to a certain extent, became a distinctive literary form in the Japanese literary circle. The magazine *Shin Seinen*, which was specially dedicated to the publication of detective works of Japanese young writers at the end of the Taisho period, was a garden for modern Japanese mystery novels. Only after that did modern detective novel masters represented by Edogawa Rampo and Matsumoto Seicho emerge.[406]

松本清张步入文坛时已有 41 岁，他只念过八年书，主要靠自学和深入生活获得渊博的学问和文学素养。1950 年，他以历史小说《西乡钞票》走上文坛。接着又以《某〈小仓日记〉传》荣获日

406　苏伦高娃撰《松本清张推理小说的艺术特色》，来源《短篇小说：原创版》，2015 年第 12Z 期

本纯文学奖——1953 年度的芥川龙之介奖，从此一发不可收。随后在 20 世纪 60 年代和 70 年代分别完成了日本战后知名度最高的小说《砂器》，以及后被评为世界十大侦探推理小说佳作之一的《点与线》。[407]

Matsumoto Seicho entered the literary circle at the age of 41. He had only studied for eight years, but he acquired profound knowledge and made significant literary achievements mainly through self-study and in-depth experience of life. In 1950, he stepped onto the literary stage with his historical novel *Saigo's Banknote*. Then, with his work *The Story of a Certain "Ogura's Diary"*, he won the Japanese Pure Literature Award - the Akutagawa Prize in 1953. After that, he could not refrain himself from creating novels. Subsequently, in the 1960s and 1970s, he respectively completed *The Castle of Sand*, which enjoyed the highest popularity in Japan after the Second World War, and *Points and Lines*, which was later rated as one of the top ten detective novels in the world.[407]

以松本清张为代表的日本社会派推理小说，摆脱过去推理小说单纯侦破案件的拘囿，对从不同途径搞到手的官方机密材料进行宏观与微观的消化，通过栩栩如生的艺术形象，揭开笼罩在日本列岛的浓重黑雾。他的小说以权与法、善与恶、罪与罚等与社会现实紧密相关的问题为题材，用敏感而犀利的笔触，披露了日本社会的瑕疵，尽可能在广阔的社会背景中展示故事情节。就反映生活的深度和广度而言，比起从前的刑事侦破小说，表现出难能可贵的拓展与超越，注意融入积极的思想意义，力求给读者以积极的人生认识和启示。作品描写的犯罪根源，也从过去那种出于个人恩怨、桃色纠纷或图财害命，发展为官僚政客和资本家为了政治上的阴谋诡计而

---

407 冯莉撰《胜利属于坚韧不拔的人——浅议大器晚成的松本清张》，来源《佳木斯教育学院学报》，2010 年 6 期

杀人灭口，体现了一种朴实而严肃的美学追求，无形中完成了一次质的飞跃，升高了视点，以更强有力的声音在时代的胸膛上搏动。同时，使得那些对推理小说睥睨不屑者认识到，必须综合地多层次地对推理小说进行科学的考察和分析，盲目的推崇和不加分析的一概否定，都是不妥当的，从而认识到不能不让社会派推理小说在日本当代文坛上占有一席之地。[408]

Japanese detective novels of the social school represented by Matsumoto Seicho have broken the constraints of the simple crime-solving in previous detective novels. Through macroscopic and microscopic digestion of the official confidential materials obtained through various channels, and through the representation of vivid artistic images, they revealed the oppressive dark fog that shrouded the Japanese archipelago. His novels, themed with matters closely related to social reality such as power and law, good and evil, crime and punishment, used sensitive and incisive descriptions to expose the flaws of Japanese society and display the plots as much as possible in a broad social background. In terms of the depth and breadth of reflecting life, compared with the previous criminal detective novels, they showed a valuable expansion and transcendence, paid attention to integrating positive ideological significance, and strove to provide readers with a positive understanding and enlightenment of life. The root causes of crimes depicted in his works also evolved from personal grudges, romantic entanglements or killing for money to murders committed by bureaucrats, politicians and capitalists for preventing disclosure out of political intrigues. This embodies a simple and solemn aesthetic pursuit. Imperceptibly, these novels have undergone a qualitative leap, elevated the perspective, and throbbed more

---

408　李德纯撰《论松本清张的创作与艺术》，来源《外国文学研究》，1989 年 2 期

powerfully in the chest of the era. At the same time, it makes those who look down on detective novels realize that it is necessary to conduct a scientific investigation and analysis of detective novels comprehensively and at multiple levels. Neither blind admiration nor complete negation without analysis is appropriate. In this way, they will realize that detective novels of the social school should be given a place in the contemporary Japanese literary circle.[408]

长期以来，人们形象地把日本政治称作"金权政治"。在"金权政治"下，政官企相互利用形成密不可分的"铁三角"：官僚管制企业活动；企业提供的政治资金控制政治家的活动；政治家奉企业的命令，施加压力影响官僚。权和钱的交换，是维系政企官三者互相牵制关系的要素。同时，为了从财政预算里得到更多的钱，他们相互之间不停地协作，其结果是政界变成"淘金场"，包括内阁总理大臣、国务院大臣和政务次官在内的特别职公务员贪污腐败，各种腐败丑闻层出不穷。1970 年代的洛克希德行贿丑闻、1980 年代的"里库路特股票丑闻"、1990 年代的"佐川快件公司贿赂丑闻"和"金丸信巨额偷税丑闻"，无一不轰动世界。[409]

Over a long time, Japanese politics has been vividly referred to as "money and power politics", under which a close "iron triangle" has been formed through mutual utilization among politicians, officials, and enterprises: Bureaucrats regulate enterprise activities; the political funds provided by enterprises control the activities of politicians; politicians, following the orders of enterprises, exert pressure to influence bureaucrats. The exchange between power and money is an element that maintains the mutual restraint relationship among the government,

---

409 刘英捷撰《日本特别职公务员腐败丑闻层出不穷》，来源《中国人才》，1995 年 6 期

enterprises, and officials. At the same time, in order to obtain more money from the fiscal budget, they maintain cooperation with one another. As a result, the political arena has become a "gold rush field", where corruption scandals of the Prime Minister, cabinet ministers, parliamentary vice-ministers, and other special civil servants have emerged one after another. The Lockheed bribery scandal in the 1970s, the "Recruit stock scandal" in the 1980s, and the "Sagawa Express bribery scandal" and the "Shin Kanemaru's massive tax evasion scandal" in the 1990s all aroused a great sensation in the world.[409]

在各个国家与地区，很多人不愿意大器晚成，反而自愿出名趁早，愿意沉沦在荣华富贵、锦衣玉食、高官厚禄、为官之道之下。甚至这些利欲熏心的人群为了自己利益最大化，不断上下勾结他人，制造出各式各样的极端事件。

In each country and region, many people are not content with achieving success late in life. Instead, they voluntarily seek fame as early as possible, willing to degenerate into a life of pursuing glory, wealth, luxury, high official positions, and the ways of being an official. Even those people who are consumed by avarice, keep colluding with others at all levels to cause all kinds of extremist incidents for the maximization of their own interests.

恐惧让人沉默，知情不报也是在纵容犯罪。各国政府牵涉诸多丑闻，已经不是新鲜事情，人民用笔杆子曝光政府肮脏的丑事，这也是在间接打击恐怖主义，将恐怖主义进行压缩。比如在 19 世纪的美国，美国女作家斯托夫人写了一本《汤姆叔叔的小屋》，此书出版传播以后，融入了美国内战的一部分，为反种族歧视做出了贡献。

Fear makes people silent, and concealing information is equivalent to abetting crimes. It is no longer news that governments of each country are involved in numerous scandals. The exposure of the dirty deeds of governments by the people is equivalent to indirectly combating terrorism and curbing its spread. For example, in the 19th century, the American female writer Mrs. Stowe wrote the book *Uncle Tom's Cabin*. After its publication and dissemination, it was linked to the American Civil War and made contributions to the fight against racial discrimination.

斯托夫人全名为哈里耶特·比彻·斯托（1811—1896），19 世纪美国著名的女作家。出生于美国北部康涅狄格州的一个牧师家庭，她自幼受父亲加尔文教信仰的影响，笃信基督教，成年后受叔父自由主义思想熏陶，关注社会问题，喜欢读英国小说家司各特的小说，这对她以后的创作有明显影响。她在 21 岁时，随全家迁往南部的辛辛那提市，那里和蓄奴的社会仅有一河之隔，从而使得她对黑奴的悲惨生活有着更为真实的认识[410]。

With the full name being Harriet Beecher Stowe, Mrs. Stowe (1811-1896) was a famous American female writer in the 19th century. Born in a pastor's family in Connecticut in the northern United States, she was influenced by her father's Calvinist belief in her childhood, and firmly believed in Christianity. After growing up, influenced by her uncle's liberal ideology, she paid attention to social issues and was fond of reading novels of the British novelist Walter Scott. This had an obvious influence on her later creation. At the age of 21, she relocated her family to Cincinnati in the southern United States. That city was only a river apart from the slave-owning society, enabling her to have a more vivid understanding of the miserable life of black slaves.[410]

1836 年她和神学教授卡尔文·斯托结婚，在家人的鼓励下，专业从事文学创作。之后，在访问活动及其周围人废奴思想影响下，

410　杨天地撰《斯托夫人〈汤姆叔叔的小屋〉赏析》，来源《电影评介》，2014 年第 2 期

坚定了她写一部以废奴思想为主旨的长篇小说。1852 年，长篇小说《汤姆叔叔的小屋》出版，使她一举成名。其他代表作有：长篇小说《德雷德，阴暗的大沼地的故事》（1856）、《老镇上的人们》（1869）、诗集《宗教诗选》（1867）、女权主义论文《我妻子和我》（1871）等 [411]。

In 1836, she married Calvin Stowe, a theology professor. Encouraged by her family members, she engaged in professional literary creation. Later, influenced by her visiting activities and the anti-slavery ideas of the people around her, she was determined to write a full-length novel with the theme of abolishing slavery. In 1852, the full-length novel *Uncle Tom's Cabin* was published, making her famous overnight. Her other representative works include the full-length novels *Dred: A Tale of the Great Dismal Swamp* (1856) and *The People of the Old Town* (1869), the poetry collection *Religious Poems* (1867), and the feminist treatise *My Wife and I* (1871).[411]

19 世纪的美国在经济发展时期涌现出很多伟大作家，创作了很多经典作品。斯托夫人的《汤姆叔叔的小屋》就是其中典型代表之一，并且受到了众多政治家和文人的高度评价。比如，美国第 16 任总统林肯（Abraham Lincoln，1809—1964）于 1862 年在白宫会见斯托夫人时，称《汤姆叔叔的小屋》是一部"引发了一场伟大战争的书"；爱默生（Ralph Waldo Emerson，1803—1882）说它可以沟通普天下的人；托尔斯泰（Leo Tolstoy，1828—1910）也曾暗示它要高于《安娜·卡列尼娜》和《战争与和平》；美国著名黑人诗人兰斯顿·休斯（Langston Hughes，1902—1967）在 20 世纪 50 年代称其为"道德层面的自由宣言"。作为美国文学历史上具有开创意义的一部社会小说，《汤姆叔叔的小屋》中所涉及的种族问题，尽

411　同上

管表现形式不同，却依然困扰着美国社会[412]。

During the economic development in the 19th century in the United States, there emerged many great writers who created a lot of classic works. As a typical representative, Mrs. Stowe's *Uncle Tom's Cabin* received high praise from many politicians and scholars. For example, when Abraham Lincoln (1809-1864), the 16th President of the United States, met Mrs. Stowe at the White House in 1862, he called *Uncle Tom's Cabin* a book that "had led to a great war"; Ralph Waldo Emerson (1803-1882) said that it could be used to communicate with people all over the world; Leo Tolstoy (1828-1910) once hinted that it was superior to *Anna Karenina* and *War and Peace*; Langston Hughes (1902-1967), a famous American black poet, called it a "declaration of freedom at the moral level" in the 1950s. As a pioneering social novel in the history of American literature, *Uncle Tom's Cabin* involved racial issues. Although these issues take on different forms of manifestation nowadays, they still trouble American society.[412]

《汤姆叔叔的小屋》自从 1851 年问世以来，一直受到世界各国读者的喜爱和众多评论者的关注。它鲜明的废奴主题在当时就引起了极大的轰动，对于美国当时的废奴主义运动起了非常大的推动作用，并且在很大程度上推动了美国南北战争的爆发[413]。

Since its publication in 1851, Uncle Tom's Cabin has been loved by readers all over the world and received the attention of many critics. Its distinct theme of slavery abolition caused a great sensation at that time, played an important role in promoting the abolitionist movement in the United States, and led to the outbreak of the American Civil War to a

---

412　吕水平撰《〈汤姆叔叔的小屋〉的文学性及其艺术呈现》，来源《上海外国语大学》，2014 年

413　李世奎撰《〈汤姆叔叔的小屋〉的主题解析》，来源《长城》，2014 年第 3 期

large extent.[413]

人类解决恐怖主义，需要营造一个健康良好的社会环境，这更加需要的是笔杆子，而非枪杆子。文化人是可以把旧文化再加工成新文化，成为正宗的文化。

To resolve the issue of terrorism, humanity needs to create a healthy social environment, which requires far more the pen than the gun. Cultural people can transform old culture into new culture and make it authentic.

东西方文化有异有同。然而，优秀的东西方文化作品都能有净化社会的作用。就像明清小说内容包含实学，其明清两朝代小说的质量也是参差不齐。同是中国章回体长篇小说的《金瓶梅》和《红楼梦》，尽管这两部中国古代小说有诸多相似之处，但论励志程度，清朝《红楼梦》远超明朝《金瓶梅》，对现代社会抵制藏污纳垢起到了积极的作用。

Eastern and Western cultures differ in some aspects while sharing similarities. However, excellent cultural works, whether from the East or from the West, can play a role in purifying society. For example, the novels of the Ming and Qing Dynasties contain practical learning, but their qualities vary. Both *Jin Ping Mei* and *A Dream of Red Mansions* are Chinese long chapter-based novels. Although the two ancient Chinese novels have many similarities, *A Dream of Red Mansions*, written in the Qing Dynasty is far more inspiring than *Jin Ping Mei*, written in the Ming Dynasty, and plays a positive role in resisting corruption and vice in modern society.

《金瓶梅》产生于明代嘉靖、隆庆、万历年间，其所反映的社会历史背景，正是正德以后到万历中期，其中特别是嘉靖年间的历史现实。这一时期，明王朝急剧地走向衰落，社会风气日益浇薄。由于社会矛盾的尖锐激化，统治阶级的腐败无能，尤其武宗的荒淫，世宗的昏愦，神宗的怠荒，遂使朝政陷于不可收拾之局。作为现实主义文学巨著的《金瓶梅》，正如同一面镜子忠实地反映了这一特定的时代，并以其全部的艺术力量，深刻地暴露了这个时代的种种黑暗与丑行。[414]

Jin Ping Mei was written during the reigns of Ming Dynasty's Emperor Jiajing, Emperor Longqing, and Emperor Wanli. The social and historical background it reflects is the historical reality from after Emperor Zhengde's Reign to the middle of Emperor Wanli's Reign, especially during Emperor Jiajing's Reign. During this period, the Ming Dynasty was rapidly declining, and the social atmosphere was becoming increasingly immoral. Due to the sharp intensification of social contradictions and the corruption and incompetence of the ruling class, especially the debauchery of Emperor Wuzong, the obtuseness of Emperor Shizong, and the idleness of Emperor Shenzong, the government affairs fell into chaos. As a great work of realistic literature, *Jin Ping Mei* faithfully mirrors this specific era, and profoundly exposes all kinds of darkness and scandals with its artistic power.[414]

在中国小说史上，关于《金瓶梅》文化身份的认知始终在色情小说与世情小说之间争论不休。究其原因，在于《金瓶梅》一书中有近万字关于色情内容的描写。明代小说创作在《金瓶梅》的影响下，色情类小说逐步发展，形成了一种不容忽视的文学现象。[415]

In the history of Chinese novels, regarding the cultural identity, whether *Jin Ping Mei* is a pornographic novel or a social-situation novel has been debated endlessly. One reason is that there are nearly ten thousand words of pornographic content in the book. Influenced by *Jin Ping Mei*, the

---

414　程良胜撰《< 金瓶梅 > 封建官场文化解读》，来源《武汉大学》，2010 年
415　周娜撰《社会问题视角下的 < 金瓶梅 > 研究》，来源《延边大学》，2019 年

creation of pornographic novels in the Ming Dynasty gradually developed, forming a literary phenomenon that cannot be ignored.[415]

以《红楼梦》比较《金瓶梅》，是两部名著间历史与美学联系的探讨与厘清。《金瓶梅》固不必攀附《红楼梦》而自有其价值与地位，但对当下《金瓶梅》文学价值的认可及其社会地位的提高，有学术以外的现实意义。"反模仿"本质上也是一种模仿。《红楼梦》对《金瓶梅》的"反模仿"，使其形象体系包括立意、结构、人物等"大处"和总体，"乃《金瓶梅》之倒影"：《红楼梦》"谈情"，是青春版的《金瓶梅》；《金瓶梅》"戒淫"，是成人版的《红楼梦》；《红楼梦》"以情悟道"，贾宝玉是迷途知返的西门庆；《金瓶梅》"以淫说法"，西门庆是不知改悔的贾宝玉。其他林黛玉与潘金莲、薛宝钗与吴月娘、袭人与春梅等，皆具此等"倒影"关系。这种"反模仿"而成"倒影"关系的过程与机制，有似于生物工程上的"转基因技术"，而《红楼梦》实可视为《金瓶梅》的"转基因产品"。在这个意义上，《红楼梦》"深得《金瓶》壸奥"，"《金瓶梅》是《红楼梦》的祖宗"。[416]

A comparison between *A Dream of Red Mansions* and *Jin Ping Mei* is an exploration and clarification of the historical and aesthetic connections between the two famous works. *Jin Ping Mei* has its own value and status, so there is no need to associate it with *A Dream of Red Mansions*. However, the recognition of its literary value and the improvement of its social status embody practical significance beyond academics. "Anti-imitation" is essentially a form of imitation. The "anti-imitation" of *A Dream of Red Mansions* to *Jin Ping Mei* makes the image system of *A Dream of Red Mansions*, including its main idea,

---

416　杜贵晨撰《<红楼梦>是<金瓶梅>之"反模仿"和"倒影"论》，来源《求是学刊》，2014 年第 4 期

structure, and characters, generally "a reflection of that in *Jin Ping Mei*": Reading *A Dream of Red Mansions*, one can perceive the theme of "love and romance" and realize that *A Dream of Red Mansions* is a youth version of *Jin Ping Mei*; reading *Jin Ping Mei*, one can perceive the theme of "warning against lust" and realize that *Jin Ping Mei* is an adult version of *A Dream of Red Mansions*; reading *A Dream of Red Mansions,* one can "gain enlightenment from emotions" and realize that Jia Baoyu is Xi Menqing who returns to the right path after going astray; reading *Jin Ping Mei*, one can "learn the doctrine through lascivious content" and realize that Xi Menqing is Jia Baoyu who refuses to repent. Other characters such as Lin Daiyu and Pan Jinlian, Xue Baochai and Wu Yueniang, and Xi Ren and Pang Chunmei also embody such "reflection" relationships. The process and mechanism of forming such a "reflection" relationship through "anti-imitation" are similar to the "genetic engineering technology" in biotechnology, and *A Dream of Red Mansions* can be regarded as a "genetically modified product" of *Jin Ping Mei*. In this sense, *A Dream of Red Mansions* "has grasped the essence of *Jin Ping Mei*," while "*Jin Ping Mei* is the ancestor of *A Dream of Red Mansions*."[416]

明清两朝代合起来统治中国仅七百多年，明清小说就有上千部以上。优秀的明清小说在中国现代社会是一种文化产品，在现代中国仍然有足够的影响力。以至于，明清小说还能在资本主义的世界里树立起一面属于自己的旗帜，对社会上一些不良现象起到有条件性的冲击。

The Ming and Qing Dynasties altogether ruled China for only seven hundred years, yet there were more than a thousand novels from these two dynasties. Excellent novels from the Ming and Qing Dynasties are cultural products in modern Chinese society and still have considerable influence in modern China. Therefore, they can stand out even in the capitalist world and conditionally influence some unhealthy phenomena in society.

写书、出书、卖书、买书都需要一个安定的社会环境。如果，人民对写作不感兴趣，就对游行示威感兴趣，就需要提防这种人类群体容易头脑发昏，做一时冲动的事情。就像日本冲绳民众经常聚众发声抗议美军暴行，却失去了大量用于写作救国的时间。

Writing, publishing, selling, and buying books all require a stable social environment. If people are not interested in writing, they may be interested in demonstrations. So, there is a need to guard against them losing their rationality and doing some impulsive things. For example, the people of Okinawa, Japan often gathered to voice their protests against the atrocities of the US military, but they lost a great deal of time that could have been used for writing to save their country.

冲绳是日本的一个由群岛组成的县，位于日本九州之南、中国台湾东北的太平洋海面上，是美国在亚洲最大的军事基地[417]。

Okinawa is a prefecture in Japan composed of archipelagos, located on the Pacific Ocean to the south of Kyushu, Japan, and to the northeast of Taiwan, China. It is the largest US military base in Asia.[417]

1945 年 3—6 月，冲绳岛战役爆发，这是美军在太平洋战场上进行的最激烈的战斗。在冲绳岛战役中，美军虽然损失惨重，但是最终还是以胜利结束。在这之后，美国开始了对冲绳长达 27 年的战略托管统治。美国为了维护其在冲绳、日本乃至东亚的利益，在托管统治时期在政治、军事、经济、文教等方面实行了一系列的措施。与此同时，美军的统治给当地带来了积极和消极的影响，冲绳

417　亢武超撰《美军会撤出冲绳基地吗?》，来源《世界知识》，1998 年第 23 期

人民在这 27 年中也一直处于抵制和反抗美军的行动中 [418]。

From March to June 1945, the Battle of Okinawa broke out, which was the fiercest battle the US military fought in the Pacific theater. Although the US military suffered heavy losses, it ultimately ended in victory. After that, the United States began a 27-year strategic trusteeship over Okinawa. In order to safeguard its interests in Okinawa, Japan, and even East Asia, the United States implemented a series of political, military, economic, cultural and educational measures during the trusteeship period. At the same time, the rule of the US military had both positive and negative impacts on the local area, and the people of Okinawa had been resisting and opposing the US military during these 27 years.[418]

2015 年 4 月底，安倍晋三展开其上台以来首次，同时也是继 2006 年 6 月小泉纯一郎之后日本首相时隔 9 年再次对美进行国事访问。美国对此也积极回应，除对安倍此次访美以国宾规格接待并安排了为期 8 天的访问行程外，还安排安倍晋三以日本首相的身份在美国参众两院做主旨演讲。[419]

At the end of April 2015, Abe Shinzo paid his first state visit to the United States since taking office. It was also the first state visit by a Japanese prime minister to the United States in nine years after Koizumi Junichiro's visit in June 2006. The United States responded positively. In addition to receiving Abe Shinzo with state guest protocol and arranging an eight-day visiting schedule, it also arranged for him as the Japanese prime minister to deliver a keynote speech in both houses of the US Congress.[419]

---

418 尹玲撰《美国占领下的冲绳（1945—1972）》，来源《白城师范学院学报》，2011 年第 4 期

419 朱博文撰《安倍内阁对美外交的两面政策》，来源《南方论刊》，2015 年 9 期

2017 年 2 月，日本共产党报刊《赤旗报》的网站 15 日刊文说，来自防卫省的资料显示，1952 年旧《日美安保协定》签署至今，驻日美军犯罪案件超过 21 万起，因此致死人数过千，其中冲绳是驻日美军犯罪重灾区。《冲绳时报》报道说，美军基地周边治安案件频发，驻日美军已经成为冲绳的沉重负担，而日本政府基于日美同盟所谓的"大局"，不响应民意将美军基地迁出冲绳，导致民怨沸腾[420]。

A report released on the website of the Japanese Communist Party newspaper *Akahata* on February 15, 2017 showed that according to the Ministry of Defense, since the signing of the old *US-Japan Security Treaty* in 1952, the US troops stationed in Japan had committed more than 210,000 criminal cases, resulting in the death of more than a thousand people. Among them, Okinawa was the hardest-hit area. According to *Okinawa Times*, security cases frequently occurred around US military bases, and the US troops stationed in Japan had become a heavy burden for Okinawa. However, based on the so-called "overall situation" of the US-Japan alliance, the Japanese government did not respond to the public opinion to relocate the US military bases out of Okinawa, leading to widespread public resentment.[420]

冲绳抵制美军基地已不是一个新话题了，美军基地对当地居民生活造成的困扰是冲绳地方对其不满的根本原因。日常的军事演习带来的噪声污染和安全威胁都令附近的居民感到不安[421]。

The issue of Okinawa's resistance to US military bases is not a new topic. The fundamental reason for the dissatisfaction of the Okinawa

---

420 《日媒：驻日美军犯案超过 21 万起，共夺走上千人命》，腾讯新闻（腾讯网），www.qq.com，2017 年 2 月 16 日

421 《多次诉求无果，冲绳民意拗不过美日同盟》，网易军事（网易网），www.163.com，2019 年 7 月 23 日

people with the US military bases is the troubles they cause to the lives of local residents. The noise pollution and security threats brought about by daily military exercises make the nearby residents feel uneasy.[421]

截至 2019 年，冲绳地方近年来多次诉求无果，当地民众的抗议效果微乎其微。《现代日刊》杂志称，安倍政府不顾曾经做出的"充分考虑冲绳民众感受"的承诺，公然向冲绳县县民施压。在对待冲绳军事基地问题上，日本中央政府选择牺牲冲绳地方民意，以满足美国同盟的军事需求[422]。

By 2019, the several local appeals in Okinawa had ended in failure in recent years, and the effect of the local people's protests was insignificant. According to the magazine *Gendai Nikkan*, the Abe government broke its promise of "fully considering the feelings of the Okinawa people", and blatantly pressured them. In dealing with the issue of military bases in Okinawa, the Japanese central government chose to sacrifice the public opinion of the local people to meet the military needs of the US alliance.[422]

政府有贪污腐败，使恐怖主义更加棘手。然而，政府为人民处理事情，要以服务人民为宗旨，人民才会对政府有起码的信任。

When there is corruption in the government, it makes terrorism a more difficult problem to tackle. However, if the government handles affairs for the people with the purpose of serving the people, the people will have basic trust in the government.

对付恐怖主义，政府要多为人民考虑，人民则是做到依法交租纳税。比如，用各种人质要挟各国政府是恐怖分子常用的伎俩，当国家遇到这种情况时，就是考验政府对待人民真实态度的时候。

In dealing with terrorism, the government should consider more

---

422　同上

for the people, and the people should pay rent and taxes according to the law. For example, using hostages to blackmail governments of different countries is a common trick used by terrorists. When a country encounters such a situation, it is a test of the government's true attitude towards the people.

2015 年 9 月 20 日，中国大陆媒体中国新闻网在文章《揭秘 IS 绑架黑色生意链：边防人员受贿为其放行》中有两段这样的文字："是否使用赎金解救人质引发很多争议，有分析认为，支付赎金正在引发连锁反应，催生了更多的人质事件。""有日本媒体指出，伊斯兰国去年 3～6 月释放 4 名法国人和 3 名西班牙人等。尽管各国未承认支付赎金，但似乎通过中介私下交涉。有美国报纸报道，去年获释的 15 名外国人平均赎金为 200 万欧元。今年初被解救的两名女性意大利医护人员，也被疑支付了 1200 万欧元巨额赎金。"

On September 20, 2015, the article *Revealing the Black Business Chain of IS Kidnapping: Border Guards Take Bribes to Let Them Pass* released by China News Service, a mainland Chinese media outlet, contained two paragraphs: "Whether to use ransom to rescue hostages has aroused much controversy. According to some analyses, ransom payment is triggering a chain reaction and giving rise to more hostage incidents." "According to a Japanese media outlet, the Islamic State released four French people and three Spanish people from March to June last year. Although each country did not admit to paying ransom, it seems that relevant parties had private negotiations through intermediaries. According to a US newspaper, the average ransom for the 15 foreigners who were released last year was 2 million euros. As to the two Italian female medical workers who were rescued early this year, it is suspected that a huge ransom of 12 million euros had been paid."

在 21 世纪，"税收取之于民，用之于民"。无论国家是大是小，

是强是弱，只要政府收税，人民交税，政府反恐就要顾虑到人民的
接受程度。

In the 21st century, "taxes are collected from the people and used for the people." No matter the size or strength of a country, as long as the government collects taxes and the people pay taxes, the government must take into account the people's acceptance level when combating terrorism.

在将来，无论国家是否有退钱机制，都离不开一个宗旨：只要
国家收入来源于人民，那么，人民允许公务员贪污腐败，公务员就
能贪污腐败。反之，人民不允许公务员贪污腐败，公务员就不能贪
污腐败。

In the future, regardless of whether a country has a refund mechanism, it cannot deviate from one principle: On the precondition that the country's revenue comes from the people, if the people allow civil servants to be corrupt, then civil servants can be corrupt. Conversely, if the people do not allow civil servants to be corrupt, then civil servants cannot be corrupt.

有些社会问题难以启齿比较敏感，需要权衡利弊，考虑到国家
贪污腐败和恐怖主义能成因果循环。据此，政府为人民妥协恐怖分
子不一定是错的，政府为反恐不屈服恐怖分子可能也是对的。

Some social issues are embarrassing and sensitive. It is necessary to balance the advantages and disadvantages. The situation where corruption in the country and terrorism form a causal cycle has to be taken into account. Therefore, it may not be wrong for the government to make concessions to terrorists for the sake of the people, and it may also be right for the government not to yield to terrorists in the fight against terrorism.

讨论"恐怖分子劫持人质，政府要不要满足恐怖分子的要求"这个论题，不能太理想化，有诸多条件限制政府解救人质，打击恐怖主义。毕竟，国家各有一秋，再强大的政府也有自身难保的时候，反恐随心所欲是一纸空谈。

When discussing "whether the government should meet the demands of terrorists when they hijack hostages", we cannot be too idealistic. There are many factors restricting the government from rescuing hostages and combating terrorism. After all, every country has its own characteristics, and even the most powerful government may sometimes find itself in a difficult situation. Acting arbitrarily in the fight against terrorism is merely empty talk.

一个人进行生活和生存都太累，以至于连累无辜容易，保全他人困难。比起无政府主义，政府主义优秀之处就在于人民知道该找谁算账，以免"错斩崔宁"，其他方面都不能确定。

Life and survival are exhausting for the people. As a result, it is easier to implicate the innocent than to protect others. As to the superiority of government governance over anarchism, only one thing is certain, that is, the people know whom they should hold accountable, less false and unjust cases occur. Other aspects are uncertain.

社会总有人愿意害人又害己，世人争论"公民生命与反恐，政府哪一方更要顾及"的命题，会逐渐朝明确"政府和恐怖分子的较量，政府必须承担人质危机事件中好和坏的全部影响"方向靠拢，以肃清政府对待恐怖主义有美化自己的元素。

In society, there are always some people who harm both others and themselves. When people debate "which side the government should give more consideration to, the lives of citizens or counter-terrorism", they should come to realize that "in the contest between the government and terrorists, the government must bear all the positive and negative consequences in hostage crisis incidents", so as to eliminate the elements that the government may use to beautify itself when it deals with terrorism.

只要恐怖分子对付人民不会停止，人民反恐就不会停止，政府反恐也不会停止。反恐大业开始于人民，不会终止于人民。在价值观混乱的年代，人民和恐怖主义之间未必明确对立，却必定对立明确。政府有公仆精神，人民和恐怖主义之间才有产生鸿沟的本质。

As long as terrorists do not stop their attacks on the people, the people's fight against terrorism will not stop, and the government's counter-terrorism efforts will not stop either. The great cause of counter-terrorism starts with the people, but it will not end with the people. In an era of confused values, the people and terrorism are not necessarily explicitly contradictory, but the opposition definitely exists. Only when the government has the spirit of serving the people can there be a real gulf between the people and terrorism.

第六章　解决有组织犯罪能打击恐怖主义

Chapter 6: Combating Terrorism by Solving Organized Crimes

恐怖组织、黑社会、邪教、土匪、雇佣兵、毒贩，这六种有组织犯罪都可以制造恐怖主义，这是这些犯罪组织的共同点。

Terrorist organizations, underworld gangs, cults, bandit gangs, mercenary groups, and drug traffickers are six types of organized crimes that can give rise to terrorism. This is a common feature of these criminal organizations.

在当今学术界，学者对恐怖组织、黑社会、邪教、土匪、雇佣兵、毒贩、有组织犯罪，这七个学术概念都没有得出一致的结论，只有一些零星散乱的词汇获得认同，例如，非法、犯罪、破坏、结构、组织、双面性等。

In today's academic community, scholars have not reached a consensus on the connotations of terrorist organizations, underworld gangs, cults, bandit gangs, mercenary groups, drug traffickers, and organized crimes from an academic perspective. Only some scattered words have been recognized, such as illegal, criminal, destructive, structural, organizational, and dual-natured.

有组织犯罪和恐怖主义都是犯罪，有组织犯罪多受经济驱使，恐怖主义多怀政治野心。这二者的犯罪目的、手段、行为、性质等介于互有互无之间。比如，搞过恐怖袭击的爱尔兰共和军就有满足被界定为有组织犯罪和恐怖组织的双重条件。

Both organized crime and terrorism are crimes. Organized crime is mostly driven by economic interests, while terrorism is often motivated by political ambitions. The criminal purposes, means, behaviors, and natures of these two types of crime are somewhat intertwined and overlapping. For example, the Irish Republican Army, which once carried out terrorist attacks, met the dual criteria of being defined as an organized criminal group and a terrorist organization.

20 世纪，爱尔兰共和军被认为是国际恐怖主义的重要力量，他们以北爱尔兰独立为名，发动了一系列恐怖袭击事件 [423]。

In the 20th century, the Irish Republican Army was regarded as an important force in international terrorism. In the name of fighting for the independence of Northern Ireland, they launched a series of terrorist attacks. [423]

真爱尔兰共和军成立于 1997 年，成员多是从爱尔兰共和军分裂出来的恐怖分子，反对和英国政府达成任何形式的停火协议。1998 年，该组织在北爱尔兰小镇奥马制造了一次汽车炸弹袭击，炸死 29 人。这是北爱历史上最恶性的恐怖炸弹案。此外，该组织还在英国制造了数起爆炸案，其中包括 2001 年 BBC 总部爆炸案 [424]。

The Real Irish Republican Army was established in 1997, and most of its members were terrorists who split from the Irish Republican Army. They opposed reaching any ceasefire agreement with the British government. In 1998, the organization carried out a car bomb attack in Omagh, a small town in Northern Ireland, causing 29 deaths. This was the most vicious terrorist bombing incident in the history of Northern Ireland. In addition, the organization carried out several bombings in the UK, including the bombing of the BBC headquarters in 2001. [424]

爱尔兰共和军则通过盗窃艺术品及古董交易为其恐怖活动筹

---

423 《没有退路的绝食：撒切尔对爱尔兰共和军不妥协》，腾讯新闻（腾讯网）www. qq.com，2012 年 7 月 19 日

424 《真爱尔兰共和军首领被判无期徒刑》，新浪军事（新浪网）www.china.com.cn，2003 年 8 月 6 日

资，还曾以归还艺术品为条件要求其他国家释放其被关押的成员。1986 年，荷兰画家维米尔的名画《读信的女子》落入爱尔兰大盗 Martin Cahill 之手。4 年后，当它被发现时，是在伊斯坦布尔的一间旅馆房间内，匪徒正用它交换海洛因。与《读信的女子》同时遭窃的维米尔作品《写信的太太与女佣》，则被匪徒当作抵押，向一位荷兰钻石商贷款 100 万美元 [425]。

The Irish Republican Army financed its terrorist activities through the theft of artworks and antique trading. It once required other countries to release the imprisoned members in exchange for the return of artworks. In 1986, the famous painting *Woman Reading a Letter* by the Dutch painter Vermeer fell into the hands of Martin Cahill, a notorious Irish thief. Four years later, it was found in a hotel room in Istanbul, and at that time, the bandits were using it to exchange for heroin. *Lady Writing a Letter and Her Maid*, which was another work of Vermeer's and was stolen at the same time as "*Woman Reading a Letter*", was used by the bandits as collateral to borrow $1 million from a Dutch diamond merchant.[425]

2005 年以前，爱尔兰共和军卷入了洗钱、抢劫银行、走私香烟和造假等各种犯罪事件，引起各方强烈抨击。但是在 2005 年 7 月 28 日发表的声明仅仅表示将停止"其他有关活动"，并没有明确承诺中止这些犯罪活动，许多民众都对此十分不满。此外，虽然解除了武装，但是爱尔兰共和军仍然存在，并没有被彻底解散，所以许多人担心爱尔兰共和军随时会拿起武器，东山再起 [426]。

Before 2005, the Irish Republican Army aroused strong

---

425 《专访"艺术犯罪学专家"诺亚—查尼》，新浪新闻（新浪网）www.sina.com.cn，2007 年 10 月 23 日

426 《爱尔兰共和军弃武从政》，搜狐新闻（搜狐网）www.sohu.com，2005 年 7 月 29 日

condemnation from all parties, because it was involved in various criminal incidents such as money laundering, bank robbery, cigarette smuggling, and counterfeiting. However, in the statement issued on July 28, 2005, it only said that it would stop "other related activities", but did not clearly commit to ceasing criminal activities. This made many people very dissatisfied. In addition, although disarmed, the Irish Republican Army still exists and has not been completely disbanded. Therefore, many people are worried that it may pick up weapons and make a comeback at any time.[426]

恐怖组织、黑社会、邪教、土匪、雇佣兵、毒贩都属有组织犯罪，谈古论今，无论有组织犯罪数量是增是减，这六种有组织犯罪都是基本模式。

Terrorist organizations, underworld gangs, cults, bandit gangs, mercenary groups, and drug traffickers are organized crimes. Since ancient times, regardless of whether the number of organized crimes increases or decreases, these six types have remained the basic forms.

这六种有组织犯罪都各可用一个字来概括其邪恶本质。恐怖组织代表"恐"字；黑社会代表"黑"字；邪教代表"邪"字；土匪代表"暴"字；雇佣兵代表"恶"字；毒贩代表"毒"字。

Each of these six types can be described by a single word to reflect its evil nature. Terrorist organizations can be described as "terror"; underworld gangs can be described as "dark"; cults can be described as "heretical"; bandit gangs can be described as "violent"; mercenary groups can be described as "evil"; and drug traffickers can be described as "ruthless".

这六种有组织犯罪是所有团伙犯罪的基调。和恐怖主义崛起雷同，警察、法院、监狱等政府部门、单位、机构、责任人腐败与无能，是有组织犯罪能够"一呼百应"的风向标。比如，在20—21

世纪，有墨西哥公务员妥协贩毒武装就是例子。

These six types have set the tone for all gang crimes. Similar to the rise of terrorism, the corruption and incompetence of government departments, units, institutions, and responsible persons such as the police, courts, and prisons are wind vanes that can "echo" organized crimes. For example, in the 20th and 21st centuries, some Mexican civil servants compromised with armed drug trafficking groups.

2019 年 10 月 17 日，墨西哥安全部队在库利亚坎市逮捕了大毒枭古兹曼的儿子奥维迪奥·古兹曼，该市随后爆发激烈枪战。据外媒最新消息，墨西哥安全部部长称奥维迪奥已被释放[427]。

On October 17, 2019, the Mexican security forces arrested Ovidio Guzmán, the son of the major drug lord Joaquín Guzmán Loera, in Culiacán. Then, intense gun battles broke out in the city. According to the latest news from foreign media, the Mexican security minister said that Ovidio had been released.[427]

据路透社 17 日报道，墨西哥安全部部长阿方索·杜拉佐（Alfonso Durazo）表示，墨西哥安全部队在 17 日短暂逮捕了奥维迪奥后已经将其释放。杜拉佐称，此举是为了保护生命[428]。

According to a Reuters report on October 17, Mexican Security Minister Alfonso Durazo said that the Mexican security forces had released Ovidio after briefly arresting him on October 17. Durazo said that this move was for the sake of protecting the lives of the people.[428]

在奥维迪奥被拘捕的消息曝出后，库利亚坎市爆发了长达数小时的激烈枪战。一些忠于贩毒头目的集团成员全副武装，向墨西哥安全部队开火。社交媒体上发布的一段视频显示，持枪的贩毒团体

427　《抓捕引发激烈枪战后 墨西哥释放大毒枭古兹曼之子》，凤凰资讯（凤凰网）www.ifeng.com，2019 年 10 月 18 日

428　同上

成员乘坐至少一辆装有机枪的卡车在城市中乱逛，对车辆和加油站纵火，堵住街道。一些当地平民躲藏在一家超市的过道中，其他人则在树叶茂密的郊区街道上藏了起来[429]。

After the news of Ovidio's arrest was released, intense gun battles lasted for several hours in Culiacán. Some group members loyal to the drug lord were fully armed and opened fire on the Mexican security forces. According to a video released on social media, members of the armed drug trafficking group were riding in at least one truck equipped with a machine gun and wandering around the city, setting fire to vehicles and gas stations and blocking the streets. Some local civilians hid themselves in the aisles of a supermarket, while others hid themselves on the leafy suburban streets.[429]

有证据表明，法学解决有组织犯罪的难度很高。从古代到现代，人类用法学无法彻底解决有组织犯罪，只能将其压制在一定的范围之内。

Evidence suggests that it is very difficult to solve organized crimes through jurisprudence. Since ancient times, people have been unable to completely solve organized crimes through jurisprudence, only suppressing them within a certain range.

如果政府用国家法律打击有组织犯罪，对付恐怖组织不是政府反恐就可以解决；对付黑社会不是政府"扫黑"就可以解决；对付邪教不是政府抵制邪教就可以解决；对付土匪不是政府剿匪就可以解决；对付雇佣兵不是政府不使用雇佣兵就可以解决；对付毒贩不是政府禁毒就可以解决。就像巴西旧都里约热内卢充斥暴力就是一个鲜活的例子。

If the government uses national laws to crack down on organized

---

429　同上

crimes, its anti-terrorism efforts are insufficient to deal with terrorist organizations; its efforts of "combating gang crimes" are insufficient to deal with underworld gangs; its efforts against cults are insufficient to deal with cults; its measures of suppressing banditry are insufficient to deal with bandit gangs; its attitude of not employing mercenary groups is insufficient to deal with mercenary groups; and its drug-control measures are insufficient to deal with drug traffickers. The prevalence of violence in Rio de Janeiro, the former capital of Brazil, is a vivid example.

巴西里约热内卢是 2014 年世界杯足球赛和 2016 年夏季奥运会举办地，但那里的高犯罪率一直被人诟病。为改善治安状况，政府先派特警突袭清剿贫民窟贩毒分子，再派维护治安力量进驻社区加强管理[430]。

Rio de Janeiro, Brazil, was the host city of the 2014 FIFA World Cup and the 2016 Summer Olympics, but its high crime rate was criticized by people. To improve the public security, the government first dispatched special police to raid and clear out the drug dealers in the slums, and then dispatched security forces to enter the communities and strengthen management.[430]

这一模式自一开始就引起诸多争议。有人说，它有效打击了黑帮势力，可以作为"楷模"在世界其他地区推广；也有人说，赶走黑帮的警察可能比黑帮更黑[431]。

The mode caused much controversy from the very beginning. Some people said that it could effectively crack down on the forces of the underworld and serve as a "model" to be promoted in other areas of the world; others said that the police who drove away the underworld gangs

---

430　《巴西军警占领最大贫民窟 市民怕警察超毒贩》，搜狐新闻（搜狐网）www.sohu.com，2011 年 11 月 15 日

431　同上

might be even more "sinister" than the gangs themselves.[431]

由于长期成为"城市孤岛"，在一定程度上，贫民窟里的黑帮扮演着"政府"的角色，他们控制着水、电、天然气等基础服务，还宣称能为居民们提供"保护"。警察和军警每次在贫民窟展开治理行动，则更像是在"他国土地"上与敌人作战[432]。

The slums having evolved into long-standing "isolated urban islands", the underworld gangs there played the role of "government" to a certain extent. They controlled basic services such as water supply, electricity, and natural gas, and even claimed to provide "protection" for the residents. Every time the police and military police carried out governance operations in the slums, it was like fighting against the enemy on "foreign soil."[432]

2014年，为了保证举办一届安全、成功的世界杯，巴西政府决定在世界杯期间动用军队维护治安。比如，里约市，届时就将进驻2500名荷枪实弹的士兵，他们将在贫民窟不断巡逻，以降低该市的犯罪率。与此同时，巴西还将向边境地区增兵3万人，动用陆海空三军，打击贩毒、走私、偷渡、贩卖军火等犯罪活动，这样可以有效改善世界杯期间巴西的治安环境[433]。

In 2014, in order to host a safe and successful World Cup, the Brazilian government was determined to deploy the military to maintain public security. For example, in Rio de Janeiro, 2,500 armed soldiers would be stationed at that time, and they would continuously patrol in the slums to reduce the crime rate in the city. At the same time, Brazil would add 30,000 soldiers to the border areas, and employ the army,

---

432 《巴西贫民窟遭黑帮占领成边缘角落 政府柔化处理》，搜狐新闻（搜狐网）www.sohu.com，2010年11月21日

433 《巴西警方提示：不要炫富！遭抢劫绝不能反抗》，腾讯体育（腾讯网）www.qq.com，2014年5月12日

navy, and air force to crack down on criminal activities such as drug trafficking, smuggling, human trafficking, and arms trafficking. These measures could effectively improve the public security environment during the World Cup.[433]

马雷贫民窟位于里约机场和市中心之间，包含16个社区、14万居民，最近几年，毒贩、民兵和军警这3大势力之间的暴力活动让这里的住户苦不堪言[434]。

Located between the Rio Airport and the urban center, the Maré slum consists of 16 communities and 140,000 residents. In recent years, the violent activities among the three major forces, namely, the drug dealers, the militias, and the military police, overwhelmed the residents with suffering.[434]

社会良莠不齐，公有制和私有制就算联手也不是假公济私的对手。即使是在国破家亡的年代，政府上下都有人公私不分，并且社会上有很多人见钱眼开，有组织犯罪有卷土重来的能力，某些方面可与政府旗鼓相当。

Society is a mixed bag. Even if public ownership and private ownership join hands, they are not necessarily able to defeat those who abuse public power for private gain. Even in the era of national subjugation and family ruin, some people in the government confuse public and private interests, and many people in society are greedy for money. Organized crimes have the ability to make a comeback and can rival the government in some aspects.

这些有组织犯罪连国家体制都能破坏，只要政府按照"制度在上，法律在下"的模式，那么，法治对付有组织犯罪就苍白无力。

---

434 《被毒贩还是被军警打死？巴西贫民窟住户苦不堪言》，新浪军事（新浪网）www.sina.com.cn，2015年4月7日

所以，"以吏为师，以法为教"解决有组织犯罪只能治标不治本。

The organized crimes can even damage the national system. As long as the government follows the mode of "institutions above, laws below," the rule of law will be powerless in dealing with organized crimes. Therefore, the approach of "taking officials as the models for learning and the law as the teaching content" can only address the symptoms rather than the root causes of organized crimes.

20 世纪 80 年代以前，雇佣兵都是以个人或小团体为单位，受雇于某国或某个利益集团，策动政变、绑架暗杀、劫掠财物，一度被称为"战争动物"。2003 年，联合国大会曾通过一项法案，禁止外籍雇佣兵这个职业，雇佣兵活动一度受到限制。此后，雇佣兵开始谋求以合法的集团公司模式即私营军事企业或保安公司出现，按照现代商业模式建立公司管理体制，并作为一种新型的"战争服务业"对外承揽业务，不断地向世界各地的热点地区"批发"雇佣兵 435。

Before the 1980s, mercenary groups, known as "war animals", were hired on the basis of individuals or small groups by a certain country or interest group to instigate coups, carry out kidnappings and assassinations, and plunder property. In 2003, the United Nations General Assembly adopted a bill to ban the profession of foreign mercenaries. As a result, mercenary activities were once restricted. After that, mercenary groups sought to take the form of legitimate corporate entities. In other words, they became private military companies or security companies. They have established company management systems according to the modern business mode and, as a new type of "war service industry",

---

435 《揭秘雇佣兵：年薪可达 20 万美元 远超美军工资》，腾讯新闻（腾讯网）www.qq.com，2015 年 5 月 29 日

undertake foreign businesses and continuously "wholesale" mercenaries to trouble spots around the world.[435]

政府无法压制住有组织犯罪，势必引起有组织犯罪反弹，犯罪便会层出不穷。

If the government is unable to curb organized crimes, it will lead to a resurgence of organized crimes, making crimes emerge endlessly.

敌不可纵，一旦江湖道义崩塌，有组织犯罪不单要与政府有对抗。在利益召唤下，为了金钱、地盘、武器、人员、情报等，"黑吃黑"和"黑黑勾结"取代了"井水不犯河水"与"老死不相往来"。这六种有组织犯罪是既能对抗，也能合作。

The enemy should not be indulged. Once the moral principles cf the underworld collapse, organized crimes will not only confront the government. Driven by interests, in contention for money, territory, weapons, personnel and intelligence resources, they will replace the situations of "never encroaching on each other" and "never having any contact with each other" with "preying on each other" and "colluding with each other". These six types of organized crimes can not only confront but also cooperate with each other.

比如，2015 年，据报道，古斯曼的开战宣言直接指向"伊斯兰国"领袖阿布·贝克尔·巴格达迪。宣言写道："你们（IS）不是战士，是懦夫。如果你们选择继续影响我的生意，我将给你们带来真正的恐怖……这个世界并不由你们决定，如果继续干涉锡那罗亚集团的事务，我们将奉陪到底！"[436] 索马里海盗每年都要上缴 20% 的"发展税"给恐怖组织索马里青年党以寻求联合[437]。报道称，意六

---

436 《墨西哥头号大毒枭向 IS 宣战　将给你们带来真正的恐怖》，国际在线新闻（国际在线）www.cri.cn，2015 年 12 月 11 日

437 《索马里"青年党"海盗都要让三分》，网易新闻（网易网）www.163.com，2015 年 7 月 28 日

利黑手党不仅同爱琴海地区的犯罪团伙有勾结，同北非的圣战者贩毒集团之间也有联系，共享通过地中海地区的毒品和人口交易。意大利警方称，一些男性难民随后会被利用来运送毒品，女性就沦为妓女 [438]。

For example, it was reported that in 2015, Joaquín Guzmán Loera directly declared war against Abu Bakr al-Baghdadi, the leader of the "Islamic State". The declaration said, "You (IS) are not warriors, but cowards. If you continue to affect my business, I will bring you real terror... This world is not decided by you. If you continue to interfere in the affairs of the Cártel de Sinaloa, we will accompany you to the end!"[436] The Somali pirates would pay 20% of their income as "development tax" to the terrorist organization Al-Shabaab every year in order to seek cooperation.[437] It was reported that the Italian mafia not only colluded with criminal gangs in the Aegean region, but also had connections with the jihadist drug trafficking groups in North Africa. They were jointly involved in the drug and human trafficking activities across the Mediterranean region. According to the Italian police, some male refugees would subsequently be employed to transport drugs, and women would be forced into prostitution.[438]

有组织犯罪再狡猾也总会有"露出马脚"的时候，政府对付有组织犯罪应该"以长胜短"，不能以"以强胜弱"。其意思是政府对付有组织犯罪不能以为自己实力胜过有组织犯罪，就幻想以泰山压顶之势清风扫落叶般解决有组织犯罪。

However cunning organized crimes are, they will sometimes "give themselves away". The government should "overcome the disadvantages

---

438 《黑手党靠难民潮赚大钱：仅意大利就有8亿欧元大生意》，网易新闻（网易网）www.163.com，2016年2月2日

with its advantages" when dealing with organized crimes, instead of "defeating the weakness with its strength". That is to say, the government should not, under the illusion that it has more strengths than organized crimes, attempt to eliminate them in a sweeping manner.

政府对付有组织犯罪有一个明面账：政府数量少，有组织犯罪数量多；政府在明，有组织犯罪在暗；政府力量分散，有组织犯罪力量集中。这种敌我态势是常态，对政府不利，对有组织犯罪有利。

When dealing with organized crimes, the government should know the following clearly: The number of governments is small while the number of organized crimes is large; the government is in the open while organized crimes are in the dark; the strength of a government is scattered while the strength of organized crimes is concentrated. This is a normal situation, which is disadvantageous to the government and advantageous to organized crimes.

打一个比方，以黑制黑是黑社会"为恶"和"为善"的历史手段之一。与此同时，黑社会开公司步入企业化也是"黑道洗白"的潮流趋势。可以说，以黑制黑是黑道的阳刚手段，黑社会做生意是黑道的阴柔手段，这两种暴力和暴利的阴阳手段，会造成民间分裂和对立的局面。

For example, fighting fire with fire is a historical means for underworld gangs to "be evil" and "be good". At the same time, it has become a tendency that underworld gangs whitewash themselves by establishing companies and corporatizing themselves. It can be said that fighting fire with fire is a tough method employed by underworld gangs while doing business is a soft method. The two methods, characterized by violence and seeking huge profits respectively, will lead to division and opposition within the society.

2015 年 1 月，外媒称，日本最大黑帮"山口组"25 日在神户总部举行了成立 100 周年纪念仪式。[439]

It was reported by foreign media that on January 25, 2015, the Yamaguchi-gumi, the largest criminal organization in Japan, held a ceremony to celebrate the 100th anniversary of its founding at the Kobe headquarters.[439]

山口组的主要收入来源是走私毒品、卖淫等相关非法事业。但除了非法事业外，该组织还涉足演艺界、房地产投资等多个领域。[440]

The incomes of the Yamaguchi-gumi were mainly from illegal businesses such as drug smuggling and prostitution. However, apart from illegal businesses, the organization was also involved in many fields such as the entertainment industry and real estate investment.[440]

山口组进入 21 世纪以后采取的生存战略是智能型经济犯罪，而不是一味地动用拳头。其中的典型事例包括 2007 年与金融、IT 领域专家合作购买著名互联网企业，通过操纵股价牟取暴利，被有关当局揭发。[441]

In the 21st century, the Yamaguchi-gumi adopted intelligent economic crime as its survival strategy rather than simply resorting to violence. A typical example is that in 2007, the organization cooperated with financial and IT experts to buy a well-known Internet enterprise and made huge profits by manipulating the stock price. This was later exposed by relevant authorities.[441]

在日本泡沫经济的 1980 年代，山口组就发生了名为"山一抗争"的黑帮血腥事件，其源头正是山口组内争，第三代帮主田冈一雄因无法摆平人事问题，而导致属下的"一和会"人马射杀第四代

---

439 《黑帮也搞企业化 外媒揭日最大黑帮生存百年秘诀》搜狐新闻（搜狐网），www.sohu.com，2015 年 1 月 27 日

440 同上

441 同上

传人。[442]

During Japan's bubble economy era in the 1980s, a bloody gang incident called the "Yamaguchi-Ichiwa Strife" occurred within the Yamaguchi-gumi. The root cause was the internal conflict within the Yamaguchi-gumi. Taoka Ichio, the third-generation leader, failed to resolve personnel issues, resulting in the members of the "Ichiwa-kai" under his command shooting the fourth-generation successor.[442]

这一事件后，黑帮势力展开大搏斗，在 1985 至 1987 年间，因火并而造成 25 人死亡。一般日本老百姓也被卷入其中，包括警察在内，有 70 人负伤。[443]

After the incident, the gang forces launched major battles. Between 1985 and 1987, 25 people were killed due to the firefights. Ordinary Japanese people were also involved. 70 people, including policemen, were injured.[443]

不管是以黑制黑，还是黑社会开公司做生意，都是需要资金在台前幕后支撑局面。可是，历朝历代做生意破产的商家到处都是，本来黑社会做生意就是一种慢性"自废武功"的方式，逐渐使黑社会丧失暴力武装技能，继而剥夺暴利经营能力，再加上黑社会得势还能风光无限，一旦黑社会失势就会遭到同行和同类，以及异类的挤压与迫害。

Whether fighting fire with fire or operating companies, underworld gangs require fund support on and off the stage. However, there are countless bankrupt businesses in all dynasties. In fact, the involvement of underworld gangs in business will lead to chronic "self-disabling". It will gradually make them lose their violent armed skills, and then deprive

---

442 《日本警方公布黑帮山口组分裂为幕 忧引发社会动乱》中国新闻网国际新闻（中国新闻网），www.chinanews.com，2015 年 09 月 08 日

443 同上

them of the ability to gain huge profits. Moreover, when underworld gangs seize the upper hand, they can be very powerful, but once they are at a disadvantage, they will be squeezed and persecuted by their peers, similar organizations, and other groups.

黑社会就算将以黑制黑和黑社会经商运用得再炉火纯青，都改变不了黑社会乃是"跳梁小丑"的事实。究其原因，黑社会怕敢于反抗和有勇气的敌人，黑社会的兴衰成败都与他人的纵容有关系，黑社会历史是一面反映政府和人民关系是否离心离德的社会镜子。

Even if an underworld gang fights fire with fire and engages in business with utmost proficiency, the fact that it is a "clown" cannot be changed. The reason is that underworld gangs fear enemies who dare to resist and have courage. The rise and fall of underworld gangs are related to others' indulgence toward them. The history of underworld gangs is a social mirror that reflects whether the relationship between the government and the people is estranged.

政府要想扭转这种颓势，就必须改变对付有组织犯罪的策略。政府应该增加自己的长处，减少自己的短处。

If the government intends to reverse this unfavorable situation, it must change its strategy for dealing with organized crimes. The government should enhance its advantages and reduce its disadvantages.

步入新世纪以后，社会信息爆炸，人与人相处要学习的技能是永远也学不完的。政府能力能够跟得上社会生产力的需求，有组织犯罪自然倒霉。

The new century is characterized by social information explosion, and there are numerous skills for people to learn when interacting with each other. If the government has the capability of meeting the requirements of social productivity, organized crimes will naturally be in trouble.

"人少好吃饭，人多好干活"，利用制度只享福不患难大有人在。"挂羊头卖狗肉"想当皇帝的人既可能是有组织犯罪，也可能是政府中人。他们有金钱、有地位、有势力、有权力，不惜祸国殃民。

"When there are fewer people, their demand for food can be easily satisfied; when there are more people, work will be more efficient." Many people are only willing to enjoy the benefits of the system but unwilling to share hardships. Those who want to obtain supreme power under some high-sounding pretexts can either be people in organized crimes or government officials. They have money, status, influence, and power, and do not hesitate to harm the country and the people.

《庄子·外篇·胠箧》有云："圣人不死，大盗不止。"一个社会要是有"圣人和大盗"，那么，这个社会就有平时社会和战时社会。这两个社会都有正面和负面的评价，即为"圣人有盗，大盗有圣"。

In *On Letting Alone, Supplementary Volume, Zhuangzi*, it is said, "As long as sages do not vanish, thieves will continue to exist." If a society has both "sages and thieves", it can be divided based on whether it's in peacetime or wartime. Both states have positive and negative evaluations, that is, "Sages have some qualities similar to those of thieves, while thieves have some qualities similar to those of sages."

中外无数事实证明，《庄子》书中"道转换盗，盗转换道"的理论思想散发着先进性、正确性、客观性，成为有组织犯罪屡试不爽能够立足于法治社会的"试金石"，是有组织犯罪必做的功课。

Numerous facts in China and other countries have proven that the philosophical theory that "good and evil can be transformed into each other in some circumstances" in the book *Zhuangzi* has the characteristics of progressiveness, correctness, and objectivity. It has become a "touchstone" for organized crimes to repeatedly succeed and stand firm in a law-based society, as well as a necessary lesson.

有组织犯罪是组织犯罪。钱粮强则力量强，钱粮弱则力量弱，钱粮尽则力量尽。有组织犯罪收买人心和坐大、坐强、坐实自己的力量，是离不开金钱的支持的。

Organized crimes are carried out by criminal organizations. An organization with ample funds will have powerful strength; an organization with insufficient funds will have weak strength; an organization with exhausted funds will lose all its strength. For organized crimes to win over people's hearts and expand, strengthen, and solidify their own strength, the support of money is indispensable.

毒品是犯罪分子的强硬市场，要解决有组织犯罪就需要禁毒。在 20—21 世纪，禁毒的主要力量是国家机器，政府强力打击毒品的标志性见证就是自己国度家园没有泛滥的毒品。

The drug trade is a lucrative business for criminals. To resolve the issue of organized crimes, we must control drugs. In the 20th and 21st centuries, the main force in drug control is the state machinery. The emblematic success of the government's strong crackdown on drugs is the eradication of widespread drug abuse in its own country.

虽然只要毒品不是从天上掉下来的，禁毒就能成功，但实际上毒品却屡禁不止。历史告诉世人，不少人物和组织从自己利益出发，在毒品面前"低下了头颅"，有受制于毒品的"黑历史"。

As long as drugs are not created out of thin air, drug control can become successful. However, in reality, drug abuse persists despite repeated prohibitions. History tells us that many individuals and organizations, driven by their own interests, tend to "bow their heads" in the face of drugs. They have a "dark history" of being controlled by drugs.

合作下的毒品问题使得有些罪恶勾结昭然若揭，这导致政府禁毒的根本目的必须是为了人民能够安定生活，而不是为了保障该政权的稳定。政府涉毒已成铁的事实，难以遮掩。负责任政府既不能推卸责任，也不能五十步笑百步，需要承认肮脏的历史，必须把整天灌输给世人的"为人民服务"，改成"游戏规则"，这是禁毒的"黑白之理"。

The issue of drugs under cooperation has made some evil collusion obvious to all. Therefore, the fundamental purpose of the government's drug control must be to guarantee the peaceful lives of the people, rather than to safeguard the stability of the regime. Government involvement in drugs has become an undeniable fact and can hardly be concealed. A responsible government should neither shirk its responsibility, nor should it only focus on the problems of others while turning a blind eye to its own. It must admit its dirty history, and change the slogan of "serving the people" that it has been instilling in the people all day long into "rules of the game". It is a "fundamental principle" for drug control.

毒品再毒，有时候也毒不过某些人的内心。国家被毒品侵害，政府和贩毒者以及吸毒者都要为毒品涂炭生灵而负上不同程度的责任。

No matter how poisonous drugs are, they are not so evil as some people's hearts. When a country is damaged by drugs, the government, drug dealers, and drug addicts should all bear responsibilities of different degrees for the great hardships caused by drugs.

推崇愚蠢显出智慧，推崇智慧显出本性。简称推愚显智，推智显性。政府再怎么推行愚民政策，到头来人民都会变得有智慧，从而人与人互相看见其本性，这一切都只是时间问题。

Promoting foolishness can give rise to wisdom, and promoting wisdom can bring about the manifestation of one's true nature. In short, this is what we mean by promoting foolishness to reveal wisdom and promoting wisdom to disclose one's true nature. No matter how strenuously the government implements an obscurantist policy, the people will ultimately become wise, and then see each other's true natures. This is just a matter of time.

物质社会只有以逸待劳，没有一劳永逸。一夜暴富和亿万富翁照样都会倾家荡产，沦为社会底层人物，违法产业却照样有人明知故犯去涉足。毒品见证人性有丑恶的一面。如果人类真想斩断毒祸，就要先从人愿意吃苦耐劳，脚踏实地做事情开始，而非总想着去做黄粱美梦。

In a materialistic society, one can never find a once-and-for-all solution. Instead, he should reserve his strength for an appropriate opportunity. Even those who get rich overnight or those who possess billions of dollars may lose everything and sink to the bottom of society. However, there are still people who deliberately engage in illegal industries despite knowing the consequences. Drugs bear witness to the ugly side of human nature. If humans really want to eliminate the disasters brought by drugs, they should be willing to endure hardships and work steadily, rather than dreaming of illusory success.

"毒品账"的罪责在人不在毒品，毒品祸国殃民已然得到历史的见证。然而，国家"有黑无白"和"有白无黑"都是不切实际的。禁毒成功的标志是人民不去碰毒品，而不是毒品沦为人类舍弃的产物。人类更不能沉浸在对毒品进行惊天动地的改造，将它称为一种"仙丹妙药"。

The blame for the "drug problem" lies with people, not with drugs. History has witnessed the harm that drugs bring to the country and the people. However, it is unrealistic for a country to be "completely black" or "completely white". The sign of successful drug control is that the people do not touch drugs, rather than that drugs become something discarded by humans. Moreover, humans should not indulge themselves in the idea of making astonishing transformations of drugs and calling them "elixirs".

政府禁毒成功，恐怖主义不一定销声匿迹，而政府禁毒没有成功，恐怖组织就有非法资金的来源，恐怖主义就早晚能够由此猖獗，全球局势势必"越反越恐"。由此，政府解决毒品问题，是人类反恐必走的道路。同时，政府禁毒成功，能够大力挫伤有组织犯罪的锐气。

If the government succeeds in drug control, terrorism may not necessarily disappear completely. But if the government fails in drug control, terrorist organizations will have a source of illegal funds, and terrorism will sooner or later become rampant. This will inevitably lead to a global situation that can be described as "the higher the intensity of counter-terrorism is, the more rampant terrorism becomes". Therefore, the government's solution to the drug problem is a necessary path for humanity's fight against terrorism. At the same time, the government's success in drug control can greatly dampen the momentum of organized crimes.

政府要想消除有组织犯罪，需要政府同时拥有四条基本主线。另外，有一条次要辅线是可有可无的。第一，政府要解决全国上下温饱问题；第二，政府道德水平高于有组织犯罪的"盗亦有道"；第三，国家没有内忧外患；第四，人民不被国内外势力压迫。另外还有一个辅助条件，法律能够洗冤禁暴，惩恶扬善，赏罚分明，会加速有组织犯罪支离破碎的步伐。在将来，政府走"四主一辅"路线对付有组织犯罪，是必经之道。

If the government wants to eliminate organized crimes, it should follow four basic lines simultaneously. In addition, there is an auxiliary line that is optional. First, the government should solve the problem of food and clothing nationwide. Second, the government should uphold a moral standard superior to the so-called "codes of conduct" adhered to by organized crimes. Third, the country should be free from internal troubles or external threats. Fourth, the people should not be oppressed by domestic and foreign forces. The auxiliary condition is that the law should be able to redress grievances, prohibit violence, punish evil, promote good, and be clear in rewards and punishments. This will promote the disintegration of organized crimes. In the future, the government must follow the "four main lines and one auxiliary line" to deal with organized crimes.

《道德经》有云："法令滋彰，盗贼多有。"自古以来，法律法规就有不能解决内忧外患，有组织犯罪却能打击内贼外敌的史实。于是，造成政府的公信力大打折扣、谋生的人民不相信法律。

The *Tao Te Ching* states, "The more detailed the laws, the more thieves there will be." Since ancient times, there have been historical facts that laws and regulations cannot solve internal troubles and external threats, but organized crimes can combat internal traitors and external enemies. As a consequence, the government's credibility is greatly reduced, and the people who make a living do not believe in the law.

1901—1905 年的拒俄运动前后持续 4 年 [444]。

The Anti-Russian Movement from 1901 to 1905 lasted for four years.[444]

在"拒俄"和"反满"舆论潮中出世的《俄事警闻》（《警钟日报》）是一个比较特别的对象。《俄事警闻》因研究应对俄国侵略的策略而创刊，1904 年 2 月，随着日俄开战，《俄事警闻》又更

444　杨天石、王学庄撰《1901 年至 1905 年的拒俄运动》，来源《社会科学战线》，1978 年第 4 期

名为《警钟日报》，报纸宣传的重点也从以爱国救亡为中心转变为以宣传推翻清朝、建立民主政权为主要传播目的的刊物，可以说是继《苏报》《国民日报》后国内当时最重要的一份革命报纸。该报创刊正值社会的"拒俄""排满"运动，"拒俄""排满"之间既独立存在又相互融合，前者针对的是以沙俄为主的帝国主义侵略者，后者的矛头指向清政府。它们都是在"夷夏"观念作用下的种族斗争，只不过前者是对外，后者是对内[445]。

The *Russian Affairs Alarm* (later renamed *Alarm Bell Daily*) emerged amid the public opinions of "resisting Russia" and "opposing the Manchus", and it was a special subject. The *Russian Affairs Alarm* was launched for studying strategies to deal with Russia's aggression. In February 1904, with the outbreak of the Russo-Japanese War, the *Russian Affairs Alarm* was renamed *Alarm Bell Daily*, and the focal points of publicity shifted from patriotic salvation to the overthrow of the Qing Dynasty and the establishment of a democratic regime. It can be considered the most important revolutionary newspaper in China at that time following *Suzhou Gazette* and *National Daily*. The establishment of the newspaper coincided with the social movements of "resisting Russia" and "opposing the Manchus". The two movements existed independently but were mutually integrated. The former targeted imperialist aggressors with Tsarist Russia as the main one, while the latter targeted the Qing government. Both were ethnic struggles under the concept of "the distinction between the barbarians and the Han people". The difference was that the former was directed externally and the latter internally.[445]

当新兴知识阶层和普通民众都无法承担抗俄救亡的理想时，会

---

445 靳金撰《舆论潮中的〈俄事警闻〉(〈警钟日报〉) 研究》，来源《湘潭大学》，2014 年 3 月 14 日

党和马贼作为某种客观存在的现实力量，受到了《俄事警闻》的高度重视。特别是马贼，作为东北地区实际存在和活动的抗俄武装力量，更是《俄事警闻》直到《警钟日报》持续关注和一直肯定的对象[446]。

When the emerging intellectuals and ordinary people were unable to shoulder the ideal of resisting Russia and saving the nation, the secret societies and bandits, as real forces that exist objectively, received great attention from the *Russian Affairs Alarm*. In particular, the bandits, as an actual anti-Russian armed force being present and active in Northeast China, received continuous attention and affirmation by the *Russian Affairs Alarm* and then the *Alarm Bell Daily*.[446]

在日军、俄军侵入东北的特殊历史背景下，有些土匪开始抗日、抗俄；有些原不是土匪的，但也以土匪的方式进行抗日、抗俄。抗击外敌、对抗官府是这个时期东北土匪的一大特点。1900年俄军入侵，被清政府追剿的土匪刘永和（绰号刘单子，又称刘弹子）和从宁古塔败下来的抗俄武装杨玉麟的镇东营、义和团余部等会师海龙，举起联合抗俄的义旗，号称忠义军。他们据海龙，进通化，痛歼俄兵于海龙南山，四进新宾堡；夺怀仁，下宽甸，陷凤城，袭安东……到处打击沙俄侵略军和清廷的武装，坚持武装斗争两年多，沉重地打击了俄国侵略军，也动摇了清王朝在东北的统治[447]。

Against the special historical background of the Japanese and Russian troops invading Northeast China, some bandits began to resist Japan and Russia, and some who were not originally bandits also resisted

---

446 季剑青撰《面向"下等社会"——拒俄运动后的〈俄事警闻〉与〈警钟日报〉（1903—1904）》，来源《汉语言文学研究》，2011年第2期

447 胡玉海著《"九一八"事变前东北境内外国军事势力研究》，北京：中国社会科学出版社，2006年7月

Japan and Russia in the form of bandits. The bandits in Northeast China during that period were characterized by resisting foreign invaders and the Qing government. In 1900, when the Russian troops invaded, Liu Yonghe (nicknamed Liu Shanzi, also known as Liu Danzi), a bandit who was being pursued and suppressed by the Qing government, joined forces with Yang Yulin's Zhendong Camp, which was an anti-Russian armed force defeated in Ningguta, and the remnants of the Boxers in Hailong. They raised the banner of jointly resisting Russia, and called themselves the Loyal and Righteous Army. They occupied Hailong, advanced to Tonghua, severely defeated the Russian troops in Nanshan, Hailong, entered Xinbinbao four times; captured Huairen, took Kuandian, occupied Fengcheng, and raided Andong... They struck the Tsarist Russian invaders and the armed forces of the Qing Dynasty everywhere, and persisted in armed struggle for more than two years, dealing a heavy blow to the Russian invaders and also shaking the rule of the Qing Dynasty in Northeast China.[447]

1901—1911年间的历史大背景赋予了东北绿林新的活动内容，他们比以往任何时候都活跃。总的来说，绿林由于思想认识的局限，没有坚定的阶级立场和民族意识，没有明确的政治目标，更提不出明确的政治纲领，表面打着反抗清政府的旗号，却屡次投诚，又屡次背叛，反复无常；对帝国主义的侵略面目缺乏正确的认识，其中有些人受利禄的诱惑，敌我不分，因此出现了被日俄争相收买，为敌所用的复杂情况。尽管如此，部分绿林英勇抗清、抗俄的历史功绩是不应被抹杀的[448]。

The historical background from 1901 to 1911 made the bandits in Northeast China engage in new activities, and they were more active

---

448　邵雍等著《中国近代土匪史》，合肥：合肥工业大学出版社，2012年4月

than ever before. Generally speaking, due to the restrictions of their ideological understanding, the bandits had no firm class stance and national consciousness, nor did they have a clear political goal. Still less could they raise a clear political program. On the surface, they fought under the banner of opposing the Qing government, but they surrendered and betrayed repeatedly, behaved capriciously, and lacked a correct understanding of the aggressive nature of imperialism. Some of them, lured by wealth and official positions, could not distinguish between the enemy and themselves. This led to complex situations where they were bribed by Japan and Russia and used by the enemy. Nevertheless, the historical contributions of some bandits in heroically resisting the Qing Dynasty and Russia should not be ignored.[448]

由于，这个社会的事情是互为因果，许多问题能够无中生有，社会上不出坏事比有好事更好。即使一个人少做好事，也是有正面评价和负面评价。要是一个人没有做坏事，就没有正面评价和负面评价。所以，人不做坏事比做好事更加重要，这就是以无胜有。

Things in this society are interrelated as cause and effect, and many problems can arise out of nothing. Therefore, it is better for society to have no evil things than to have some good things. Even if a person does fewer good deeds, he may receive positive and negative evaluations simultaneously. However, if a person does not do any evil things at all, he will receive neither positive nor negative evaluations. Therefore, it is more important for a person not to do evil things than to do good things, and this can be called the victory of non-action over action.

故此，道德乃是以德催道，并非以道催德。政府大公无私是消灭有组织犯罪的基础，"道"能让天下太平不少，杜绝恐怖主义才不是纸上谈兵。

Therefore, morality is to promote the Tao with virtue, rather than to promote virtue with the Tao. The selflessness of the government is the foundation for eliminating organized crimes. The "Tao" can make the world much more peaceful, and make the eradication of terrorism no longer just empty talk.

后记
Postscript

　　笔者是一个出生于 20 世纪末期，成长于 21 世纪的中国人。在这个时间段，有的外国人很喜欢中国文化，更加刺激了中国文化能够大放异彩，融入世界反恐文化之中。在晚清民国时期，就有博学多才的中国人辜鸿铭预料到中国文化能够为世界消灾解难。

　　I am a Chinese person who was born in the late 20th century and grew up in the 21st century. During this period, some foreigners are very fond of Chinese culture, and this further stimulates Chinese culture to shine brightly and integrate into the global anti-terrorism culture. During the late Qing Dynasty and the Republic of China era, the erudite Chinese scholar Gu Hongming predicted that Chinese culture was able to relieve the world of disasters.

　　民国出大儒，辜鸿铭（1857.7.18—1928.4.30）学博中西，号称"清末怪杰"，精通英、法、德、拉丁、希腊、马来亚等 9 种语言，获 13 个博士学位，是清朝时期精通西洋科学、语言兼及东方华学的中国第一人[449]。

　　Many great scholars emerged during the Republic of China. Well-versed in both Chinese and Western learning, Gu Hongming (July 18,

---

449 《辜鸿铭：中国人的精神》，腾讯网，www.qq.com，2018 年 1 月 17 日

1857 - April 30, 1928) was known as a "genius scholar at the end of the Qing Dynasty". He was proficient in 9 languages including English, French, German, Latin, Greek, and Malay, and was conferred 13 doctoral degrees. He was the first Chinese person in the Qing Dynasty who was proficient in Western sciences, languages, and traditional Chinese culture.[449]

晚清以来，中国形象被严重扭曲。学贯中西、特立独行的辜鸿铭，于 1915 年出版用英文写成的《中国人的精神》(*The spirit of the Chinese people*)，用自己的笔维护了中国文化的尊严，改变了部分西方人对中国的偏见。此书一出，轰动西方，后被译为多种文字。正如大师林语堂用英文写《京华烟云》(*Moment in Peking*)，辜鸿铭同样是英文写《中国人的精神》，他翻译了中国"四书"中的三部——《论语》《中庸》《大学》，创获甚巨；著有《中国的牛津运动》(原名《清流传》)等英文书，热衷向西方人宣传东方的文化和精神，并产生了重大的影响。西方人曾流传一句话：到中国可以不看三大殿，不可不看辜鸿铭。辜鸿铭在西方获得赫赫之名，多半由于他那机智有余、火花四溅、酣畅淋漓的英文实在太出色，他那专搔痒处、专捏痛处、专骂丑处的文化观点实在太精彩，令欧洲学者为之心折，敬佩有加[450]。

From the late period of the Qing Dynasty, China's image was seriously distorted. In 1915, Gu Hongming, who had a comprehensive understanding of both Chinese and Western cultures, and a unique personality, published *The Spirit of the Chinese People* in English, which safeguarded the dignity of Chinese culture and changed some Westerners' prejudices against China. The book caused a sensation in the West, and was later translated into different languages. Just as the master Lin

---

450 同上

Yutang wrote *Moment in Peking* in English, Gu Hongming wrote *The Spirit of the Chinese People* in English. He translated three of the "Four Books" of China, namely *The Analects of Confucius*, *The Doctrine of the Mean*, and *The Great Learning*, thus making great contributions. He also wrote English books such as *The Story of a Chinese Oxford Movement* (originally named *The Qingliu Faction*). He was enthusiastic about promoting Eastern culture and spirit to Westerners, and caused a significant influence. There was a saying among Westerners: When visiting China, one can miss the Three Great Halls, but one must visit Gu Hongming. His high reputation among Westerners can largely be attributed to his extremely brilliant, witty, and incisive English, as well as his wonderful cultural viewpoints that precisely targeted the sensitive points, weaknesses, and ugliness. All these qualities deeply convinced European scholars and won their admiration.[450]

辜鸿铭觉得西方文明太注重实证，而科学越进步、战争越激烈，最终还是要靠中国的道德文明来消弭灾祸。东方的特点是深沉、博大、纯朴、灵敏，相较而言，美国人失之深沉，英国人失之博大，德国人失之纯朴，都不足以相提并论，唯有法国人勉强过得去。辜鸿铭的这些见解，国内不以为然，在国外却预言了一战等，深得俄国皇储、伊藤博文、托尔斯泰等人推崇，连圣雄甘地都称他为"最尊贵的中国人"。1913 年，辜鸿铭和泰戈尔同时被提名为诺贝尔文学奖候选人[451]。

In Gu Hongming's opinion, Western civilization places excessive emphasis on empirical evidence. As more scientific progress is made and wars become more intense, the resulting disasters can only be eliminated

---

451 《辜鸿铭：古老中国的最后一个代表》，新浪读书（新浪网），www.sina.com.cn，2017 年 3 月 23 日

by China's moral civilization. Eastern culture is characterized by depth, vastness, simplicity, and sensitivity. In comparison, Americans lack depth, the British lack vastness, and the Germans lack simplicity. None of them are comparable. Only the French are somewhat acceptable. These views of Gu Hongming were disagreed with in China. However, in foreign countries, his views were verified by his prediction of the First World War, and were thus advocated by people such as the Russian Crown Prince, Ito Hirobumi, and Leo Tolstoy. Even Mahatma Gandhi called him "the most honorable Chinese person". In 1913, Gu Hongming and Rabindranath Tagore were nominated as candidates for the Nobel Prize in Literature.[451]

诸子百家是中国文化的灵魂。诸子百家包含诸多学术流派和治国理念。在 21 世纪，随着时间的推移，这些方家文化照样也是有长有短，都属于"时势造英雄，英雄造时势"的一部分。

As the soul of Chinese culture, the Hundred Schools of Thought include many academic schools and concepts of governing the country. In the 21st century, as time goes by, these cultures still have their own strengths and weaknesses. They all belong to the situation that "the times produce heroes, and heroes shape the times".

倘若中国出现文化浩劫，道家思想生命力是最为顽强，能够坚韧挺拔，却依旧无法换来高额的经济报酬；无论是中国古代还是现代，兵家思想照样能够服务各种类型的战争，却终究仍是一种轩兵杀将的杀戮武器；即便中国现代政府下达何种政策，小说家所撰写的作品都足以展示社会的另一面，是在发现事物隐藏属性，却要满足读者的口味和需求；尽管在现代中国，中国政府强调要构建法治社会，成就法家思想趁势崛起，法家能够充分与法治社会紧密相连，却也暴露了"法家与政府"唇齿相依的尴尬局面；如果现代中国人要团结一致，纵横家思想就会甚嚣尘上，帮人和害人的社会事件会经常发生，极有可能造就出一种危害社会的群体；哪怕中国再怎么强大，只要中国人追求吃喝玩乐，就要关注农家思想，并付出一定的实践，然而中国政府大力提倡农家思想，确实会妨碍本国工业化快速发展⋯⋯

If a cultural holocaust takes place in China, the Taoist ideology has the most tenacious vitality and can stand firm and be resilient, but it cannot bring high economic returns. Whether in ancient or modern China, the military strategist's ideology can serve different types of wars, but after all, it is a weapon for slaying soldiers and generals. No matter what policies the modern Chinese government formulates, the works written by novelists are sufficient to show another side of society. However, the novelists, aiming to discover the hidden attributes of things, have to meet the tastes and needs of readers. Even though in modern times, the emphasis of the Chinese government on building a law-based society has led to the rise of the Legalist ideology, and closely linked the Legalist ideology with a law-based society, this situation has exposed the awkward situation of the close interdependence between "the Legalist ideology and the government". If modern Chinese hope to unite as one, the thought of the School of Diplomacy will become prevalent. However, if social events of helping and harming others frequently take place, this tends to create a group that endangers society. However powerful China becomes, as long as the Chinese people pursue pleasure and enjoyment, they have to pay attention to the Agrarianist ideology and put it into practice. However, if the Chinese government strongly promotes the Agrarianist ideology, it will indeed hinder the rapid development of the national industrialization...

从诸子百家在现代中国的发展，就足以看出国家大事从来就是犬牙交错。无论东西方，一次性解决国家问题从来就是"欲速则不达", 恐怖主义就是其中一个经过日积月累产生积压的国际问题。

From the development of the thoughts of the Hundred Schools of Thought in modern China, we can clearly see that national affairs are intertwined. Whether in the East or the West, solving national problems all at once will lead to the situation of "more haste, less speed". Terrorism is one of the international issues that result from long-term accumulation.

中国文化讲究平和, 排斥极端文化。在中国文化史, 中国汉字 "极"这个字, 包含"极端、顶点、尽头、最终、最高"等多个意思。在 21 世纪, 倘若将中国哲学"太极"二字, 运用于解释反恐问题, 能够通称为"太极, 即使再极端, 也照旧很平和"。

Chinese culture emphasizes harmony and rejects extremes. In the history of Chinese culture, the character "极" (jí) encompasses multiple meanings such as "extreme", "peak", "end", "ultimate", and "highest". In the 21st century, if the Chinese philosophical concept of "Taiji" is applied to explain the issue of counter-terrorism, it can be generally stated as "With Taiji as a weapon, even the most extreme situations can become harmonious."

中国文化重视基本功, 中国人发扬反恐文化不能纠结一击必杀, 轻易下手对付恐怖主义, 自己学富五车, 解决恐怖主义才会行之有效。就像在日本现代社会, 有人赞同保留天皇制, 有人力挺废除天皇制, 去留和改变日本天皇制, 决定了日本社会的安定与稳定, 极有可能引爆日本的政变或者内战, 从而催生出新的恐怖主义历史事件。

Chinese culture attaches great importance to basic skills. When the Chinese promote the counter-terrorism culture, they should avoid being obsessed with the idea of a single decisive strike. It is not advisable to deal with terrorism rashly. Only when one is extremely knowledgeable can he effectively resolve the issue of terrorism. For example, in modern

Japanese society, some people supported the retention of the imperial system, while others strongly advocated its abolition. Whether to retain or change the Japanese imperial system determined the stability of Japanese society. If this issue had not been handled properly, it would have probably triggered a coup or civil war in Japan, thus giving rise to new historical events related to terrorism.

在日本，曾一度流行的皇国史观宣称，日本自神武天皇以来，天皇治世一脉相承，即所谓"万世一系"，从无间断。毋庸赘言，这种日本天皇乃"万世一系"之说缺乏根据，但若称其"千世一系"倒还基本符合史实。总体来看，尽管日本的政局经常风云变幻，政权由摄政、关白、幕府将军到藩阀官僚几经易手，但直至21世纪，天皇作为日本唯一合法的君主地位始终没有改变[452]。

According to the once popular view of Japanese imperial family, since Emperor Jimmu, the rule of the emperors has been passed down in an unbroken line, which is called "unbroken line of emperors for thousands of generations". However, the claim that the Japanese emperors have followed an "unbroken line for thousands of generations" lacks basis. It is more accurate to describe it as an "unbroken line of emperors for a thousand generations". Generally speaking, although the political situation in Japan often changes dramatically, with regime shifting from regents, Kampaku, shoguns to feudal-clique bureaucrats, the status of the emperor as the only legitimate monarch has never changed until the 21st century.[452]

世界近代史上亚洲地区的资产阶级革命中，日本明治维新是比较成功的。明治政权的建立，结束了统治日本265年的幕府封建制

---

452 张建立撰《日本天皇世袭制延续至今的原因研究述评》，来源《日本研究》，2014年第 2 期

度，确立了地主和资产阶级联合专政的资本主义制度。明治维新挽救了日本沦为半殖民地的危机，促进了日本资本主义经济的发展，使日本迅速成为资本主义的统一强国。[453]

Among the bourgeois revolutions in Asia in modern world history, the Meiji Restoration in Japan was relatively successful. The establishment of the Meiji regime ended the feudal shogunate system that had ruled Japan for 265 years and established a capitalist system of joint governance by landlords and the bourgeoisie. The Meiji Restoration saved Japan from the crisis of becoming a semi-colonial country, promoted its capitalist economy, and made it a unified and powerful capitalist country within a very short time.[453]

在幕府统治时期，国家大权掌握在幕府将军手中，天皇被剥夺了一切大权，只不过是全日本精神上的最高统治者。[454]

During the period of shogunate rule, the national power was in the hands of the shogun. The emperor was deprived of all power, only serving as the supreme spiritual ruler of Japan.[454]

19 世纪末，明治维新开始，其中在军事上明确改革封建军制，建立近代化军队，对日本军人进行武士道教育，意图建立一支崇尚"武士道"精神、效忠天皇的军队。[455]

At the end of the 19th century, the Meiji Restoration began. In terms of military affairs, measures were taken to explicitly reform the feudal military system, establish a modern army, and carry out Bushido education for Japanese soldiers, aiming to establish an army that

---

453　杨惠萍撰《试论明治维新成功的原因》，来源《内蒙古民族师院学报（哲学社会科学汉文版)》，1991 年 2 期

454　李琼、郭南南撰《日本近代武士道的产生与嬗变》，来源《牡丹江教育学院学报》，2012 年 4 期

455　同上

advocated the "Bushido" spirit and was loyal to the emperor.[455]

2019 年 5 月，共同社 1、2 两日实施的日本全国紧急电话舆论调查结果显示，82.5% 的受访者表示对已即位的新天皇"有亲切感"，11.3% 的人回答"没有亲切感"。围绕《皇室典范》规定的仅"男系男子"可继承皇位，对允许女性天皇表示赞成的受访者占 79.6%，超过了反对者的 13.3%。[456]

According to a nationwide emergency telephone public opinion survey conducted by Kyodo News on May 1 and 2, 2019, 82.5% of the respondents said they had a "sense of closeness" with the newly enthroned emperor, and 11.3% said that they had no "sense of closeness". Regarding the provision in the *Imperial Household Law* that only "male descendants in the paternal line" can inherit the throne, 79.6% of the respondents supported amending the law to allow for the accession of a female emperor. This exceeded the percentage of those opposing it, which was 13.3%.[456]

退位仅限前天皇（现上皇）一代。关于今后的天皇退位，多达 93.5% 的受访者回答"应该允许"，回答"不应该允许"的占 3.5%。[457]

The abdication system is only applicable to the generation of Emperor Akihito (the current retired emperor). Regarding the future abdication of the emperor, 93.5% of the respondents answered that it "should be allowed", and only 3.5% answered that it "should not be allowed".[457]

进入"平成"时代不久的 1989 年 1 月的舆论调查中，认为天皇"中途退位也可以"的人占 60.5%。因为设问不同无法进行单纯

---

456 《日民调：逾 8 成日本人对新天皇"有亲切感"》观察者网 www.guancha.cn，2019 年 5 月 2 日

457 同上

比较，不过对退位的肯定意见可能较约 30 年前深入人心。[458]

In a public opinion survey in January 1989, that is, in the early "Heisei" era, 60.5% of the people thought that the emperor "could abdicate his throne during his reign". Because the questions are different, we cannot make a simple comparison. However, the positive attitude towards abdication may be more deeply rooted in people's hearts as compared with about 30 years ago.[458]

关于天皇制的应有形式，回答"和现在一样的象征（天皇制）就好"的受访者最多，占 80.9%。回答"不是象征而是成为神圣的存在"的占 7.3%，回答"废除天皇制"的占 4.8%，回答"较现在赋予政治权限"的占 4.3%。[459]

Regarding the appropriate form of the monarchy system, 80.9% of the respondents answered that "the emperor should remain a symbol as now", accounting for the largest percentage. 7.3% of the respondents answered that the emperor should be "a sacred existence rather than a symbol", 4.8% answered that the monarchy system should be "abolished", and 4.3% answered that the emperor should be "given more political power".[459]

有关期待天皇从事的活动（最多两项），回答"国际亲善"的最多，占 35.1%，之后依次为"慰问灾民"（34.0%）、"激励社会弱者"（33.0%）、"从事宪法规定的国事行为"（17.4%）和"访问地方"（16.4%）。[460]

Regarding the activities anticipated from the emperor (up to two choices), 35.1% of the respondents answered "promoting international goodwill", accounting for the largest percentage. Other answers

---

458　同上

459　同上

460　同上

include "consoling disaster victims" (34.0%), "encouraging the socially vulnerable" (33.0%), "performing state affairs as stipulated in the constitution" (17.4%), and "visiting local areas" (16.4%).[460]

从日本皇室角度出发，即使现代日本天皇真的大权在握，再次拥有了实际权力，可是日本天皇身体健康最重要，诛杀罪臣乃是其次。这就预示着，在权力世袭的日本政坛，中国古代"挟天子以令诸侯"的傀儡政策依然有市场需求，何人何时何地实行"削藩政策"仍不失为一种政治游戏的攻防转换。

From the perspective of the Japanese imperial family, even if the modern Japanese emperor really holds great power and regains actual power, the emperor's physical health should be given the highest priority, and punishing guilty ministers comes second. This indicates that in the Japanese political arena where power is hereditary, there is still a demand for the puppet policy similar to "holding the emperor hostage to command the vassals" in ancient China. When, where, and by whom the "policy of weakening the local warlords" is implemented can still be regarded as an offensive and defensive transformation in the political game.

忍一时风平浪静，退一步海阔天空。古今中外，即使是超凡入圣的大人物也要学会能屈能伸，方能立足于世界。例如基督教的耶稣被钉在十字架上；伊斯兰教创始人穆罕默德惨遭迫害，被迫迁往他处；在中国古代，来华的印度僧人达摩就算真会七十二绝技，也需要后继有人；中国道家创始人老子思想，是"善退不善进"等。

Endure for a moment, and things will calm down; yield a little, and there will be a broader future. Throughout history, whether in China or foreign countries, even extraordinary and saintly figures have to learn to be flexible, capable of bending and stretching. Only in this way can they find a foothold in the world. For example, Jesus in Christianity was crucified on the cross; Muhammad, the founder of Islam, was brutally persecuted and forced to move elsewhere; in ancient China, even though Bodhidharma, an Indian monk who came to China, truly possessed seventy-two extraordinary skills, he needed successors; Laozi, the founder of Taoism in China, advocated "being good at retreating but not at advancing".

中国文化否定极端思想和恐怖行为，中国文化土壤容不下敏感事物。即使是社会黑暗和国仇家恨，也不代表任何人可以为所欲为，名人胡作非为反而能让人看出此人的有何不足。例如在中国明清时期，都有做人偏激的代表人物，他们这些人代表不了中国正统思想。

Chinese culture negates extremist thoughts and terrorist behaviors. The soil of Chinese culture cannot tolerate sensitive things. Even in a period of social darkness, national humiliation, and family suffering, no one can act willfully. In fact, the wanton behaviors of famous people will reveal their own shortcomings. For example, both the Ming and Qing Dynasties produced radical representative figures, but these people could not represent the orthodox Chinese ideology.

李贽（1527—1602），号卓吾，人称温陵居士，福建泉州晋江县人，生长于破落的航海商人家庭，从小接受儒家传统思想教育，五十四岁前走与一般文人士子相同的道路——读书做官，官至姚安知府。几十年的官场生活，加上接触社会实际，目睹当时社会政治腐败，不满封建社会的黑暗统治，不满儒家正宗即道学的说教，这使他思想发生深刻变化，"眼高一世"。五十四岁后，李贽毅然辞官，在湖北等地广交名士，招徒讲学，评点诸书，宣传自己的学说见解。在他出版的《焚书》、《藏书》和所评点的《水浒传》等书中，表现出他"独创特解""别出于眼"。他公开指出，那些道学家"阳为道学，阴为富贵，被服儒雅，行若狗彘"。他以辛辣的笔

锋，向道学家宣战，说出别人想说而不敢说的话。在同道学作斗争
中，他不怕围攻，不怕杀头，孤军作战，表现出硬骨头精神。李贽
反对道学的主张和行动，在中国传统思想史上呈现出奇光异彩，成
为儒家学说的异端。就因此，封建统治者视他为洪水猛兽，把他说
成"人妖""魔鬼"，多次寻找借口，欲置他于死地。最后于李贽
七十六岁那年，封建统治者以"敢倡乱道，惑世诬民"的罪名，将
他逮捕，逼死于北京通州狱中。[461]

Li Zhi (1527-1602), known as Zhuowu by literary name, also
known as Wenling Jushi, was a native of Jinjiang County, Quanzhou,
Fujian Province. He grew up in a declining maritime merchant family
and received traditional Confucian ideological education from a young
age. Before the age of 54, he followed the same path as ordinary literati
and scholars, studying for official positions. He attained the position
of the Magistrate of Yao'an Prefecture. During his official career for
decades, he was exposed to social realities, and witnessed the political
corruption of the society. Therefore, he was dissatisfied with the dark rule
of the feudal society and the preaching of Confucian orthodoxy, i.e. Neo-
Confucianism. This led to a profound change in his thoughts, making him
"look down upon the world". After the age of 54, he resolutely resigned
from his official post. In Hubei and other places, he made friends with
many famous scholars, recruited disciples, gave lectures, commented
on various books, and spread his own academic views. In his published
works such as *The Book to Be Burned*, *The Book to Be Hidden*, and his
commentary on *The Story of the Water Margin*, he showed "original
opinions" and "distinctive perspectives". He openly pointed out that

---

461　林其泉撰《试论李贽思想对日本的影响》，来源《长沙理工大学学报：社会科学
　　　版》，1990 年第 1 期

those Neo-Confucian scholars "pretended to be Confucian moralists in public, but sought wealth and status in private. They dressed elegantly but behaved like beasts". With pungent strokes, he attacked the Neo-Confucian scholars, saying what others wanted to say but dared not. In the struggle against Neo-Confucianism, he did not fear being besieged or killed. Instead, he fought alone and showed a spirit of integrity. His claims and actions against Neo-Confucianism shone brightly in the history of traditional Chinese thought, but made him a heretic of Confucianism. As a result, the feudal rulers regarded him as a scourge, called him a "monster" and a "devil", and attempted to kill him on all kinds of pretexts. Finally, at the age of 76, he was arrested by the feudal rulers on the charge of "spreading heresy and misguiding the people", and was forced to death in a prison in Tongzhou, Beijing.[461]

泰州学派自始祖王艮起，就在思想上主张个性价值，在行动上特立独行。李贽作为泰州后学，则进一步突出了主体意识中的个体性规定。他所提出的"天生一人，自有一人之用"的命题，既肯定了个体的价值，又蕴含了对人之独特个性的多样化确认，因而表现为具有积极意义的自我意识觉醒。然而他在确认个体价值的同时，却又走向了另一极端，导致个体与群体之间的紧张对立。[462]

Starting with Wang Gen, the founder of the Taizhou School, the school advocated personal values in thought and uniqueness in action. As a later scholar of the Taizhou School, Li Zhi further highlighted the individualistic elements in subjective consciousness. His proposition that "everyone is born useful" not only affirms the value of the individual but also implies the recognition of the diversity of people's unique personalities. Therefore, it is manifested as the awakening of self-

---

462　于云瀚、全晰纲撰《从王艮到李贽》，来源《潍坊学院学报》，2003 年 3 期

awareness, which is of positive significance. However, while confirming the value of the individual, he went to the other extreme, leading to a tense opposition between the individual and the group.[462]

清朝自入关立国以来，朝野上下怀抱"四海之内，天朝为大"的观念，长期闭关锁国。对西洋的历史、地理、军事、经济、政治、外交、教育等，几乎"浑然不知"。[463]

Since the Qing Dynasty entered the Central Plains and established its rule, both the court and the common people held the concept that "within the Four Seas, the Celestial Empire is supreme" and remained isolated from the outside world for a long time. They almost knew nothing about the history, geography, military affairs, economy, politics, diplomacy, and education of the West.[463]

借助于坚船利炮，西方列强在清朝晚期强行敲开了中国的大门，传教士也由此获得了在中国合法传教的权利。基督教此后在华迅猛发展，与中国固有的儒教伦理产生了越来越严重的冲突。深感于洋教带来的危机，各地士绅官吏奋起抗争。其中，湖南道员周汉以"崇正黜邪、杀身报国"为旗帜，煽动暴力仇杀，试图发动底层民众武力驱逐洋教、重振儒教。这一举动引发了多次外交纠葛，张之洞、陈宝箴等封疆大吏纷纷出面干预，甚至于光绪帝也为此颁发上谕，此即牵动晚清朝野的周汉反洋教案。[464]

With powerful warships and cannons, the Western powers forcefully opened the gate of China in the late Qing Dynasty, and missionaries obtained the legal right to preach in China. Christianity then developed rapidly in China, leading to an increasingly serious conflict with the inherent Confucian ethics. Deeply concerned about the crisis brought

---

463　李素平撰《＜海国图志＞和师夷之长技以制夷》，来源《北京印刷学院学报》，2001 年第 3 期

464　刘锟撰《晚清周汉反洋教案》，来源《中国审判》，2015 年第 4 期

about by foreign religions, gentry and officials in each area rose up against it. Among them, Zhou Han, a Taoist official in Hunan, incited violent hatred and killing under the banner of "upholding the orthodox, eliminating the heretic, and sacrificing one's life for the country", attempting to mobilize the low-class people to expel foreign religions by force and revive Confucianism. This action triggered several diplomatic disputes. High-ranking officials such as Zhang Zhidong and Chen Baochen intervened successively, and even Emperor Guangxu issued an imperial edict regarding it. The Zhou Han Anti-Foreign Religion Incident affected both the court and the public in the late Qing Dynasty.[464]

中国自古以来就有鼓励生育的文化传统，"多子多孙多福气"，"不孝有三，无后为大"等等古训。况且在手工劳动的生产技术条件下，家庭生产经营的状况和收入多寡在相当大程度上要依赖人手的多少。因此，在"老有所养"和预期劳动力收益的驱使下，人们并不在意由于多生多育而引起的生活水平下降。除非天灾人祸等迫不得已的原因，人们不会有意识地控制人口的增长。但由于生产水平以及相应的健康水平的低下，传统社会几千年来人口的增长并不很快，只是到了明清时期，才出现了人口增长的几次高峰期。对明清时期人口迅速增长的史实，学者们普遍认同。[465]

China has had a cultural tradition of encouraging childbearing since ancient times. There are many ancient sayings such as "More children and grandchildren bring more blessings" and "Among the three unfilial acts, the greatest is to have no descendants". Moreover, under the production and technical conditions of manual labor, the status of family production and operation and the income largely depended on the number

---

465　于秋华撰《明清时期人口快速增长对经济发展的影响》，来源《财经问题研究》，2008 年 12 期

of laborers. Therefore, driven by the desire for "old-age support" and expected labor income, people did not care about the decline in living standards caused by having more children. Unless there were irresistible factors such as natural disasters and man-made calamities, people would not consciously control population growth. However, due to the low production level and the relatively unhealthy condition of the people, the population growth in traditional society remained slow for thousands of years. It was only during the Ming and Qing Dynasties that several peaks of population growth emerged. Scholars generally acknowledge the rapid population growth during the Ming and Qing Dynasties as a historical fact.[465]

即使中国国家版图再大，人民做生意不能发财的事情照样有之。何况，中国历朝历代的国土面积都是有鼎盛时期和衰落时期，中国版图没有固定的疆域。于是，在中国人口激增之下，中国人不会做生意的人口基数也在增长，中国人做生意不能发财的确定性也在增加，中国人做生意发家致富的难度也在逐步升高。

Even if China has a large territory, there are still cases where people cannot make big money in business. Moreover, throughout Chinese history, the territorial areas in any dynasty witnessed both golden and declining ages, and there was no fixed boundary for China's territory. Therefore, with the sharp increase in China's population, the population base of Chinese people who are not good at doing business is also growing, the likelihood that Chinese people cannot get rich in business is increasing, and the difficulty for Chinese people to make a fortune through business is gradually rising.

为此，像明人"为我"李贽和清人"排外"周汉所作所为，贪图一时之快，不计较后果冲动行事，恰恰加速了他们二人思想会身死道消，根本不符合中国修身、齐家、治国、平天下的标准。如此一来，明朝人李贽和清朝人周汉只能是中国历史上一闪而过的两个异类。

Therefore, the "For Myself" concept of Li Zhi in the Ming Dynasty and the "anti-foreign sentiment" of Zhou Han in the Qing Dynasty are embodied in their behaviors of seeking momentary pleasure and acting impulsively without considering the consequences. This actually accelerated the withering of their thoughts after their death, because their thoughts were completely incompatible with the Chinese standards of cultivating one's moral character, regulating the family, governing the state, and bringing peace to the world. As a result, Li Zhi in the Ming Dynasty and Zhou Han in the Qing Dynasty can only be regarded as two heterodox figures who shone briefly in Chinese history.

在地球上，每个时期都是狼多肉少，每个人享福和受罪都是并存的，没有例外可言。既然有反恐失败的历史人物，那么，也就有反恐成功的历史人物，成为正反两面的反恐史例。在中国古代时期，汉朝司马迁和明朝方孝孺二人都是正直的个性，他们分别触怒当时的权威者，被泄私愤迫害，就是证明"伴君如伴虎"的恐怖史例。

On this planet, in any period, there are too many people competing for too few resources, and everyone experiences both happiness and hardship. There is no exception. Although some historical figures failed in their anti-terrorism efforts, others achieved success. They have become positive and negative examples in counter-terrorism history. In ancient China, both Sima Qian in the Han Dynasty and Fang Xiaoru in the Ming Dynasty had upright personalities. They respectively offended the authorities of their times and were persecuted out of personal grudges. These are terrible examples to prove that "serving a monarch is as dangerous as accompanying a tiger".

宫刑是汉朝承袭秦朝旧制，除大辟（死刑）之外，最惨无人道、侮辱人格的刑罚。司马迁在《报任安书》中说："最下腐刑，极矣！"腐刑即宫刑（一种破坏男子或女子生殖的刑罚）[466]。

In the Han Dynasty, castration was the most inhumane and insulting punishment next to the capital punishment (execution). It was inherited from the Qin Dynasty. In *A Letter to Ren An*, Sima Qian said, "The lowest is the 'rotting' penalty, which is extremely harsh!" The 'rotting' penalty refers to castration (a punishment that damages the reproductive organs of men or women).[466]

公元前 99 年，正当司马迁草创《史记》，壮志未酬的时候，由于他出自良心为李陵说了几句公道话，因而触怒了汉武帝，被打入了牢狱，处以腐刑。如此不幸的严峻考验，使他的思想发生了深刻的变化，对人生的意义有了更新的理解，也给他的写作带来了巨大的力量，赋予更为深刻的思想内容[467]。

In 99 BC, when Sima Qian was starting to write *Records of the Grand Historian* and his ambition remained unfulfilled, he offended Emperor Wu of Han due to speaking up for Li Ling out of conscience. Then, he was thrown into prison and sentenced to castration. Such an unfortunate and severe ordeal transformed his thinking, enabling him to gain new insights into the meaning of life. It also brought great strength to his writing, endowing it with more profound ideological depth.[467]

司马迁的人格结构特质有明显的前后期之分。前期以"不应美、不隐恶"的求实精神和爱奇志趣体现了他正直进取、壮美的人格；后期因身心遭受严重打击，人格结构扭曲变形，形成了外在的随波逐流与内在的人格升华双重人格，而升华了的人格表现在由

466　王正权撰《司马迁"宫刑"小考》，来源《涪陵师范学院学报》，2002 年第 6 期

467　沈新林、孙应杰撰《司马迁的生死观》，来源《人文杂志》，1984 年第 5 期

"立功"转向"立言"，这使他完成了巨著《史记》的创作，实现了他人生的价值[468]。

There are obvious differences in Sima Qian's personality characteristics between the early and later periods. In the early period, his realistic spirit of "not flattering certain people and not concealing their evil aspects" and his love for extraordinary aspirations reflected his upright, proactive, and lofty personality. In the later period, due to the severe physical and mental traumas, his personality structure was distorted, leading to the formation of a dual personality of outward conformity and inward sublimation. The sublimated personality was manifested in the shift from "establishing merits" to "establishing words", which enabled him to complete the great work *Records of the Grand Historian* and realize the value of his life.[468]

1402 年，明首都应天（今南京）城内发生了一起骇人听闻的冤杀事件[469]。

In 1402, a horrifying unjust execution occurred in Yingtian (now Nanjing), the capital of the Ming Dynasty.[469]

这一年，朱元璋第 4 子燕王朱棣发动靖难之役，篡夺了侄子建文帝朱允炆的皇位。朱棣命令建文帝遗臣方孝孺草拟即位诏书时，遭到了拒绝和痛骂。朱棣恼羞成怒，下令灭方氏九族。为泄私恨，又将方孝孺的朋友、门生另凑成一族磔于市。圣旨颁布之后 7 天方行刑完毕，共杀戮 873 人，开创了中国历史上株连之最[470]。

That year, Zhu Di, the fourth son of Zhu Yuanzhang and the Prince of Yan, launched the Jingnan Campaign and usurped the throne of his

---

468 高益荣撰《试论司马迁的人格结构特质》，来源《北华大学学报：社会科学版》，1994 年第 4 期

469 张群撰《方孝孺后人之谜》，来源《寻根》，2002 年第 6 期

470 同上

nephew, the Jianwen Emperor Zhu Yunwen. When Zhu Di ordered Fang Xiaoru, a surviving official of the Jianwen Emperor, to draft the imperial enthronement edict, Fang Xiaoru refused and vehemently cursed him. Zhu Di flew into a rage and ordered that Fang Xiaoru and nine categories of his relatives be executed. To vent his personal hatred, Zhu Di gathered Fang Xiaoru's friends and disciples as another category and dismembered them in the marketplace. The execution was not completed until seven days after the imperial decree was issued, with a total of 873 people killed. This set a record for the largest number of implicated people in Chinese history.[470]

宁海方孝孺身受有明开国君臣的特别器重，无论是君王的仁政构想，还是儒者的明道寄托，均将其定位为有明一代承续道统、昌明圣学的读书种子。方孝孺亦每以承续前贤，阐明王道为念，立身行事，谈诗论道，莫不合节中礼。建文被夺位后，一介书生方孝孺以荷道之身独抗万乘君威，虽罹极刑，然持道守节之士人志行已凛然驾于君权之上，天下读书种子亦自此断绝，君主心理与士人志行间的隔阂遂被推至极端[471]。

Fang Xiaoru from Ninghai was held in high esteem by the founding emperor and ministers of the Ming Dynasty. Both the monarch's vision of benevolent governance and the Confucians' aspiration to expound the truth regarded him as the "seed of scholars" in the Ming Dynasty, who carried on the Confucian orthodoxy and promoted the great learning. Valuing the continuation of his predecessors' teachings and the exposition of the kingly way, Fang Xiaoru conducted himself with propriety in all his words and deeds, and his discussions of poetry and the Tao also

---

471　郭万金撰《"天下读书种子绝矣"——方孝孺之死的文化阐释》，来源《浙江学刊》，2007 年第 6 期

conformed to the rules of propriety. After the Jianwen Emperor lost his throne, Fang Xiaoru, a scholar, defied the imperial might with his moral integrity alone. Although he suffered the most severe punishment, the lofty aspiration of a scholar who upheld the Tao and kept his integrity towered above the imperial power with a dignified air. After that, the "seed of scholars" in China was cut off, and the estrangement between the monarch's will and the scholars' aspiration was pushed to the extreme.[471]

汉朝司马迁生不如死，明代方孝孺被诛十族，前者是身残志坚选择继续活下去，还要完成自己尚未完成的作品和为家人的以后打算。后者是以身殉道，以死明志，自己一了百了，却也精神永存，能够鞭策世人。相同的是，这两位历史名人都是不趋炎附势的杰出代表人物，此二人都是愿意牺牲自己的身体，保全自身的仁义道德，用抵制全面合作或执行部分合作来实现本人的价值，成为中国文化人的不朽丰碑，令后人汗颜。

Sima Qian in the Han Dynasty endured a life worse than death, while Fang Xiaoru in the Ming Dynasty was executed along with ten categories of people related to him. The former, despite his physical disability, chose to survive with a strong will, determined to complete his unfinished works and make arrangements for his family's future. The latter sacrificed his life for a just principle and proved his loyalty with his death. Though his life came to an end, his spirit continues and inspires the people. Both historical celebrities had something in common. Both were outstanding representatives who refused to fawn on the powerful. Both were willing to sacrifice their bodies to preserve their benevolence and righteousness, and realize their own value by resisting full cooperation or executing part cooperation. They have become immortal monuments for Chinese intellectuals, making later generations feel ashamed.

面对与国家有关的问题，小至个人安危，大至国际事件，一旦政府采取极端手段，都容易出现不良症状。从主观和客观两个层面来讲，朝野上下处理国家问题，都需要先经过多年的市场调查，将敏感成分逐步淡化，方能一一实行，让信者更信，让疑者不疑，皆心悦诚服。就像在中国东汉末年，外戚宦官专政和道教分支太平道创始人张角率众起义，就有实质性的因果关联。

Regarding national matters, ranging from personal safety on a small scale to international events on a large scale, once the government takes extreme measures, negative consequences are likely to occur. From both subjective and objective perspectives, when dealing with national issues, both the government and the people need to conduct market surveys for several years and gradually dilute the sensitive elements before implementing the measures one by one. In this way, those who believe will have stronger faith, and those who doubt will no longer have misgivings, and everyone will be convinced. For example, in the late Eastern Han Dynasty, there was a real causal relationship between the usurpation of power by imperial relatives and eunuchs and the peasant uprising led by Zhang Jiao, the founder of Taipingdao, a branch of Taoism.

总的来说，道家与道教是两个不同的概念。道家的学术思想属于哲学范畴，是对社会现实的抽象反映；道教则属于宗教范畴，是人们对现实世界虚幻的、歪曲的反映。这是两者的本质区别。但是，二者也是相互联系的。道教来源于道家，同时也承袭了中国古代的巫术和神仙方术，在发展过程中还糅合了儒家、佛教的某些思想和教规、仪式；二者在内容与形式上既有联系的地方，又有区别之处。[472]

472　黄颖、梁家胜撰《"道"亦有道：道家与道教》，来源《枣庄学院学报》，2014 年
　　第 3 期

Generally speaking, the Taoist School and Taoism are two different concepts. Belonging to the philosophical category, the academic thoughts of the Taoist School are an abstract reflection of social reality. Belonging to the religious category, Taoism is a distorted and illusory reflection of the real world. This is the essential difference between the two. However, they are also interrelated. Tacism originated from the Taoist School. At the same time, it inherited ancient Chinese witchcraft and immortal arts, and incorporated some thoughts, religious rules, and rituals from Confucianism and Buddhism in the process of development. Therefore, there are both connections and differences in content and form between the two.[472]

两汉时期道家到早期道教的嬗变是一个重要的思想演变过程。首先是汉初道家的勃兴与衰落，然后是道家宗教化趋势的加强和黄老道的形成，最后是东汉末年太平道和五斗米道等早期道教的出现。这个过程贯穿了两汉思想史的全过程，对中国宗教的发展也有重要意义。[473]

The evolution from the Taoist School to early Taoism in the Han Dynasty is an important process of ideological evolution. The first is the rise and fall of the Taoist School in the early Han Dynasty. The second is the strengthening of the religiousization of the Taoist School's thoughts and the formation of Huanglao Taoism, which combines the Yellow Emperor's ideas and Laozi's Taoism. The third is the emergence of early forms of Taoism such as Taipingdao (Way of Great Peace) and Wudoumi Dao (Way of the Five Bushels of Rice) in the late Eastern Han Dynasty. This process ran through the entire intellectual history in the Han Dynasty and was of great significance to the development of Chinese religion.[473]

473　于斌撰《两汉时期的道家和早期道教》，来源《重庆师范大学》，2007 年

东汉后期，外戚宦官交替擅权，政治黑暗腐败，豪强地主势力不断发展，土地兼并越来越严重。[474]

In the late Eastern Han Dynasty, imperial relatives and eunuchs alternately held power, the politics was dark and corrupt, the power of powerful landlords continued to grow, and land annexation became increasingly serious.[474]

钜鹿人张角生活在东汉末年社会矛盾激化的年代，起初奉事黄老道，后来创立太平道，中平元年（184 年），发动八州并起的黄巾大起义，虽然由于各种原因失败了，但却沉重地打击了东汉皇朝，使其陷入土崩瓦解的过程之中。[475]

Zhang Jiao, a native of Julu, lived in the late Eastern Han Dynasty, an era of intensifying social contradictions. At first, he followed Huanglao Taoism. Then, he established Taipingdao (Way of Great Peace). In the First Year of Emperor Zhongping's Reign (184 AD), he launched the Yellow Turban Uprising in which people rose up simultaneously in eight prefectures. Although the uprising failed for various reasons, it dealt a heavy blow to the Eastern Han Dynasty and promoted its disintegration.[475]

太平道是黄巾起义的组织形式，在太平道 10 余年的发展、壮大过程中，数十万起义民众被严密地组织了起来。[476]

Taipingdao was the organizational form of the Yellow Turban Uprising. During its development and growth for more than ten years, hundreds of thousands of rebels formed a closely-knit organization.[476]

张角之所以创立"太平道"，当然不是出于纯粹的个人动机，

474　王震亚撰《东汉后期的"凉州三杰"》，来源《西北师大学报（社会科学版)》，1985 年 2 期

475　秦进才撰《黄巾起义领袖张角》，来源《邢台学院学报》，2003 年 2 期

476　徐难于撰《论黄巾起义宗教色彩和规模巨大的成因》，来源《西南师范大学学报（哲学社会科学版)》，1998 年 6 期

而是严重的社会危机的产物。东汉中叶以来，宦官和外戚轮流专政，政府腐败，巧取豪夺，民不聊生，疫病流行。安桓二帝时期大疫记载，史不绝书，灵帝年间，更为频繁。面对日益猖獗的传染病，东汉朝廷却束手无策，任其流行。而病魔缠身的劳动人民，只得祈求神灵与方术，于是迷信和巫师乘势大兴。古代方士和巫医，往往兼具迷信与医学的特点。他们以咒除病固然荒唐，但也身挂药囊，能用中草药和针刺治病，又有科学的成分。张角就属于此类。因此，东汉末年原始道教广泛地流传，是跟现实生活中病疫蔓延紧密相关的。它完全适应苦难的人们祈求精神安慰的心情。[477]

As a matter of course, Zhang Jiao established Taipingdao not purely out of personal motives, but due to serious social crises. Since the mid Eastern Han Dynasty, eunuchs and imperial relatives took turns to hold power, the corrupt government robbed the people by force and trickery, the people lived in misery, and epidemics were prevalent. According to historical records, serious epidemics occurred in succession during Emperor An's Reign and Emperor Huan's Reign, and they became even more frequent during Emperor Ling's Reign. In the face of the increasingly rampant infectious diseases, the Eastern Han court was at a loss and allowed them to spread. The working people, afflicted by diseases, could only pray to ceities and resort to witchcraft. As a result, superstition and witchcraft thrived. Ancient alchemists and witch doctors usually had the characteristics of superstition and medicine. It was of course absurd for them to cure diseases with incantations. However, they also carried medicine bags, and were able to use Chinese herbs and acupuncture to treat diseases. This embodied a certain degree of

---

[477] 刘旭初撰《论黄巾起义与太平道》，来源《阜阳师范学院学报：社会科学版》，2001 年第 4 期

scientificity. Zhang Jiao belonged to this type. Therefore, the widespread dissemination of primitive Taoism in the late Eastern Han Dynasty was closely related to the spread of diseases and epidemics in real life. It fully met the suffering people's need for spiritual comfort.[477]

黄巾起义，八州并发，烟炎烽天，规模之大，威力之猛，超过了过去几次大规模的农民起义。这次起义不仅只是声势浩大，而且阶级意识比过去几次更加为之明朗，响亮地喊出"苍天已死，黄天当立"的革命口号，有力地粉碎了统治阶级套在人民身上的精神枷锁，锋芒直指汉家天子和地方官吏。虽然张角利用特殊的时代背景，以"太平道"为掩护煽动、鼓惑民众，组织发动起义，并猛烈地冲击了封建统治秩序，但"太平道"归根到底只不过是由一些晦涩的迷信思想和肤浅的说教拼凑的大杂烩。虽然它在一定的程度上反映了农民阶级对社会黑暗现状的不满和对未来社会的憧憬，对这次起义产生过一些积极作用，但这种作用毕竟是短暂的，而它的消极作用随着起义的发展和深入逐步暴露无遗。加之敌我力量悬殊，张角死得过早，起义军缺乏领导，因此失败不可避免。[478]

The Yellow Turban Uprising broke out simultaneously in eight prefectures, with flames and smoke billowing across the sky. Its scale and power surpassed those of previous major peasant uprisings. This uprising not only gained great momentum, but also embodied a clearer class consciousness than previous ones. The rebels loudly shouted the revolutionary slogan "The Blue Heaven is dead, and the Yellow Heaven shall rise," effectively shattering the spiritual shackles that the ruling class had imposed on the people and directly targeting the emperor and local officials of the Han Dynasty. Against the backdrop of this special historical period, Zhang Jiao used Taipingdao as a cover to incite

---

478　同上

the people and launch the uprising, which severely shook the feudal ruling order. However, in essence, Taipingdao was nothing more than a hodgepodge of obscure superstitious ideas and superficial teachings. To a certain extent, it reflected the peasant class's dissatisfaction with the dark social reality and their longing for a better future, causing some positive effects. However, these effects were temporary, and with the development and deepening of the uprising, its negative effects gradually emerged. Owing to a huge disparity in strength between the two sides, Zhang Jiao died prematurely. The lack of leadership in the peasant army made the failure inevitable.[478]

任何人都是可以被替代的，这个世界没有谁都可以正常运转。官逼民反下的恐怖分子还是恐怖分子，贪污腐败还是贪污腐败，反恐和反贪污反腐败都会有人来接手完成其目标，不必杞人忧天。

Anyone is replaceable, and the world can go on as normal without anyone. Terrorists under the oppression of officials are still terrorists, and corruption is still corruption. There will always be people to take over the anti-terrorism and anti-corruption campaigns and complete their goals, so there is no need to worry unnecessarily.

哲学讲究顺势而行，引导势利，宗教讲究顺天而行，难违天命。哲学是基础力量，宗教是高等产物。这二者是有本质的不同。

Philosophy emphasizes acting in accordance with natural tendencies and making the best of the situation, while religion emphasizes acting in accordance with the will of heaven rather than going against fate. Philosophy is the fundamental force, while religion is a higher-level product. There is an essential difference between the two.

要想解决复杂局面，先解决简单问题。人会变，事会变，物会变，有些本质则是不变的。这些变化之道都需要顺应时代的发展，才能保证彼此之间互相不落伍，相得益彰有结果。

In order to deal with a complex situation, one should first solve simple problems. People may change, things may change, and objects may change, but some essences remain the same. Only when the principles of change conform to the development of the times can everything keep up with each other and enhance each other's effect.

美化和包装自己是恐怖分子的邪恶文化攻势，成为了恐怖主义的一部分。明是非，辨道理，可以粉碎虚假宣传，打击恐怖主义。即使社会现实真的太残酷，但战胜和战败都能够波及敌我双方及第三方，有"柔非柔，刚非刚，强非强，弱非弱"局面。所以，一时的得失算不上什么，不能注定你以后的人生是光明还是黑暗。

As a part of terrorism, self-beautification and self-packaging is part of the evil cultural offensive launched by terrorists. Only by distinguishing right from wrong and understanding the truth can we shatter deceptive publicity and crack down on terrorism. Even if the social reality is really harsh, both victory and defeat can have an impact on the enemy, our side and third parties, creating a situation where "softness is not really softness, hardness is not really hardness, strength is not really strength, and weakness is not really weakness." Therefore, temporary gains and losses mean little. They cannot determine whether your future life will be bright or dark.

华夏文明几千年历史，产生了无数的历史人物和历史事件。这些历史人物和历史事件都不是单独存在，而是依附于各种群体之中，杜绝他人在自我世界里获得成功。

With a history of thousands of years, Chinese civilization has given rise to countless historical figures and events, which do not exist in isolation but are attached to different groups. This attachment can prevent others from achieving success in their own world.

在中国古代，有些著名的兵法家、军事家、战争家有属于自己的文化符号。中国每个朝代的社会规则都不尽相同，他们这些人在历史上，都留下了自己的优缺点，留给后人来评说。像深思熟虑要学习"姜尚择主"；军法无情要学习"司马穰苴执法"；军事演习要学习"孙武练兵"；养家糊口要学习"范蠡求人不如求己"；善待下属要学习"吴起爱兵"；身残志坚要学习"孙膑对决庞涓"；选择敌人要学习"韩信背水一战"；有求于人要学习"诸葛亮联外"；破敌顺序要学习"刘基献计"；训练战力要学习"戚继光练兵"……

In ancient China, some famous strategists, military leaders, and war experts had their own cultural symbols. The social rules of each dynasty were different. These people have left behind their strengths and weaknesses in history for future generations to evaluate. For example, if one wants to think carefully, he should study "Jiang Shang's choice of a lord"; if one wants to understand that military law is ruthless, he should study "Rangju's enforcement of military law"; if one wants to conduct military drills, he should study "Sun Wu's military training"; if one wants to make a living, he should study "Fan Li's relying on himself rather than others"; if one wants to treat his subordinates kindly, he should study "Wu Qi's love for his soldiers"; if one wants to be firm in spirit despite physical disability, he should study "Sun Bin's confrontation with Pang Juan"; if one wants to choose the right enemy, he should study "Han Xin's fighting with his back to the river"; if one wants to seek help from others, he should study "Zhuge Liang's alliance with external forces"; if one wants to know the order of breaking the enemy, he should study "Liu Ji's strategies"; if one wants to cultivate combat effectiveness, he should study "Qi Jiguang's military training"...

公元前 21 世纪，夏王朝逐渐形成，这是中国历史上人类组织的最高形式。夏朝建城邑，组军队，制刑法，兴监狱，具备了国家的雏形。公元前 17 世纪，商汤灭夏，建立商王朝，国家行政组织更加完备。公元前 11 世纪，武王伐纣，西周王朝兴起。西周实行宗法分封制，统治秩序进一步完善，周公旦制礼作乐，为巩固西周政权做出了重要贡献。西周灭亡后，周平王迁都洛邑，史称东周。春秋战国时期开始，诸侯争霸，战争连年。各国为求生存和发展，招贤纳士，改革图新，管理思想不断涌现，管理人才层出不穷。公元前 221 年，秦灭六国，建立起中央集权的国家，标志着夏商周时期的结束。[479]

In the 21st century BC, the Xia Dynasty gradually emerged. This was the highest form of human organization in Chinese history at that time. Through building cities, organizing troops, formulating criminal laws and establishing prisons, the Xia Dynasty took on the embryonic form of a state. In the 17th century BC, Shang Tang overthrew the Xia Dynasty, and established the Shang Dynasty, which had a more complete national administrative structure. In the 11th century BC, King Wu of Zhou launched a campaign against King Zhou of Shang and established the Western Zhou Dynasty. The Western Zhou Dynasty implemented the patriarchal enfeoffment system, and further improved the ruling order. Duke Dan of Zhou formulated rituals and composed music, making important contributions to the consolidation of the Western Zhou regime. After the downfall of the Western Zhou Dynasty, King Ping of Zhou relocated the capital to Luoyang, and that period was historically known as the Eastern Zhou Dynasty. The Spring and Autumn Period and the Warring States Period began, with the feudal lords vying for hegemony and wars lasting year after year. In order to survive and develop, each

---

[479] 王忠伟、王书汉、张琦撰《夏商周时期管理思想的产生》，来源《鞍山科技大学学报》，2006 年 5 期

state recruited talents and implemented reforms, leading to continuous emergence of management ideas and management talents. In 221 BC, the Qin Dynasty destroyed the six states and established a centralized state, marking the end of the Xia, Shang, and Zhou Dynasties.[479]

姜太公即姜子牙，名尚。史称吕尚，以其德高望重又高寿故称姜太公。他在中国历史上是大器晚成的典型，年逾古稀仍怀才不遇，默默无闻；后来听说周文王很尊重人才，便持竿到渭水之滨终日借垂钓修养心志，磨炼毅力，他钓鱼从来不用鱼饵，正所谓"姜太公钓鱼，愿者上钩"，传为佳话。上天不负有心人，终于在姜子牙80岁时被周文王访贤发现，拜为西周朝丞相；他不负信任，励精图治，安邦治国，为灭纣兴周做出了贡献[480]。

Jiang Ziya, named Shang and also known as Jiang Taigong, was the founding father of the Zhou Dynasty. Historically, he was called Lv Shang. Because of his noble character and longevity, he was honored with the title of Jiang Taigong. He was a typical example of achieving success late in life in Chinese history. Even in his seventies, he remained an unrecognized talent. Later, he heard that King Wen of Zhou attached great importance to talents, so he went to the bank of the Wei River with a fishing rod, and spent his days fishing to cultivate his mind and hone his will. He never used bait when fishing. As the saying goes, "Jiang Taigong fished with a straight hook, and only the willing ones would take the bait." This is a well-known story. Finally, at the age of 80, he was found by King Wen of Zhou during his search for talents and was appointed as the prime minister of the Western Zhou Dynasty. He lived up to the trust placed in him, made great efforts to govern the country, and made contributions to overthrowing the Shang Dynasty and establishing the

---

480　曲顺章撰《话说姜太公钓鱼》，来源《河南水产》，1997 年第 2 期

Zhou Dynasty.[480]

约公元前 1066 年的西方周族，在经过先前周文王的苦心经营后，由一个蕞尔小邦发展成拥有数十万大军的强国，为灭殷帝国打下了坚实的基础。武王继位，在孟津观兵之后二年，这时期的周族已在政治上，军事上都取得了能与殷帝国抗衡的优势后，从而发动了中国历史上著名的"牧野之战"（即"武王伐纣"之战）。[481]

Around 1066 BC, the Zhou clan in the west, thanks to the painstaking efforts of King Wen of Zhou in the previous period, evolved from a significant small state into a powerful country with hundreds of thousands of troops, thus laying a solid foundation for the destruction of the Yin Empire. Two years after King Wu's accession to the throne and the military review at Mengjin, the Zhou clan gained political and military advantages that could rival those of the Yin Empire. Therefore, it launched the famous "Battle of Muye" (that is, the campaign against King Zhou of Shang) in Chinese history.[481]

牧野之战，就是周武王在吕尚等人辅佐下，率军直捣商都朝歌（今河南淇县），在牧野（今淇县以南卫河以北地区）大破商军遂使商朝灭亡的一次战略性决战[482]。

The Battle of Muye was a strategic decisive battle in which King Wu of Zhou, assisted by Lü Shang and others, led his army directly to Chaoge, the capital of the Shang Dynasty (now Qi County, Henan Province), and defeated the Shang army in Muye (now the area south of Qi County and north of the Wei River). This battle caused the downfall of the Shang Dynasty.[482]

---

481 李卫红、杨华撰《论"武王伐纣"战役中的巴、蜀之师》，来源《三峡大学学报（人文社会科学版）》，2006 年 2 期

482 刘岳撰《试析牧野之战与商朝灭亡的原因》，来源《河南商业高等专科学校学报》，2015 年第 2 期

司马穰苴是田完的后裔，他的原名叫田穰苴，曾为大司马一官，所以也被称为司马穰苴。[483]

Originally called Tian Rangju, Sima Rangju was a descendant of Tian Wan. He once held the position of Grand Marshal (Da Sima), so he was also known as Sima Rangju.[483]

《史记·司马穰苴列传》记载了这样一件事：司马穰苴被齐景公任命为将军，但他又觉得自己出身卑贱，于是要求齐景公选派一个宠臣做监军。景公选派了庄贾，司马穰苴与庄贾约定，第二天中午到军门会集。司马穰苴一早就到了军中，准备好记时的表柱和沙漏等待庄贾的到来，但庄贾过了中午还未到，于是司马穰苴命人撤去表柱和沙漏，向部队申明了纪律。到黄昏的时候，庄贾才到军中，司马穰苴问他怎么迟到了，庄贾说是亲戚置酒相送，因此迟了。司马穰苴教训了他一顿之后，问掌管军法的军吏按军法应当怎么处理，军吏回答："当斩"。庄贾害怕了，派人飞马向景公求救，援救未至，司马穰苴已当众斩了庄贾。这时景公的使者飞马到了军中，宣读景公赦免庄贾的命令，司马穰苴说："将在军，君令有所不受。"又问军法吏对使者在军中驰马，应当如何处理，军吏曰："当斩。"使者大惊，司马穰苴说国君的使者不能杀，于是杀了使者的奴仆，砍了左边马的头，割断了马车左边的车驸。为了维护军纪，国君的宠臣可杀，代表国君的使者可以冒犯，可见，"杀之贵大"，在兵家绝非空谈。[484]

In *Biographies of Sima Rangju, Records of the Grand Historian*, there is such a story: Sima Rangju was appointed as a general by Duke Jing of Qi. However, he felt that he was born in a humble family, so he asked Duke Jing of Qi to appoint a confidant as a military supervisor.

483　扶栏客撰《司马穰苴：不战而屈人之兵》，来源《各界》，2009 年第 12 期
484　车远鸿撰《先秦兵家法律思想述评》，来源《肇庆学院学报》，2003 年第 3 期

Duke Jing chose Zhuang Jia. Sima Rangju made an appointment with Zhuang Jia to meet at the military gate at noon the next day. Sima Rangju arrived at the army early in the morning, prepared the timekeeping sundial and hourglass, and waited for Zhuang Jia's arrival. However, Zhuang Jia did not arrive even after noon. So Sima Rangju ordered the sundial and hourglass to be removed, and declared the military discipline to the troops. It was not until at dusk that Zhuang Jia finally arrived. Sima Rangju asked him why he was late. Zhuang Jia said that his relatives had held a farewell banquet for him, so he was late. After rebuking him, Sima Rangju asked the official in charge of military law how Zhuang Jia should be dealt with according to the military law. The military official replied, "He should be beheaded." Zhuang Jia was scared and sent someone posthaste on horseback to plead with Duke Jing for help. Before the rescue arrived, Sima Rangju had already beheaded Zhuang Jia in public. At this time, the messenger of Duke Jing arrived on a fast horse and announced Duke Jing's order to pardon Zhuang Jia. Sima Rangju said, "A general in the army can disregard orders from the monarch." He then asked the military official how the messenger who rode a horse in the army should be dealt with. The military official said, "He should be beheaded." The messenger was greatly shocked. Sima Rangju said that the messenger of the monarch could not be killed, so he killed the messenger's servant, chopped off the head of the horse on the left, and cut off the left carriage shaft of the carriage. In order to maintain military discipline, a favored courtier of the monarch could be killed, and a messenger representing the monarch could be offended. It can be seen that the saying "the execution of a person of eminent status can shock the entire army" is by no means an empty statement among the military strategists.[484]

穰苴杀了庄贾，军营上下为之震动，自此以后，穰苴令行禁止，在军中树立了威信。同时，穰苴对于宿营、打井、垒灶、饮食、疾病这样一些关乎士兵疾苦的事情都亲自过问，又把自己作为将军应得的口粮拿出来分给士兵，而自己则和士兵一起排序分配口粮，经过排队，他所得到的口粮只是相当于军中瘦弱者的口粮量。因此他深得士兵的信任和爱戴。三天以后，穰苴勒兵进发，军中老弱都争先恐后随军出战，士气之高前所未有。晋、燕两国军队听到消息，纷纷解兵而去。齐军乘胜追击，收复了全部失地。为了褒奖穰苴的功劳，齐景公任他为大司马，掌管全国军务，因此后人便称他为司马穰苴。[485]

The execution of Zhuang Jia by Sima Rangju shocked all the soldiers in the military camp. After that, Sima Rangju realized the prompt execution of orders and strict enforcement of prohibitions, thus establishing his prestige in the army. At the same time, he personally inquired into the soldiers' well-being, including aspects like camping arrangements, pit digging, stove building, food supply and their health conditions. He also distributed the rations due to him as a general to the soldiers, and then lined up with the soldiers to receive his share. After queuing up, he only received rations that were equivalent to those of the weak soldiers in the army. Therefore, he won the trust and love of the soldiers. Three days later, he assembled the troops and set out. The old and weak soldiers in the army all rushed to go into battle, making the morale unprecedentedly high. When the armies of the Jin and Yan States heard the news, they withdrew their troops. The Qi army followed up its victory and regained all the lost territory. In order to commend Rangju's contributions, Duke Jing of Qi appointed him as the Grand Marshal,

---

485 孙晓春撰《司马穰苴斩庄贾》，来源《现代交际》，2006 年 8 期

in charge of the state's military affairs. Therefore, he was called Sima Rangju by later generations.[485]

论辈分司马穰苴是孙武的叔父，孙武原本是齐国大夫，避祸越国，认识了伍子胥被越王重用，著名的孙武练兵，即使用后宫的美姬也能训练有素，令行禁止[486]。

In terms of seniority, Sima Rangju was Sun Wu's uncle. Sun Wu was originally a minister of the State of Qi. In order to avoid disaster, he fled to the State of Yue, where he met Wu Zixu and was highly valued by the King of Yue. In the famous incident of Sun Wu training the troops, he managed to train the beautiful concubines in the inner court into an orderly unit, making them strictly follow orders.[486]

吴越争霸是春秋争霸的尾声。它是吴越两国开发南方、国力强大的结果，也是中原各诸侯国争霸战争的连锁反应。春秋中期，晋楚争霸，晋联吴制楚，楚却联越制吴，因此造成了吴越长期对立，互为水火的局面。[487]

The struggle for hegemony between the State of Wu and the State of Yue marked the end of the struggle for hegemony in the Spring and Autumn Period. It resulted from Wu and Yue's gaining strength through developing the south, and it was also a chain reaction of the struggles for hegemony among the vassal states in the Central Plains. In the middle of the Spring and Autumn Period, the State of Jin and the State of Chu struggled for hegemony. Jin united with Wu to contain Chu, while Chu united with Yue to contain Wu. As a result, a situation of long-term opposition and extreme hostility between Wu and Yue was formed.[487]

公元前 584 年，楚国一个臣子申公巫臣逃亡到晋国，建议晋国

---

486 《孙武和司马穰苴居然是同族，＜司马法＞足以和＜孙子兵法＞比肩》，腾讯网，www.qq.com，2019 年 10 月 20 日

487 朱耀廷撰《用贤而兴，失贤而亡》，来源《人才研究》，1986 年 7 期

扶植吴国以对付楚国。晋派申公巫臣到吴，把中原的乘车、射御、战阵之法教给吴人，又"教之叛楚"。从此吴国寿梦称王，开始对楚进行骚扰。公元前 515 年，吴王阖闾用伍子胥之谋，收买勇士专诸，刺杀吴王僚，夺得王位，重用伍子胥、伯嚭、孙武等人。伍子胥、伯嚭都是楚国亡臣。[488]

In 584 BC, Wuchen, the Duke of Shen, who was a courtier of the State of Chu, fled to the State of Jin, and suggested that the State of Jin support the State of Wu to deal with the State of Chu. The State of Jin dispatched Wuchen to the State of Wu. Wuchen taught the local people there the methods of riding chariots, shooting, defending themselves, and the techniques of military formations of the Central Plains, and also "incited them to rebel against the State of Chu". After that, Shoumeng of the State of Wu proclaimed himself king and started harassing the State of Chu. In 515 BC, King Helü of Wu adopted Wu Zixu's strategy, bribing the warrior Zhuan Zhu to assassinate King Liao of Wu. Then, he seized the throne. He highly valued people such as Wu Zixu, Bo Pi and Sun Wu. Both Wu Zixu and Bo Pi were officials who fled from the State of Chu.[488]

夫差，生年不详，卒于公元前 473 年，吴王阖闾之子，春秋末年吴国君，公元前 496 ～ 473 年在位。在位期间，曾连续 4 次开凿运河，为中国早期水利事业的发展做出了贡献。[489]

Fuchai, whose year of birth is unknown and whose year of death is 473 BC, was the son of King Helü of Wu and the ruler of the State of Wu in the late Spring and Autumn Period. During his reign from 496 to 473 BC, he launched four consecutive projects of canal digging, thus making contributions to the development of China's early water conservancy

488　同上

489　廖高明撰《吴王夫差凿运河》，来源《水利天地》，2002 年 4 期

undertakings.[489]

孙武，生长于齐，建功立业于吴。中原地区的齐鲁文化与南方地区的吴文化共同孕育了孙武这位春秋时期伟大的军事家。孙武因助吴败楚、辅佐吴王夫差确立了春秋霸主地位而在当时扬名天下；又因其名著《孙子兵法》而被称誉为兵家鼻祖，流芳百世。孙武的军事思想因其谋略突出而被班固列为兵权谋家的代表。然而孙武的军事谋略与普通的军事谋略不同，这种谋略是建立在"安国全军"的仁德基础上的大智慧、大谋略。[490]

Sun Wu grew up in the State of Qi and achieved accomplishments in the State of Wu. The Qi and Lu cultures in the Central Plains and the Wu culture in the southern region jointly nurtured Sun Wu, a great military strategist in the Spring and Autumn Period. Due to assisting the State of Wu in defeating the State of Chu and supporting King Fuchai of Wu as the overlord of the Spring and Autumn Period, he became well-known at that time. He was also praised as the founder of the Military Strategists for his famous work *The Art of War*, and his reputation has been remembered through the ages. With excellent strategies in his military thoughts, Sun Wu was regarded by Ban Gu as the representative of the Military Strategists. However, his military strategies were distinct from ordinary ones. These strategies embodied great wisdom and tactics based on the benevolence concept of "ensuring national security and preserving the army".[490]

《史记·孙子吴起列传》中记载：吴王阖闾让孙武训练宫女，孙武将宫女编成两队，派吴王的两个宠妃分任队长。开始那些女子们嘻嘻哈哈，不听指挥。孙武三番五次作了说明，并告诫她们："约

490　张杰、张斌撰《论孙武军事思想中的仁德》，来源《山东理工大学学报（社会科学版）》，2010 年 5 期

束不明，申令不熟，将之罪也。"那些宫女仍不听指挥，把军令当儿戏。于是，孙武不顾吴王的阻挡和反对，毅然将二妃斩首，另派两名分任队长，继续训练。此后无一人不服从命令，"皆中规矩绳墨，不敢出声"。孙武这一招高就高在他敢拿王妃开刀，以正军纪。他清楚地知道斩杀一个王妃所产生的效应远比斩杀 10 个宫女要明显得多。孙武敢来真的，动硬的，做到了令行禁止，为后世提供了一条经验。[491]

According to *Biographies of Sun Tzu and Wu Qi, Records of the Grand Historian*, King Helü of Wu asked Sun Wu to train the palace maids. Sun Wu divided them into two teams and appointed the king's two favorite concubines as team leaders. At first, the palace maids laughed and joked, refusing to follow the commands. Sun Wu repeatedly explained the rules and warned them, "Failure to issue clear orders or ensure that soldiers master them is the commander's fault." The palace maids still refused to follow the commands and treated the military orders as a trifle. As a result, ignoring the obstruction and opposition of the king, Sun Wu resolutely beheaded the two concubines, appointed two others as team leaders, and continued the training. After that, no one disobeyed the orders. "All of them strictly abode by the rules, daring not to make a sound." The wisdom of Sun Wu lies in his daring to target the concubines as an example to reinforce the military discipline. He clearly knew that the effect of beheading one concubine was much better than that of beheading ten palace maids, so he dared to be serious and tough, and achieved prompt execution of orders and strict enforcement of prohibitions. This provides some experience for future generations.[491]

范蠡者，楚国宛三户人（今河南南阳），字少伯，生卒年不可

491　子胜撰《从孙武斩二妃说起》，来源《党的建设》，1995 年 4 期

考，是春秋末年的政治家，事越王勾践二十余年，助勾践灭吴兴越，称霸中国，建立不世之功业，官至越上将军，功成书辞勾践，乘扁舟浮于江湖。[492]

Fan Li, whose courtesy name was Shaobo, was a native of Sanhu, Wan, the State of Chu (now Nanyang, Henan Province). The exact years of his birth and death are unknown. He was a statesman in the late Spring and Autumn Period. He served King Goujian of the State of Yue for more than twenty years, assisting Goujian in destroying the State of Wu and rejuvenating the State of Yue. He helped the State of Yue achieve hegemony, thus accomplishing extraordinary feats. He was promoted to the highest-ranking general of Yue. After achieving success, he submitted his resignation to Goujian, and floated on a small boat in rivers and lakes.[492]

范蠡之所以抛弃权位，坚决出走，毅然斩断名缰利锁的羁绊，是由于他对服侍多年的越王勾践的为人有深刻了解。语云："勇略震主者身危，功盖天下者不赏。"历代君王，对于天下独尊的座位总是怀着深深的忧虑，生怕被他人夺去，因此便疑心重重，总觉得有人在觊觎，于是就要残酷地消灭已知的或潜在的争夺者。勾践就正是一个这样的心地偏狭的君王，他胁迫曾经为他出过死力的功臣文种自杀就是其阴暗灵魂的大暴露。而此点，早已在范蠡的意料之中。[493]

The reason why Fan Li abandoned his power and resolutely resigned, breaking free from the fetters of fame and fortune, lies in his profound understanding of the character of King Goujian of Yue, whom he had served for many years. As the saying goes, "Those whose bravery and strategy threaten the ruler are in danger of their lives, and

---

492　陈红兵撰《范蠡的商业思想解析》，来源《中国商界（下半月）》，2010 年 1 期

493　商聚德撰《范蠡的品格及思想试论》，来源《河北大学学报（哲学社会科学版）》，1998 年 3 期

those whose merits surpass all the others are not rewarded." Throughout history, monarchs were deeply concerned about the throne that made them supreme rulers of the land, worrying that it might be taken away by someone. Therefore, they were full of suspicion, always feeling that someone was coveting it. As a result, they would brutally eliminate known or potential competitors. Goujian was such a narrow-minded king. He once coerced Wen Zhong, a meritorious official who had exerted great efforts for him, to commit suicide. This incident fully exposed his dark nature. In fact, this was within Fan Li's expectations.[493]

范蠡是中国古代的著名人物，在中国军事史、商业史、思想史以及外交史上占有重要地位。他生活于群雄并起、思想激荡的春秋战国之际。在这样一个社会变动的时代，范蠡所展示的杰出政治、军事、外交智慧和经商治产的成功实践，对中国历史文化的发展产生了重要的影响。[494]

As a famous figure in ancient times, Fan Li holds an important position in China's military history, business history, ideological history, and diplomatic history. He lived during the Spring and Autumn Period and the Warring States Period when numerous powerful states coexisted and thoughts were surging. In such an era of social change, Fan Li demonstrated outstanding political, military, and diplomatic wisdom, as well as successful practices in business management, which had a significant impact on the development of Chinese historical culture.[494]

吴起，约生于公元前 440 年（周考王元年），死于前 381 年（周安王二十一年），卫国左氏人。他是战国前期著名的法家学派的代表人物之一，新兴封建地主阶级的政治家，又是当时著名的军事家，历任鲁国的将军，魏国的大将、西河郡守，楚国的苑守、令尹等军

494　刘纪兴撰《范蠡思想研究简论》，来源《江汉论坛》，2006 年 7 期

政要职。[495]

Wu Qi was born around 440 BC (the First Year of King Kao of Zhou) and died in 381 BC (the Twenty-first Year of King An of Zhou). He was a native of Zuoshi, the State of Wei. As a representative of the famous Legalist School in the early Warring States Period, a statesman of the emerging feudal landlord class, and a renowned military strategist at that time, he successively held important military and political positions. These included general in the State of Lu, general and magistrate of Xihe Prefecture in the State of Wei, and official in charge of the imperial garden and prime minister in the State of Chu.[495]

吴起是战国初期著名的军事家、政治家、改革家。一生历仕鲁、魏、楚三国，在内政、军事上都有极高的成就，仕鲁时曾击退齐国的入侵；仕魏时屡次破秦，尽得秦国河西之地，成就魏文侯的霸业；仕楚时主持改革，史称"吴起变法"。后世把他和孙武并称为"孙吴"，著有《吴子》。《吴子》与《孙子》又合称《孙吴兵法》，在中国古代军事典籍中占有重要地位，尤其他与士卒同甘共苦，爱兵如子，为士卒吮疽的团队精神深得后世景仰并成为楷模[496]。

Wu Qi was a famous military strategist, statesman, and reformer in the early Warring States Period. He served in the states of Lu, Wei, and Chu successively and achieved extremely high accomplishments in internal and military affairs. When serving in the State of Lu, he repelled the invasion of the State of Qi; when serving in the State of Wei, he repeatedly defeated the State of Qin and captured all Qin's land west of the Yellow River, contributing to the hegemony of Marquis Wen of Wei; when serving in the State of Chu, he presided over the reform, which

---

495 王贝贝撰《战国时代急需人才的研究》，来源《曲阜师范大学》，2011 年第 4 期

496 叶建华撰《吴起的爱兵效应》，来源《现代企业文化》，2012 年第 10 期

is historically known as "Wu Qi's Reform." Wu Qi and Sun Wu were together called by later generations as "Sun and Wu". Wu Qi's major work was *Wuzi*. *Wuzi* and *Sunzi* are collectively known as *The Art of War of Sun and Wu*, which holds an important position among ancient Chinese military classics. In particular, due to his team spirit of sharing weal and woe with the soldiers, loving them as if they were his own children, and even sucking the carbuncle for the soldiers, Wu Qi was revered by later generations and served as a model for them to learn.[496]

孙膑，战国时期齐国人，据史书记载，"膑生阿鄄之间，膑亦孙武之后世子孙也"（《史记·卷六十五·孙子吴起列传》），因曾受膑刑（去掉膝盖骨），古世人称之为孙膑。其生卒年月史无记载，主要活动于齐威王、齐宣王在位期间（公元前 357 年—前 301 年），著有《孙膑兵法》，是中国战国中期杰出的军事理论家和军事谋略家。庞涓，战国时期魏国人。其出生地、出生年月史无记载，主要活动于魏惠王在位期间（公元前 370—前 319 年），是战国中期魏国的主要将领。庞涓与孙膑青年时曾共学兵法于鬼谷子门下，庞涓早于孙膑出师，后至魏国任将军。因嫉妒孙膑的才能，将其诱至魏国，加以迫害，借故处以膑刑。孙膑逃至齐，成为齐统治集团的智囊人物。孙膑一生的战绩主要是辅佐田忌，在桂陵、马陵两次大战中，大败魏军，创造了"围魏救赵"与"减灶诱敌"两种战法的范例，使齐的霸业奠定了基础。从此，魏国一蹶不振，"诸侯东而朝齐"，孙膑也因之名扬天下。马陵之战后，齐统治集团内部矛盾激化，始终支持孙膑的田忌，在内部斗争中失败，被迫逃去楚国，孙膑从此也不知所终，仅有所著《孙膑兵法》传世。庞涓曾于周显王十五年（公元前 354 年）率八万魏军攻赵，包围赵都邯郸，次年克之。然而在随后的桂陵之战中败于孙膑之手。周显王二十七年（公元前 343 年）庞涓伐韩，后中孙膑减灶之计，在马陵全军覆没，庞涓因此羞愤自杀。[497]

Sun Bin was a native of the State of Qi during the Warring States Period. According to historical records, "Sun Bin, born in the area between E and Juan, was a descendant of Sun Wu" (*Biographies of Sun Tzu and Wu Qi, Volume 65 of Records of the Grand Historian*). He once suffered the Bin penalty (removal of the kneecaps), so he was called Sun Bin. The exact years of his birth and death are unknown. He was mainly active during the reigns of King Wei of Qi and King Xuan of Qi (357 BC - 301 BC). He wrote *The Art of War* and was an outstanding military theorist and strategist in the mid Warring States Period. Pang Juan was a native of the State of Wei during the Warring States Period. His birthplace and birth year are unknown. Mainly active during the reign of King Hui of Wei (370 - 319 BC), he was a major general of the State of Wei in the mid Warring States Period. When Pang Juan and Sun Bin were young, they studied the art of war together under Guiguzi. Pang Juan graduated earlier than Sun Bin and later became a general in the State of Wei. Out of jealousy of Sun Bin's talent, he lured Sun Bin to the State of Wei and persecuted him by deliberately imposing the kneecap-removing penalty on him. Sun Bin escaped to the State of Qi and became a think-tank member for the ruling group of Qi. Sun Bin made great achievements in assisting Tian Ji. In the two major battles in Guiling and Maling, he defeated the Wei army, and created two battle strategies: "besieging Wei to rescue Zhao" and "reducing the number of cooking stoves to lure the enemy," thus laying the foundation for the hegemony of the State of Qi. After that, the State of Wei declined, and "the prince of each state went

---

497　周勋撰《从桂陵、马陵之战看孙膑、庞涓》，来源《海南广播电视大学学报》，2005 年 1 期

eastward to pay homage to the King of Qi." This made Sun Bin a well-known figure. After the Battle of Maling, the internal contradictions within the ruling group of the State of Qi intensified. Tian Ji, who had been supporting Sun Bin, failed in the internal struggle and was forced to flee to the State of Chu. Sun Bin's subsequent whereabouts are unknown, and only his book *The Art of War* has been passed down. In the 15th year of King Xian of Zhou (354 BC), Pang Juan led 80,000 Wei soldiers to attack Zhao. The army surrounded Handan, the capital of Zhao, and captured it the next year. However, Pang Juan was defeated by Sun Bin in the subsequent Battle of Guiling. In the 27th year of King Xian of Zhou (343 BC), Pang Juan attacked the State of Han, but he fell into Sun Bin's trap of reducing the number of cooking stoves. His entire army was annihilated at Maling, and Pang Juan committed suicide out of shame and indignation.[497]

兵书云：陷之死地而后生，置之亡地而后存。把这一策略运用得最成功，最著名的战例，莫过于汉代韩信的背水一战了。公元前204年10月，刘邦派韩信攻取赵国。韩信遂率三军东进，直逼太行山交通要冲井陉。赵王和成安君陈余闻讯，忙调集20万重兵，把住了井陉的重要隘口。地形、兵力众寡对比对韩信都十分不利。继而，韩信又一反常规把军队排布在绵蔓河边，面对强敌，背后浊浪滔滔，实乃死地也。陈余大喜，自以为韩信必败无疑。事实恰恰相反，鏖战之后，陈余被斩，赵王被俘，赵国一战而亡。[498]

As the military classics state, "Only in a desperate situation can one fight back and survive." The most famous and successful case in which this strategy is applied is undoubtedly Han Xin's battle of fighting with his back to the river in the Han Dynasty. In October 204 BC, Liu Bang

498　韩宝章撰《从绝境求生说起》，来源《中国企业家》，1996年8期

dispatched Han Xin to attack the State of Zhao. Han Xin led his army eastward and directly approached Jingxing, a strategic pass of the Taihang Mountains. Upon hearing the news, the King of Zhao and Chen Yu, the Lord of Cheng'an, immediately mobilized 200,000 elite soldiers to hold the important pass of Jingxing. The terrain and the troop-number contrast were quite unfavorable to Han Xin. Then, contrary to the normal practice, Han Xin arranged his troops by the Mianman River. Facing the powerful enemy and having the surging turbid waves behind, it was indeed a desperate situation. Chen Yu was overjoyed, believing that Han Xin was bound to be defeated. However, the fact was just the opposite. After a fierce battle, Chen Yu was beheaded, the King of Zhao was captured, and the State of Zhao was destroyed.[498]

诸葛亮，字孔明，琅邪阳都人，是诸葛丰的后人。诸葛亮幼年时父亲诸葛珪就去世了，跟随叔父诸葛玄。诸葛玄曾在袁术手下做官，后来投奔了刘表。诸葛玄死后，诸葛亮便隐居起来，耕种田地，他身高八尺，喜好吟诵《梁父吟》。他常常自比管仲、乐毅，而当时的人都不这样认为，只有少数的有识之士才知道他真的有这样的才能。刘备屯兵新野的时候，徐庶向刘备推荐诸葛亮，刘备于是到隆中见诸葛亮，一共去了三次才见到。这也就是历史上著名的三顾茅庐。诸葛亮最终加入了刘备的军事集团，在回答刘备的询问时，他总结历史，预测形势，向刘备提出了一个转弱为强的战略，也就是《隆中对》[499]。

Zhuge Liang, known as Kongming by courtesy name, was a native of Yangdu, Langya. He was a descendant of Zhuge Feng. When Zhuge Liang was a child, his father Zhuge Gui died, so he was brought up by his uncle Zhuge Xuan. Zhuge Xuan once served as an official under Yuan

---

499 《正史上真实的诸葛亮到底有多厉害?》，腾讯网 www.qq.com，2019 年 1 月 28 日

Shu and later sought refuge with Liu Biao. After Zhuge Xuan's death, Zhuge Liang went into seclusion and worked in the fields. He was eight feet tall and fond of reciting *Ode to Liangfu*. He often compared himself to Guan Zhong and Yue Yi, but at that time, most people did not think so. Only a few insightful people knew that he truly had such talents. When Liu Bei stationed his troops in Xinye, Xu Shu recommended Zhuge Liang to him. Liu Bei then went to Longzhong to meet Zhuge Liang. He didn't meet him until the third visit. This is the famous story of "Three Visits to the Thatched Cottage". Eventually, Zhuge Liang joined Liu Bei's military group. When answering Liu Bei's questions, he summarized history, predicted the situation, and put forward a strategy to turn weakness into strength, which was embodied in the *Longzhong Plan*.[499]

诸葛亮在隆中对没有实现的情况下去世，使其成为夸谈。但依据史书，纵观时下情形，隆中对绝对是刘备最好的选择。所谓谋事在人，成事在天[500]。

Zhuge Liang died before the "Longzhong Plan" was realized, making it seem like an empty talk. However, according to historical records and considering the current situation at that time, this was definitely the best choice for Liu Bei. As the saying goes, "Man proposes, God disposes."[500]

《隆中对》是诸葛亮"观其大略"之结晶，也是他在刘备三顾茅庐时向其提出的兴复汉室、谋取天下的战略策划书。刘备说："孤之有孔明，犹鱼之有水也。"最看重的就是诸葛亮这种运筹帷幄的战略谋划才能。曹操率军南下的时候，诸葛亮的自然反应是"事急矣，请奉命求救于孙将军"。后孙刘联军打败曹操，奠定了三国鼎

500　《百年动乱——诸葛亮的"隆中对"为什么会实现不了》，腾讯新闻（腾讯网）www.qq.com，2019 年 12 月 27 日

立的基础。尽管孙刘也存在很多矛盾，但诸葛亮一直主张坚持"联孙抗曹"，即使在夷陵之战后，也主动缓和吴蜀关系。这就是"大略"，大略是管根本的和管长远的。诸葛亮的聪明，不是所谓的"机灵"和"精明"，而是战略上的远见和定力。[501]

The *Longzhong Plan* fully embodied Zhuge Liang's vision of "grasping the overall situation". It was also the strategic plan he presented to Liu Bei when Liu Bei paid three visits to him in the thatched cottage, aiming to restore the Han Dynasty and seize power. Liu Bei said, "For me, Kongming is like water to a fish." What he valued most was Zhuge Liang's ability to formulate strategies and make decisions. When Cao Cao led his army southward, Zhuge Liang's natural reaction was, "The situation is urgent. Please allow me to seek help from General Sun." Later, the alliance of Sun Quan and Liu Bei defeated Cao Cao, laying the foundation for the tripartite confrontation of the Three Kingdoms. Although there were many contradictions between Sun Quan and Liu Bei, Zhuge Liang stuck to the policy of "allying with Sun Quan to resist Cao Cao". Even after the Battle of Yiling, he took the initiative to ease the relationship between the Kingdom of Shu and the Kingdom of Wu. This was the "overall situation", which concerned the fundamental and long-term aspects. Zhuge Liang's intelligence was not the so-called "cleverness" and "shrewdness", but rather strategic foresight and determination.[501]

"三分天下诸葛亮，一统江山刘伯温。前朝军师诸葛亮，后朝军师刘伯温"是民间广泛流传的说法[502]。

---

501 《毛泽东评点〈隆中对〉：诸葛亮致命战略失误在何处》，新浪军事（新浪网），www.sina.com.cn，2017 年 3 月 2 日

502 《明代刘基：三分天下诸葛亮，一统江山刘伯温》，温都王 wendu.cn，2018 年 10 月 23 日

The saying "Zhuge Liang brought about the tri-partition of the country, while Liu Bowen reunified the country. Zhuge Liang was the military advisor of the previous dynasty, and Liu Bowen was the military advisor of the later dynasty" is widely spread among the people.[502]

刘基（1311.7.1—1375.5.16），汉族，字伯温，处州青田县南田乡（今属浙江省温州市文成县）人，故称刘青田，元末明初军事家、政治家、文学家，明朝开国元勋。明洪武三年（1370）封诚意伯，故又称刘诚意。武宗正德九年追赠太师，谥号文成，后人称他刘文成、文成公[503]。

Liu Ji (July 1, 1311 - May 16, 1375), of the Han ethnicity, with the courtesy name Bowen, was a native of Nantian Town, Qingtian County, Chuzhou (now part of Wencheng County, Wenzhou City, Zhejiang Province). Therefore, he was also known as Liu Qingtian. He was a military strategist, statesman, and litterateur in the late Yuan Dynasty and the early Ming Dynasty, as well as one of the founding fathers of the Ming Dynasty. In the Third Year of Emperor Hongwu's Reign (1370), he was conferred the title of Marquess of Cheng Yi, so he was also known as Liu Chengyi. In the Ninth Year of Emperor Zhengde's Reign, he was posthumously granted the title of Grand Preceptor, with the posthumous title Wencheng. Therefore, he was called Liu Wencheng or Duke Wencheng by later generations.[503]

是时，群雄并立，天下未定，朱元璋为求尽快翦灭群雄，急于向刘基问征讨大计。刘基从容分析大势，他为朱元璋制订"征讨大计"。并提出先灭陈友谅，后取张士诚的战略，为朱元璋所采纳。[504]

At that time, numerous figures rose simultaneously, and the country

---

503 《三分天下诸葛亮，一统江山刘伯温?》，腾讯网 www.qq.com，2018 年 2 月 10 日

504 陈守文、何向荣撰《论刘基在建立朱明王朝中的历史作用》，来源《浙江工贸职业技术学院学报》，2006 年第 2 期

was in a chaotic state. In order to quickly eliminate the warlords, Zhu Yuanzhang earnestly solicited a grand strategy of conquest from Liu Ji. Liu Ji calmly analyzed the general situation and formulated one for Zhu Yuanzhang. He proposed the strategy of eliminating Chen Youliang first and then dealing with Zhang Shicheng, which was adopted by Zhu Yuanzhang.[504]

为辅佐朱元璋完成帝业、开创明朝，刘基做出了杰出贡献：在军事上，刘基不仅提出了"时务十八策""先陈后张"的战略性规划，而且作为朱元璋的最主要参谋，策划了"龙江之战""江州战役""鄱阳湖战役"等关键性与决定性的战役[505]。

Liu Ji made outstanding contributions to assisting Zhu Yuanzhang in achieving the imperial cause and establishing the Ming Dynasty. Militarily, he put forward strategic plans such as "eighteen strategies on current affairs" and "eliminating Chen Youliang before dealing with Zhang Shicheng". In addition, as Zhu Yuanzhang's most important advisor, he planned decisive battles such as the "Battle of Longjiang", the "Battle of Jiangzhou", and the "Battle of Poyang Lake".[505]

明代后期，统治者自身统治已病入膏肓，并在内地农民起义和东北建州女真的联合打击下趋于衰亡，其军事重心仍偏重于北方。而明代中叶，统治者所面临的军事压力是全方位的。不仅要面对前期未处理彻底的北方威胁，"在整个明代中叶，蒙古人是中国的民族敌人。在北方边境与蒙古人的战争是最持久、费用最大和最危险的战争"，是为"北虏"问题。在南方，特别是嘉靖中期以后，倭患问题亦凸显出来，亦如王世贞所言："自壬子始，而东南之兵亡日不与倭战。"是为"南倭"问题。[506]

505　同上

506　李德锋撰《唐顺之军事思想探析》，来源《宁夏师范学院学报》，2011 年 4 期

In the late Ming Dynasty, the rulers themselves were on their last legs in terms of governance. Under the joint attacks of peasant uprisings in the interior and the Jianzhou Jurchen in the northeast, the Ming Dynasty was on the verge of collapse, but it still placed military focus on the north. In the mid Ming Dynasty, the rulers faced all-round military pressure. They had to deal with the northern threat that had not been completely resolved in the previous period. "Throughout the mid Ming Dynasty, the Mongols were China's ethnic enemies. The wars with the Mongols on the northern border were the most enduing, costly, and dangerous." This was the problem of the "Northern Barbarians". In the south, especially after the middle period of Emperor Jiajing's Reign, the problem of Japanese pirates became prominent. As Wang Shizhen said, "From the Renzi year, the soldiers in the southeast fought against the Japanese pirates every day." This was the problem of the "Southern Japanese Pirates".[506]

嘉靖至万历年间，明朝遭受"南倭北虏"的双重危机。戚继光训练"戚家军"，创立"鸳鸯阵"，南灭倭寇北上戍边，为明朝消除倭患、维护边疆稳定做出了重要贡献。[507]

From Emperor Jiajing's Reign to Emperor Wanli's Reign, the Ming Dynasty was plagued by the dual crisis of "the Southern Japanese Pirates and the Northern Barbarians". Qi Jiguang trained the "Qi Family Army" and created the "Mandarin Duck Formation". He eliminated the Japanese pirates in the south and then went north to garrison the border, making important contributions to eliminating the Japanese pirate menace and maintaining border stability.[507]

---

507 王建超撰《戚继光对中国武术和军事发展的影响研究》，来源《武术研究》，2018年2期

戚继光创建的戚家军在明朝抗倭过程中独放异彩，先是转战东南各省无一败绩，与其他友军一起平定了肆虐百年之久的倭寇之患。尔后戚继光又到蓟镇训练军队，守护北京数十年不受侵犯。在这个过程中随着环境和作战对象的改变，戚家军的作战模式也随之改变，战斗力快速提升。但戚家军并非完美无缺，其也有众多局限。[508]

The Qi Family Army shone brightly during the Ming Dynasty's resistance against Japanese pirates. First, the soldiers fought in the southeastern provinces without a single defeat. Together with other friendly troops, they eliminated the Japanese pirate menace that had been rampant for a hundred years. Then, Qi Jiguang trained the army in Jizhen, protecting Beijing from being invaded for decades. During this process, with the changes in the environment and combat targets, the Qi Family Army changed its combat modes accordingly, and rapidly improved its combat effectiveness. However, the Qi Family Army was not perfect and still had many limitations.[508]

历史人物常常以个人带动他人或者多人，致使更多人进行效仿，从而解封落后的社会生产力。每个历史事件都有正反两面的历史影响，其历史事件的正面效果也有负面评价，负面效果也有正面评价，形成一种唯物主义的历史。

Historical figures often inspire others with their own actions, causing more people to imitate them. This will literate the backward social productive forces. Every historical event has both positive and negative impacts. The positive effects of historical events may be negatively evaluated, while their negative effects may be positively evaluated. This is a materialist view of history.

508　马冲、赵毅撰《戚家军战力发展研究——从浙江到蓟镇》，来源《辽宁师范大学学报（社会科学版）》，2018 年 2 期

一天只有二十四小时，工作和休息已经占据了每个人绝大多数的固有时间。故此，人类顺势而行和顺天而行能够降低动乱，进而解放生产力，获得更多的生产资料，都是一种势在必行的举动。

There are only 24 hours in a day, and work and rest already occupy most of everyone's fixed time. Therefore, it is imperative for human beings to act in line with the trend and the will of nature. This helps reduce turmoil so as to liberate the productive forces and get more means of production.

人类如果放眼宇宙，就会得出这样一个结论：天无尽，地可测，人有寿。这句话意思是：天是没有尽头的，地是可以测量的，人的寿命是有限的。

If human beings look at the universe, they will come to the conclusion: The sky is boundless, the earth can be measured, and human life is limited.

其要表达的意思是天比地大，地比人大。寿命有限的人不是天下无敌，无论做什么事情都只能有限地斗争，不能掌握全局。世人应该顺天应地解决诸多问题。

This means that the sky is bigger than the earth, and the earth is bigger than humans. People with a limited lifespan are not invincible in the world. No matter what they do, they can only make limited efforts instead of controlling the overall situation. People should solve problems in accordance with the will of nature.

先明察秋毫，后秋毫无犯。做人做事用刚用柔，都离不开实际情况，反恐亦是如此。即根据反恐刚柔程度可以划分为"阴柔反恐""阳刚反恐""刚柔并济反恐"三种方式。

One should be perceptive of the slightest detail before committing no offense. Whether one conducts himself and handles affairs toughly or flexibly depends on the actual situation, and this is also the case for counter-terrorism. That is to say, based on the level of toughness, there are three counter-terrorism methods: "tackling terrorism flexibly", "tackling terrorism toughly", and "tackling terrorism both flexibly and toughly".

在中国传统文化里，阳刚和阴柔的文化特征是共存的，只有主次之别。在一决胜负的情况下，比起"阳刚反恐"和"刚柔并济反恐"，"阴柔反恐"不缺客观性、科学性、基础性，成为"幼、童、少、青、壮、中、老"这七类人统一合理的选择。就以中国黑社会问题为例子，则能看出阴柔反恐，是如何不输给阳刚反恐和刚柔并济反恐。

In traditional Chinese culture, the elements of toughness and flexibility coexist. The only difference is which one takes precedence. In a case of determining the final result, compared with "tackling terrorism toughly" and "tackling terrorism both flexibly and toughly", "tackling terrorism flexibly" is more objective, more scientific and more fundamental. Therefore, it is a unified and reasonable choice for people in seven age brackets, namely, infants, children, adolescents, young adults, prime adults, middle-aged adults, and senior adults. When addressing the underworld problem in China, we can see how "tackling terrorism flexibly" is not inferior to "tackling terrorism toughly" and "tackling terrorism both flexibly and toughly".

在现代中国，有一种解决黑社会问题的思路，乃是大家不跟黑社会说话，黑社会就会慢性消亡。然而，有的中国人没有骨气，向黑恶势力屈服，愿意给国家丢脸。再加上中国现代社会，长期女少男多，有男人愿意和女黑社会成员结婚，这也助长了黑社会继续存活于中国社会的势头。

In modern China, there is a way to address the underworld problem, that is, if people refuse to associate with underworld gangs, they will gradually decline. However, some spineless people are willing to yield to evil forces and bring shame to the country. In addition, in modern Chinese society, there has been a long-term imbalance with more men than women. Some men are willing to marry female members of the underworld, which contributes to the survival of the underworld in society.

在 20—21 世纪，中国社会有很多的势利眼，愿意和黑社会同流合污。为此，站在黑社会对立面的这些中国人就要做到多柔少刚，少争少斗，达到柔弱胜刚强的效果，避免自己也触犯法律，这就是中国法治社会的势头。

In the 20th and 21st centuries, there are many snobs in Chinese society. They are willing to collude with underworld gangs. Therefore, people who stand on the opposite side of the underworld should be more flexible than tough, and engage in less contention and fighting. In this way, they can achieve the effect of flexibility overcoming toughness, and avoid violating the law. This is a tendency in China's law-based society.

有人爱用柔弱政策不代表这个人软弱可欺。毕竟，"自然而然"也是公事公办的一种，而且，还能代替"人定胜天"，故此，多柔易胜，多刚易败。

Some people prefer applying flexible policies, but this does not mean that they are weak. After all, "following the natural course" is a way of handling affairs impartially, and it can even replace the idea of "man can conquer nature". Therefore, more flexibility tends to lead to success, while more toughness tends to lead to failure.

兵法贵守不贵攻，建功立业之心不死，生产资料被消灭，民不聊生必定降临。人在乱世社会生死未卜如常事，和平规律是阴是柔，战争规律是阳是刚，将和平规律与战争规律进行对比，能悟出似阴非阴，似柔非柔，似阳非阳，似刚非刚的道理。比如，在二战时期前后，德国纳粹元首希特勒也没有办法逃脱"趁势崛起""落井下石""雪中送炭""锦上添花""墙倒众人推"等一系列的历史命运。

The art of war values defense more than offense. If the ambition to attain supreme dominance is not abandoned, the means of production will be destroyed, and the people will inevitably suffer. In a chaotic society, people's lives are often at stake. The law of peace is flexibility, while the law of war is toughness. By comparing the law of peace with the law of war, we can realize that there is no absolute flexibility or absolute toughness. For example, before and during the Second World War, Adolf Hitler, the head of Nazi Germany, could not escape a series of historical destinies, which can be described as "rising with the trend", "striking a person when he is down", "giving help in time of need", "making something already good even better", and "kicking a falling man".

阿道夫·希特勒，纳粹德国元首，第二次世界大战元凶。1889年4月20日生于奥地利。曾自学绘画与建筑。1913年移居慕尼黑。"一战"时在陆军服役，并获铁十字勋章。1919年9月加入德国工人党（纳粹党）从事宣传工作。1921年成为该党主席。1923年11月策划啤酒店暴动，事败被捕，在狱中写成《我的奋斗》一书，宣扬复仇主义和种族主义。1933年1月制造"国会纵火案"，夺取政权，任总理。1934年自称元首。开始疯狂迫害与屠杀共产党人、进步人士和犹太人，镇压工人运动、实行法西斯独裁，并积极扩军备战。1936年武装干涉西班牙内战，并与日本签订反共条约。1938年任德军最高统帅，并占领奥地利和捷克斯洛伐克的苏台德地区。1939年3月占领捷全境，9月入侵波兰，挑起世界大战。1941年6月撕毁《苏德互不侵犯条约》，进攻苏联。在北非阿拉曼和斯大林格勒战役后，军队实力大减。1945年4月30日，在柏林被苏军攻占后，他和爱娃同时自杀，结束了罪恶的一生[509]。

---

509 《1945年4月30日 战争狂人希特勒自杀》，中国网 www.china.com.cn，2009年4月27日

Adolf Hitler, the head of Nazi Germany, was the prime culprit of the Second World War. He was born in Austria on April 20, 1889. He once studied painting and architecture by himself. In 1913, he moved to Munich. During the First World War, he served in the army and was awarded the Iron Cross. In September 1919, he joined the German Workers' Party (the Nazi Party), and engaged in propaganda work. In 1921, he became the chairman of the party. In November 1923, he plotted the Beer Hall Putsch, but he failed and was arrested. While in prison, he wrote the book *My Struggle*, preaching revenge and racism. In January 1933, he staged the "Reichstag Fire" to seize power and became the chancellor. In 1934, he proclaimed himself the head of Nazi Germany. Then, he began to brutally persecute and massacre Communists, progressives and Jews, suppress the labor movement, implement fascist dictatorship, and actively expand the military and prepare for war. In 1936, he intervened in the Spanish Civil War by force and signed an anti-communist treaty with Japan. In 1938, he served as the Supreme Commander of the German army and occupied Austria and the Sudetenland region of Czechoslovakia. In March 1939, he occupied the whole territory of Czechoslovakia. In September 1939, he invaded Poland and initiated the Second World War. In June 1941, he tore up *Non-aggression Pact between Germany and the Soviet Union* and launched an attack on the Soviet Union. After the battle of El Alamein in North Africa and the Battle of Stalingrad, the military strength of the German army was greatly weakened. On April 30, 1945, after Berlin was captured by the Soviet army, he and Eva simultaneously committed suicide, bringing an end to his sinful life.[509]

"大鱼吃小鱼，小鱼吃虾米"和"比上不足比下有余"是一对富有强弱属性的辩证法。大自然的淳朴是将无私和有私相结合，不管一个人先天优势和缺陷有多少，都要提高自己，而不是摧毁他人。这是努力在弱肉强食的社会里面进行艰苦卓绝的奋斗方式，避免腐朽文化侵蚀自己，毁了自己都不自知。

Sayings such as "Big fish eat small fish, and small fish eat shrimps" and "Not good enough to compare with those above, but better than those below" represent a pair of dialectical relationships concerning the nature of strength and weakness. The simplicity of nature lies in its combination of selflessness with self-interest. No matter how many innate advantages and disadvantages one has, he should strive to improve himself instead of destroying others. This is a way of arduous struggle in a society where the strong prey on the weak, and one should avoid being imperceptibly eroded by decadent culture.

国家长期反恐，需要个人身心都健康，政府还要规范人群行为准则，协调统一部署和规划行为准则，避免国家卷入太多是是非非之中，反恐才能一帆风顺。比如伊斯兰教的穆罕默德发动过圣战，他是伊斯兰教教徒口中的"圣者"。可就是这样一位开宗立派的大人物，其宗教教义也被邪恶人士利用，加以"发扬光大"。由此，我们可以看出阳刚反恐的缺陷有多么严重，其反恐功效充其量只能算是一把"双刃剑"。

A country's long-term anti-terrorism campaign requires people to be healthy both physically and mentally. The government should regulate people's behavior, carry out coordinated and unified deployment, and formulate the code of conduct. Only when the country is not involved in too many disputes can the anti-terrorism campaign be promoted smoothly. For example, Muhammad of Islam launched a jihad, and he is regarded as the "saint" by Muslims. However, even for such a great figure who established a religion, his religious teachings have been exploited by evil people and "carried forward" in a distorted matter. From this, we can see that the approach of tackling terrorism toughly has serious flaws, and its anti-terrorism effect is at best a double-edged sword.

穆罕默德出生于麦加古来氏部落的哈希姆家庭。他建立了一个今天拥有信徒数约占地球总人口数五分之一的宗教——伊斯兰教，建立了世界上第一个伊斯兰国家，许多人认为穆罕默德是历史上最有影响的人物之一。他是穆斯林公认的伊斯兰教的先知，中国的穆斯林普遍尊称为穆圣。[510]

Muhammad was born into the Hashim family of the Quraysh tribe in Mecca. He established Islam, a religion whose followers account for about one-fifth of the world's total population, and established the first Islamic state in the world. Therefore, he is regarded by many people as one of the most influential figures in history. He is recognized by Muslims as the Prophet of Islam. Among the Chinese Muslims, he is respectfully called the Prophet Muhammad.[510]

穆罕默德（570—632 年）出生于麦加城古来氏部落的哈希姆家族，生前丧父，六岁丧母，后由伯父艾布抚养成人。穆罕默德创立伊斯兰教，并统一阿拉伯半岛，经过了一个斗争的过程。12 岁时，他随伯父到叙利亚和巴勒斯坦经商，游历了许多地方，积累了丰富的社会知识和经验。大约在 25 岁时，他受雇于麦加富孀赫蒂彻，为她经商，后来又与赫蒂彻结婚，进入上层社会。穆罕默德的这次成婚，为其以后事业的成功提供了优厚的物质条件和社会地位。[511]

Muhammad (570 - 632) was born into the Hashim family of the Quraysh tribe in Mecca. He lost his father before his birth and his mother at the age of six, and was later raised by his uncle Abu. Muhammad established Islam and unified the Arabian Peninsula through a series of

---

510 张畅撰《穆罕默德平等思想探析》，来源《太原大学学报》，2010 年 2 期

511 高岚撰《伊斯兰教的起源和阿拉伯的政治统一》，来源《云南教育学院学报》，1994 年 4 期

struggles. At the age of 12, he accompanied his uncle on business trips to Syria and Palestine, traveling to many places and accumulating abundant social knowledge and experience. At around the age of 25, he was employed by Khadijah, a wealthy widow in Mecca, to conduct business for her. Later, he married her, thus entering the upper social circles. Muhammad's marriage provided him with favorable material conditions and social status for the success of his later career.[511]

麦加是阿拉伯半岛的宗教和商业中心，地位十分重要，要完成统一大业，必须征服麦加。因此，穆罕默德决心实行"圣战"揭开统一战争的序幕。"圣战"是为了信仰而战，为保卫安拉之道而战，它的原则是为了"自卫、名誉、财产、传道"而战。圣战是每个穆斯林应尽的一项宗教义务。参加"圣战"的人可分得战利品，殉道者可升天堂。参加"圣战"的穆斯林必须奋勇前进，"不得以背向敌"。"圣战"实质上是在伊斯兰教旗帜下进行的统一战争。在这样的名义下，通过一系列的武装斗争，穆罕默德率领穆斯林军队于630年征服了麦加，使伊斯兰教力量空前壮大，并迅速向这个半岛的各地传播。到632年穆罕默德去世时，阿拉伯半岛的政治统一已大体实现。[512]

As the religious and commercial center of the Arabian Peninsula, Mecca holds a very important position. To complete the great cause of unification, one must conquer Mecca. Therefore, Muhammad was determined to launch the war of unification with a "jihad". "Jihad" is a fight for faith, a fight to defend the path of Allah. Sticking to principles of "self-defense, honor, property, and preaching", Jihad is a religious obligation that every Muslim should fulfill. Those who participate in

---

512　高岚撰《伊斯兰教的起源和阿拉伯的政治统一》，来源《云南教育学院学报》，1994 年 4 期

the "jihad" can share spoils, and those who were martyrized can enter paradise. Muslims participating in the "jihad" must move forward bravely and "should not turn their backs to the enemy." In essence, the "jihad" was a war of unification carried out under the banner of Islam. Under this name, through a series of armed struggles, Muhammad led the Muslim army to conquer Mecca in 630, making the strength of Islam grow unprecedentedly and spread rapidly to various parts of the Arabian Peninsula. When Muhammad died in 632, the political unification of the Arabian Peninsula had been largely achieved.[512]

伊斯兰教是主张宗教信仰自由，倡导和平、博爱、宽容及完善一切美德的宗教。作为伊斯兰教的核心理念，宽容仁爱主要表现在尊重人类尊严、认同人类差异、主张信仰自由、提倡宽以待人、秉持平和心态、构建和谐关系[513]。

Islam advocates freedom of religious belief and promotes peace, fraternity, tolerance, and the improvement of all virtues. As the core concepts of Islam, tolerance and benevolence are mainly manifested in respecting human dignity, recognizing human differences, advocating freedom of belief, promoting leniency towards others, maintaining a peaceful mindset, and building harmonious relationships.[513]

可是，在伊斯兰教中却出现了伊斯兰极端主义。伊斯兰极端主义在全球范围内都有"苗头"，有反社会和反人类的势头。

However, Islamic extremism has emerged within Islam. Islamic extremism has shown signs globally and has a tendency to be anti-social and anti-human.

与其他当代伊斯兰思潮相比，伊斯兰极端主义具有以下鲜明特

---

513 《专家学者谈伊斯兰教：宽容仁爱是处世基本原则》，中国新闻网新闻（中国新闻网），www.chinanews.com，2014 年 7 月 16 日

点：一是披着宗教外衣且有明确的政治主张；二是具有一定的组织基础和经济基础；三是以暴力、恐怖为主要活动形式；四是往往与恐怖主义、民族分裂主义相纠合。[514]

Compared with other contemporary Islamic ideological trends, Islamic extremism has the following distinct characteristics: First, it is under the guise of religion and has clear political claims; second, it has a certain organizational and economic foundation; third, it mainly takes violent and terrorist activities as its form; fourth, it is often entangled with terrorism and ethnic separatism.[514]

伊斯兰教教义裂变出伊斯兰极端主义，这是邪恶分子在"拉大旗作虎皮"，他们用他人思想来包装自己，伪装自己是好人在做好事。实际上，伊斯兰极端主义就是一种破坏思想，伊斯兰极端主义分子就是一群寄生虫，他们就是在从事破坏活动。

The splitting of Islamic extremism from Islamic doctrines shows that some evil people are "using a great banner as a protective shield." They use the ideas of others to package themselves and pretend to be good people doing good deeds. In fact, Islamic extremism is a destructive ideology, and Islamic extremists are parasites who are engaged in destructive activities.

十年河东，十年河西。在 21 世纪，伊斯兰教圣战思想已经失去了昔日崇高的光环，成了恐怖主义的一部分，是极端化的代名词，成为恐怖分子从事危害社会的思想工具。

"The wheel of fortune turns every ten years." In the 21st century, the idea of jihad in Islam has lost its lofty halo. It has become part of terrorism, a synonym for extremism, and an ideological tool used by

---

514　徐浩淼撰《伊斯兰极端主义的概念阐释》，来源《俄罗斯中亚东欧研究》，2006 年
　　2 期

terrorists to engage in activities harmful to society.

由于阳刚反恐有浓浓历史后遗症的缘故，阳刚反恐不能算是解决恐怖主义的百年大计。在很长的一段时间内，阳刚反恐只能作为解决恐怖主义的后备道路。

The approach of tackling terrorism toughly has strong historical aftermaths, so it cannot be regarded as a long-term solution to the issue of terrorism. For a long time in the future, this approach can only serve as a backup option for dealing with the issue of terrorism.

这也足以证明众口难调，人各有志，其道路都是自己选择的，与人无干。故此，有人幻想改变社会并不可取，人类顶多只能将事物的版本进行改变，其本质还是同出一辙。

This is sufficient to prove that it is difficult to satisfy all people's tastes, because different people have different aspirations. The paths they choose are based on their own decisions and have nothing to do with others. Therefore, it is not advisable to attempt to transform society. Humanity can at most change the version of things, but the essence remains the same.

最好的准备，最坏的打算。历史证明，连不义之师都不敢"处处用刚"，也需要韬光养晦，正义之师更要"多柔少刚"，以免矫枉过正。

Prepare for the best and expect the worst. History has proven that even an unjust army dare not "use toughness all the time". Instead, it needs to hide its capabilities and bide its time. A just army should "be more flexible than tough" to avoid going to extremes in rectifying a deviation.

休养生息在现代社会也不会过时，这是阴柔反恐的魅力，阳刚反恐所不能及，实乃以柔克刚。虽然，刚柔并济反恐，能够有轻有重，柔为轻，刚为重，避免反恐隔靴搔痒和过犹不及，取得较好的平衡点，有比较强的实用性。但是，刚柔并济反恐是一种混合手段，反恐和恐袭都可以使用。

The concept of recuperation is not obsolete even in modern society. This is the charm of the approach of tackling terrorism flexibly, which is absent in the approach of tackling terrorism toughly. It can be called beating toughness with flexibility. The approach of tackling terrorism both flexibly and toughly embody different degrees of intensity. It can avoid the pitfalls of dealing with terrorism superficially or going too far, and achieve a better balance. Therefore, it is practical. However, the combination of toughness and flexibility is a mixed method, which can be applied by both anti-terrorism forces and terrorists.

犹如面对国家恐怖主义，侵略和反侵略都可以一手为刚，一手为柔，这就证明刚柔并济反恐，也会被侵略者所利用。国家反抗暴行判断正确能使自己耀武扬威，判断错误则使自己弃甲曳兵。

When facing national terrorism, both aggressors and anti-aggressors can adopt a combination of toughness and flexibility. This shows that the combination of toughness and flexibility can also be exploited by aggressors. When a country resists atrocities, a correct judgment can make it demonstrate its power, while an incorrect judgment can make it vanquished by the enemy.

灭亡中国是抗日战争时期日本侵华的基本政策，但其侵华策略则根据形势的变化而不断改变。纵观日本的侵华策略，主要经历了从不扩大方针向全面侵华战争的转变；从速胜决战向持久消极战的转变；从以军事进攻为主向军事进攻与政治攻势并举的转变；从有条件求和向无条件投降的转变。这些转变并非日本侵略者的主观意愿，而是决定于中日双方军事力量的消长，中国和世界反法西战场胜负的趋向。[515]

The annihilation of China was Japan's basic policy during its invasion of China, but its invasion strategies constantly changed according to the situation. Generally speaking, Japan's invasion strategies mainly underwent the transformation from the non-expansion policy to comprehensive aggression; from a quick victory strategy to a protracted and passive war strategy; from mainly relying on military offensives to combining military offensives with political offensives; and from seeking peace with conditions to unconditional surrender. These transformations were not driven by the subjective wishes of the Japanese invaders but were determined by the changes in the military strength of China and Japan as well as the trend of victory or defeat in the Chinese and global anti-fascist battlefields.[515]

1931 年的九一八事变，揭开了中国人民全民族抗击日本侵略者的历史序幕。面对日本帝国主义的入侵，作为执政党的国民党，经历了一个不抵抗、抵抗、消极抵抗的转变过程；而对中共，国民党也经历了一个军事解决到政治解决的策略变迁。纵观九一八事变到 1945 年 8 月日本宣布投降这 14 年的历史，国民党的政策变化大致经历了反共和日、准备抗日、联共抗日、消极抗日四个阶段。[516]

The September 18th Incident in 1931 marked the beginning of the Chinese people's nationwide resistance against the Japanese invaders. In the face of the invasion by Japanese imperialism, the Kuomintang, as the ruling party, went through a transformation from non-resistance to resistance and then to passive resistance. In dealing with the Communist

---

515　于耀洲撰《试分析日本在全面侵华战争中策略的演变》，来源《辽宁师范大学学报》，2003 年 2 期

516　杨志文撰《抗日战争中国民党对日、对中共政策变迁浅析》，来源《党史研究与教学》，1996 年 5 期

Party of China, the Kuomintang also underwent a strategic change from pursuing a military solution to seeking a political one. From the September 18th Incident to Japan's announcement of surrender in August 1945, a period that spanned 14 years, the policies of the Kuomintang roughly went through four stages: opposing the CPC and allying with Japan, preparing for the War of Resistance against Japan, allying with the CPC to resist Japan, and passively resisting Japan.[516]

国家有难，恐怖主义就会猖獗，个人就会不幸。人步入社会就要学会努力奋斗，自强不息。人是有缺陷的，人不互相比较长处，而是去弥补自己短处，才能在社会上有所作为。所以，在反恐领域，"阳刚反恐"输给"刚柔并济反恐"，"刚柔并济反恐"输给"阴柔反恐"。

When a country is in distress, terrorism will run rampant, and people will suffer misfortunes. Once a person enters society, he should learn to strive unremittingly for self-improvement. Everyone has flaws. Only when people focus on making up for their own weaknesses rather than comparing their strengths can they achieve success in society. Therefore, as far as anti-terrorism methods are concerned, "tackling terrorism toughly" is inferior to "tackling terrorism both flexibly and toughly", and "tackling terrorism both flexibly and toughly" is inferior to "tackling terrorism flexibly".

中国五行学说认为世间万物相生相克。恐怖主义是一种唯我独尊的思想，中国文化博大精深，兼容并蓄，薪火相传。中国文化对付恐怖主义乃是以强胜弱，以大吃小，以多压少，以明照暗，总有一天会成为对付罪恶文化的法宝。

According to the theory of the Five Elements in traditional Chinese culture, all things in the world are interconnected, with each element both generating and restraining the others. Terrorism is an ideology of extreme egotism. Chinese culture, characterized by its breadth, depth and inclusiveness, has been passed down from generation to generation. Chinese culture can defeat terrorism with its inherent advantages in strength, size, quantity, and uprightness. It will one day become a powerful tool for addressing evil cultures.

作者简介
ABOUT THE AUTHOR

张子良，男，中国人，1989 年 12 月出生，高中学历。在 2008 年，作者高中毕业以后，就开始步入社会。先后从事过五金行业、卖过餐具、销售过电动车、干过搬货，应聘过仓管，和维修过打印机，以及当过便利店营业员。从 2025 年 6 月开始，笔者任职外卖员来养家糊口。虽然，作者本人没有上过大学，并非高学历。但是，本著作人从小爱看课外书，家里有属于自己的独立书房。这为本作者写作打下了坚固的文化基础。

The author is Zhang Ziliang, male, a Chinese national, born in December 1989, with a high school education. After graduating from high school in 2008, he entered the workforce. He has held various jobs successively, including working in the hardware industry, selling tableware, selling electric vehicles, carrying goods, managing warehouses, repairing printers, and working as a convenience store clerk. Since June 2025, he has been working as a delivery rider to support his family. He has not attended college and has no advanced academic credentials. However, he has loved reading extracurricular books since childhood and owns an independent study. All these have laid a solid cultural foundation for his writing.

Author's contact information:

Mobile phone number: +8615280002057
WhatsApp: +8615280002057
Email: 694413898@qq.com